# Texts in Theoretical Computer Science
## An EATCS Series

R. Kurki-Suonio

# A Practical Theory of Reactive Systems

## Incremental Modeling of Dynamic Behaviors

With 112 Figures and 20 Tables

 Springer

*Authors*

Reino Kurki-Suonio
Tampere University of Technology
Box 553
33101 Tampere
Finland
reino.kurki-suonio@tut.fi

*Series Editors*

Prof. Dr. Wilfried Brauer
Institut für Informatik der TUM
Boltzmannstrasse 3
85748 Garching
Germany
Brauer@informatik.tu-muenchen.de

Prof. Dr. Arto Salomaa
Turku Centre for Computer Science
Lemminkäisenkatu 14 A
20520 Turku
Finland
asalomaa@utu.fi

Prof. Dr. Grzegorz Rozenberg
Leiden Institute of Advanced Computer Science
University of Leiden
Niels Bohrweg 1
2333 CA Leiden
The Netherlands
rozenber@liacs.nl

ACM Computing Classification (1998): D.2.1, F.3.1

ISBN 978-3-642-06237-7        e-ISBN 978-3-540-27348-6

Springer is a part of Springer Science+Business Media
springeronline.com

© Springer-Verlag Berlin Heidelberg 2010
Printed in Germany

Cover design: KünkelLopka, Heidelberg

Printed on acid-free paper        45/3142/YL - 5 4 3 2 1 0

*To Elina (1966–1988)*

# Preface

*A man may imagine he understands something,*
*but still not understand anything in the way that he ought to.*
(Paul of Tarsus, 1 Corinthians 8:2)

Calling this a 'practical theory' may require some explanation.

Theory and practice are often thought of as two different worlds, governed by different ideals, principles, and laws. David Lorge Parnas, for instance, who has contributed much to our theoretical understanding of software engineering and also to sound use of theory in the practice of it, likes to point out that 'theoretically' is synonymous to 'not really'.

In applied mathematics the goal is to discover useful connections between these two worlds. My thesis is that in software engineering this two-world view is inadequate, and a more intimate interplay is required between theory and practice. That is, both theoretical and practical components should be integrated into a practical theory.

It should be clear from the above that the intended readership of this book is not theoreticians. They would probably have difficulties in appreciating a book on theory where the presentation does not proceed in a logical sequence from basic definitions to theorems and mathematical proofs, followed by application examples. In fact, all this would not constitute what I understand by a practical theory in this context.

Instead, the book is intended for software engineers, whose interest in theory depends on its usefulness and maturity for practical purposes. The emphasis is not on mathematical results but on their support for realistic specification and design methods, which are themselves an essential part of the theory. The presentation and the abstractions used in the theory aim at making the results natural and easy to use.

Throughout my career in computing since 1960 I have found myself somewhere between theory and practice. With a background in mathematics I have always believed in its power. When computer science was emerging as a discipline, I was especially fascinated by the effect of mathematics on the definition and implementation of programming languages. Inspired by the advanced facilities that this made possible, it was a slow process to grow in understanding the teachings of Edsger W. Dijkstra, the apostle of simplicity, who wrote in 1997 [47]: "All through history, simplifications have had a much greater long-range scientific impact than individual feats of ingenuity."

For my ideals of computing research I owe much to Alan J. Perlis, under whose supervision I had the privilege to do postdoctoral research before permanently moving to a university environment. As I understood him, computing practice is the primary source and ultimate criterion for a theory of computing. Theoretical formalizations for their own sake will miss the point and will lead to 'theoretical practice', in which 'theoretical' stands for 'not really'.

From Alan I also learned that one man's theory is another man's practice. My theory may sound like practice to theoreticians, and my practice may sound like theory to practitioners. Instead of theoretical practice, which is uninteresting to all except its developers, I hope, however, to have provided essential components for a practical theory, with contributions that are worthwhile to both sides.

In the mathematical formalization of a specific problem area, like the syntax and parsing of programming languages, the role of theory is, in principle, straightforward. Once a useful theory has been developed, it can be taken as a basis for how programs in this particular area operate. In a general-purpose formalization of software the situation is different in the sense that a theory cannot be encapsulated in special-purpose tools.

It is a common mistake to equate theory with the use of formal methods, for which a rigorous theoretical basis is, of course, necessary. A solid theoretical foundation is not, however, needed only for formal methods and associated tools, but also for all design documentation and human communication in different stages of the software process. This makes it a major challenge to develop a practical theory for software engineering.

In software engineering a good theory is not just an add-on to current practices, in order to add better quality to software by more advanced tools. By providing better understanding of problems it should affect our thinking independently of available tools. For this reason it should not be surprising that some of the ideas in this book are not direct formalizations of conventional wisdom on software. Well-established concepts will not be abandoned, but some new insight will be provided to understand better their role in specification and design.

For me, the purpose of theory is to help in understanding what I do, at a level of abstraction that is appropriate for the problems at hand. As a side-effect, it should allow me to use formal methods to ascertain that I have not made mistakes in my informal reasoning.

In academia, better understanding of (toy) problems is important in itself. In software-intensive industry, the goal is not to understand, but to make profit by constructing useful (non-toy) products. Since understanding is not achieved for free, it can be afforded only by the advantages gained by it. With increasing complexity of evolving products it is, however, not uncommon to eventually face the situation: when nothing else helps, try to understand better what you are doing. To cite Dijkstra [47] again: "Because we are dealing with artifacts, all unmastered complexity is of our own making."

New ways of thinking can be recommended only if they help in dealing with some important issues for which previous practices are ineffective. For the theory presented in this book I argue this to be the case for reasoning on collective behaviors of objects – both at an informal level and also with rigorous formality – and for incremental derivation of specifications and designs of reactive systems. It is my hope that the simplicity of the fundamentals of the theory and its intuitively natural relationship to familiar notions will also persuade the reader of this.

It has taken a long time for the ideas in this book to take their present shape. Their origins are in joint work with Ralph-Johan Back in the early 1980s, in which the advantages of a simple action-oriented execution model were recognized in stepwise design of distributed algorithms [20]. Zohar Manna's and Amir Pnueli's work on using temporal logic in the modeling of distributed programs and reactive systems [151, 172] had a strong influence on the formal aspects of that work.

In the mid-1980s, when I was still interested in programming languages rather than formal specification, I was asked to coordinate some cooperative projects between Finnish industry and academia within a research programme sponsored by TEKES (Technology Development Centre of Finland). Among other things, some formal approaches were tried in these projects on certain strongly simplified problems given by industry. I was then badly disappointed to realize how unmanageable the suggested formal models were for humans even in extremely idealized situations.

This gave me a strong feeling that it all could be done a lot better, and in a subsequent TEKES project (1988–1991) my group got a chance to try it. As a result, the earlier ideas were extended into an experimental specification language *DisCo (distributed cooperation)*, which supported multi-object actions and an incremental approach to specification, and also had tools for graphical animation of specifications [127, 93, 92, 187].

When the DisCo project was started we learned that Mani Chandy and Jayadev Misra had in the meantime used a similar execution model as an operational basis for a comprehensive theory called *UNITY* [36]. We also got familiar with related work by Paul Attie, Michael Evangelist, Ira Forman, Nissim Francez, Shmuel Katz, and others [59, 14, 64, 53, 105]. Having experienced difficulties in convincing either theoreticians or practitioners of the advantages of our non-conventional approach, it was reassuring to find others who sought solutions from similar directions, although with somewhat different aims.

Having started with programming languages we were still mainly concerned about the capabilities to be provided by a specification and modeling language. Temporal logic and Back's extension of refinement calculus to deal with reactive systems [17] were only in the background, to allow precise discussion of language semantics. Unlike in UNITY, programming logic was not yet an integral part of our approach. It was discussions with Leslie Lamport that made me realize the central role of logic, and I was especially encouraged by noticing how closely the canonical expressions in his *temporal logic of actions (TLA)* [141] corresponded to what we had been developing at the language and design methodology levels.

In addition to the people mentioned above, this work has been influenced by many more, too numerous to list here. Interaction with industry has also been essential in trying to develop the approach into a comprehensive theory that would be useful for practice. In its various stages, the work has been supported by Instrumentointi, Kone, several branches of Nokia, Space Systems Finland, Valmet Automation, TEKES, and the Academy of Finland.

Of the members of the DisCo team, with whom all the ideas have been developed, and who have been responsible for all tool development and practical experimentation, I am especially indebted to Hannu-Matti Järvinen, Kari Systä, Pertti Kellomäki, Tommi Mikkonen, Mika Katara, Timo Aaltonen, and Risto Pitkänen, without whom this book would never have reached its present shape. My warm thanks also go to Ingeborg Mayer and other members of the editorial staff at Springer for their extremely helpful and efficient cooperation in the final stages of this writing project.

Finally, I want to thank my wife Liisa, whose loving support and patience always encouraged me to continue with this work. I dedicate the book to our youngest daughter Elina (1966–1988), who during her last year of life taught me more than I have ever been able to teach anybody, about the inadequacy of both theory and practice, about our inability to understand in the way we ought to, and about the reality of a pure abstraction – love.

Tampere, Finland, December 2004                    *Reino Kurki-Suonio*

# Contents

## Part III  Building a Practical Theory

## Part IV  Distributed and Real-Time Systems

## Part V  Epilogue

# Part I

## Prologue

# 1

## Components of a Theory

*Software engineering* is about specification, design, implementation, and maintenance of software artifacts. Like any engineering profession, it requires various kinds of knowledge and skills. One of the necessary ingredients is a theory that makes it possible

- to formulate, discuss, and reason about the properties that are essential in software artifacts,
- to specify and design software systems that have the desired properties, and
- to verify that software designs actually meet the given requirements.

The characteristic properties that such a theory should help to deal with are those of the *dynamic behaviors* that are generated by the execution of software.

Since it is software that has made it possible to create artifacts with involved dynamic behaviors, managing this kind of complexity has become an issue only with the proliferation of software. The same problem arises, however, in any engineering of complex systems. Therefore, a theory that helps in managing the logical complexity of dynamic behaviors is also applicable more generally. Due to the non-physical character of software, software engineering faces the problem, however, in a pure form, where physical theories play no essential role.

Dealing with the complexity of dynamic behaviors is what this book is all about. The main emphasis is on a theoretically justified specification and design method, which supports incremental derivation of operational specifications that have the desired properties. The specific focus of this book is on *reactive systems*, i.e., on systems that are in continual interaction with their environments. By the environment we understand in this context human users, physical environment, and other reactive systems that interact with the system under consideration.

Although the attribute 'reactive' emphasizes the most distinctive characteristic of the systems that we are interested in, there are other frequently used terms that characterize some more technical aspects of such systems:

- Reactive behavior is usually associated with *embedded systems*, in which software is an integral part of devices that have been designed for specific purposes. The hardware and the software of such dedicated systems have to be designed together, which is usually referred to as *codesign*.
- Real-time properties are often crucial in the requirements for reactive systems, in which case the term *real-time system* is used. Depending on whether real-time requirements are essential for correct behavior, or are formulated as statistical requirements that have to be satisfied on the average, real-time systems are called *hard* or *soft*.
- When a system consists of cooperating subsystems that are physically or even geographically distributed, it is called a *distributed system*. The subsystems of a distributed system are often reactive, and real-time requirements may also be associated with them.
- The purpose of a real-time system may be to *monitor* and *control* some physical phenomena in its environment. In addition to discrete states, the specification of such a system may need to refer to physical quantities that change as continuous functions of time. Such systems are referred to as *hybrid systems*.

The purpose of this introductory chapter is to outline the components that are needed in a theoretically justified approach to reactive systems. The structure of the chapter is as follows:

- In Sect. 1.1 we briefly analyze the relationship between theory and practice in software specification.
- Section 1.2 outlines some general requirements for a theory that would provide comprehensive support for the specification and design of reactive systems.
- Section 1.3 gives a brief outline of the rest of this book.

## 1.1 The Role of Theory

We start by inspecting the role of an underlying theory in the specification and design of software.

### 1.1.1 Theory and Practice

The history of software engineering is still very brief. In just a few decades, software has become a ubiquitous basic technology for the implementation of complex systems. The size and complexity of software artifacts have grown immensely at the same time, and the qualitative character of software and its applications have also changed rapidly.

These advances in the state of the art have been largely based on practical rather than theoretical understanding of software. Also, due to the speed of development, theoretical understanding of software has not had much time to mature. As a result, the need of theory is often underestimated in the practice of software engineering.

Although the driving forces for theoretical and practical developments are different, useful theory of software cannot be developed in isolation from understanding what the essential practical problems in software and software engineering are. Otherwise, theoretical work would remain as useless formalization. On the other hand, the need for a solid underlying theory is also becoming more and more evident in software practice. We are already facing the situation where some software cannot – or should not – be developed without theoretically justified confidence in its behavior.

### 1.1.2 What Is Theory?

In a broad sense, anything that provides understanding at some level of generality can be called theory. The Oxford English Dictionary explains theory, among other things, as "systematic conception or statement of something; abstract knowledge, or the formulation of it."

For theoretical understanding of practical artifacts it is important that a theory supports thinking in terms of *abstractions*, which allows us to omit those aspects of the reality that can be managed trivially, and to concentrate on those aspects that at least potentially may cause problems. Different theories may support different kinds of abstractions, which is useful for taking multiple views of the same artifacts. For instance, focusing on logical behaviors abstracts away all physical characteristics, which are also important in all digital devices.

In particular, a theory of software (or any systems with behavioral complexity) should provide a rigorous basis for

- *specification*, i.e., formulation of the required behavioral properties,
- *design methods*, i.e., systematic methods for developing systems that meet the given requirements, and
- *verification*, i.e., reasoning on whether the required properties are, indeed, satisfied by the design.

In addition, effective use of a theory should also be helpful for

- *validation*, i.e., checking that the design (or its eventual implementation) meets the actual needs from which the requirements were derived.

### 1.1.3 Reality and Abstractions

Every theory has some inherent limitations. Since abstractions do not model all properties of reality, a theory can be used only for those properties for which it has been designed.

Since a theory deals with abstractions, it does not say anything about the reality itself. Therefore, theoretical results and proofs are relevant for reality only as far as this obeys the basic assumptions that have been made in the theoretical models. The validity of such assumptions will always remain beyond the reach of mathematical proofs. In addition, no formal proof of software can show that the original informal requirements have been correctly formalized. This is why formal methods can never remove the need for validation.

Although these remarks about distinguishing between the reality and abstract models are a truism, there is considerable danger for confusion between the two, especially in connection with software.

A written program seems to belong to reality, as its execution on real computers gives rise to those real phenomena that we are interested in. We are not, however, interested in these physical phenomena as such, but on their interpretation as computations. Since widely different physical representations can be used for computations, a program is, in fact, an abstraction that is independent of the actual phenomena that arise in its real executions, and it can therefore be subjected to formal analysis and proofs.

The relevance of any proofs of programs always depends on some assumptions, like absence of ambiguities in the programming language that is used, correctness of all system software that it relies on (compilers, operating systems, database systems, communication protocols, etc.), fault-free operation of the hardware involved, and satisfaction of (often implicit) assumptions on ranges of numbers, amounts of data, frequencies of communication, etc. All these are non-trivial assumptions, as is shown by the multitude of bugs in commonly used system software, famous design errors in hardware, and the Y2K problem, for instance.

Worse still, abstractions of interactive behavior make assumptions on all partners of interaction. Therefore, reactive systems cannot be specified independently of modeling the environments in which the systems are intended to be used. Although assumptions on the environment can be formalized in more and more detail when increased confidence in the satisfaction of these assumptions is required, it is important to understand that the reality itself always escapes full formalization.

For all these reasons, theoretically well-justified formal methods and proof techniques can never replace testing and validation. Instead, the two kinds of approaches complement each other and should be used in tandem to increase our confidence in complex systems.

### 1.1.4 Role of Theory in Engineering

Natural sciences and the associated mathematical theories provide the basis for theoretical understanding in traditional engineering disciplines. In practical engineering work one may not need to go to these fundamentals all the time, but it is always possible to resort to them when necessary.

These fundamentals are considered essential in engineering education, and one would not think of teaching only practical engineering skills without associated theoretical understanding. This shows that the importance of a universally accepted theoretical framework is recognized, even though practical engineering standards and industrial practices may be more important in everyday engineering work.

In software engineering the situation is a bit different. Obviously, physics and calculus do not provide a useful basis for understanding software. Since no comparable and generally accepted theoretical basis has been agreed on, software-engineering education typically concentrates on programming skills, available tools, standard practices, organization and leadership of software projects, etc. Instead of a general theory of programs, discrete mathematics is taught, as well as specialized mathematical theories that are relevant in computer science, like those needed for understanding compilers, computability and complexity issues, efficiency of algorithms and data structures, etc. Although all of these are essential for the software-engineering profession, they are no replacement for an underlying theory of software.

### 1.1.5 Emerging Need for a Theory

The need for a general theory depends greatly on the size and complexity of the artifacts to be constructed, and on the severeness of the potential consequences of errors in them. Just plain logical thinking without any special theory is sufficient for understanding short and simple programs. In larger programs, simple programming errors can be avoided by using appropriate tools, and an error can often be understood and corrected without much theory, once somebody points out under which circumstances it occurs.

This has led to a situation where the significance of high-level programming languages and other tools, maintainable software architectures, teamwork skills, systematic testing methods, good management of the software process, etc., is recognized in software-intensive industry, but no stringent need is felt for competence in an underlying theory of software.

With growing requirements for the degree of confidence in software, the situation is, however, becoming unsatisfactory. This is the case, in particular, with software that is used to control life-critical systems, and also with embedded consumer products like automobiles, where human control more and more often takes place through software interfaces. Networking of systems has also greatly increased the need for trustworthiness even in the presence of deliberate misuse and malicious attacks.

Although understanding of theoretical foundations is only one aspect in producing high-quality software, its importance will necessarily increase when the field becomes more mature, and when consumers become more conscious about software quality.

### Review Questions

QUESTION 1.1.1 What are the main purposes for which a theory of software can be used?

QUESTION 1.1.2 What makes interactive behaviors more difficult to specify than non-interactive behaviors?

QUESTION 1.1.3 What makes software engineering fundamentally different from other engineering disciplines?

## 1.2 Parts of a Comprehensive Theory

In computer science and software engineering, people are used to develop and deal with different kinds of abstractions. The problem is therefore not in the lack of useful abstractions, but in their incompatibilities, and in the lack of a comprehensive theory that would support them.

In this section we discuss different kinds of abstractions that should fit together in a balanced manner and without incompatibilities, in order that a theory would be useful for the practice of software specification.

### 1.2.1 Spectrum of Abstractions

Specification formalisms are often classified into *property-oriented* and *model-oriented* ones. The purpose of the former is to express required properties independently of how they can be implemented. In the latter, specifications are given as *operational models*, which can be understood as 'abstract implementations'.

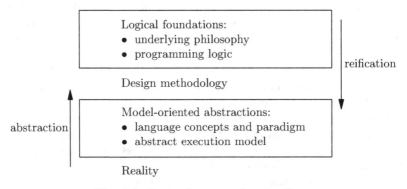

**Fig. 1.1.** Parts of a comprehensive theory

A practical theory cannot be limited to either category alone, since it has to support both kinds of views. Figure 1.1 outlines the spectrum of abstractions that a successful theory has to address. *Logical foundations* constitute the high end, which has to support property-oriented abstractions. *Design methodology* has been placed in the middle, between logical foundations and *model-oriented abstractions*, since it deals with the design of operational models and requires language support for this, but also needs to be based on solid logical foundations.

### 1.2.2 Development of Abstractions

Two opposite directions can be seen in the process of developing abstract concepts for software, *abstraction* and *reification*, as shown in Fig. 1.1.

#### Abstraction

Historically, and in programming education, the dominating direction for developing understanding of software is to start with concrete programs and to design abstractions in the *bottom-up* direction. Real computer architectures and machine languages are then taken as the reality, for which useful higher-level abstractions are gradually developed in terms of language ideas and language-related programming concepts.

This approach has been very successful, and has led to effective machine-independent *languages* and *tools*, to reusable *design patterns*, and to informal *design methods* for managing the complexity associated with software. In particular, these abstractions help in the *architecture* of software, i.e., in structuring it into units that have well-defined properties and relationships.

Together with a specification of what a program is intended to accomplish, such concepts make it easier to check whether a final product meets the intentions. However, this abstraction process assigns no abstract meaning to programs as such. Therefore, these concepts are not directly suited for addressing semantically relevant relationships between programs, such as program equivalence.

On the other hand, being independent of the meaning of programs, these abstractions are relatively insensitive to what kinds of essential properties programs are interpreted to possess. As an extreme example of our freedom in this interpretation, consider being interested only in the side-effects on console lamps, for instance. In this connection it may be interesting to recall that the machine instructions of some early computers had side-effects on a loudspeaker, which allowed us to interpret the meaning of a program as the tune played by its execution.

#### Reification

The reification process starts with the fundamental question of what the essential properties of programs really are. Mathematical abstraction of the meaning of programs allows us to discuss rigorous reasoning on these properties, and can also give a solid basis for design methods.

One of the problems with this *top-down* direction is that it is possible to start with different kinds of underlying philosophies. It may, in fact, be the case that no single philosophy will ultimately be good for all kinds of programs. The essential properties in mathematical subroutines, interactive systems, and real-time control software, for instance, seem to be very different, and specialized theories for them may therefore give better results than a single unified theory of programs.

Another problem with top-down development of abstractions is how to integrate the resulting rigorous methods smoothly into the software process. In particular, bottom-up development of abstractions has led to extremely complicated languages like C++, and gaps and incompatibilities are therefore unavoidable between mathematically manageable basic concepts and those that are currently advocated in practice.

### 1.2.3 Execution Models

Abstract *execution models*, or *abstract machines*, provide a possible first step in providing abstractions of software. In the specification of software, such models are important for operational specifications that can be executed, simulated, or animated. To allow effective reasoning, the models should, however, be simpler than real execution of programs on existing computer architectures.

*Turing machines*, *finite automata*, and *Petri nets* are examples of abstract execution models that have been designed for different theoretical purposes. The notion of Turing machines has been used successfully as a basis for the theory of computability and for complexity theory, but it would be totally inapplicable as a basis for discussing the specification and design of software. Finite automata, on the other hand, are suitable for modeling special classes of software, like communication protocols, for instance, and Petri nets have been designed for the modeling of parallelism in concurrent systems.

The execution model to be used in this book is a simple *action-oriented* execution model, which will be explained in Chap. 2.

To distinguish between executions of real systems and those in a model, the former will be called *computations* in the following, whereas those in abstract machines will be referred to as *executions*.

Formal execution models allow rigorous reasoning on executions in abstract machines, but they do not assign abstract mathematical meanings to the models. Therefore, they may be useful in the modeling of software, but as such they are insufficient to support a comprehensive theory. In particular, without additional information they cannot be used to address the fundamental question of whether two different systems are equivalent or not, or whether one of them models a correct implementation of the other.

### 1.2.4 Language Concepts

*Programming concepts* and *paradigms* provide the conceptual basis for the constructs and facilities in programming languages. Therefore, the history of high-level languages and the associated paradigms reflects the development of our conceptual understanding of programs.

Programming language mechanisms are, however, often treated as if they would be the primary objects of concern, instead of the underlying concepts that they should be designed to reflect. For instance, extending programming languages to deal with concurrency has often been discussed as if this would primarily be a question of language constructs and their implementation mechanisms, not a question of how concurrency affects the fundamental properties of programs.

In each case, language concepts are an important step beyond execution models. In particular, high-level programming languages have declarative features, which allow much freedom in algorithmic implementation. Programming language concepts therefore also provide useful abstractions for operational specifications, although the latter may have features that prevent automatic compilation into executable programs, in general.

One of the idealistic goals in developing high-level languages has been that they would by themselves be sufficient for discussing the properties of programs, so that no higher-level abstractions would be needed on top of them. For large and complex programs this has, however, turned out to be unrealistic.

One reason for this is that, although high-level languages aim at simplicity, they are not at all simple. In fact, when all the ingredients for a modern high-level language are put together, their combined effects are bound to lead to complexities and ambiguities that are difficult to foresee and to manage. For this reason, some theoreticians have often argued for much simpler programming languages, but the practice has not followed their advice – and often with good reason. In each case, much of the complexity of current programming languages has to be abstracted away in order to obtain a practical theory.

A good example of current trends in programming languages is object orientation, which has proved to be a very successful paradigm. However, if the facilities in object-oriented programming languages are adopted in specifications as such, without abstracting away some of the associated complications, specifications are not any easier to reason about than programs.

### 1.2.5 Underlying Philosophy

Each theory has an *underlying philosophy*, which determines informally the semantic properties that one wishes to express and reason about.

One of the fundamental distinctions to be made at this level is whether the purpose of executions in a model is thought of as transforming input to output, or as continued interactions between a system and its environment. Depending on this distinction, the semantics of an approach is either *transformational* or *reactive*.

In this connection it should be noticed that a program itself is always just a program, not a transformational, reactive, real-time, or some other kind of a program. Such distinctions are not in the programs themselves, but in the theories that are useful for reasoning on their properties. This is analogous to having just one physical reality, but different kinds of physical theories, like classical Newtonian physics, theory of relativity, and quantum mechanics. Different theories of software make it possible to concentrate on different kinds of properties, and the properties that are crucial depend on the intended use of a program in its intended application environment.

## Transformational Philosophy

With *transformational* semantics, a program can be visualized as a black box, which, for any input x, determines a corresponding output f(x), as illustrated in Fig. 1.2. Instead of a purely functional correspondence between input x and output f(x), a specification may also allow several alternatives for f(x), and for some x it may allow the program to give no output at all.

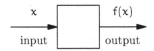

**Fig. 1.2.** A transformational system as a black box

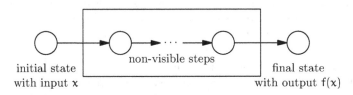

**Fig. 1.3.** Illustration of a transformational black-box execution

In an operational model of a transformational system, computations are modeled to proceed in *discrete steps*, starting from an *initial state*, where input x has already been read in. Intermediate steps take place in a black box and are therefore not visible. If the execution terminates, output f(x) is eventually available in the *final state* as shown in Fig. 1.3. Nonterminating and aborted computations give no value for f(x).

## Reactive Philosophies

With *reactive* semantics, a system is assumed to be in continual interaction with its environment. Described as a black box, the input–output relationship

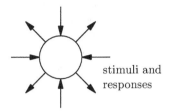

**Fig. 1.4.** A reactive system as a black box

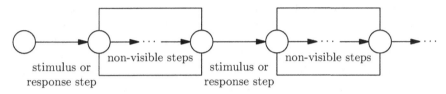

**Fig. 1.5.** Illustration of a reactive black-box execution

of transformational systems then generalizes to *stimuli* and *responses* with more complex causal–temporal relationships (see Fig. 1.4).

In an operational model of a reactive system, computations are normally understood to be nonterminating. In *interleaving models*, stimulus steps, response steps, and non-visible internal steps are all interleaved as illustrated in Fig. 1.5, i.e., all steps are assumed to be taken in some sequential order independently of the 'execution agents' by which they are performed. In contrast, *true concurrency* means that the concurrency of execution steps is also modeled. Instead of total ordering, this leads only to a *partial order* between the steps in an execution.

Under the so-called *synchrony hypothesis*, which essentially states that the system is 'infinitely fast' in comparison to its environment, no new stimuli can appear while a response is being computed. This leads to simpler models, since it is then possible to consider a reactive execution as a sequence of transformational executions. The initial state of each execution is then, however, affected by the history of previous executions.

In principle, execution steps can be understood either as *state changes* or as *events* with identification labels. Depending on this choice, an approach is called either *state-based* or *event-based*.

In general, there are several possible continuations for a given prefix of a reactive execution. Therefore, another basic question in reactive philosophies is whether one wishes to express properties of individual *sequences* of executions or of the whole *trees* that contain all possible continuations of an initial prefix. Depending on this choice, an approach is called *linear-time* or *branching-time*. The most obvious limitation of linear-time approaches is that *stochastic properties* of possible executions cannot be formulated as properties of individual linear executions.

Since different approaches to the modeling of reactive systems differ in their basic philosophies, they cannot be directly mapped into each other. This has caused some misunderstanding between their proponents. Such misunderstanding is often a sign of confusion between reality and a theory. Once one learns to think in terms of a given theory, one starts to consider only those aspects of the reality to be important that this theory is able to describe, and tends to ignore those aspects that have been abstracted away. Since different theories abstract away different kinds of properties, it may then be that only one's own theory can express what one considers important.

In choosing between different alternatives for a reactive philosophy, decisions are mostly based on intuition and subjective preferences. Ultimately, to understand the consequences of such selections, one should compare all aspects of fully developed theories, including their support for languages, tools, and design methods. An important point that needs to be understood in this context is that increasing the expressiveness of a formalism also adds to its logical complexity, and the main enemy of intellectual management is unnecessary complexity.

The choices on which the theory of this book is based are the following:

- The approach is *truly reactive* in the sense that it is not based on the synchrony hypothesis.
- The approach is *state-based*, although one can also see some event-oriented flavor in it.
- Reasoning in the approach is based on the *interleaving* model, which is simpler than true concurrency, but can still also be used for the modeling of distributed concurrency.
- The approach is *linear-time*, which means that specifications determine properties that must be satisfied by all execution sequences.

### 1.2.6 Programming Logic

*Programming logic* is a formal system for expressing properties of programs and to reason about them. In connection with state-based reactive philosophies, *temporal logics* are the primary vehicles for this. The choice in this book is a variant of linear-time temporal logic called *temporal logic of actions (TLA)*, which will be discussed in Chaps. 3 and 4.

In principle, an expression in a programming logic is a specification for a software system in the sense that it expresses the logical meaning of such a system.[1] In other words, expressions in the logic constitute the *semantic domain* for the systems. Two systems are equivalent if they have the same meaning in this logic, and a system is a correct implementation of a given specification if its meaning logically implies the specification.

---

[1] To be more precise, the logical expressions that will be used in this book describe not only software, but any reactive systems together with their intended environments.

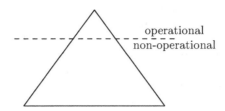

**Fig. 1.6.** The 'iceberg' of specifications

No matter how the logical meaning of systems is defined, if the semantic domain is restricted to correspond to operational systems only, it does not possess mathematical properties that would be easy to manage. However, by allowing the domain to contain also non-operational 'meanings' that have no operational interpretation, mathematically more elegant structures can be achieved. This is illustrated in Fig. 1.6 as an 'iceberg', where the tip corresponds to those specifications that have an operational interpretation. The purpose of a specification process is to lead to specifications with their meanings within this tip, but the full range of the 'iceberg' needs to be available during this process.[2]

### 1.2.7 Design Methodology

As such, *design methods* do not provide additional abstractions to a theory. However, as shown in Fig. 1.1 (p. 8), they have a central position in a practical theory, providing a link between logical foundations and model-oriented abstractions.

Traditionally, design methods have been developed with a view on model-oriented abstractions that can be supported by programming languages and various kinds of tools for manipulating software modules. This means that the emphasis has been on *structural* aspects of software, and on issues of *syntactic* compatibility.[3] In particular, attention has been paid to structural modularity, encapsulation of design decisions within modules, and to the design of module interfaces. The role of design methods has then largely been in providing guidelines for proper module design, in graphical illustrations for the structural aspects of the design, and in systematic documentation of design decisions.

---

[2]The same phenomenon is well known from extending the set of natural numbers to real and complex numbers. In electrical engineering, for instance, one frequently needs complex numbers in calculations, even when the final results are known to be real.

[3]In syntactic aspects we also include 'static semantics', which makes it possible to check that variables, objects, modules, etc., are utilized in accordance with their definitions.

The main problem with such design methods is that no *meaning* is associated with the system under design, except in terms of some scenarios of the intended 'dynamic properties'. Since such methods support rigorous inspection of only syntactic and structural properties, until the dynamic properties have been determined by an essentially implementation-oriented description, the slogan 'correctness by design' remains an empty phrase with them.

This problem can be overcome if design methods have a solid foundation in programming logic. Such a foundation makes it possible to reason about the semantic properties of a design already before any implementation-oriented descriptions are available.

Design methodology is, in fact, a crucial part in integrating the various aspects of a practical theory. It has to be rooted in the logical foundations of the approach, but it also affects the concepts of modularity that need to be supported by the design language. In fact, design methods that are supported by a theory reveal whether the abstractions at the different levels fit together in a reasonable manner. It should not be expected, as it is often done, that one could build a useful approach by taking a heterogeneous set of abstractions and associated tools, and constructing artificial bridges between them to overcome gaps and incompatibilities.

In other words, a good theory is not for constructing tools by which theoretically justified quality could be added to an arbitrary software process. A theory is a basis for thinking and understanding, and it necessarily also affects the software process, in particular the methods and ways of thinking that are used in early stages of specification and design. This is perhaps the biggest obstacle in adopting a theory in practice.

## Review Questions

QUESTION 1.2.1 Why is an execution model insufficient as such as a basis for a theory of programs?

QUESTION 1.2.2 Why is any classification of programs (into transformational, reactive, and real-time programs, for instance) actually a classification of theories, not of programs?

QUESTION 1.2.3 What is the difference between transformational and reactive philosophies?

QUESTION 1.2.4 What is meant by an interleaved execution model?

QUESTION 1.2.5 What is meant by the synchrony hypothesis?

QUESTION 1.2.6 What is the difference between state-based and event-based approaches?

QUESTION 1.2.7 What is the difference between linear-time and branching-time approaches?

QUESTION 1.2.8 Why is it reasonable that the semantic domain also contains other 'meanings' than those that have operational interpretations?

QUESTION 1.2.9 What is the role of design methodology in a theory of programs?

## 1.3 The Structure of the Book

A comprehensive theory for reactive systems will be described in this book. The core chapters of the book have been grouped into three parts. These three parts are preceded by Part I, Prologue (this chapter), and followed by Part V, Epilogue (Chap. 11), which take a more general look at the characteristics of the approach.

Although mathematical concepts and results are effectively utilized in the book, formal theorems and proofs are avoided in the presentation. At the end of most sections, some of the key points are reiterated in the form of simple review questions given to the reader, and exercises of varying difficulty are also given. Each chapter ends with some notes on related history and literature.

No single running example was found suitable to illustrate the different topics discussed in the book. Instead, example specifications of varying size and complexity are given throughout the book. Although these are only 'academic exercises', the reader is encouraged to study them also in those chapters that he/she will not otherwise read carefully. Although the examples are mostly placed after the text that they are supposed to illustrate, it may often be wise·to study them in parallel with the text.

### 1.3.1 Part II: Fundamentals

Part II of the book addresses the fundamental ideas of the approach and consists of three chapters.

Since model-oriented abstractions are the most natural starting point for software engineers,

- Chapter 2 introduces the *execution model* of *action systems*, which provides the basis for operational interpretation of specifications in this theory.

This execution model is *action-oriented* in the sense that execution consists of an interleaved sequence of *actions*, which are considered to be *atomic* units of execution. To fulfill its role in the theory, the execution model is very simple, and has no built-in support for any program structures. For instance, unlike commonly used execution models, it has no inherent bias towards sequential control threads. As such it provides, however, a suitable basis for operational specification of reactive systems, and of any systems in which concurrency and distributed execution is essential. Although the execution model could also be used as a basis for a programming language, this is not a relevant question in the context of this book.

To give a solid basis for the theory,

- Chapter 3 is devoted to the *logical foundations* of the approach.

As the logical basis we take temporal logic of actions (TLA), which is a variant of linear-time temporal logics. TLA is used here to express and reason about properties of 'closed systems', where the environment of a reactive system is also included. An important point in fitting the different parts of the theory together is that the action-oriented execution model provides a natural operational interpretation for TLA expressions in a certain canonical form.

To help readers who do not have strong background in logic, but who would like to understand what it means to carry out formal proofs in detail,

- Chapter 4 gives an introduction to *formal reasoning* in TLA.

The deduction rules that are discussed in this chapter are not essential for understanding how the theory can be used in practice. In particular, the reader is warned of the fact that even 'obvious' properties may lead to long and complicated proofs, when carried out in detail, and that less formal proofs in English may be perfectly adequate in practice.

## 1.3.2 Part III: Building a Practical Theory

Part III of the book addresses questions on building a practical theory on the fundamentals described in Part II, and consists of four chapters.

Since practical use of the theory requires a specification and design language,

- Chapter 5 is devoted to *language aspects*, by which notions like types, finite-state structures, object-oriented classes, relations between objects, and multi-object actions can be built on top of the primitive execution model and can be rigorously reasoned about.

The language ideas presented in this chapter will be used in the rest of the book. The main purpose of the chapter is not, however, to give a detailed language, but to present the main problems in designing a language as part of the theory.

Of special importance in this chapter is how the facilities of object-oriented programming languages can be abstracted to a level that is appropriate for specifications. In particular, single-object 'methods' and communication protocols between objects are abstracted into *multi-object actions*, which allows reasoning on *collective behaviors* even in early stages of specification and design.

As presented in Fig. 1.1 (p. 8), design methods have a central role in our theory. To discuss them,

- Chapter 6 introduces the basic mechanisms to support *design methods*.

The main principle here is that specifications are constructed in incremental layers, and that the design can therefore proceed incrementally, with rigorous support for the preservation of behavioral properties in each step. The modularity of the design language has been designed to support such a layered structure, where a specification layer need not correspond to a natural module in an implementation, but may, instead, correspond to a concern that cuts across them in an *aspect-oriented* manner.

The methodology gives a theoretically solid foundation for a specification and design process that can start at a high level of abstraction and proceed by stepwise refinements towards an implementable form. It also supports the preservation of certain crucial properties (safety properties) in each refinement step, without a need to resort to explicit proofs.

To allow object-oriented specification in the full meaning of the word,

- Chapter 7 extends the discussion of language aspects to *aggregate objects* and to object-oriented *inheritance*.

This is done in such a manner that objects of a subclass always satisfy all properties specified for the base class. This also holds when multiple inheritance is used.

Modeling reactive systems as closed systems raises issues of *partitioning* a closed system into independently implementable components. To deal with such matters,

- Chapter 8 analyzes how *interfaces* can be defined in closed-system specifications, and under which conditions components in a closed-system specification can be refined independently.

A special characteristic of the design method is that interfaces between components can first be given at a high level of abstraction; a form that models their implementation can then be achieved by refinements.

Although partitioning of closed systems has both theoretical and practical interest, no language support is provided for it, and the reader may wish to skip this chapter during the first reading of the book.

### 1.3.3 Part IV: Distributed and Real-Time Systems

Part IV of the book provides excursions to two more specific areas, which may not interest all readers.

Historically, the development of this theory started with an attempt to model *distributed systems* at a high level of abstraction, and the notion of multi-object actions was originally proposed for this purpose. Addressing the specific problems of distribution,

- Chapter 9 analyzes the applicability of the interleaved execution model to distributed systems, and how action systems can be implemented in a distributed fashion.

In particular, it is shown in this chapter that the simple interleaved execution model does, indeed, also provide a suitable basis for the modeling of distributed systems, in which real concurrency is involved.

Since real time is essential for many reactive systems,

- Chapter 10 describes how the theory can be applied to model and reason about *real-time properties*.

The treatment in this chapter also covers *hybrid systems*, in which *continuous state functions* of the environment are also relevant.

## Bibliographic Notes

Model-oriented abstractions have a long history in computing, and are primarily reflected in the evolution of programming languages.

The idea of rigorous reasoning on programs can be found even in some early papers by Goldstine and von Neumann [68] and by Turing [190]. Serious interest in this topic did not, however, arise before Floyd's seminal paper [57]. At the same time, similar ideas were presented independently in a less widely known paper by Naur [163].

The next step towards a theory of programs was Hoare's work on associating axioms and logical deduction rules directly with the definition of a programming language [83]. *Hoare logic* involved triples of the form {P}S{Q} with the following transformational meaning: if the execution of a program statement S starts in a state where *precondition* P holds, then its execution terminates in a state where *postcondition* Q holds.

Based on Hoare's work, Dijkstra observed [43, 44] that each program statement S can be given an abstract meaning as a *predicate transformer* $\Phi_S$, which for any postcondition Q gives the *weakest precondition* P for which {P}S{Q} holds, i.e., $\Phi_S(Q) = P$. This was a crucial step in making mathematical manipulation of programs possible with the transformational basic philosophy. The associated *refinement calculus* gave a solid foundation for rigorous programming methods, as developed further by Gries [71], Hehner [79], Morgan [161], and Back and von Wright [21], for instance.

As for the more established specification languages and formal methods that are essentially based on transformational semantics, the reader is referred to *VDM* [96], *Z* [184], and *B* [9]. For a more detailed history of formal reasoning on programs the reader is referred to an extensive survey by Jones [97].

In dealing with reactive systems, the *synchrony hypothesis* provides the basis for Harel's *statecharts* [76] and the associated tools called *STATE-MATE* [77], as well as for a family of synchronous programming languages that includes *Esterel, Lustre*, and *Signal* [73].

As for theories with 'truly reactive' semantics, *event-based* approaches were pioneered by Hoare's *communicating sequential processes (CSP)* [86] and Milner's *calculus of communicating systems (CCS)* [159, 160]. *LOTOS* [26] is a specification language that combines such a *process-algebraic* approach with an *algebraic specification* of data structures.

Event ordering in distributed systems, which is essential for *interleaving* models, was first discussed by Lamport [136]. An early example of such execution models is the one given by Lynch and Fischer [149]. *Partial-order* and interleaving semantics for CSP-like languages have been compared by Reisig [176].

*Temporal logic* was introduced to *state-based* reasoning on reactive systems by Pnueli [170, 171]. More recent textbooks by Manna and Pnueli [152, 153] give a comprehensive treatment of this. The term 'reactive system' was coined by Harel and Pnueli [78]. The inherently greater complexity of reactive systems, when compared to transformational systems, has been discussed by Wegner [193], for instance.

Temporal logic of actions (TLA) was developed by Lamport [138, 141]. One of its goals was to achieve the situation that an implementation relationship between specifications corresponds to logical implication. *TLA*[+] [144, 145] is a language for constructing TLA specifications. The approach in this book is based on experiences with an experimental specification language *DisCo* [93, 124, 49], in which TLA has been used as the logical basis.

While most research has concentrated on limited aspects of a theory, Chandy's and Misra's *UNITY* [36] was an important milestone in developing a comprehensive theory for distributed systems. Its essential components are an execution model and an associated language (the UNITY language), a temporal logic tuned to deal with this language (UNITY logic), and modularity constructs that support certain design methods.

Although the theory presented in this book has been developed independently of UNITY, and its goals are somewhat different, there is much similarity between the two approaches. The most important differences will be discussed at the end of those chapters where the different parts of the theory are addressed.

# Part II

Fundamentals

# 2

# Towards an Action Language

Operational specifications are based on an abstract *execution model*. On one hand, this makes specifications useful as models for implementation in terms of programming concepts. This viewpoint dominates for execution models that are derived from real computations by abstraction (see Fig. 1.1, p. 8). On the other hand, an abstract execution model can also serve for operational interpretation of expressions in a programming logic, which is emphasized by the reification direction in Fig. 1.1.

The approach in this book is based on an action-oriented execution model, which provides a basis for an *action language*. Specifications given in the action language are called *action systems*. Action systems are operational models that have a close connection to a programming logic.

Every piece of software consists of data structures and of instructions for their manipulation. Correspondingly, an operational model needs to model the *state* of a system and the *events* by which this state can be changed. These questions are discussed for action systems in this chapter, which has the following structure:

- Section 2.1 discusses the use of *variables* for modeling the state of a system.
- The notion of *actions* for modeling dynamic events in a system is introduced in Sect. 2.2.
- Models that are not restricted by the idea of sequential execution threads need a notion for an 'execution force' that can enforce the execution of actions. Such a force is provided by the notion of *fairness*, which is described in Sect. 2.3.
- Section 2.4 discusses how an action system can be used as a model for an implementation.

A simple example of an embedded system is used throughout this chapter to illustrate the concepts introduced.

## 2.1 Modeling of System State

The notion of state is obviously central in a state-based approach. Before elaborating on it, we introduce the example that will be used in this chapter.

### 2.1.1 An Introductory Problem: Gas Burner

Controling a gas burner will be used to illustrate the idea of action systems. The problem is discussed here in a somewhat unstructured and informal manner; the main purpose is to give an intuitive idea of the action-oriented execution model, and to provide motivation for the more formal and structured discussions that will follow.

In this example we assume that there are actuators by which a computer can open and close a *gas valve*, as well as turn an *ignition transformer* on a gas burner on and off. In addition, two sensors are assumed, by which the computer can sense whether a thermostat indicates a *heat request* from the environment, and whether there is a *flame* in the burner.

The requirements for the design are given in an informal and incomplete form. In particular, we ignore here all real-time requirements, to which we will return in Chap. 10. The following initial formulation of the required properties is given:

- A heat request from the environment should cause the system to open the gas valve and to turn the ignition transformer on.
- When the flame has ignited, the ignition transformer should be turned off.
- When the heat request goes off, burning should be stopped by closing the gas valve.
- If the flame does not ignite, the ignition transformer should be turned off, and the gas valve should be closed.
- If the flame goes off during normal burning (flame failure), the gas valve should be closed.

### 2.1.2 State Variables

At any moment of time during an execution, the *state* of an action-system model is composed of the current values of some *state variables*. When there is no danger for confusion, state variables are just called *variables*.

Some of the variables in a model are *essential variables* in the sense that the whole purpose of the model is to specify how the values of these variables are changed in executions. In addition to essential variables one usually needs *auxiliary variables*, the purpose of which is to make it possible (or at least easier) to describe how the values of the essential variables are changed.

The essential variables in the gas-burner example are four Boolean variables that model the states of the two sensors and two actuators attached to the burner:

- variable req_e indicates whether a heat request has been turned on by the environment,
- variable flam_e indicates whether a flame is sensed by the flame sensor,
- variable flow_e indicates whether the control system has opened the valve for gas flow, and
- variable ign_e indicates whether the ignition transformer has been turned on by the control system.

The suffix 'e' is used here in order to emphasize that these variables model the state of the *environment* of the control system. Initially, all of them are assumed to have the value false.

Since it seems unreasonable that the control system could always access environment variables directly, corresponding variables are also needed in it:

- variable req_s indicates whether the control system has registered a heat request from the environment,
- variable flam_s indicates whether the control system has registered that a flame is sensed by the flame sensor,
- variable flow_s indicates whether the control system has opened the valve for gas flow, and
- variable ign_s indicates whether the ignition transformer has been turned on by the control system.

Also these are assumed to be initialized as false. Suffix 's' is used to indicate that they model the state of the control system itself. Although the explanations for the two flow and ign variables are identical, these are not the same: flow_e and ign_e model the physical states of the two actuators, whereas flow_s and ign_s model the information that the control system has about these states.

Since the purpose of the model is to specify how the actuators should behave as a response to state changes in the sensors, the four system variables are auxiliary variables, whose purpose is only to make it possible for the control system to control the actuators appropriately.

The *state space* of an action system consists of all possible states in it, i.e., of all possible assignments of values to its state variables. With eight Boolean variables the gas-burner system is a *finite-state system* with $2^8 = 256$ possible different states. All of these will not, however, be reachable in the executions that will be specified for the system.

In general, state variables could also have infinite ranges of values, like integers. Notice that the fact that every variable in a compiled program has a finite range does not imply that a theory should be built on this assumption.

### 2.1.3 Components and Interfaces

Action systems will be used in this book as *closed-system models*, in which the system to be implemented and its environment are both included as a *system part* and an *environment part*, respectively. More generally, a closed system may be seen to consist of any number of interacting parties, each of them having all the others as its environment. Such parties in a closed-system model will be called its *components.*

Each state variable belongs to a specified component and is said to be *local* to that component. In particular, variables that are local to the system part are called *system variables*, and those in the environment part are called *environment variables.*

Interaction between components takes place by changes in the values of shared *interface variables.* These are state variables that are accessible also to other components than the one to which they belong. Other variables are *private* variables in the components to which they belong.

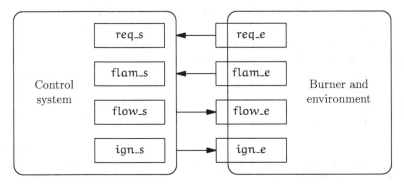

**Fig. 2.1.** Illustration of components and variables in the gas-burner example

The gas-burner example has already been described as consisting of two components: the system component, which consists of the control system, and the environment component, which encompasses all the rest. Since it is reasonable to assume that the environment has in this case no access to variables in the system component, these are assumed to be private to that component, whereas the four environment variables are considered as interface variables that can be accessed by both parties The situation is illustrated in Fig. 2.1, where interface variables have been drawn to stick out from a component, and the arrows show the direction in which information is supposed to flow, when these variables are accessed from outside.

### 2.1.4 Input and Output Variables

In traditional (non-reactive) models of software there is a clear separation of when input can be accepted from the environment, and when output can be given to it. When the synchrony hypothesis is not made (see Sect. 1.2.5, p. 13), this is no longer true for models of reactive systems: stimuli from the environment and responses by the system can usually be interleaved in a more liberal manner. For instance, in the gas-burner example it is reasonable to assume that a heat request may go off already before the system has had time to react to it.

This freedom of the components to compete for accessing interface variables is often managed by partitioning the interface variables of a component into input variables, through which its environment can give input (stimuli) to it, and output variables, through which it can give output (reactions to stimuli) to its environment. The component itself can only read its input variables, whereas other components can only write to them. Correspondingly, a component can write to its output variables, whereas other components can only read these.

In the gas-burner example, variables req_e and flam_e are output variables in the environment component, i.e., their values can be affected only by this component itself. Correspondingly, flow_e and ign_e are its input variables, whose values are assumed to be controlled by the system component.

**Review Questions**

QUESTION 2.1.1 What is meant by a closed-system model?

QUESTION 2.1.2 What are the different kinds of state variables that appear in action system models?

QUESTION 2.1.3 What is the role of auxiliary variables in operational specifications?

QUESTION 2.1.4 How do components communicate with each other in state-based models?

QUESTION 2.1.5 Why are interface variables often partitioned into input variables and output variables?

QUESTION 2.1.6 Why was variable req_e in the gas-burner example called an output variable, although it gives input to the control software?

**Exercises**

EXERCISE 2.1.1 Considering programs in high-level languages, which are the different aspects that may lead to (potentially) infinite state spaces in them?

## 2.2 Executions and Actions

Operational models specify executions in which the system state is changed in discrete steps. In this section we discuss the modeling of such steps in action systems.

### 2.2.1 Executions

An *execution* in an action system consists of *steps* in which the state of the total system is modified.[1] Figure 2.2 illustrates an execution that generates the state sequence $\langle s_0, s_1, s_2, \ldots \rangle$. Each step in an execution corresponds to the execution of some *action*. The execution in Fig. 2.2 is generated by executing the sequence $\langle A_1, A_2, \ldots \rangle$ of actions.

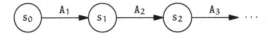

**Fig. 2.2.** Execution in an action system

Depending on the state of the total system, each action is either *enabled* in that state or not. An action can be executed only when it is enabled. In Fig. 2.2, action $A_1$, for instance, is enabled in state $s_0$.

The first state in an execution ($s_0$) is called its *initial state*. An initial state has to belong to a set that has been specified as the set of permissible initial states.

An execution may be terminating, in which case it has a *final state*. If an execution is non-terminating, the associated state sequence $\langle s_0, s_1, s_2, \ldots \rangle$ is infinite.

A state in the state space is said to be *reachable* if it appears in some possible execution that starts from a permissible initial state.

In the gas-burner example it is natural to assume that all four variables have value false in the initial state, and that executions are non-terminating.

### 2.2.2 Actions

Actions are the basic units of execution in action systems. Each action is *local* to a specified component, i.e., an action of this component. In addition to local variables of the component, an action can also access and modify interface variables in other components.

When executed, an action is said to be executed by the component to which it is local.[2] In particular, actions of the system part are called *system actions*, and those of the environment part are called *environment actions*. Obviously, an implementation of the system part needs to implement only

---

[1] Notice the overloading of the word 'system', used both for the 'system part', i.e., the 'system' to be implemented, and for the 'total system' that consists of a 'system part' and an 'environment part'.

[2] This deviates from the principle followed in CSP and other process algebraic approaches, where the responsibility for executing an action is shared by a process and its environment.

system actions; environment actions are ones that are assumed to be executed by the environment, when it cooperates with the system part.

The total effects of execution in a closed system are independent of how the actions are assigned to the components. Therefore, we keep this assignment as an extralinguistic issue for which no special facilities will be provided in the action language. However, since this assignment is important for implementing a component, we will return to the associated question of *partitioning* (of both variables and actions) into components in Chap. 8.

### 2.2.3 Nondeterminism

As illustrated in Fig. 2.3, there may be several alternatives – nondeterministic choices – for the next step in an execution. In this figure there is a choice between actions A and B, both of which are enabled in state s.

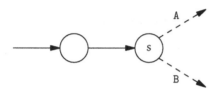

**Fig. 2.3.** Illustration of nondeterministic alternatives

Taking *nondeterminism* as an inherent characteristic of the execution model is a clear departure from deterministic control, which is a natural assumption in sequential algorithms. In operational specifications, especially in the modeling of reactive systems, nondeterminism is a necessity. The reasons for this are the following:

- Environment behavior cannot be modeled deterministically, in general. Therefore, there may be several alternatives for an environment action to be executed next.
- Without the synchrony hypothesis (see Sect. 1.2.5, p. 13), there are situations where the next action to be executed can be either a system action or an environment action.
- Alternative choices for a system action to be executed next are needed in the modeling of concurrent and distributed systems.
- In operational specifications it is important to be able to leave more freedom for the action to be executed next than what will be utilized in implementations.

Basically, nondeterminism reflects lack of information.[3] Instead of deterministic modeling, the best we can then do is to give approximations that are

---

[3] It is a philosophical question that is irrelevant for this book whether there exists nondeterminism in the real world, or only in our incomplete models of it.

'safe' for reasoning. This is essential especially in the modeling of the environment, which we wish to treat similarly to the system part in closed-system modeling of reactive systems.

As for system actions, concurrency is an important source for lack of information. Due to unknown relative speeds and communication delays, or to the freedom left for schedulers, the exact order of events in concurrent processes is unpredictable, and a specification should therefore be prepared for the different possibilities by nondeterminism.

A different reason for lack of information is that this lack is a deliberate choice of the specifier, who wants to avoid *overspecification*, i.e., unnecessary constraints for implementations.

### 2.2.4 Absence of Probabilities

When nondeterminism is used in quantum physics, for instance, probabilities are assigned to the different alternatives that can take place. This is natural when nondeterministic models are associated with physical systems that can be observed.

In contrast, our specifications are for describing required properties of all individual executions in a reactive system. Therefore, the nondeterminism that is used here is 'pure' nondeterminism without probabilities. In other words, we are interested only in the possibility of executing different actions, not in their stochastic properties or execution frequencies.

Lack of information then means that nothing is known (or specified) about the process by which nondeterministic alternatives are selected. In other words, an implementor (or the environment) has complete freedom to use any policy – systematic or random – in this selection.

This simplifies our models essentially, but it also restricts the kinds of properties that can be modeled and talked about. In particular, it is then not possible to rely on the idea that zero probability would exclude some (infinite) executions. Also, it is not possible to specify stochastic properties of executions.

### 2.2.5 Atomicity of Actions

Actions are assumed to be *atomic* units of execution. The meaning of this is that, once the execution of an action has started, it will eventually be completed without interruption or interference from any other actions. Obviously, atomicity is essential for modeling executions as sequences of state transitions of the kind illustrated in Fig. 2.2 (p. 30), where each step is associated with some action. In Chap. 9 we will take a closer look at why the idea of atomic state changes is applicable in the modeling of both sequential and concurrent computations.

The significance of atomicity is illustrated in Fig. 2.4, where action A of the upper part is divided in the lower part into two consecutive actions $A_1$ and $A_2$

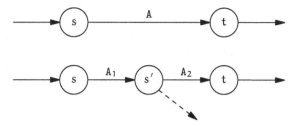

**Fig. 2.4.** Illustration of the significance of atomicity

with the same combined effect. The emerging intermediate state s' now has the consequence that some other actions than $A_2$ may also be possible in this state. As a result, some executions may become possible that were excluded by the atomicity of A. Obviously, phenomena of this kind cannot appear in sequential programming, but in concurrent and distributed systems they are a dangerous source for time-dependent errors, since the programmer's intuitive idea of atomicity may easily differ from the one actually implemented. Such errors may also be impossible to find by systematic testing.

The notion of atomicity is fundamental for operational specification of concurrent and distributed systems, and therefore also for reactive systems.[4] It can, however, be seen as a specification-level concept that cannot be directly utilized (at least in current) programming languages for concurrent and distributed computing. Instead, various mechanisms for communication and synchronization between concurrent processes are available in them, in terms of which the desired atomicity can be built into systems.

Unfortunately, the significance of atomicity as a basic notion is not yet commonly understood in the literature on design methods. Instead, concurrency is usually discussed in the light of mechanisms to control it in sequential execution threads, rather than in terms of the intended degree of atomicity.

Notice that the execution of an atomic action may take time, i.e., atomicity is not synonymous to instantaneity. The discussion of time-related aspects will be postponed to Chaps. 9 and 10.

### 2.2.6 Interleaving

Atomicity, as defined above, does not exclude concurrent execution of several actions in an implementation, provided that their combined effect is as if they were executed in some sequential order. In an interleaved model of executions (see Fig. 2.2, p. 30) actions can then be thought of to be executed in such

---

[4]Notice that even in the presence of a single thread of execution in software, a reactive system is always a concurrent system in the sense that the environment 'executes' concurrently with the system part. At the machine-language level this concurrency is reflected in the use of an interrupt mechanism, or in systematic polling of interface variables.

an order. It is the responsibility of an implementor to ensure the validity of the non-interference assumption of actions that can be executed concurrently in different threads of control, by using the concurrency mechanisms that are available in the programming language. These problems will be discussed in more detail in Chap. 9.

In particular, reactive systems have potential concurrency in what happens in the environment and what happens in the system part. As an example, consider the situation that the heat request in the gas burner is turned off while the control system is executing some action. Because of the atomicity assumption this has no affect on the action that the control system is currently executing, and the total effect is as if the heat request had gone off immediately after this action.

Obviously, the atomicity assumption of actions is what makes it possible to use an interleaved execution model, and thereby to avoid the complications that would follow from explicit modeling of concurrency. This is essential in making the execution model as simple as possible without affecting its applicability to distributed and concurrent systems.

In particular, an interleaved execution model makes it possible to utilize the notion of a *global state*, which consists of the current values of all variables. In distributed systems, where several actions may be executed concurrently in different parts of the system, there need not exist any moments (except the initial state) where all variables would have well-defined values. Therefore, the global state is a theoretical notion that need not exist in reality. In Chap. 9 we will also discuss this question in more detail.

### 2.2.7 Absence of Processes

Concurrency is usually described in terms of concurrent processes or execution threads. This reflects a desire not to change the conceptual basis that has been successful for sequential programming, but to develop add-ons to it, in order to cope with the additional problems. It is, however, unreasonable to expect that a well-developed but inherently sequential basis could be extended to cover concurrency in a conceptually elegant manner. After all, sequential execution is a reduced special case of concurrency, and extending a specific solution to a more general situation easily burdens the more general case with unnecessary complications.

The action-oriented execution model is not an extension of an inherently sequential model of computing. In particular, there are no built-in control threads or implicit program counters. Instead, any action that is enabled in the current state can be executed next, and competition between different actions is always resolved by a nondeterministic choice. If sequential threads are required, these can always be imposed by using explicit program-counter variables and utilizing them in the enabling conditions of actions. Questions related to concurrent processes will be discussed in more detail in Chap. 9.

Comparing the roles of actions and processes, an action describes *what* is done, while processes are for describing *who* does it, or *how* the responsibilities are divided between different execution agents. Obviously, 'what' questions are essential in specification, while 'who' and 'how' questions can be postponed to later stages of design. This provides further justification for abandoning process-oriented execution models in operational specifications. In closed-system modeling of reactive systems one cannot, however, ignore the question of assigning the responsibility for each action to some component in the total closed system. This question will be discussed in more detail in Chap. 8.

### 2.2.8 Actions as Syntactic Entities

In conventional programming languages for concurrent and distributed systems, atomic actions emerge as 'dynamic' run-time entities, which have no explicit representation in program text. For instance, when a programming language provides a mechanism for synchronous communication between two processes, no corresponding syntactic entities are provided: such events just take place whenever the communicating processes execute matching send and receive statements in their own codes.

This situation can be compared to how subroutines, loops, and other sequential programming structures were dealt with in early programming languages, where even these notions had no clearly defined syntactic representations. Since atomic actions are a fundamental concept for an execution model for concurrent and reactive systems, they are taken as explicit syntactic entities in our action language.

An action consists of an enabling *guard* and a *body*. The guard is a Boolean expression that determines whether or not the action is *enabled* for execution in the current state, and the body is a multiple-assignment statement to be executed when the action is executed. Syntactically an action A will be written in the form

$$
\begin{aligned}
\text{A}: \ & g \\
\to \ & x_1' = e_1 \\
\land \ & x_2' = e_2 \\
& \cdots \\
\land \ & x_k' = e_k \ ,
\end{aligned}
$$

where $g$ is the guard, and $x_i' = e_i$, $i = 1, \dots, k$, denote the individual assignments in the body. Each assignment is written as an equation between the new (primed) value of a variable $x_i$ and an expression $e_i$, which is given in terms of the old (unprimed) values of variables. Also, conditional assignments of the form

$$ \text{if } p \text{ then } x' = e $$

will be used, which is equivalent to

$$x' = \text{if } p \text{ then } e \text{ else } x \ .$$

### 2.2.9 Example: Gas-burner Actions

As an example we discuss actions for the gas-burner problem introduced above.

**Environment Actions**

What the environment can do is to turn the two sensors on and off.

For the temperature sensor this leads to two simple actions, which we call Req_on_e and Req_off_e. The former can be executed when req_e is false, and it turns it into true. Correspondingly, the latter can be executed when req_e is true, and it turns it into false. In the action language we give these in the following form:

$$\text{Req\_on\_e}: \neg \text{req\_e}$$
$$\rightarrow \ \text{req\_e}' = \text{true} \ ,$$

$$\text{Req\_off\_e}: \text{req\_e}$$
$$\rightarrow \ \text{req\_e}' = \text{false} \ .$$

For the flame sensor the situation is analogous and leads to the following actions:

$$\text{Flame\_on\_e}: \neg \text{flam\_e}$$
$$\rightarrow \ \text{flam\_e}' = \text{true} \ ,$$

$$\text{Flame\_off\_e}: \text{flam\_e}$$
$$\rightarrow \ \text{flam\_e}' = \text{false} \ .$$

In the absence of a model of how the temperature develops, it is natural to assume that the heat request can go on and off arbitrarily, as modeled here. For the flame sensor one might suggest, instead, that it would not be possible to sense a flame unless the gas valve has been opened and the ignition transformer is on. Discussing the feasibility of including these conditions in the model is left to the reader (Exercise 2.2.4).

**Input from Sensors**

Since the interface variables that model the state of the two sensors belong to the environment, system actions are needed for transmitting this information to the control software. This leads to the following system actions:[5]

---

[5] The meaning of prefix [SF] on action names will be explained below in Sect. 2.3.3.

$$^{\mathrm{SF}}\mathsf{Req\_on\_s} : \mathsf{req\_e} \wedge \neg\mathsf{req\_s}$$
$$\rightarrow \mathsf{req\_s'} = \mathsf{true} \,,$$

$$^{\mathrm{SF}}\mathsf{Req\_off\_s} : \neg\mathsf{req\_e} \wedge \mathsf{req\_s}$$
$$\rightarrow \mathsf{req\_s'} = \mathsf{false} \,,$$

$$^{\mathrm{SF}}\mathsf{Flame\_on\_s} : \mathsf{flam\_e} \wedge \neg\mathsf{flam\_s}$$
$$\rightarrow \mathsf{flam\_s'} = \mathsf{true} \,,$$

$$^{\mathrm{SF}}\mathsf{Flame\_off\_s} : \neg\mathsf{flam\_e} \wedge \mathsf{flam\_s}$$
$$\rightarrow \mathsf{flam\_s'} = \mathsf{false} \,.$$

In other words, whenever the values of the corresponding variables in the two components disagree, those in the system component can be updated. It is left unspecified how the communication for noticing these situations should take place. Some alternatives are that the control software would periodically poll the states of the sensors, or that each change in these would transmit an interrupt signal that invokes a suitable code in the control software.

**Phases of Control**

To describe how the system should react to environment stimuli, we observe that a normal operation cycle consists of phases that can be described as follows (see the state diagram in Fig. 2.5, where the asterisk indicates the initial state):

- Initially, and between consecutive heating cycles, the state of the control component can be characterized by state predicate $\mathsf{Idle}$,[6]

$$\mathsf{Idle} \triangleq \neg\mathsf{flow\_s} \wedge \neg\mathsf{ign\_s} \,,$$

expressing that the gas valve is closed and the ignition transformer is off. We say that the state then is $\mathsf{Idle}$.

- As a response to a heat request, state $\mathsf{Starting}$ is entered,

$$\mathsf{Starting} \triangleq \mathsf{flow\_s} \wedge \mathsf{ign\_s} \,,$$

in which the gas valve has been opened and the ignition transformer has been turned on. The action that causes this will be called $\mathsf{Start\_s}$.

- If the flame sensor then indicates a flame, state $\mathsf{Ignited}$ is entered (action $\mathsf{Ign\_off\_s}$),

$$\mathsf{Ignited} \triangleq \mathsf{flow\_s} \wedge \neg\mathsf{ign\_s} \,,$$

in which the gas valve is still kept open, but the ignition transformer has been turned off. Otherwise state $\mathsf{Idle}$ is re-entered (action $\mathsf{Stop\_s}$).

---

[6]The symbol '$\triangleq$' is used to stand for 'is defined as', or 'is defined to be equivalent to'.

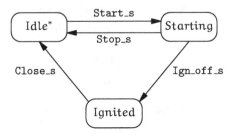

**Fig. 2.5.** Phases of a gas burner

- As a response to the heat request or the flame sensor going off in state Ignited, state Idle is re-entered (action Close_s).

This leads to the following formulation of system actions for controling the burner:

$$^{SF}\mathtt{Start\_s}:\ \mathtt{Idle} \wedge \mathtt{req\_s} \wedge \neg\mathtt{flam\_s}$$
$$\rightarrow\ \mathtt{flow\_s}' = \mathsf{true}$$
$$\wedge\ \mathtt{flow\_e}' = \mathsf{true}$$
$$\wedge\ \mathtt{ign\_s}' = \mathsf{true}$$
$$\wedge\ \mathtt{ign\_e}' = \mathsf{true}\ ,$$

$$^{SF}\mathtt{Ign\_off\_s}:\ \mathtt{Starting} \wedge \mathtt{flam\_s}$$
$$\rightarrow\ \mathtt{ign\_s}' = \mathsf{false}$$
$$\wedge\ \mathtt{ign\_e}' = \mathsf{false}\ ,$$

$$^{SF}\mathtt{Stop\_s}:\ \mathtt{Starting} \wedge \neg\mathtt{flam\_s}$$
$$\rightarrow\ \mathtt{flow\_s}' = \mathsf{false}$$
$$\wedge\ \mathtt{flow\_e}' = \mathsf{false}$$
$$\wedge\ \mathtt{ign\_s}' = \mathsf{false}$$
$$\wedge\ \mathtt{ign\_e}' = \mathsf{false}\ ,$$

$$^{SF}\mathtt{Close\_s}:\ \mathtt{Ignited} \wedge (\neg\mathtt{req\_s} \vee \neg\mathtt{flam\_s})$$
$$\rightarrow\ \mathtt{flow\_s}' = \mathsf{false}$$
$$\wedge\ \mathtt{flow\_e}' = \mathsf{false}\ .$$

As for other details, these actions are relatively straightforward, but the conjunct ¬flam_s may at first sight seem superfluous in the guard of Start_s. It disallows, however, restarting the burner when some fault prevents the flame sensor from going off. This is an example of properties that a specification formalism should allow us to discuss and analyze properly, before implementation strategies are considered.

It should be noticed that predicates Idle, Starting, and Ignited are just a shorthand for three value combinations for the Boolean variables flow_s and ign_s, which are controlled by the above system actions. The fourth possible value combination, ¬flow_s ∧ ign_s, is obviously undesirable, and is unreachable from the initial state by these actions.

### Review Questions

QUESTION 2.2.1  Why is nondeterminism essential in operational models of reactive systems?

QUESTION 2.2.2  What is meant by pure nondeterminism, and why is it useful in specifications?

QUESTION 2.2.3  What is meant by atomicity of actions, and why is it a fundamental notion in the specification of distributed and concurrent systems? Why is atomicity not usually discussed as a basic notion in connection with programming languages?

QUESTION 2.2.4  What is meant by time-dependent errors, and how do they relate to atomicity?

QUESTION 2.2.5  Why is it possible to use an interleaving model for reasoning, even though actions can be executed concurrently in reality?

QUESTION 2.2.6  Why is it so that global states need not exist in the reality of distributed systems?

QUESTION 2.2.7  Why are concurrent processes not fundamental concepts in the specification of reactive systems?

### Exercises

EXERCISE 2.2.1  Discuss the difference between the impossibility of a non-terminating execution and its zero probability in the light of repeated coin tossing, or repeated collisions in Ethernet-like protocols.

EXERCISE 2.2.2  Which of the 256 possible states in the gas-burner example are not reachable from the initial state? Which state transitions would be possible for a state where flow_s = false and ign_s = true?

EXERCISE 2.2.3  Variables flow_s and flow_e have the same value in all reachable states, and the same holds for ign_s and ign_e. Why are they all included in the model?

EXERCISE 2.2.4 Consider adding the assumption to the gas-burner model that a flame cannot be sensed unless the gas valve is open and the ignition transformer is on. How would this affect environment actions and the states that are reachable? Discuss whether this would be a reasonable assumption to make.

## 2.3 Fairness as an Execution Force

Since a sequential program has exactly one control thread, there is no need for an explicit notion of an execution force that would ensure and control progress in executions. With nondeterminism the situation is different in models of concurrent and distributed systems. A suitable notion for this purpose is *fairness*, which will be introduced in this section.

### 2.3.1 Need to Control Nondeterminism

In execution models for sequential programs, execution always proceeds to the next statement, as long as there exists one.

With concurrency the situation is more complex, since the next statement (or action) is no longer uniquely defined because of nondeterminism. Unrestricted nondeterminism is obviously insufficient as such, since some control may be needed to disallow systematic bypassing of some enabled actions. For instance, one of environment actions Req_on_e and Req_off_e is always enabled in the gas-burner example, but executing only those would not generate the kinds of executions we want. The problem would not be solved by requiring that system actions – or actions of each component – must also be executed, since similar competition may also appear between different actions of the same component.

For concurrent processes a practical solution is to use a scheduler to control their execution. For an action language a similar solution would be to assign priorities to system actions, and to postulate a scheduler that would utilize these priorities to dispatch system actions into execution in a deterministic fashion. This would, however, be an implementation-oriented solution that would remove nondeterminism from system actions, which is not desirable, as was discussed in Sect. 2.2.3 (p. 31). What is needed instead is an abstraction that captures the essential properties of schedulers, but without enforcing determinism.

The solution should also be such that it applies in a similar fashion to all kinds of components in a closed system. For instance, considering the modeling of environment behavior, it is quite reasonable that the environment may remain continually silent in spite of enabled environment actions. Therefore, in addition to selecting an action nondeterministically for execution, it should also be possible that none of the enabled actions is selected, which would terminate the execution.[7]

### 2.3.2 Fairness

An appropriate abstraction of schedulers and an execution force is provided by the notion of *fairness*. Informally, fairness with respect to an action guarantees fair treatment of this action in the sense that, when enabled, this action cannot be systematically bypassed in legal executions.

Two varieties of fairness are distinguished, *strong fairness* and *weak fairness*. The former allows us to express that a *repeatedly* enabled action cannot be systematically bypassed. Weak fairness is a weaker force that enforces the execution of *continually* enabled actions only.

To be more precise, an execution is *strongly fair* with respect to an action A if it is not the case that A is enabled infinitely often (or, in the final state, if the execution terminates), but is not executed from some point on.

Correspondingly, an execution is *weakly fair* with respect to action A if it is not the case that, from some point on (or, in the final state, if the execution terminates), A is continually enabled but not executed.

Since 'continually' implies 'infinitely often', strong fairness is properly stronger than weak fairness.

### 2.3.3 Fairness in the Action Language

The first question in including the notion of fairness in the action language is whether some uniform fairness assumption – like weak fairness with respect to each individual action – would be sufficient for our purposes. This is not the case, since different actions may need to be treated differently. For instance, we would not like to exclude the possibility that some environment stimuli are not at all given in some executions, even though the corresponding actions are enabled, but the system component should never stop responding to those stimuli that have been given to it. Therefore, we choose to express fairness assumptions explicitly and individually for each action.

The next question is whether both kinds of fairness assumptions should be supported. On one hand, it can be argued that all direct possibilities to enforce fairness properties in an implementation are restricted to weak fairness. On the other hand, there is no reason to require specifications to be directly implementable, and strong fairness assumptions are more stable in some transformations of action systems, which makes them more appealing for specifications (see Exercise 2.3.1, for instance). Therefore, we decide to accept the slight notational complexity of allowing them both.

---

[7]It would, of course, be possible to add an explicit action that terminates the execution by entering a state in which no actions are enabled, but this would only increase the complexity of modeling.

The convention that will be adopted here is to prefix the names of actions by $^{SF}$ or $^{WF}$ to indicate strong or weak fairness assumptions with respect to them. Actions for which such fairness assumptions are given will be called (strongly or weakly) *fair*. In the gas-burner example, each system action was marked as strongly fair.

Legal executions in an action system are now assumed to satisfy also the fairness requirements specified for its actions. To emphasize this, such executions are also called *fair* executions. In contrast, executions that are not acceptable because they do not satisfy the given fairness requirements are called *unfair*.

It should be pointed out that giving fairness assumptions only with respect to those actions that have been given in the action system constrains what can be conveniently expressed in the action language. For instance, no fairness marking on the actions given in the gas-burner example could express the environment property that action Req_off_e will eventually be executed, if it stays continually enabled with flam_e = true. Therefore, requiring this property would require changes in environment actions (see Exercise 2.3.4). This restriction allows us, however, to keep the execution model of action systems relatively simple also with respect to fairness properties.

### 2.3.4 The Effect of Fairness

Fairness assumptions express how the execution force is controlled. In their absence there would be no need for an execution to take any steps at all. That is, an execution could terminate in the initial state, or in any other state afterwards. With fair actions, on the other hand, an execution cannot terminate in a state in which one of these is enabled. That is, fairness then enforces the execution of some action (which need not be a fair action).

In nonterminating executions fairness forbids only infinitely often repeated (or continual) bypassing of fair actions. In other words, fairness can only guarantee eventual execution of a fair action, but it states nothing about how soon this will take place. The effect of fairness therefore becomes visible only 'in the infinity', which means that any finite sequence of steps, starting from an admissible initial state and proceeding by enabled actions, can be completed into a fair execution.

Since 'eventually' is obviously insufficient for specifying deadlines for action execution, fairness has sometimes been considered a purely theoretical notion that is useless for practical purposes. Another view has been that it is useful when only temporal ordering of events is of concern, but has to be replaced by something else when quantitative time is introduced. In Chap. 10 we will see how fairness can also be used as the execution force when real-time properties of executions are significant.

## 2.3.5 Example: Gas Burner

The strong fairness assumptions given in the actions of the gas-burner example require that no system action can be continually or repeatedly enabled without eventual execution. This has some important consequences for the executions that are allowed.

Obviously, no fairness assumptions could guarantee that each individual change in the states of the two sensors would be observed by the control system, if these states are very unstable. This is related to the symmetry of the modeling formalism with respect to components in the model. In contrast to the synchrony hypothesis, this symmetry would also allow the environment to be fast in comparison to the control system. Strong fairness ensures in this example, however, that continual instability of environment variables req_e and flam_e will be observed by the control system.

Without Start_s being a fair action, its execution would not be enforced even if its guard would continually stay true. This would allow executions where the system does not react to any stimuli. Although Start_s can be executed only when req_s indicates a heat request, strong fairness guarantees that it is not possible for req_s always to be turned off before the system has reacted to the request. (Whether this is a desirable property in a specification, or how to implement it, will not be discussed here.)

Similarly, if flam_s goes repeatedly on and off in state Starting, strong fairness eventually forces either Ign_off_s or Stop_s into execution. This disallows indefinite gas leakage while the ignition transformer is on.

No fairness requirements were given for environment actions. With such requirements one could model, for instance, the property that the heat request will eventually go off, if the flame is burning sufficiently long. This would, however, need slight changes in environment actions (see Exercise 2.3.4).

## 2.3.6 Fundamental Liveness

As already mentioned, the possibilities of expressing fairness assumptions are not as general in the action language as they could be. The basic restriction is that fairness requirements can only be associated with those actions that are given as syntactic entities. A slight generalization would be to consider fairness also with respect to collections of such actions. A set of actions would then be considered to be enabled when at least one action in the set is enabled, and it would be considered to be executed when any of them is executed.

Using this generalization, *fundamental liveness (FL)* in a reactive system is defined as weak fairness with respect to the set of all system actions. Informally this can be understood as follows: if the system can continually do something, it will eventually do something.

In conventional programming languages fundamental liveness is an implicit assumption. If there are no sources for nondeterminism (like concurrency), this is a natural basic assumption. At most one action is then enabled at any time, which means that fundamental liveness is in this situation equivalent to (both weak and strong) fairness with respect to each individual system action.

### 2.3.7 Example: Fair Scheduling of Processes

As an example, consider the scheduling of $n$ independent, non-terminating, concurrent processes that run on a single processor. In modeling this situation we can assume for each process a single action $A_i$, which is always enabled:

- Action $A_i$, $1 \leq i \leq n$, models the event that process $i$ executes for a finite time slice allocated to it.

If all actions $A_i$ are assumed to be (at least weakly) fair, then we have a model of fair scheduling in the sense that each process will always eventually get its next chance to proceed, and no execution with this property is made impossible. In other words, the crucial property of reasonable scheduling algorithms can be specified using fairness, without going into details of how to implement it.

This shows that fair scheduling – or fairness, in general – is an abstraction that is not intended to be implemented as such, i.e., in a manner that would allow only fair executions, but would not exclude any one of them. Instead, one usually needs to implement some deterministic policy that implies fairness but also excludes some fair executions.

For instance, a simple round-robin policy could be used for scheduling of independent processes in practice. In more sophisticated scheduling algorithms the processes could have different priorities for execution, but fairness would then require that high-priority processes still cannot permanently block the execution of low-priority processes (see Exercises 2.3.6 and 2.3.7).

### 2.3.8 Theoretical Power of Fairness

Since algorithms are deterministic by definition, nondeterminism is algorithmically unimplementable. For implementing a nondeterministic choice – for instance a nondeterministic assignment of either 0 or 1 to a variable – one can, however, use such interactions with other concurrent processes or the environment in which the outcome is unpredictable. An example of this is to use the last bit of the clock reading. This shows that interaction provides possibilities that exceed those of algorithms.

Nondeterministic choice between an infinite number of alternatives is called *unbounded nondeterminism*. This is unimplementable not only algorithmically but also using nondeterministic choice between a finite number of alternatives (see Exercise 2.3.10).

Unbounded nondeterminism could, however, be implemented if fairness were available as such, i.e., if action systems could be implemented so that no fair executions would be excluded (see Exercise 2.3.12). Conversely, if unbounded nondeterminism is available, then it is possible to construct a theoretical *fairness scheduler* for an arbitrary action system, so that none of the fair executions are excluded (see Exercise 2.3.15). Fairness and unbounded nondeterminism therefore have the same theoretical power.

### 2.3.9 Probabilistic Implementation

If probabilities can be assigned to the alternatives in selecting between a finite number of alternatives, then *probabilistic implementation* of unbounded nondeterminism is possible, where any one of the alternatives has a non-zero probability, and the selection is completed in finite time with probability 1 (see Exercise 2.3.11). Comparing to 'pure' nondeterminism, this still leaves the possibility that the selection is never completed, but the probability for this to happen is 0.

Correspondingly, in probabilistic implementation of strong (weak) fairness with respect to action A, action A is eventually executed with probability 1 if it is infinitely often (continually) enabled from some point on. Such an implementation is obviously possible if probabilities can be assigned to the alternatives in a boundedly nondeterministic choice. This would still leave the possibility for unfair executions, but their probability would be 0.

A practical example of probabilistic implementation of fairness is the treatment of collisions in Ethernet-like protocols. If several processes try to broadcast a message at the same time, then each of them observes the collision and waits for a random time before retrying. Although renewed attempts may lead to repeated collisions, the probability of eventually getting through is 1 for each process. That is, eventual execution of a continually enabled broadcast action will succeed with probability 1, and the probability for the (theoretically still existing) possibility for not succeeding is 0.

### 2.3.10 Critique and Defence of Fairness

On one hand, fairness provides a very weak way to control the execution of concurrently enabled actions – no matter whether weak or strong fairness is used. In particular, fairness does not provide any direct means to bound the time (or number of times) for which a fair action can be bypassed when it is enabled. On the other hand, fairness is a theoretically very powerful notion that cannot be directly enforced as such.

For these reasons it should not be surprising that fairness is often considered to be totally useless for the practice of software engineering. This critique is, however, usually based on misplaced expectations of its role. Comparing to practical facilities, like priorities, by which process scheduling can be affected, fairness is not intended to be a programming mechanism that could be directly utilized in implementations. Instead, it is an abstraction that has a fundamental role in an execution model for specifications.

On a high level of abstraction it is sufficient for a specification to indicate which actions have to be treated fairly. A model of an implementation needs, however, a concrete solution of how this can be done. In practice this usually requires exclusion of some executions that would not be incorrect as such, and the associated decision can be seen as an implementation-oriented one. It is important, however, that fairness still remains a useful notion for an execution force also on such lower levels of abstraction.

An advantage of the notion of fairness is that it keeps the execution model of specifications simple. Still, it provides a sufficient basis for also specifying properties with practical characteristics. As such it allows us, for instance, to deal effectively with stimulus–response properties at a logical level of causality, where real time is not considered. Furthermore, such logical models can be extended to specify also real-time properties, as will be discussed in Chap. 10.

## Review Questions

QUESTION 2.3.1 Why is there no need for the notion of fairness in deterministic systems?

QUESTION 2.3.2 What is the difference between strong and weak fairness?

QUESTION 2.3.3 What is the main restriction of the action language in expressing fairness properties?

QUESTION 2.3.4 What is meant by fundamental liveness?

QUESTION 2.3.5 How can fairness be enforced in practical implementations?

QUESTION 2.3.6 Why is nondeterminism not algorithmically implementable?

QUESTION 2.3.7 What is meant by a fairness scheduler?

QUESTION 2.3.8 What is the difference between unbounded nondeterminism and its probabilistic implementation?

## Exercises

EXERCISE 2.3.1 Consider the situation illustrated in Fig. 2.4 (p. 33). If no other action except $A_2$ is enabled in the intermediate state $s'$, is it still possible that the splitting of action $A$ has some effect on the legal executions that can be generated by the action system? Notice that there may be fairness assumptions on the actions of the system.

EXERCISE 2.3.2 If only weak fairness would be required with respect to each system action in the gas-burner example, what effect would this have on executions? Analyze this separately for each system action.

EXERCISE 2.3.3 How would the executions in the gas-burner example be affected if only fundamental liveness would be required? Would the executions be the same as in the situation of Exercise 2.3.2?

EXERCISE 2.3.4 Modify the environment model in the gas-burner example so that req_e will eventually turn false, if the flame is continually burning.

EXERCISE 2.3.5 Does fundamental liveness imply weak fairness with respect to each system action, or conversely?

EXERCISE 2.3.6 Consider the situation with several independent, concurrent and non-terminating processes on two levels of priority. Assume also additional actions by which these processes can be nondeterministically disabled and enabled. Give an action-system model in which fair scheduling is violated only by always giving preference to higher-priority processes.

EXERCISE 2.3.7 Modify the model constructed in Exercise 2.3.6 so that every continually enabled process will eventually proceed, even though higher-priority processes may get their chances more often.

EXERCISE 2.3.8 The use of shared resources can be controlled by semaphores. Let the following actions be used in the modeling of a semaphore:

- Action $A_i$, $1 \leq i \leq n$: process $i$ executes code where the shared resource is not used.
- Action $B_i$, $1 \leq i \leq n$: process $i$ requests permission to enter its critical region, in which it is allowed to use the shared resource.
- Action $P_i$, $1 \leq i \leq n$: process $i$ enters its critical region (P operation on the semaphore).
- Action $C_i$, $1 \leq i \leq n$: process $i$ executes code within its critical region.
- Action $V_i$, $1 \leq i \leq n$: process $i$ exits its critical region (V operation on the semaphore).

Add suitable variables to these actions, to model their intended sequencing, as well as the associated P and V operations on the semaphore.

EXERCISE 2.3.9 A *fair semaphore* is a semaphore that eventually gives every requesting process a permission to use the resource. Add fairness requirements to the actions of Exercise 2.3.8 to model the use of a fair semaphore.

EXERCISE 2.3.10 König's Lemma states that a finitely branching tree with an infinite number of leaf nodes necessarily contains infinitely long paths. Use this to show that a nondeterministic choice between a finite number of alternatives is insufficient for implementing unbounded nondeterminism.

EXERCISE 2.3.11 Assume that a probabilistic assignment of either 0 or 1 is available, where the probability for each alternative is 0.5. Show how to implement nondeterministic assignment of an arbitrary natural number to a variable, so that the probability for completing this in finite time is 1.

EXERCISE 2.3.12 Give actions that use fairness to implement a nondeterministic assignment of an arbitrary natural number to a variable in a finite number of action executions.

EXERCISE 2.3.13 Assume that nondeterministic assignment is available for assigning an arbitrary natural number to a variable. Outline a theoretical construction of a fair scheduler for $n$ independent non-terminating processes (as discussed in Sect. 2.3.7, p. 44), so that no fair executions are excluded. Hint: in a fair schedule, each execution of a process is followed by some finite number of scheduling decisions in which other processes are selected.

EXERCISE 2.3.14 Modify the construction outlined in Exercise 2.3.13 to the situation where the scheduling concerns $n$ actions $A_1, \ldots, A_n$ that may also affect each other's guards. The scheduler is assumed to be able to evaluate the guards of all of them, and strong fairness is required with respect to each.

EXERCISE 2.3.15 Generalize the construction outlined in Exercise 2.3.14 to cover the possibility that actions may also have weak fairness requirements or no fairness requirements at all.

## 2.4 Implementation of Action Systems

Operational specifications in the action language can be used as models for implementation. In this section we discuss this in the light of the gas-burner example.

### 2.4.1 Operational Specifications vs. Programs

In principle, the action language could be developed into a programming language. This is not, however, the goal in this book. Instead we are interested in

- giving operational specifications at a high level of abstraction, where human assistance may be needed in their execution (or simulation and animation), and in
- refining operational specifications into a form that reflects the possibilities that are available in actual implementations.

For these reasons, the action language, as developed in this book, deviates from programming languages in the following respects:

- Action systems provide closed-system models that also describe the behavior of the environment.
- Interaction between the environment and the system can be modeled at a level of abstraction which differs from the direct physical possibilities of implementations.
- The types of state variables are mathematical abstractions, like integers of arbitrary size.
- The language is open for additional mathematical concepts.
- Actions may contain expressions that cannot be evaluated mechanically, or whose efficient evaluation is not directly possible.
- No attention is paid to the possibility of efficient schedulability of actions.
- Operational specifications in the action language cannot be directly transformed into implementations that satisfy the real-time properties specified.

### 2.4.2 Example: Gas Burner

Being operational, the above gas-burner specification can be used as a model for an implementation. Still, an implementor has to decide how the interaction between the system and environment parts is implemented, and human assistance may also be needed in translating the given system actions into executable code in a conventional programming language.

In the following we use the specification as a basis for an implementation in *Ada 83*, which is a language that has high-level facilities for writing embedded software. No prior familiarity with Ada is expected of the reader.

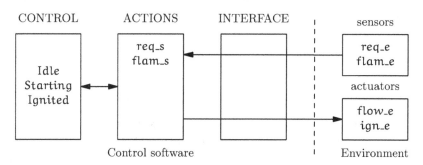

**Fig. 2.6.** Illustration of a gas-burner implementation

### General Structure

The structure of the implementation is shown in Fig. 2.6. The states of the two actuators are controlled by the main program (procedure CONTROL, given in Table 2.3 on p. 53). This program, which will be discussed below in more detail, is a nonterminating loop with statement labels that correspond to the three control states Idle, Starting, and Ignited. The program counter of CONTROL will then always show the control state and, hence, the currently assumed states of the two actuators. Therefore, variables flow_s and ign_s need no explicit representation as program variables.

All code that corresponds to the bodies of system actions is contained in process[8] ACTIONS, which will be discussed below. Actions that control the actuators require cooperation between CONTROL and ACTIONS, whereas actions for registering the sensor states are executed in cooperation between ACTIONS and INTERFACE. Variables req_s and flam_s, whose values indicate the most recent sensor readings, are local to process ACTIONS.

INTERFACE is a module which observes (or is notified of) changes in sensor states, and communicates these changes to process ACTIONS. It also contains subroutines for operating the two actuators. This module is implementation-dependent and will therefore not be discussed here in more detail.

**Actions**

In Ada, process communication takes place through 'entries', which are declared in separate specification modules for processes. An entry of a process can be called from other processes as if it were a subroutine, and such a call can be accepted with an accept statement.

For process ACTIONS we declare entries that correspond to the different system actions (see Table 2.1). Actions Ign_off_s and Stop_s have been combined here, since the decision between their execution is based on the value of variable flam_s, which is local to process ACTIONS.

**Table 2.1.** Entries in process ACTIONS

| | |
|---|---|
| **task** ACTIONS **is** | |
| **entry** Req_on_s; | − − called from INTERFACE |
| **entry** Req_off_s; | − − called from INTERFACE |
| **entry** Flame_on_s; | − − called from INTERFACE |
| **entry** Flame_off_s; | − − called from INTERFACE |
| **entry** Start_s; | − − called from CONTROL |
| **entry** Ign_off_or_Stop_s(b: **out** BOOLEAN); | |
| | − − called from CONTROL |
| **entry** Close_s; | − − called from CONTROL |
| **end**; | |

Corresponding to the simple execution model of action systems, the code of process ACTIONS consists of a nonterminating loop, in which one system

---

[8]In Ada terminology, processes are called 'tasks'.

**Table 2.2.** Process ACTIONS

---

**with** INTERFACE; **use** INTERFACE;
**task body** ACTIONS **is**
   req_s, flam_s: BOOLEAN;
**begin**
   **loop**
      **select**
         **accept** Req_on_s **do**         – – action **Req_on_s**
           req_s := TRUE;
         **end;**
        **or accept** Req_off_s **do**       – – action **Req_off_s**
           req_s := FALSE;
         **end;**
        **or accept** Flame_on_s **do**     – – action **Flame_on_s**
           flam_s := TRUE;
         **end;**
        **or accept** Flame_off_s **do**    – – action **Flame_off_s**
           flam_s := FALSE;
         **end;**
        **or when** req_s **and not** flam_s $\Rightarrow$
         **accept** Start_s **do**         – – action **Start_s**
           turn_gas_valve_on;       – – subroutine in INTERFACE
           turn_ignition_on;        – – subroutine in INTERFACE
         **end;**
        **or accept** Ign_off_or_Stop_s(b: **out** BOOLEAN) **do**
              – – action **Ign_off_s** or Stop_s, depending on flam_s
           **if not** flam_s **then**
              turn_gas_valve_off;     – – subroutine in INTERFACE
           **end if;**
           turn_ignition_off;       – – subroutine in INTERFACE
           b := flam_s;           – – indication of choice
         **end;**
        **or when not** req_s **or not** flam_s $\Rightarrow$
         **accept** Close_s **do**        – – action **Close_s**
           turn_gas_valve_off;       – – subroutine in INTERFACE
         **end;**
      **end select;**
   **end loop;**
**end;**

---

action is executed in each cycle (see Table 2.2). The select statement in the loop therefore has seven alternative accept statements, one alternative for each entry, and one of these is selected in each cycle.

A necessary condition for one of the alternative accept statements to be selected is that the entry in question has been called (either from CONTROL or from INTERFACE), and that the Boolean guard expression (if any) in front of the accept statement is true. These conditions represent, in fact, exactly the guards of the corresponding actions.

Once an alternative is accepted, the associated statements are executed. The caller waits at the entry call until the accept statement is finished, and after that both processes are free to continue their execution. The atomicity assumption of system actions is obviously satisfied, since the control thread of process ACTIONS is involved in each of them. Therefore, there is no possibility for the bodies of two actions to interfere with each other. For instance, the two uses of variable flam_s in the accept statement for entry Ign_off_or_Stop_s necessarily give the same value.

If none of the alternatives can be accepted, then the execution of process ACTIONS waits at the select statement until this becomes possible. If several alternatives could be accepted, then the choice between them is arbitrary, corresponding to nondeterministic selection of an enabled action.

As mentioned above, actions Ign_off_s and Stop_s have been combined here into one accept statement, where the current value of flam_s determines the action to be chosen. An indication of the selection is also given to the caller in a Boolean return parameter b.

**The Main Program**

As already mentioned, the main program (CONTROL; see Table 2.3) is a loop that corresponds to the cycle in Fig. 2.5 (p. 38). Except for the delay statements, which have no counterparts in the specification, the primitive statements in it are entry calls to process ACTIONS.

When at label ⟨⟨Idle⟩⟩, the main program issues an entry call that corresponds to an attempt to initiate action Start_s. As long as this entry call cannot be accepted by process ACTIONS, the main program waits at this point. Once the code for action Start_s has been executed in the corresponding accept statement in process ACTIONS, the main program continues execution, but waits then in a delay statement for 10 seconds, in order to give the flame in the burner some time to stabilize.

After that, at label ⟨⟨Starting⟩⟩, another entry call is issued, corresponding to an attempt to execute either Ign_off_s or Stop_s. Once this entry call has been accepted and the associated code has been executed in process ACTIONS, the return parameter in variable 'success' indicates which of the two actions was executed. If it was action Ign_off_s, an entry call is issued for Close_s, but this can be accepted by process ACTIONS only after the as-

**Table 2.3.** The main program

---

```
with ACTIONS; use ACTIONS;
procedure CONTROL is
   success: BOOLEAN; – – auxiliary variable
begin
   loop
   ⟨⟨Idle⟩⟩                  – – statement label for state Idle
      Start_s;                – – entry call for action Start_s
      delay 10;               – – give the flame 10 seconds to stabilize
   ⟨⟨Starting⟩⟩              – – statement label for state Starting
      Ign_off_or_Stop_s(success);
                              – – action Ign_off_s or Stop_s
                              – – as indicated in return parameter
      if success then
      ⟨⟨Ignited⟩⟩            – – statement label for state Ignited
         Close_s;             – – action Close_s
      end if;
      delay 60;               – – wait one minute before next cycle
   end loop;
end;
```

---

sociated guard has become true. In each case, execution of the main program can go back to label ⟨⟨Idle⟩⟩ only after a one-minute delay.

### 2.4.3 Validation: Satisfaction of Specification

Ultimately, a program running on a computer is not a formal mathematical object – not to speak of closed systems with different kinds of components. Therefore, conformance to a formal specification always depends on some assumptions that are beyond the reach of mathematics. Even when implementation code has been derived from the specification by a formal process, its correctness depends on the validity of some basic assumptions. The more critical a system is, the more effort one should spend in reducing these assumptions to the minimum, and in making them explicit.

In non-critical systems one may, for instance, take it for granted that

- the underlying hardware is reliable,
- one can rely on the correctness of the operating system, compiler, and other basic software that is utilized,
- the environment is non-hostile and does not try to misuse or break the system, and that
- some reasonable assumptions on ranges of input data, frequencies of external events, the capacity and processing speed of the system, etc., are satisfied,

but in critical systems all of these have to be carefully considered. This can be done in two ways:

- On one hand, the specification can be made more and more detailed in reflecting the practical details of implementations.
- On the other hand, implementations can be designed to make weaker assumptions about the conditions under which they work as specified.

An important point in considering the satisfaction of a specification is whether it is reasonable to assume that the required fairness properties are also satisfied. After all, fairness is an abstraction, and its satisfaction may depend, for instance, on various physical properties of the system, as well as on implementation details of the system software that is used. Depending on the criticality of the system, different levels of precision can be used in showing that unfair executions are impossible or sufficiently unlikely in a given implementation.

Concerning the above gas-burner example one can notice that the select statement in Ada does not guarantee fair selection between the different accept alternatives. In fact, it is possible, for instance, that an implementation always selects the first alternative that is ready to be accepted. Therefore, if it is possible for the sensors and module INTERFACE to invoke entry calls for updating variable req_s in each cycle of process ACTIONS, then this process can spend all its time in accepting these calls, and fairness with respect to other system actions will be violated. Reasonable assumptions on the physical characteristics of the different components are, however, sufficient in this case to convince us about the impossibility of such scenarios.

Another abstraction in specifications is the atomicity of actions, which implies that possible intermediate states in the execution of an action need not be considered. As an example, consider actions Start_s and Stop_s in the gas-burner example, which abstract away the intermediate states in which only one of the actuators has been operated.[9] Suppose now that such an intermediate state would be physically dangerous if the actuators were operated in a wrong order. Then the atomicity assumption of actions Start_s and Stop_s could be violated in the implementation, since another environment action, which has not been modeled, could interfere with their execution.

### 2.4.4 Validation: Non-formalized Requirements

Another aspect in validation is that a specification never formalizes all requirements. To be useful, a formal specification concentrates on those properties that are considered non-trivial for the problem at hand. Therefore, an implementation cannot be validated merely by comparing it to the specification.

---

[9]The Ada program is even insufficient for determining how long the system could stay in such an intermediate state.

In the gas-burner example, for instance, all real-time properties were left unspecified,[10] but the Ada implementation explicitly enforced some by delay statements. In validating this implementation one should also consider whether these are appropriate, taking into account that the semantics of the delay statement in Ada 83 only requires that a process be delayed for *at least* the time indicated.

### Review Questions

QUESTION 2.4.1 Why is it not possible, in general, to translate action systems automatically into executable code?

QUESTION 2.4.2 Why is the atomicity assumption of system actions satisfied in the Ada implementation of the gas-burner example?

QUESTION 2.4.3 Admitting that implementations are not formal objects, how can one increase one's confidence in the satisfaction of specifications in life-critical systems?

### Exercises

EXERCISE 2.4.1 Discuss the assumptions under which the gas-burner implementation can be considered to be an acceptable implementation of the given specification.

## Bibliographic Notes

The idea of *closed-system* operational specifications is well known, and has been advocated, for instance, by Zave [195]. Feather has also elaborated on this idea [54]. Most specification approaches deal, however, with *open systems*, which are specified without explicit modeling of the environments in which they are to be used.

The origins of the action language used in this book are in the DisCo language [93], which is an action-oriented language developed by Kurki-Suonio et al. for closed-system specifications. For the current state of DisCo-related research, the reader is referred to [126] and to the DisCo home page [49].

The action-oriented execution model can be traced back to *production systems* for generating sentences in formal languages. In them, the system state is a string of nonterminal and terminal symbols, the initial state being a single start nonterminal, and the 'actions' are rules for replacing some part of the

---

[10]Notice that time-related properties are relevant in *all* systems, not only those that are called real-time systems. In 'non-real-time systems' they are, however, not considered worth making explicit.

string by another string according to given patterns. With nondeterminism, an arbitrary sentence of a language is then generated.

In practical programming languages this kind of an execution model has been used in *production system languages*, notably *OPS5* [58], which have been used for writing expert systems. In these, the goal is to find a terminating execution with a 'successful' final state, and backtracking is essential in this search. A crucial problem then is to control nondeterminism so that this search becomes efficient.

As a language construct for high-level languages the idea of nondeterministic choice appeared first in the iteration statement of Dijkstra's *guarded command language* [43, 44]. This was also the first language that was intended for refining programs (or specifications) into more concrete or efficient forms by systematic transformations. Unbounded nondeterminism was, however, explicitly rejected by Dijkstra [44] as "an insurmountable barrier to the possibility of implementation."

For the specification and design of concurrent and distributed systems an action-oriented execution model was proposed by Back and Kurki-Suonio [20], and also independently by Chandy and Misra in the UNITY language [33, 36]. In contrast to action systems, as presented here, UNITY has a uniform fairness assumption that corresponds to weak fairness with respect to each individual action.

An action-oriented execution model has also been proposed under the name *abstract state machines* (previously also called dynamic structures or evolving algebras) [27]. Otherwise, the characteristics of the associated approach to high-level modeling are, however, rather different from the ideas on which this book is based.

Process communication by *semaphores* is due to Dijkstra [41]. Although fair implementation is essential for them, Dijkstra rejected the theoretical notion of fairness in one of his notes as "unworkable" [46]. This raised immediate responses by Schneider and Lamport [180] and by Chandy and Misra [35], which are instructive reading about the essence of fairness. The conclusion in [180] is that "anyone who accepts the argument of [46], that fairness can be ignored, must also be prepared to ignore termination and all other liveness properties."

The relationship between fairness and unbounded nondeterminism was first shown by Olderog and Apt [164]. The textbook [61] by Francez has an extensive treatment of fairness, mainly from the viewpoint of termination in CSP-like languages for distributed programming.

The gas-burner example of this chapter appeared originally in [75] and was also used in several papers in [72].

# 3

# Formal Properties of Behaviors

In this chapter we take a more formal look at reactive executions, whose abstractions will be called *behaviors*. Temporal expressions and associated mathematics will be introduced to express properties of behaviors and to reason about them. This gives a formal foundation for the action language and for the design methodology to be used with it.

The logic that will be used is a variety of linear-time temporal logics, temporal logic of actions (TLA), in which the expressive power is constrained in a manner that makes it better suited for our purposes.

Temporal logic will not be considered here as an axiomatic system. Instead, it will be discussed from the viewpoint of its semantic interpretation in terms of (linear) behaviors. A number of rules will be derived for the mathematical manipulation of temporal expressions, in order that the reader gets some familiarity with their use.

The structure of this chapter is as follows:

- In Sect. 3.1 we analyze the basic notions of *state* and *state functions* from the viewpoint of using them in *state predicates*.
- Section 3.2 discusses the formalization of executions as sequences of states, called *behaviors*. The notions of *safety* and *liveness properties* are introduced and analyzed at a general level.
- Section 3.3 gives an introduction to temporal logic expressions in terms of their semantic interpretation on behaviors, and to the basic mathematics associated with them.
- Section 3.4 discusses how liveness properties can be expressed in TLA using derived and combined operators.
- Relation to action systems, and various aspects of using TLA for specification, are the topics of Sect. 3.5.

## 3.1 States and State Functions

The notion of state is fundamental in all state-based approaches to reactive systems. We start with discussing how state variables and other state functions are understood in state predicates.

### 3.1.1 State Variables

A countably infinite number of *state variables* (or variables, for short) is assumed. This set, denoted by $\mathsf{Var}$, is universal and consists of all variables that we can name. Since syntactic details are not of interest here, no fixed format is given for the names of variables. The naming conventions that will be used resemble those in programming languages.

All variables in $\mathsf{Var}$ are assumed to 'exist' in each state. In a specification one can, however, make use of some subset $\mathsf{X}$ of these variables only, $\mathsf{X} \subseteq \mathsf{Var}$. All other variables in $\mathsf{Var}$ are then of no concern to the specification. This is in contrast to programming languages, where only those variables are considered to exist that are used. Notice that the variables in conventional programs also include the program counters of the control threads involved.

Unlike in most programming languages, variables have no types. That is, a universal set $\mathsf{Val}$ of possible values is assumed. Set $\mathsf{Val}$ will not be explicitly defined, but it is assumed to contain such countable sets[1] as Booleans ($\mathbb{B}$), natural numbers ($\mathbb{N}$), integers ($\mathbb{Z}$), characters ($\mathbb{C}$), strings ($\mathbb{S}$), etc. In addition, to deal with real-time properties (to be discussed in Chap. 10), we will also assume real numbers ($\mathbb{R}$) to be included in $\mathsf{Val}$, even though they make $\mathsf{Val}$ an uncountable set. Structured and aggregated values, like *lists*, *records*, *sequences*, *sets*, and *multisets*[2] will also be used.

The subset $\mathsf{X} \subseteq \mathsf{Var}$ of variables referred to in the gas-burner example of Chap. 2 was

$$\mathsf{X} = \{\mathsf{req\_e}, \mathsf{flam\_e}, \mathsf{flow\_e}, \mathsf{ign\_e}, \mathsf{req\_s}, \mathsf{flam\_s}, \mathsf{flow\_s}, \mathsf{ign\_s}\} \,.$$

Like all variables, these are understood to be untyped, in principle. They are, however, Boolean variables in the sense that they do not possess any other kinds of values in those states that are reachable in legal executions of the given action system, and this property can also be mechanically checked. This kind of typing of untyped variables will be discussed in more detail in Chap. 5.

### 3.1.2 States

The notion of *state* is another basic notion. It is assumed that each variable has a unique value in every state and, conversely, all possible assignments of

---

[1]A set is countable if it is finite or if its elements can be mapped one-to-one on natural numbers.

[2]A multiset is like a set that may contain several 'copies' of the same element. Multisets are also called *bags*.

values to variables constitute the different states. The set of all possible states will be denoted by $\Sigma$, and symbols s and t will be used in the following to denote individual states.[3]

The value of variable $x \in Var$ in state $s \in \Sigma$ will be denoted by $s[\![x]\!]$. Here $[\![x]\!]$ stands for the 'meaning' of x, and the prefix s indicates that this meaning is evaluated or interpreted in state s.

By definition, every variable $x \in Var$ has some value $s[\![x]\!]$ in each state $s \in \Sigma$. For instance, variable z is understood to have some value in each state discussed in the gas-burner example. However, since we were not interested in z in this example, we did not specify how its value would change, and z is therefore allowed to change arbitrarily.

### 3.1.3 State Functions

Any expression f that has a unique value (that belongs to $Val$) in each state $s \in \Sigma$ is called a *state function*. For state s the value of f will be denoted by $s[\![f]\!]$.

State variables are a special case of state functions. Intuitively, state variables can be thought of as primitive state functions whose values are 'stored' or represented in each state as such. Other state functions are non-primitive, and can be expressed in terms of state variables. In order to allow freedom in choosing the representation of state functions we do not, however, determine which of them are primitive and which are not.

Notations of arithmetic and set theory will be used in state functions without further explanation.

Allowing variables to have arbitrary values in $Val$ has the consequence that expressions for state functions need not be well defined in all states. For instance, arithmetic does not define the values of $x/y$ and $z+1$ when $y = 0$ and $z = \mathsf{true}$. Each state function is, however, assumed to have a unique value in each state, although this value is unknown when the associated expression cannot be uniquely evaluated.

To avoid the problems that are caused by undefined or unknown values we will make sure that we need not evaluate a state function in states in which it is not well defined. We will return to this question in more detail in Sect. 3.5, where the relationship between action systems and TLA will be discussed.[4]

### 3.1.4 State Predicates

A (concrete) *state predicate* P (or just predicate, for short) is an expression that has a truth value $s[\![P]\!]$ in each state $s \in \Sigma$. State predicates are otherwise

---

[3]Notice that with an infinite $Var$, the state space $\Sigma$ would be uncountably infinite even if $Val$ were finite.

[4]In theoretical approaches to computing there are several different ways to deal with undefined values, none of which is good for all purposes. The solution adopted here serves best the purposes of this book.

like truth-valued state functions, but the logical truth values, denoted by **T** and **F**, are assumed not to belong to Val. Symbols P, Q, ... will be used in the following to denote state predicates.

The problem of undefined or unknown values also arises in connection with expressions that represent state predicates, and the solution is the same as for state functions: we will make sure that an expression for a state predicate need not be evaluated in states in which its truth value is not well defined.

When s⟦P⟧ is true for a concrete state predicate P, we say that state s *satisfies* P, or that P *holds* in s. If there exists a state s ∈ Σ that satisfies P, P is *satisfiable*. If P is satisfied by all states s ∈ Σ, it is a *tautology*.

Logical operators ($\land$, $\lor$, $\neg$, $\Rightarrow$, $\Leftrightarrow$) and quantifiers ($\exists$ for 'there exists', and $\forall$ for 'for all') are used in the normal manner in the construction of state predicates. As for syntactic priorities, we adopt the convention that negation ($\neg$) and quantifiers ($\exists$, $\forall$) are the strongest, that conjunction ($\land$) binds more strongly than disjunction ($\lor$), and that implication ($\Rightarrow$) and equivalence ($\Leftrightarrow$) are the weakest. Arithmetic and relational operators are assumed to bind more strongly than binary logical connectives.

As an example, if $x, y \in$ Var, then the expression

$$\exists m : (m \in \mathbb{Z} \land x = m^2 \land y = m^3)$$

is a concrete state predicate, which can also be written as

$$\exists m \in \mathbb{Z} : (x = m^2 \land y = m^3) \, ,$$

and which is true in those states where $x$ is the square and $y$ is the cube of some integer $m$. In this expression $m$ is not a state variable, but a 'logical variable' that is local to that expression. To distinguish such 'logical' variables from state variables, whose values may change from one state to another, they are also called *rigid variables*.

As further examples, consider state predicates on the variables in the gas-burner example. Taking the definitions of Idle, Starting, and Ignited on p. 37,[5] state predicates

$$\text{Idle} \Rightarrow \neg(\text{Starting} \lor \text{Ignited}) \, ,$$
$$\text{Starting} \Rightarrow \neg(\text{Idle} \lor \text{Ignited}) \, ,$$
$$\text{Ignited} \Rightarrow \neg(\text{Idle} \lor \text{Starting})$$

are tautologies, whereas predicates

---

[5]When a variable b is understood to possess only Boolean values, as those in the example are, its name b may also be used as such for the truth-valued expression b = true. Notice that ¬b then stands for b ≠ true, not for b = false. The two Boolean values, true and false, belong to Val, and should not be confused with the truth values **T** and **F** of predicates.

$$\text{flam\_s} = \text{true} \lor \text{flam\_s} = \text{false} , \tag{3.1}$$

$$\text{ign\_s} = \text{true} \Rightarrow \text{flow\_s} = \text{true} , \tag{3.2}$$

$$\text{Idle} \lor \text{Starting} \lor \text{Ignited} \tag{3.3}$$

are not, although they happen to be satisfied by all states that are reachable in the gas-burner example.

### 3.1.5 Predicate Expressions and Laws

In addition to concrete state predicates, predicate expressions may contain *predicate symbols*, which then stand for arbitrary concrete state predicates.[6] Such an expression is satisfiable if there exists an assignment of concrete state predicates to predicate symbols so that the resulting concrete predicate is satisfiable, and it is a tautology if all such assignments yield tautologies.

A tautology of the form $P \Rightarrow Q$ or $P \Leftrightarrow Q$ is called a (non-temporal) *law*. If $P \Rightarrow Q$ is a law, then every state that satisfies $P$ (for some assignment of concrete state predicates to the predicate symbols in $P$) also satisfies $Q$ (for the same assignment). Obviously, a law of the form $P \Leftrightarrow Q$ can be understood as shorthand for two laws, $P \Rightarrow Q$ and $Q \Rightarrow P$.

As an example, the expression

$$\neg(P \land Q) \Leftrightarrow \neg P \lor \neg Q ,$$

where $P$ and $Q$ are predicate symbols, is a law that is known as de Morgan's law.

In proving that a predicate expression $P \Rightarrow Q$ is a law we can utilize transitivity: if $P \Rightarrow R$ and $R \Rightarrow Q$ are laws, then so also is $P \Rightarrow Q$. Furthermore, if $P \Leftrightarrow Q$ is a law, and $\Phi(P)$ is a predicate expression that contains $P$ as a subexpression, then $\Phi(P) \Leftrightarrow \Phi(Q)$ is also a law.

### Review Questions

QUESTION 3.1.1 What are the differences between state variables, as discussed here, and variables in conventional programming languages?

QUESTION 3.1.2 How do we deal with undefined values of expressions?

QUESTION 3.1.3 What is the difference between state variables and rigid variables?

QUESTION 3.1.4 What is the difference between true and **T**?

---

[6]Quantification of predicate symbols will not be allowed. Therefore, predicate symbols are always free variables in predicate expressions.

QUESTION 3.1.5 Why is predicate $b = \mathsf{true} \lor b = \mathsf{false}$ not a tautology for a state variable $b$ that is known to have only Boolean values?

QUESTION 3.1.6 What is meant by a predicate expression being satisfiable, a tautology, or a law?

**Exercises**

EXERCISE 3.1.1 Formulate further state predicates that are satisfied by all states that are reachable in the gas-burner example of Chap. 2.

## 3.2 Properties of Behaviors

Executions of a reactive system generate sequences of states. In this section we discuss the logical properties of such sequences at a general level, without yet introducing a language of temporal logic to express them.

### 3.2.1 Behaviors

While a state $s \in \Sigma$ models an instantaneous situation in an execution, a complete execution can be modeled as a sequence of states. Such executions are, in general, nonterminating. Therefore, we are interested in infinite sequences of states $\sigma = \langle s_0, s_1, s_2, \ldots \rangle$, $s_i \in \Sigma$, which are called *behaviors*. The set of all possible behaviors $\sigma$ is denoted by $\Sigma^\infty$.

Assuming all behaviors to be infinite is no essential restriction, since terminating executions can always be modeled as ones where the final state is repeated indefinitely. Notice that, although we can in practice generate only *prefixes* (i.e., finite initial parts) of behaviors, a behavior is defined as a completely given infinite sequence of states.[7]

The first state $s_0$ of a behavior $\sigma = \langle s_0, s_1, s_2, \ldots \rangle$ is called its *initial state*. Each pair of consecutive states $(s_i, s_{i+1})$ in $\sigma$ is called a *step* in $\sigma$.

Let $X$ be the set of variables that are of interest in a specification. A step $(s_i', s_{i+1})$ in which all variables in $X$ have the same values in both $s_i$ and $s_{i+1}$ is then called a *stuttering* step, or an $X$-stuttering step, if we wish to make $X$ explicit. A terminating execution now corresponds to a behavior that ends in indefinite stuttering.

---

[7]Therefore, even when only one Boolean state variable is of interest, we can distinguish between an uncountably infinite number of different behaviors, although the number of different finite prefixes of them is still countable (see Exercise 3.2.1).

### 3.2.2 Properties and Characteristic Sets

By a (logical) *property* (of behaviors) we understand a mapping of behaviors to truth values. For a property $\phi$ and a behavior $\sigma \in \Sigma^\infty$ we say that $\sigma$ *satisfies* $\phi$, or that $\phi$ *holds* for $\sigma$, if $\phi(\sigma)$ is true.

For any property $\phi$, its *characteristic set* is defined as the set $S_\phi$, $S_\phi \subseteq \Sigma^\infty$, of those behaviors for which the property $\phi$ holds. Denoting identically true and false properties by $\mathbf{T}$ and $\mathbf{F}$, respectively, we have $S_{\mathbf{T}} = \Sigma^\infty$ and $S_{\mathbf{F}} = \emptyset$. That is, the identically true property is satisfied by all behaviors, but the identically false property is satisfied by none of them.

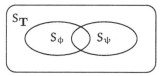 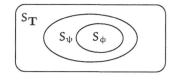

**Fig. 3.1.** Venn diagrams for properties; the one on the right illustrates the situation where $\phi \Rightarrow \psi$

Obviously, logical combinations of properties correspond to set-theoretic operations on their characteristic sets,

$$S_{\phi \wedge \psi} = S_\phi \cap S_\psi ,$$
$$S_{\phi \vee \psi} = S_\phi \cup S_\psi ,$$
$$S_{\neg \phi} = \overline{S_\phi} ,$$

and can therefore be illustrated by *Venn diagrams*, where properties are represented by their characteristic sets (see Fig. 3.1). In particular, implication between properties corresponds to set inclusion in Venn diagrams,

$$\phi \Rightarrow \psi \quad \text{iff} \quad S_\phi \subseteq S_\psi ,$$
$$\phi \Leftrightarrow \psi \quad \text{iff} \quad S_\phi = S_\psi .$$

### 3.2.3 Safety Properties

*Safety properties* are an important class of formal properties of behaviors. Informally, a safety property can be characterized as a property of the form 'something bad never happens'.

The crucial characteristic of a safety property is that its violation can always be detected from some finite prefix of a behavior. Operationally speaking, once a safety property has been violated in an execution, this cannot be remedied in the future. More precisely, every behavior $\sigma = \langle s_0, s_1, s_2, \ldots \rangle$ not satisfying a safety property $\phi$, i.e., $\sigma \notin S_\phi$, has a finite prefix $\langle s_0, \ldots, s_n \rangle$ that cannot be extended to any (infinite) behavior in $S_\phi$.

As an example, consider a property $\phi$ that is satisfied by a behavior $\sigma$ if state predicate (3.1) on p. 61 is true in all states of $\sigma$. The 'bad thing' that should not happen is then that flam_s is neither true nor false in some state. Obviously, if $\sigma$ does not have property $\phi$, then there is a first state $s_n$ in $\sigma$ where (3.1) does not hold, and the prefix $\langle s_0, \ldots, s_n \rangle$ cannot be extended to any $\tau$, $\tau \in \Sigma^\infty$, that would satisfy $\phi$. Therefore, $\phi$ is a safety property.

In ordinary non-reactive executions, *partial correctness* is an example of a safety property. Informally it means that a program never terminates with an incorrect result. In terms of behaviors, we can understand 'terminal' and 'the value of the result variable is correct' as two state predicates P and Q, respectively. The 'bad thing' that should not happen is then to enter a state that satisfies $P \land \neg Q$.

Another typical example of safety properties is that no wrong or superfluous messages are received in a message-transfer system. That is, every message that is received has also been sent, and no message is received more than once.

### 3.2.4 Liveness Properties

*Liveness properties* are another important class of formal properties of behaviors. Informally, a liveness property is characterized to have the form 'something good will eventually happen'.

The crucial characteristic of a liveness property is that its violation cannot be detected from any finite prefix of a behavior. In other words, given a liveness property $\psi$, every finite sequence of states $\langle s_0, \ldots, s_n \rangle$ can be extended to some (infinite) behavior that belongs to $S_\psi$.

As an example, consider a property $\psi$ that is satisfied by a behavior $\sigma$, if predicate flam_s = true holds in some state of $\sigma$. The 'good thing' that should happen is then that flam_s = true holds in some state. Since any finite sequence of states can be extended to contain such a state, this is a liveness property.

In ordinary non-reactive programs, *termination* is an example of a liveness property. Reaching a terminal state (i.e., one that satisfies the state predicate P defining a state to be terminal) then is the 'good thing' that should happen. Since every state sequence can be extended to contain a state that satisfies P, this is a liveness property.

In message transmission, the property that every message that has been sent will also be received is another liveness property.

### 3.2.5 Mixed Properties

It will be shown below that each formal property of behaviors can be expressed as a conjunction of a safety property and a liveness property. That is, each property is either a (pure) safety or a liveness property, or a *mixed* property that consists of a safety part and a liveness part.

*Total correctness* of a non-reactive program is an example of a mixed property, defined as the conjunction of partial correctness and termination. Similarly, correctness of message transmission is the conjunction of not receiving anything that has not been sent (or receiving a message more than once), and eventually receiving every message.

### 3.2.6 Limitations of Potential Infinity

In practice one can deal with infinity only as 'potential' infinity, which can be managed in terms of arbitrarily large finite approximations, but cannot be 'observed' in its entirety. The execution of a nonterminating program, for instance, can be observed for any finite number of steps but, in its entirety, an infinite execution is beyond any practical possibilities for observation.

Our definition of behaviors as infinite state sequences means that they provide a model of nonterminating executions, which cannot be observed in their entirety.[8] This has some important consequences for the properties that are of interest to us.

As an example, consider two properties defined as follows:

- Property $\phi$: the value of state variable $x$ is always either 0 or 1, and $x = 1$ at least once.
- Property $\psi$: the value of state variable $x$ is always either 0 or 1.

Obviously, $S_\phi$ is a proper subset of $S_\psi$, since a behavior with $x$ constantly 0 satisfies property $\psi$ but not $\phi$. Suppose now that we can observe only finite prefixes of behaviors. Then, for an arbitrary behavior $\sigma \in S_\psi$ we cannot distinguish whether it belongs to $S_\phi$ or not, since the value of $x$ may remain 0 for any finite number of steps and then turn into 1.

### 3.2.7 The Closure of a Property

To deal with the above phenomenon formally, we define a metric for measuring distances between behaviors in $\Sigma^\infty$ as follows. For two behaviors $\sigma = \langle s_0, s_1, \ldots \rangle$, $\tau = \langle t_0, t_1, \ldots \rangle$, their *distance* $\text{dist}(\sigma, \tau)$ is defined to be $2^{-n}$ if they first differ in their $(n+1)$st states, i.e., $s_i = t_i$ for $i < n$, but $s_n \neq t_n$.

Obviously, distance $\text{dist}$ satisfies the crucial characteristics of metric that $\text{dist}(\sigma, \tau) = \text{dist}(\tau, \sigma) \geq 0$ for all $\sigma, \tau \in \Sigma^\infty$, and $\text{dist}(\sigma, \tau) = 0$ if and only if $\sigma = \tau$. The maximum distance in this metric is 1, and the longer the prefixes are for which $\sigma$ and $\tau$ agree, the closer they are to each other.

As an example, let $1 \ldots$ denote (the set of) behaviors $\langle s_0, s_1, \ldots \rangle$ in $S_\phi$ where $s_0[\![x]\!] = 1$. Similarly, let $01 \ldots, 001 \ldots$, etc., denote those where $s_0[\![x]\!] =$

---

[8]Since there is an infinite number of variables, no state can be observed in its entirety, either. In the following we assume, however, that for each state it is possible to observe whether it satisfies those state predicates that we are interested in.

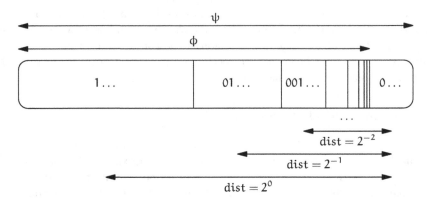

**Fig. 3.2.** Illustration of the closure of a property $\phi$, $\psi = Cl(\phi)$

0 and $s_1[\![x]\!] = 1$, $s_0[\![x]\!] = s_1[\![x]\!] = 0$ and $s_2[\![x]\!] = 1$, etc., and let $0 \ldots$ denote those in $S_\psi$ where $x = 0$ in all states. Figure 3.2 then illustrates the above properties $\phi$ and $\psi$. Obviously, for any behavior $\sigma \in 0 \ldots$ (with $x$ constantly 0) and any $\epsilon > 0$ there are behaviors $\tau \in S_\phi$ for which $dist(\sigma, \tau) < \epsilon$. That is, there is a sequence of behaviors $\tau_0, \tau_1, \ldots \in S_\phi$ such that $\lim_{i \to \infty} dist(\sigma, \tau_i) = 0$ or, in other words, $\lim_{i \to \infty} \tau_i = \sigma$.

For any property $\phi$ we now define its *closure* $Cl(\phi)$ so that its characteristic set $S_{Cl(\phi)}$ contains all behaviors in $S_\phi$ and also all limits of infinite sequences of behaviors in $S_\phi$, i.e.,

$$S_{Cl(\phi)} \stackrel{\Delta}{=} \{\tau \mid \forall \epsilon > 0 : \exists \sigma \in S_\phi : dist(\sigma, \tau) < \epsilon\}.$$

Intuitively, behaviors in $S_{Cl(\phi)}$ either belong to $S_\phi$ or cannot be distinguished from these by looking at finite prefixes only. More formally, $S_{Cl(\phi)}$ is the smallest superset of $S_\phi$ that is closed under the metric defined by $dist$.

Obviously, implications

$$\phi \Rightarrow Cl(\phi), \tag{3.4}$$

$$\text{if} \quad \phi \Rightarrow \psi \quad \text{then} \quad Cl(\phi) \Rightarrow Cl(\psi), \tag{3.5}$$

$$Cl(Cl(\phi)) \Leftrightarrow Cl(\phi) \tag{3.6}$$

hold for all properties $\phi$ and $\psi$ (see Exercise 3.2.7).

### 3.2.8 Formal Characterization of Safety and Liveness

Property $\phi$, and correspondingly also its characteristic set $S_\phi$, is said to be *closed* if it is equivalent to its closure, i.e., if $\phi \Leftrightarrow Cl(\phi)$ or $S_\phi = S_{Cl(\phi)}$. It now follows from the above definition of safety properties that these are exactly those properties that are closed under $dist$ (Exercise 3.2.8). In other words, safety properties $\phi$ can be formally characterized by

$$\varphi \Leftrightarrow Cl(\varphi) \quad \text{or} \quad S_\varphi = S_{Cl(\varphi)} \, . \tag{3.7}$$

Correspondingly, from the above definition of liveness properties it follows that liveness properties are exactly those properties whose closure under $\mathrm{dist}$ is the identically true property (Exercise 3.2.9). That is, liveness properties $\varphi$ can be formally characterized by

$$Cl(\varphi) \Leftrightarrow \mathbf{T} \quad \text{or} \quad S_{Cl(\varphi)} = \Sigma^\infty \, . \tag{3.8}$$

By (3.6), the closure $Cl(\varphi)$ is a safety property for any $\varphi$. More exactly, it is the strongest safety property that is implied by $\varphi$. In terms of characteristic sets, $S_{Cl(\varphi)}$ is the smallest closed set that contains $S_\varphi$.

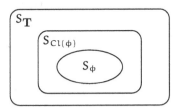

**Fig. 3.3.** Illustration of $\varphi = Cl(\varphi) \wedge (\neg Cl(\varphi) \vee \varphi)$

Each property $\varphi$ of behaviors can now be expressed as

$$\varphi \Leftrightarrow Cl(\varphi) \wedge (\neg Cl(\varphi) \vee \varphi) \, , \tag{3.9}$$

which corresponds in a Venn diagram (see Fig. 3.3) to

$$S_\varphi = S_{Cl(\varphi)} \cap (\overline{S_{Cl(\varphi)}} \cup S_\varphi) \, .$$

It will be left to the reader to show that $\neg Cl(\varphi) \vee \varphi$ is a liveness property (Exercise 3.2.4). Equivalence (3.9) therefore shows that each property of behaviors is a conjunction of a safety property and a liveness property.

## Review Questions

QUESTION 3.2.1 What is meant by stuttering?

QUESTION 3.2.2 What is meant by a property of behaviors?

QUESTION 3.2.3 What is meant by safety and liveness properties?

QUESTION 3.2.4 How can total correctness be characterized as a conjunction of a safety property and a liveness property?

QUESTION 3.2.5 What does it mean that a set is closed under a given metric? Why is $\mathrm{dist}$, as defined in the text, a reasonable metric for behaviors?

QUESTION 3.2.6 What are the formal characterizations of safety and liveness properties?

**Exercises**

EXERCISE 3.2.1 Show that the number of different finite strings of 0's and 1's is only countably infinite, but the number of infinite strings of them is uncountably infinite.

EXERCISE 3.2.2 Check that the metric determined by dist satisfies the triangle inequality $\mathrm{dist}(\sigma_1, \sigma_2) \leq \mathrm{dist}(\sigma_1, \tau) + \mathrm{dist}(\tau, \sigma_2)$ for all $\sigma_1, \sigma_2, \tau \in \Sigma^\infty$, and that equality holds only when $\tau = \sigma_1$ or $\tau = \sigma_2$.

EXERCISE 3.2.3 Show that $\psi = \mathrm{Cl}(\phi)$ in Sect. 3.2.6 (p. 65).

EXERCISE 3.2.4 Show that the property $\neg\mathrm{Cl}(\phi) \vee \phi$ is a liveness property for every property $\phi$.

EXERCISE 3.2.5 Show that only the identically true property is both a safety property and a liveness property.

EXERCISE 3.2.6 Is the identically false property a safety property or a liveness property?

EXERCISE 3.2.7 Check that (3.4)–(3.6) on p. 66 hold for all properties $\phi$ and $\psi$.

EXERCISE 3.2.8 Show that the formal characterization of safety properties in (3.7) on p. 67 follows from the definition given in Sect. 3.2.3 (p. 63).

EXERCISE 3.2.9 Show that the formal characterization of liveness properties in (3.8) on p. 67 follows from the definition given in Sect. 3.2.4 (p. 64).

EXERCISE 3.2.10 Considering the variables in the gas-burner example in Chap. 2, give an infinite sequence of behaviors that correspond to fair executions of the action system, but whose limit is a behavior that does not.

EXERCISE 3.2.11 Consider the following properties of behaviors:
- Property $\phi_1$: The value of variable x is always 0, 1, or 2.
- Property $\phi_2$: $\phi_1$ and, in addition, x will be turned from 1 to some other value at most once.
- Property $\phi_3$: $\phi_1$ and, in addition, x = 1 in infinitely many states.
- Property $\phi_4$: $\phi_1$ and, in addition, either $\phi_2$ or x ≠ 2 in all states.

For each $\phi_i$, give an action system to generate behaviors where the value of x changes arbitrarily, as allowed by property $\phi_i$.

EXERCISE 3.2.12 What are the closures of the properties in Exercise 3.2.11?

EXERCISE 3.2.13 Is it reasonable to say that all interesting properties of programs are formalizable in terms of safety and liveness properties?

# 3.3 Temporal Expressions

*Temporal expressions* are logical expressions that can be interpreted as properties of behaviors. The associated logics for reasoning are called *temporal logics*. In this section temporal expressions will be introduced in the form they are used in TLA, temporal logic of actions.

### 3.3.1 Semantic Interpretation

The *semantics* of temporal logic is provided by evaluating (concrete) temporal expressions E for behaviors $\sigma \in \Sigma^\infty$. The truth value obtained by evaluating E for a behavior $\sigma \in \Sigma^\infty$ is denoted by $\sigma[\![E]\!]$. Symbols E, F, ... will be used in the following to denote temporal expressions.

If $\sigma[\![E]\!]$ is true, we say that $\sigma$ *satisfies* E, or that E *holds* for $\sigma$. A set of behaviors satisfies E if all its behaviors satisfy E.

A (concrete) temporal expression is (temporally) *satisfiable* if there exists a behavior that satisfies it. It is a (temporal) *tautology* if all behaviors $\sigma \in \Sigma^\infty$ satisfy it.

In addition to concrete temporal expressions, a temporal expression may contain symbols that represent arbitrary temporal expressions, state predicates, or actions (to be introduced below). Such an expression is (temporally) *satisfiable* if there exists an assignment of concrete counterparts to these symbols that makes the resulting concrete expression satisfiable. It is a (temporal) *tautology* if all such assignments yield a tautology.

### 3.3.2 Extending Predicate Logic

Temporal logic is an extension of predicate logic. All non-temporal expressions therefore also have meanings as temporal expressions, where predicate symbols now stand for arbitrary concrete temporal expressions. Such expressions are also temporally satisfiable or temporal tautologies iff their non-temporal interpretations are satisfiable or tautologies, respectively. In particular, all non-temporal laws generalize into temporal laws. For instance, de Morgan's law is a (temporal) tautology for all temporal expressions E and F:

$$\neg(E \wedge F) \Leftrightarrow \neg E \vee \neg F .$$

Semantically, when a state predicate is used as a temporal expression, it is interpreted as an *initial condition* for a behavior. That is, for any state predicate P and behavior $\sigma = \langle s_0, s_1, s_2, \ldots \rangle$, the meaning of P for $\sigma$ is the same as its meaning for $s_0$ as a state predicate, i.e.,

$$\sigma[\![P]\!] \overset{\Delta}{=} s_0[\![P]\!] . \tag{3.10}$$

To make temporal logic an extension of predicate logic, logical operators $(\wedge, \vee, \neg, \Rightarrow, \Leftrightarrow)$ have to be used in the same meanings. That is, for any temporal expressions E, F, and behavior $\sigma = \langle s_0, s_1, s_2, \dots \rangle$,[9]

$$\sigma[\![E \wedge F]\!] \stackrel{\Delta}{=} \sigma[\![E]\!] \wedge \sigma[\![F]\!] , \tag{3.11}$$

$$\sigma[\![E \vee F]\!] \stackrel{\Delta}{=} \sigma[\![E]\!] \vee \sigma[\![F]\!] , \tag{3.12}$$

$$\sigma[\![\neg E]\!] \stackrel{\Delta}{=} \neg \sigma[\![E]\!] , \tag{3.13}$$

$$\sigma[\![E \Rightarrow F]\!] \stackrel{\Delta}{=} \sigma[\![E]\!] \Rightarrow \sigma[\![F]\!] , \tag{3.14}$$

$$\sigma[\![E \Leftrightarrow F]\!] \stackrel{\Delta}{=} \sigma[\![E]\!] \Leftrightarrow \sigma[\![F]\!] . \tag{3.15}$$

### 3.3.3 Temporal 'Always' Operator

In addition to operators of predicate logic, a unary *temporal operator* is needed, denoted by $\Box$ and read as *box* or *always*. For any temporal expression E and behavior $\sigma = \langle s_0, s_1, s_2, \dots \rangle$ its semantics is defined by

$$\sigma[\![\Box E]\!] \stackrel{\Delta}{=} \bigwedge_{i \geq 0} \sigma_i[\![E]\!] , \tag{3.16}$$

where $\sigma_i$ denotes the suffix $\langle s_i, s_{i+1}, s_{i+2}, \dots \rangle$ of $\sigma$. In other words,

- a behavior $\sigma \in \Sigma^\infty$ satisfies $\Box E$ iff $\sigma$ and all its suffixes satisfy E.

As a unary operator, $\Box$ is used as a syntactically more binding operator than any binary operators.

Using the above semantic definitions it is easy to prove the following temporal laws for $\Box$:

$$\Box \mathbf{T} \Leftrightarrow \mathbf{T} , \tag{3.17}$$

$$\Box \mathbf{F} \Leftrightarrow \mathbf{F} , \tag{3.18}$$

$$\Box \Box E \Leftrightarrow \Box E , \tag{3.19}$$

$$\Box E \Rightarrow E , \tag{3.20}$$

$$\Box E \wedge \Box F \Leftrightarrow \Box(E \wedge F) . \tag{3.21}$$

To check (3.21), for instance, we have for an arbitrary $\sigma \in \Sigma^\infty$:

$$\sigma[\![\Box E \wedge \Box F]\!] \Leftrightarrow \sigma[\![\Box E]\!] \wedge \sigma[\![\Box F]\!] \quad \text{by (3.11)}$$
$$\Leftrightarrow (\sigma_0[\![E]\!] \wedge \sigma_1[\![E]\!] \wedge \cdots) \wedge (\sigma_0[\![F]\!] \wedge \sigma_1[\![F]\!] \wedge \cdots) \quad \text{by (3.16)}$$
$$\Leftrightarrow (\sigma_0[\![E]\!] \wedge \sigma_0[\![F]\!]) \wedge (\sigma_1[\![E]\!] \wedge \sigma_1[\![F]\!]) \wedge \cdots \quad \text{by commutativity}$$
$$\Leftrightarrow \sigma_0[\![E \wedge F]\!] \wedge \sigma_1[\![E \wedge F]\!] \wedge \cdots \quad \text{by (3.11)}$$
$$\Leftrightarrow \sigma[\![\Box(E \wedge F)]\!] \quad \text{by (3.16)} .$$

---

[9]On the left-hand side the operators are part of the language for temporal expressions; on the right-hand side they denote operators for truth values.

### 3.3.4 State Invariants

For a state predicate P, $\Box$P expresses that P is a *state invariant* that holds in all states of a behavior. Obviously, both P (understood as a temporal predicate) and $\Box$P are safety properties. If P is a tautology as a state predicate, then both P and $\Box$P are temporal tautologies.

As examples of state invariants, consider

$$\Box(\mathsf{flam\_s} = \mathsf{true} \vee \mathsf{flam\_s} = \mathsf{false}) ,$$
$$\Box(\mathsf{ign\_s} = \mathsf{true} \Rightarrow \mathsf{flow\_s} = \mathsf{true}) ,$$
$$\Box(\mathsf{Idle} \vee \mathsf{Starting} \vee \mathsf{Ignited}) ,$$

which are satisfied by all behaviors that are generated by executions in the gas-burner example. In other words, (3.1), (3.2), and (3.3) on p. 61 are state invariants for the behaviors in this example.

In this connection a warning is in place about substituting subexpressions in temporal expressions by ones that may be mistakenly considered as equivalent. For instance, if one has shown that both $P \Leftrightarrow Q$ and $\Box P$ hold for a behavior $\sigma \in \Sigma^\infty$, one still cannot decide that $\Box Q$ would hold for it. This is because, as a temporal expression, $P \Leftrightarrow Q$ refers only to the initial state of $\sigma$. However, if $P \Leftrightarrow Q$ is a law (which is true for an arbitrary state), then the conclusion is correct.

In fact, it can be immediately checked that, if $P \Rightarrow Q$ ($P \Leftrightarrow Q$) is a non-temporal law, then $\Box P \Rightarrow \Box Q$ ($\Box P \Leftrightarrow \Box Q$) is a temporal law.

### 3.3.5 Actions

In programming languages, the same name can be used of a variable on both sides of an assignment statement, even though the value before the assignment differs from the value afterwards. In a language of logic the situation is different. Therefore, in order to speak about steps in a behavior, we need a 'mirror set' of Var, denoted by Var', so that variables in Var will refer to state variables before a step is taken, and those in Var' will refer to them after the step.

Let Var' therefore denote the set which for any state variable $x \in$ Var contains a corresponding *primed variable* $x'$,

$$\mathsf{Var}' \stackrel{\Delta}{=} \{x' \mid x \in \mathsf{Var}\} .$$

For any state function f, we will write $f'$ to denote the expression obtained by replacing all state variables in f by the corresponding primed variables. Similarly, for a state predicate P this replacement gives an expression that will be denoted by $P'$.

An *action* is defined as a truth-valued expression that depends on both unprimed and primed variables. Symbols $A, B, \ldots$ will be used in the following to denote actions. A concrete action A assigns a truth value $s[\![A]\!]t$ to any pair of states $(s, t)$, $s, t \in \Sigma$. This truth value is obtained by evaluating expression A so that unprimed variables $x \in Var$ are replaced by their values in state $s$, i.e., by $s[\![x]\!]$, and primed variables $x' \in Var'$ are replaced by their values in state $t$, i.e., by $t[\![x]\!]$.

When $s[\![A]\!]t$ is true, step $(s, t)$ is said to *satisfy* (a concrete) action A, and it is then called an A step. An action expression may also contain symbols for state predicates (both unprimed and primed) and for actions. An action expression A is *satisfiable*, if there exists an assignment of concrete counterparts to these symbols so that some pair of states $(s, t)$ is an A step for this assignment. An identically true action expression, which for all such assignments is satisfied by all steps, is a *tautology*.

Two actions A and B are said to be *disjoint* if their logical conjunction is identically false, i.e., if

$$A \wedge B \Rightarrow \mathbf{F}$$

is a tautology.

In the semantic interpretation of temporal expressions, (a concrete) action A is *satisfied* by behavior $\sigma = \langle s_0, s_1, s_2, \dots \rangle$ if the first step in $\sigma$ is an A step,

$$\sigma[\![A]\!] \overset{\Delta}{=} s_0[\![A]\!]s_1 . \tag{3.22}$$

Similarly to state predicates, if A is a tautology as an action expression, then both A and $\square A$ are temporal tautologies, and if $A \Rightarrow B$ $(A \Leftrightarrow B)$ is a non-temporal law for action expressions A and B, then $\square A \Rightarrow \square B$ $(\square A \Leftrightarrow \square B)$ is a temporal law.

A state predicate P can be understood as a special case of an action where no primed variables appear. Obviously, the temporal interpretation of P is then independent of whether it is considered a state predicate or an action. As an action, a primed state predicate $P'$ is an action that contains only primed state variables.

### 3.3.6 Stuttering

Notation $Stutter_X$ will be used to denote an X-stuttering action, which changes no variables in X:

$$Stutter_X \overset{\Delta}{=} \forall x \in X : (x' = x) . \tag{3.23}$$

An action A is *non-X-stuttering* (or non-stuttering, for short, when X is understood from context) if it changes at least one variable in X,

$$A \Rightarrow \exists x \in X : (x' \neq x) .$$

For any action A and a set of variables X, the *stuttering closure* $[A]_X$ and *non-stuttering restriction* $\langle A \rangle_X$ of A are defined as

$$[A]_X \triangleq A \vee \text{Stutter}_X , \tag{3.24}$$

$$\langle A \rangle_X \triangleq A \wedge \neg \text{Stutter}_X , \tag{3.25}$$

which are each other's duals in the following sense:

$$\neg \langle A \rangle_X \Leftrightarrow [\neg A]_X . \tag{3.26}$$

We take it as a convention that, whenever subscript X appears in these kinds of contexts, no variables outside X are referenced. For simplicity we will also omit subscript X, when X consists of all variables that we are interested in, or is otherwise understood from context.

Obviously, for any two actions A and B we have

$$[A] \wedge [B] \Leftrightarrow [A \wedge B] , \tag{3.27}$$

$$[A] \vee [B] \Leftrightarrow [A \vee B] , \tag{3.28}$$

and also dually,

$$\langle A \rangle \wedge \langle B \rangle \Leftrightarrow \langle A \wedge B \rangle , \tag{3.29}$$

$$\langle A \rangle \vee \langle B \rangle \Leftrightarrow \langle A \vee B \rangle . \tag{3.30}$$

### 3.3.7 Enabling of Actions

For any action A we will write Enabled A to denote the state predicate which is true exactly when there is a possible assignment of values to primed variables so that A evaluates to true:

$$s[\![\text{Enabled } A]\!] \triangleq \exists t \in \Sigma : s[\![A]\!]t . \tag{3.31}$$

Expression (Enabled A)′ will be abbreviated as Enabled′ A.

The following are some obvious laws for actions and state predicates:[10]

$$\text{Enabled Stutter}_X \Leftrightarrow \mathbf{T} , \tag{3.32}$$

$$\text{Enabled } P \Leftrightarrow P , \tag{3.33}$$

$$P \wedge \text{Stutter}_X \Rightarrow P' , \tag{3.34}$$

$$A \Leftrightarrow \text{Enabled } A \wedge A , \tag{3.35}$$

$$\text{Enabled } (P \wedge A) \Leftrightarrow P \wedge \text{Enabled } A , \tag{3.36}$$

$$\text{Enabled}(A \wedge B) \Rightarrow \text{Enabled } A \wedge \text{Enabled } B , \tag{3.37}$$

$$\text{Enabled}(A \vee B) \Leftrightarrow \text{Enabled } A \vee \text{Enabled } B , \tag{3.38}$$

$$(A \Rightarrow B) \Rightarrow (\text{Enabled } A \Rightarrow \text{Enabled } B) . \tag{3.39}$$

---

[10]In (3.34), X is assumed to contain all variables that may appear in the concrete predicates by which the predicate symbol P can be replaced.

### 3.3.8 TLA: Insensitivity to Stuttering

According to the semantic definition of $\Box$, a behavior $\sigma = \langle s_0, s_1, s_2, \ldots \rangle$ satisfies $\Box A$ if all its steps $(s_i, s_{i+1})$ satisfy action $A$. In general, inserting additional stuttering steps into $\sigma$ may destroy this satisfaction. There are, however, reasons not to make a distinction between behaviors that differ from each other only by the X-stuttering steps that they contain.

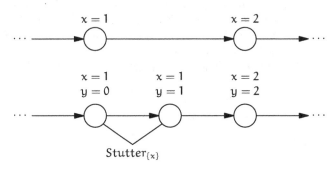

**Fig. 3.4.** Illustration of need for insensitivity to stuttering

To explain the intuitive background for this, let acceptable behaviors be specified by temporal expression $E$ that involves variables in $X \subseteq Var$. When $E$ is refined into temporal expression $F$ that describes behaviors in an implementation (or in a more detailed specification), set $X$ is, in general, extended by further variables into a larger set $Y$, $X \subseteq Y$. Expression $F$ (which uses this extended set) may then be satisfied by behaviors that contain such X-stuttering steps where variables in $Y \setminus X$ are modified[11] (see Fig. 3.4, where $X = \{x\}$ and $Y = \{x, y\}$). It would then be unreasonable if these additional X-stuttering steps would make the implementation (or refinement) not to satisfy $E$. If the satisfaction of $E$ is insensitive to addition and removal of stuttering steps, then this cannot happen.

Another way to look at this is to understand a behavior as a sequence of observations of how the variables in a given set $X$ behave in program executions. The minimum requirement for such observations is that all changes in these variables are recorded. Otherwise, there are no special reasons for determining what the 'correct' frequency of observations should be. Increasing it from this minimum will only insert X-stuttering steps. Intuitively, this does not add any information but does not yield essentially different behaviors either.

Constraining temporal expressions so that their satisfaction is guaranteed to be insensitive to stuttering will decrease their expressive power. Notice, however, that expressive power is not as such a measure for the goodness of a

---

[11]Operator '$\setminus$' is used to denote set difference.

language of logic. Obviously, one has to be able to express what is considered important, but additional power may only increase complexity.

The desired insensitivity to stuttering is achieved by weakening the expressive power of temporal expressions so that actions are allowed to appear only in subexpressions of the forms $\Box[A]_X$ and Enabled A. With this constraint, temporal logic is called temporal logic of actions or TLA.

### 3.3.9 Step Invariants

An expression of the form $\Box[A]$ expresses that $[A]$ is a *step invariant*. According to the semantic definition of the box operator (see Sect. 3.3.3, p. 70),

- behavior $\sigma = \langle s_0, s_1, s_2, \ldots \rangle$ satisfies $\Box[A]_X$ if each step $(s_i, s_{i+1})$, $i \geq 0$, in $\sigma$ either satisfies A or is an X-stuttering step,

as illustrated in Fig. 3.5. For instance, all legal behaviors in the gas-burner example satisfy the step invariant expression

$$\Box[\neg flow\_s' \land flow\_s' \Rightarrow ign\_s'] .$$

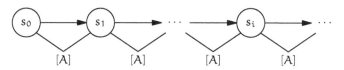

**Fig. 3.5.** Illustration of a behavior satisfying a step invariant

Comparing state invariants and step invariants one can notice that $\Box P$ is stronger than $\Box[P]$ or $P \land \Box[P]$ (see Exercise 3.3.7). In fact, we have the following laws (Exercise 3.3.11):

$$\Box P \Leftrightarrow P \land \Box[P \land P'] \tag{3.40}$$
$$\Leftrightarrow P \land \Box[P'] \tag{3.41}$$
$$\Leftrightarrow P \land \Box[P \Rightarrow P'] . \tag{3.42}$$

The validity of these laws can easily be checked by considering their semantic interpretations for arbitrary behaviors $\sigma = \langle s_0, s_1, s_2, \ldots \rangle$. As an example, consider the direction $\Leftarrow$ in (3.40). For this it is sufficient to show that, if $\sigma$ does not satisfy $\Box P$, then it does not satisfy either P or $\Box[P \land P']$.

If $\sigma$ does not satisfy $\Box P$, there is a first state $s_i$ in $\sigma$ that does not satisfy P. If $i = 0$, then $\sigma$ does not satisfy P (see top part in Fig. 3.6). Otherwise, step $(s_{i-i}, s_i)$ does not satisfy $[P \land P']$, and $\sigma$ therefore cannot satisfy $\Box[P \land P']$ (see bottom part in Fig. 3.6).

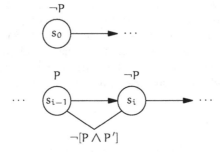

**Fig. 3.6.** If $\sigma$ does not satisfy $\Box P$, it does not satisfy either P or $\Box[P \land P']$

As an example of how temporal laws can be used in deductions, let us see how the law

$$P \land \Box[\neg P] \Rightarrow \Box[\mathbf{F}] \qquad (3.43)$$

follows from those given above. On one hand, the left-hand side of (3.43) implies[12] $\Box[\neg P]$. On the other hand, since $\neg P \Rightarrow \neg P \lor P'$ is identically true, then also $\Box[\neg P] \Rightarrow \Box[\neg P \lor P']$ is identically true, and we have

$$
\begin{aligned}
P \land \Box[\neg P] &\Rightarrow P \land \Box[\neg P \lor P'] \\
&\Rightarrow P \land \Box[P \Rightarrow P'] \\
&\Rightarrow \Box P \qquad \text{by (3.42)} \\
&\Rightarrow \Box[P \land P'] \qquad \text{by (3.40)} \\
&\Rightarrow \Box[P] \land \Box[P'] \qquad \text{by (3.27) and (3.21)} \\
&\Rightarrow \Box[P] \,.
\end{aligned}
$$

Therefore,

$$
\begin{aligned}
P \land \Box[\neg P] &\Rightarrow \Box[\neg P] \land \Box[P] \\
&\Rightarrow \Box[\neg P \land P] \qquad \text{by (3.21) and (3.27)} \\
&\Rightarrow \Box[\mathbf{F}] \,.
\end{aligned}
$$

### 3.3.10 Stability Predicates

Law (3.42) contains a step invariant $\Box[P \Rightarrow P']$, which states that, once P is true, it will never turn false again. If a set of behaviors satisfies this step invariant, then P is called *stable* (for this set of behaviors). A special notation is introduced for such stability predicates:

$$\mathbf{stable}\ P \overset{\Delta}{=} \Box[P \Rightarrow P'] \,. \qquad (3.44)$$

---

[12]Non-temporal laws, such as the one used here, will not be explicitly mentioned.

A related but weaker property is that, once P is true, it will stay true unless action A is executed. The following notation will be used to express such *unless predicates*:

$$\textbf{stable P unless } \langle A \rangle \stackrel{\Delta}{=} \Box[P \Rightarrow P' \vee A] . \tag{3.45}$$

The unless operator is often convenient for properties that appear in requirements specifications. As can be seen from its definition, it always gives a safety property.

Analogous notations are also introduced for state functions that are *steady* in the sense that their values are not changed (except possibly by a given action):[13]

$$\textbf{steady f} \stackrel{\Delta}{=} \Box[f' = f] , \tag{3.46}$$

$$\textbf{steady f unless } \langle A \rangle \stackrel{\Delta}{=} \Box[f' = f \vee A] . \tag{3.47}$$

### 3.3.11 Quantification of State Variables

In specification it is often convenient (or even necessary) to utilize also *auxiliary variables*. These are state variables that are not of interest as such, but serve an auxiliary role in the actions. If such auxiliary variables have no effect on those variables that are considered to be *essential*, they can be compared to 'instrumenting' a program to record some properties of its execution history explicitly. More generally, they can also be used to control how the essential state variables are changed in actions.

In TLA the auxiliary role of a state variable is indicated by boldface existential quantification ($\boldsymbol{\exists}$). For instance, if E is a TLA expression (presumably involving variable $x \in Var$), then

$$\boldsymbol{\exists} x : E$$

is also a TLA expression, but this quantified expression no longer specifies anything about variable $x \in Var$. Since quantification can be understood as 'hiding' of variables, quantified state variables are also called hidden variables.

Intuitively, quantification of state variables means that it does not really matter what the actual values of these variables are in behaviors, or how they change, provided that all essential variables behave as specified. More precisely, let E be a TLA expression involving variables in $X \subseteq Var$. A behavior $\sigma \in \Sigma^\infty$ then satisfies $\boldsymbol{\exists} x : E$ if it can be transformed by the following steps into a behavior $\tau \in \Sigma^\infty$ that satisfies E:

- Insert finite numbers of X-stuttering steps arbitrarily before any steps in $\sigma$, yielding some behavior $\sigma'$.
- Replace the values of variable $x$ in the states of $\sigma'$ by arbitrary values.

---

[13]Notice the difference between constants, which cannot change by definition, and steady values, which do not change in the behaviors satisfying a given steadiness property.

## Review Questions

QUESTION 3.3.1 What is meant by semantic interpretation of temporal expressions?

QUESTION 3.3.2 How are state predicates interpreted as actions and as temporal expressions?

QUESTION 3.3.3 What is the syntactic restriction that TLA imposes on temporal expressions?

QUESTION 3.3.4 Why has TLA been designed to be insensitive to stuttering?

QUESTION 3.3.5 What is meant by quantified state variables, and why are they needed?

## Exercises

EXERCISE 3.3.1 Verify the laws in Sect. 3.3.3 (p. 70) using the semantic interpretation of temporal expressions.

EXERCISE 3.3.2 Show that, if $E \Rightarrow F$ is a law for some temporal expressions $E$ and $F$, then so is $\Box E \Rightarrow \Box F$.

EXERCISE 3.3.3 The converse of the statement in Exercise 3.3.2 is not true. Give temporal expressions $E$ and $F$ for which $\Box E \Rightarrow \Box F$ is a law, but $E \Rightarrow F$ is not.

EXERCISE 3.3.4 Give a state invariant that characterizes the set of reachable states in the gas-burner example of Chap. 2.

EXERCISE 3.3.5 Explain the meanings of the following temporal expressions: $P \Rightarrow Q$, $\Box(P \Rightarrow Q)$, $\Box[P \Rightarrow Q]$, $\Box P \Rightarrow \Box Q$.

EXERCISE 3.3.6 Which behaviors satisfy $\Box[\mathbf{F}]$?

EXERCISE 3.3.7 Which behaviors satisfy $\Box[P]$ but not $\Box P$? Which behaviors satisfy $P \wedge \Box[P]$ but not $\Box P$?

EXERCISE 3.3.8 Why is Enabled $P' \Leftrightarrow \mathbf{T}$ not a law?

EXERCISE 3.3.9 Why is the law (3.37) on p. 73 only an implication, not an equivalence?

EXERCISE 3.3.10 Discuss different interpretations of the statement 'When P is true, it will stay true at least until Q is true' and formulate them in TLA.

EXERCISE 3.3.11 Verify laws (3.40)–(3.42) on p. 75 using their semantic interpretations.

## 3.4 Expressing Liveness Properties

The basic temporal operator in TLA is the box operator and, in principle, no further temporal operators are required. Derived operators are, however, needed for convenience in formulating liveness properties, and are introduced in this section. The discussion is restricted to expressions without quantified state variables.

### 3.4.1 Eventualities

Negation and $\Box$ can be used to express liveness properties. For instance, the property that state predicate P is satisfied in at least one state can be expressed as $\neg\Box\neg P$. This would, however, lead to complicated formulation of properties that are intuitively simple.

The derived operator $\Diamond$ (read: *diamond* or *eventually*) is therefore defined for an arbitrary temporal expression E by

$$\Diamond E \triangleq \neg\Box\neg E . \tag{3.48}$$

The semantics of the box operator (3.16) then gives us

$$\sigma[\![\Diamond E]\!] = \bigvee_{i \geq 0} \sigma_i[\![E]\!] , \tag{3.49}$$

where $\sigma = \langle s_0, s_1, s_2, \ldots \rangle$ and $\sigma_i = \langle s_i, s_{i+1}, s_{i+2} \ldots \rangle$. In particular, the meaning of $\Diamond P$ is that P holds in at least one state $s_i$, $i \geq 0$.

The following is a useful law about the relationship between $\Box$ and $\Diamond$:

$$\Diamond E \wedge \Box F \Rightarrow \Diamond(E \wedge F) . \tag{3.50}$$

It is left as an exercise to the reader (Exercise 3.4.13) to show how this can be deduced from previously given temporal laws.

The restrictions on using actions in TLA apply, of course, also to eventualities. Therefore, $\Diamond E$, for instance, is not a legal TLA expression for all TLA expressions E. It is easy to see, however, that the following equivalences hold:

$$\Diamond\langle A\rangle_x \Leftrightarrow \neg\Box\neg\langle A\rangle_x \tag{3.51}$$
$$\Leftrightarrow \neg\Box[\neg A]_x . \tag{3.52}$$

This shows that expressions of the form $\Diamond\langle A\rangle$ do not violate the rules for using actions in TLA expressions, and will therefore be allowed in TLA.

### 3.4.2 Arity of Operators

The number of operands for an operator is called its *arity*. Negation ($\neg$), as well as existential and universal quantification of rigid variables ($\exists m :$,

$\forall m :$), are unary operators with arity 1, while conjunction ($\wedge$), disjunction ($\vee$), implication ($\Rightarrow$), and equivalence ($\Leftrightarrow$) are binary operators with arity 2. Temporal operators box ($\Box$), diamond ($\Diamond$), stuttering closure ($[\cdots]_X$), and non-stuttering restriction ($\langle\cdots\rangle_X$) are all unary.

The notion of operators can be extended to *nullary* operators with arity 0, which are the primitive expressions of which temporal expressions are constructed, i.e., concrete state predicates and actions, and symbols representing temporal expressions, actions, or state predicates.

### 3.4.3 Duality of Operators

Two k-ary operators $\Phi$ and $\Psi$ are *dual* to each other if

$$\Phi(E_1, \ldots, E_k) \Leftrightarrow \neg\Psi(\neg E_1, \ldots, \neg E_k) . \tag{3.53}$$

In particular,

- the dual of a nullary operator is its logical complement, expressed as negation,
- negation ($\neg$) is self-dual,
- conjunction ($\wedge$) and disjunction ($\vee$) are each other's duals,
- existential and universal quantification of rigid variables ($\exists m :$, $\forall m :$) are each other's duals,
- box ($\Box$) and diamond ($\Diamond$) are each other's duals, and
- stuttering closure ($[\cdots]_X$) and non-stuttering restriction ($\langle\cdots\rangle_X$) are each other's duals.

For any temporal expression $E$ in which all rigid variables are either existentially or universally quantified, let $E^\dagger$ denote the expression obtained from $E$ by replacing each operator – including the nullary ones – by its dual. The generic *duality law*

$$E \Leftrightarrow \neg E^\dagger \tag{3.54}$$

then holds as a generalization of (3.53). Verification of this is left as an exercise to the reader (Exercise 3.4.5). De Morgan's law is a non-temporal instance of (3.54).

### 3.4.4 Duality Principle

The duality law leads to the following *duality principle*, which for any law gives another law:

- For each law

$$E \Rightarrow F , \quad \text{respectively} \quad E \Leftrightarrow F$$

there is a dual law[14]

$$F^\dagger \Rightarrow E^\dagger , \quad \text{respectively} \quad E^\dagger \Leftrightarrow F^\dagger .$$

Verification of this is left as an exercise to the reader (Exercise 3.4.5).

As an example of applying this principle, we get the law

$$\Box(E \vee F) \Rightarrow \Box E \vee \Diamond F \tag{3.55}$$

as the dual of (3.50) on p. 79.

### 3.4.5 Derived Operators for Temporal Relations

In requirements specifications one often has situations where causal or at least temporal relations exist between the states or steps that appear in behaviors. For instance, a state that satisfies P may be required to lead to a state that satisfies Q, or an $\langle A \rangle$ step may be required to lead to a $\langle B \rangle$ step. Operator symbol '$\rightsquigarrow$' (read: *leads to*) will be used in expressing such relations.

More generally, for any temporal expressions E and F we define

$$E \rightsquigarrow F \overset{\Delta}{=} \Box(E \Rightarrow \Diamond F) . \tag{3.56}$$

If operand E in E $\rightsquigarrow$ F is of the form $\langle A \rangle$, then this definition does not seem to satisfy the syntactic constraints of TLA. However, since

$$\Box(E \Rightarrow \Diamond F) \Leftrightarrow \Box(\Diamond E \Rightarrow \Diamond F) \tag{3.57}$$

is identically true, expressions of the form $\langle A \rangle \rightsquigarrow$ F can also be used (see Exercise 3.4.16).

Syntactically we use $\rightsquigarrow$ as a less binding operator than $\wedge$ and $\vee$, but more binding than $\Rightarrow$ and $\Leftrightarrow$.

Obviously, $\rightsquigarrow$ is both *reflexive* and *transitive*. That is, the following are tautologies:

$$E \rightsquigarrow E , \tag{3.58}$$

$$(E \rightsquigarrow F) \wedge (F \rightsquigarrow G) \Rightarrow E \rightsquigarrow G . \tag{3.59}$$

For two state predicates P and Q we obviously have the law

$$P \rightsquigarrow Q \Leftrightarrow P \wedge \neg Q \rightsquigarrow \langle Q' \rangle . \tag{3.60}$$

Combining 'leads to' with the stability operator (**stable unless**) gives the stronger but often useful *until* predicate (**stable until**), which expresses that a given state predicate will not be turned false except by a given action, and that this will eventually take place:

$$\textbf{stable } P \textbf{ until } \langle A \rangle \overset{\Delta}{=} (\textbf{stable } P \textbf{ unless } A) \wedge (P \rightsquigarrow \langle A \rangle) . \tag{3.61}$$

---

[14]Obviously, systematic negation of symbols for arbitrary temporal expressions, state predicates, and actions can be omitted from $E^\dagger$ and $F^\dagger$.

### 3.4.6 Combined Temporal Operators

Combining operators $\Box$ and $\Diamond$ gives us $\Box\Diamond$, which stands for *infinitely often*, and $\Diamond\Box$, which stands for *eventually always*. As an instance of the duality law (3.54) on p. 80 we have

$$\Box\Diamond E \Leftrightarrow \neg\Diamond\Box\neg E \qquad (3.62)$$

for them.

The following useful laws also hold for them:

$$\Diamond\Box E \Rightarrow \Box\Diamond E , \qquad (3.63)$$

$$\Box\Diamond\Box E \Leftrightarrow \Diamond\Box E , \qquad (3.64)$$

$$\Diamond\Box E \wedge \Diamond\Box F \Leftrightarrow \Diamond\Box(E \wedge F) . \qquad (3.65)$$

Of course, the duals for (3.64) and (3.65) also exist; law (3.63) is self-dual.

Properties of the form $\Diamond\Box P$ (eventually always P) require that P is at least eventually stable. The following laws can be used to deduce such properties:

$$\Diamond P \wedge \textbf{stable } P \Rightarrow \Diamond\Box P , \qquad (3.66)$$

$$\Box\Diamond P \wedge \Diamond \textbf{ stable } P \Leftrightarrow \Diamond\Box P . \qquad (3.67)$$

The relationship between $\Box\Diamond$ and $\leadsto$ is established by laws

$$\Box\Diamond E \Leftrightarrow \textbf{T} \leadsto E , \qquad (3.68)$$

$$\Box\Diamond E \Leftrightarrow \neg E \leadsto E . \qquad (3.69)$$

### 3.4.7 Stuttering Steps and Fairness

An action system may lead to a situation where the execution of an action corresponds to a stuttering step. This is the case when the guard is true but the body makes no changes in variables. To discuss such situations, let A be an action that deals with variables in X, and for which $A \wedge \text{Stutter}_X$ is not identically false, i.e., it is possible for an A step to leave all variables in X unchanged.

The question now is whether an X-stuttering step that satisfies $\text{Enabled} A$ should be considered an 'execution' of A or not. This is a relevant question, since the execution or non-execution of an action makes a difference for the satisfaction of possible fairness requirements for it.

There are two points to be noticed in answering this question. On one hand, the presence or absence of stuttering steps should not affect the satisfaction of any TLA expression. On the other hand, in the execution of an action system it is reasonable to think of evaluating a guard without executing the associated action – this is, in fact, needed for fairness considerations – but it does not sound reasonable to check in a similar manner whether an execution of the body could lead to a stuttering step.

These points are taken into account by adopting the following interpretation:

- An occurrence of a state satisfying $\mathsf{Enabled}\,(A \wedge \mathsf{Stutter}_X)$ will always be counted as an 'execution' of A.

### 3.4.8 Stutter-excluding Part of Actions

In order to formalize fairness properties in TLA, the above interpretation of stuttering executions means that we need to be able to talk separately about non-stuttering and stuttering A steps. For this purpose we define the *stuttering part* $A_X^0$ of action A as[15]

$$A_X^0 \;\stackrel{\Delta}{=}\; A \wedge \mathsf{Stutter}_X \,. \tag{3.70}$$

This allows partitioning of action A into three mutually exclusive cases,

$$A \Leftrightarrow A^0 \vee (A \wedge \neg\mathsf{Enabled}\,A^0) \vee (\langle A \rangle \wedge \mathsf{Enabled}\,A^0)\,. \tag{3.71}$$

The second part, the *stutter-excluding part* of A, is enabled only when the stuttering part is not, and will be denoted by $A^+$,

$$A^+ \;\stackrel{\Delta}{=}\; A \wedge \neg\mathsf{Enabled}\,A^0 \,. \tag{3.72}$$

Obviously, $A^+$ implies $\langle A \rangle$,

$$A^+ \Rightarrow \langle A \rangle \,, \tag{3.73}$$

but may be properly stronger than it, since the enabling conditions of $\langle A \rangle$ and $A^0$ need not exclude each other (see Exercise 3.4.7).

### 3.4.9 Weak Fairness

Fairness conditions can be expressed using the combined operators $\Box\Diamond$ and $\Diamond\Box$.

An operational definition of *weak fairness* with respect to an action A, WF(A), is that A cannot be continually enabled without being executed. Since enabling of $A^0$ will also be counted as an execution of A, as was discussed above, we only need to pay attention to enabling of $A^+$.

Formalizing this in TLA gives us a definition of weak fairness,

$$\mathrm{WF(A)} \;\stackrel{\Delta}{=}\; \Diamond\Box\mathsf{Enabled}\,A^+ \Rightarrow \Box\Diamond\langle A^+ \rangle \,, \tag{3.74}$$

which states that, if $A^+$ is eventually always enabled in a behavior, then the behavior must have infinitely many $A^+$ steps. This condition can also be formulated as

$$\mathrm{WF(A)} \Leftrightarrow \mathsf{Enabled}\,A^+ \rightsquigarrow \langle A^+ \vee \neg\mathsf{Enabled}'\,A^+ \rangle \,. \tag{3.75}$$

The following law is useful when dealing with actions with strengthened enabling conditions:

$$\mathrm{WF(A)} \Rightarrow \mathrm{WF(P \wedge A)} \,. \tag{3.76}$$

---

[15] Assuming that X consists of all those variables that we are interested in, subscripts X can again be omitted.

### 3.4.10 Strong Fairness

Correspondingly, formalization of *strong fairness* gives the following definition:

$$\text{SF(A)} \overset{\Delta}{=} \Box\Diamond\text{Enabled}\,A^+ \Rightarrow \Box\Diamond\langle A^+\rangle \vee \Box\Diamond\text{Enabled}\,A^0 \,. \qquad (3.77)$$

Compared to (3.74), we now need the disjunct $\Box\Diamond\text{Enabled}\,A^0$ on the right-hand side of the implication, since this possibility is in this case not excluded by the condition on the left.

The following laws hold for strong fairness:

$$\text{SF(A)} \Rightarrow \text{WF(A)} \,, \qquad (3.78)$$

$$\text{SF(A)} \wedge \text{SF(B)} \Rightarrow \text{SF}(A \vee B) \,. \qquad (3.79)$$

In the counterpart of law (3.76) we have to make an additional assumption about eventual stability of the added strengthening condition:

$$\text{SF(A)} \wedge \Diamond(\textbf{stable}\,P\,\textbf{unless}\,\langle A\rangle) \Rightarrow \text{SF}(P \wedge A) \,. \qquad (3.80)$$

### Review Questions

QUESTION 3.4.1 What is meant by the duality law and the duality principle?

QUESTION 3.4.2 What makes it desirable to be able to talk about stuttering executions of actions?

### Exercises

EXERCISE 3.4.1 Are properties of the form $\Diamond P$ or $P \rightsquigarrow Q$ always liveness properties?

EXERCISE 3.4.2 Give an example of two liveness properties $E$ and $F$ for which the conjunction $E \wedge F$ is identically false.

EXERCISE 3.4.3 There are $2^4 = 16$ binary Boolean operators. Given the 'multiplication table' for any of them, how do you get the table for its dual? Which of them are self-dual?

EXERCISE 3.4.4 Show that any law of the form $E \Rightarrow \neg E^\dagger$ or $E \Leftrightarrow \neg E^\dagger$ is effectively self-dual.

EXERCISE 3.4.5 Show that the duality law and principle in Sects. 3.4.3 (p. 80) and 3.4.4 (p. 80) are valid.

EXERCISE 3.4.6 Give duals for the temporal laws given in Sect. 3.3 (p. 69). Use the definition of $\diamond$ to prove directly that the dual of (3.19) on p. 70 follows from it.

EXERCISE 3.4.7 In which situations is it possible for $A^+$ and $\langle A \rangle$ to be different?

EXERCISE 3.4.8 Express in TLA the following property related to the gas-burner example of Chap. 2:

• If req_e is repeatedly true in state Idle, then state Starting will eventually be entered.

Does this property hold for all legal executions of the action system?

EXERCISE 3.4.9 Show that, if $E \Rightarrow F$ is a law for some temporal expressions $E$ and $F$, then so is $\diamond E \Rightarrow \diamond F$. Give a counterexample to demonstrate that the converse is not true.

EXERCISE 3.4.10 Explain the difference between $P \rightsquigarrow Q$ and $P \Rightarrow \diamond Q$. Does one of them imply the other?

EXERCISE 3.4.11 Show that the laws in Sect. 3.4.6 (p. 82) hold.

EXERCISE 3.4.12 Can the number of consecutive box and diamond operators always be reduced to two?

EXERCISE 3.4.13 Deduce law (3.50) on p. 79, or its dual (3.55) on p. 81, without resorting to its semantic interpretation.

EXERCISE 3.4.14 Deduce law (3.66) on p. 82 from other laws. Hint: utilize laws (3.50) on p. 79 and (3.42) on p. 75.

EXERCISE 3.4.15 Deduce law (3.67) on p. 82 from other laws. Hint: utilize laws (3.50) on p. 79 and (3.66) on p. 82.

EXERCISE 3.4.16 Deduce law (3.57) on p. 81 from other laws. Hint: utilize law (3.55) on p. 81.

EXERCISE 3.4.17 If $A \Rightarrow B$ is identically true, does either $WF(A) \Rightarrow WF(B)$ or $WF(B) \Rightarrow WF(A)$ hold?

EXERCISE 3.4.18 Show that condition (3.75) on p. 83 is equivalent to the one in the definition (3.74) of weak fairness (p. 83).

EXERCISE 3.4.19 Show that the conditions for weak and strong fairness could also be formulated in the following more symmetric forms:

$$WF(A) \Leftrightarrow (\Diamond\Box Enabled\ A \Rightarrow \Box\Diamond\langle A \rangle \vee \Box\Diamond Enabled\ A^0)\ ,$$

$$SF(A) \Leftrightarrow (\Box\Diamond Enabled\ A \Rightarrow \Box\Diamond\langle A \rangle \vee \Box\Diamond Enabled\ A^0)\ .$$

EXERCISE 3.4.20 Verify laws (3.76), (3.79), and (3.80) on pp. 83–84.

## 3.5 TLA-based Specifications

TLA gives a formal basis for the specification of behavioral properties and for rigorous reasoning on them. The relationship between TLA and operational specifications in the action language will be analyzed in this section.

### 3.5.1 Behaviors and Executions

According to the terminology suggested in Sect. 1.2.3 (p. 10), when real systems are modeled as action systems, concrete *computations* in the former correspond to abstract *executions* in the latter. *Behaviors*, on the other hand, are abstractions of executions as state sequences. The relationship between the associated levels of system modeling and specification is then as follows:

- TLA is a temporal logic for reasoning.
- The standard semantic interpretation of TLA is given in terms of behaviors, which means that TLA can be used to specify and reason on properties of behaviors.
- Behaviors are abstractions of executions in action systems. Operational modeling in terms of action systems therefore generates behaviors.
- Executions in action systems model computations in system implementations.

### 3.5.2 Operational Safety Specifications in TLA

Let $X \subseteq Var$ be the set of state variables that are of interest to us in a specification. By definition, all variables in $Var$ have unique values in each state $s \in \Sigma$, including those variables that are not in $X$. Ignoring variables in $Var \setminus X$, we use the words 'state' and 'behavior' in the following to denote such (projections of) states and behaviors, where only variables in $X$ are considered.

If $P$ is a satisfiable state predicate and $A$ is an action, each involving only variables in $X$, TLA formula $S$,

$$S \stackrel{\Delta}{=} P \wedge \Box[A]_X\ , \tag{3.81}$$

has a natural operational interpretation for producing arbitrary behaviors that satisfy $S$:

1. Start execution in an arbitrary state $s_0$ that satisfies the initial condition P.
2. Take a finite number (possibly zero) of X-stuttering steps.
3. If A is not enabled in the current state $s_i$, repeat X-stuttering indefinitely.
4. Otherwise, either repeat X-stuttering indefinitely, or enter state $s_{i+1}$ by an arbitrary step $(s_i, s_{i+1})$ that satisfies A, and return to step 2.

Ignoring variables in $Var \setminus X$, this nondeterministic procedure generates exactly those behaviors that satisfy S, since any such behavior can be generated by it. If some constraints are imposed on how the next execution step is selected in step 4, the procedure still produces behaviors that satisfy S, but not all of them. Obviously, if we are not interested in X-stuttering steps, step 2 can be omitted, and indefinite X-stuttering in steps 3 and 4 can be replaced by termination.

Although this procedure can be considered as an operational execution model for TLA formulas of the form (3.81), it relies on operations that need not be effectively executable. More specifically, it assumes that

- one can generate an arbitrary initial state $s_0$ that satisfies P,
- one can evaluate the enabling of A in an arbitrary state $s_i$, and
- if A is enabled in state $s_i$, one can generate an arbitrary step $(s_i, s_{i+1})$ that satisfies A.

Even assuming that an arbitrary state can be effectively constructed, and that the satisfaction of P and A can be effectively tested for arbitrary states, it need not be possible to determine in a finite time whether A is enabled or not. Still, the intuition provided by this operational model is important for understanding the relationship between TLA and action systems.

Since (3.81) defines a pure safety property, expressions of this form give safety specifications only. Conversely, one can claim that all operational specifications that specify only safety properties can be formalized as a TLA expressions of this form. Such a statement cannot, however, be proved, since it compares an informal concept to a formal one.

### 3.5.3 Feasible Liveness Conditions

If S is a pure safety property, and L is a pure liveness property, then L is said to be *feasible* for S if any finite prefix of a behavior satisfying S can be extended into an infinite behavior that satisfies both S and L. In other words, $S \wedge L$ then differs from S only by the liveness properties imposed by L. This can be expressed formally as

$$Cl(S \wedge L) \Leftrightarrow S .$$

As an example of a non-feasible liveness property, consider safety expression

$$S \overset{\Delta}{=} x = 0 \wedge \Box[x' = x + 1 \vee x' = x - 2]$$

and the effect of conjoining liveness expression

$$L_1 \triangleq \mathrm{SF}(x' = x - 1)$$

with it. Obviously, S does not allow any steps $x' = x - 1$, since all steps either increment $x$ by 1 or decrement it by 2. However, since action $x' = x - 1$ is always enabled, $S \wedge L_1$, and hence also its closure, are identically false.

On the other hand, liveness expression

$$L_2 \triangleq \mathrm{SF}(x = 0 \wedge x' = 1)$$

would require that, if $x = 0$ is true infinitely often, then step $x = 0 \wedge x' = 1$ is also taken infinitely often. Since such steps are never made impossible by S, $L_2$ is feasible for S.

More generally, let S be of the form (3.81), and let L be restricted to a (strong or weak) fairness condition with respect to some action B, i.e., to have the form $\mathrm{SF}(B)$ or $\mathrm{WF}(B)$. In this case, L is said to be *strongly feasible* for S if S implies

$$\Box(\mathrm{Enabled}\, B \Rightarrow \mathrm{Enabled}(A \wedge B)) \,. \tag{3.82}$$

In other words, strong feasibility of a fairness condition for B requires that, if B is enabled in a state that is reachable under S, then a B step cannot be excluded by S. In the above example, $L_1$ was not strongly feasible for S, but $L_2$ was. It is easy to see that strong feasibility always implies feasibility.

For two liveness conditions $L_1$ and $L_2$ that are feasible for a safety property S, the conjunction $L_1 \wedge L_2$ does not, in general, have this property (see Exercise 3.5.1). However, if $L_1$ and $L_2$ are fairness conditions that are strongly feasible for a safety property S of the form (3.81), then $L_1 \wedge L_2$ is feasible for S. More generally, if $L_1, L_2, \ldots$ is a finite or countably infinite collection of fairness conditions that are strongly feasible for a safety property S of the form (3.81), then their conjunction $L_1 \wedge L_2 \wedge \ldots$ is feasible for S (see Exercise 3.5.2).

### 3.5.4 Canonical TLA Expressions

Liveness properties can be added to a safety specification as (strong and weak) fairness conditions that are strongly feasible for it.

Let S be an arbitrary safety specification of the form (3.81), and let $\{B_i^s\}$ and $\{B_i^w\}$, $i = 1, \ldots,$ be finite or countably infinite sets of actions for which the strong feasibility condition (3.82) is satisfied for S. Defining

$$F^s \triangleq \bigwedge_i \mathrm{SF}(B_i^s) \,,$$

$$F^w \triangleq \bigwedge_i \mathrm{WF}(B_i^w) \,,$$

$$F \triangleq F^s \wedge F^w, \tag{3.83}$$

the TLA expression

$$T \triangleq S \wedge F$$
$$\Leftrightarrow P \wedge \Box[A] \wedge F^s \wedge F^w \tag{3.84}$$

is said to be in the *canonical form*.[16]

More generally, a canonical TLA formula may also contain quantified state variables, and can therefore have the form

$$\exists x : (P \wedge \Box[A] \wedge F) \,,$$

where x denotes a collection of quantified state variables in X.

The operational interpretation discussed in Sect. 3.5.2 (p. 86) can be generalized to all canonical TLA expressions with a satisfiable initial condition P. Step 4 then needs to be modified so that all fairness requirements will also be satisfied. The feasibility of F for S guarantees that this can be done so that arbitrary finite prefixes of behaviors satisfying S are allowed (see Exercise 3.5.2). Quantification of state variables has no importance for the operational model.

### 3.5.5 Action Systems and TLA

Canonical formulas of the form (3.84) and their operational interpretation are very similar to action systems and their execution model. Despite this similarity, they are conceptually different and serve for different purposes. The latter will be used as a language for constructing operational models; the former will be used as a vehicle for expressing their logical properties and for reasoning on them. Some of the consequences of this difference will be discussed in the subsequent subsections.

Thanks to the similarity, the action language can be understood as a bridge between implementation-oriented engineering of reactive systems and their formal analysis (see Fig. 3.7). As a language with an interpretation in TLA it serves as a basis for common understanding between those who specify and design reactive systems with a constructive engineering view, and those who take a more formal analytical view to prove that the designs satisfy their critical requirements. Some combination of both views is always needed in a serious review of specifications. Mixing the two views makes it possible, for instance, to talk about executions of a TLA formula in the canonical form, instead of behaviors that are satisfied by it.

As for the viewpoint of logical analysis and proofs, TLA can be understood as a logical 'machine language' of action systems, into which translation is needed. A conceptually simple mapping to TLA is therefore essential. On

---

[16]For mathematical completeness, the initial condition P is allowed to be unsatisfiable, even though no operational interpretation then exists. The possibility for an infinite number of fairness conditions will be needed in Chap. 7. It is therefore important that F is feasible for S also in that case.

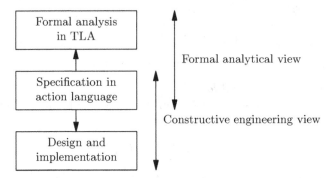

**Fig. 3.7.** Action language as a bridge between specification logic and implementation languages

the other hand, a designer who uses the action language like a programming language needs facilities that have proved useful in programming languages, and which also provide support for managing the complexity of large specifications. Such extensions of the action language will be discussed in Part III of this book.

In principle, translation of action systems into TLA is straightforward:

- The variables that are used in an action system are taken as the set X in (3.84).
- Requirements for the initial state of an action system are taken as P in (3.84).
- Each action $A_i$, $i = 1, \ldots, n$, in an action system is transformed (see below) into a corresponding TLA action $A_i$, and the expression $A_1 \vee \cdots \vee A_n$ is taken as A in (3.84).[17]
- Each strong (weak) fairness requirement for an action $A_i$ is translated directly to the corresponding fairness condition $\mathrm{SF}(A_i)$ $(\mathrm{WF}(A_i))$ in (3.84).

In the gas-burner example of Chap. 2, X, P, A, $\mathrm{F^s}$, and $\mathrm{F^w}$ would be defined as

$$X \overset{\Delta}{=} \{req\_e, flam\_e, flow\_e, ign\_e, req\_s, flam\_s, flow\_s, ign\_s\} ,$$

$$P \overset{\Delta}{=} req\_e = flam\_e = flow\_e = ign\_e$$
$$= req\_s = flam\_s = flow\_s = ign\_s = false ,$$

$$A \overset{\Delta}{=} Req\_on\_e \vee Req\_off\_e \vee Flame\_on\_e \vee Flame\_off\_e$$
$$\vee Req\_on\_s \vee Req\_off\_s \vee Flame\_on\_s \vee Flame\_off\_s$$
$$\vee Start\_s \vee Ign\_off\_s \vee Stop\_s \vee Close\_s ,$$

---

[17]Same names but different fonts will be used in the following for corresponding actions in an action system and in TLA.

$$F^s \overset{\Delta}{=} SF(Req\_on\_s) \wedge SF(Req\_off\_s) \wedge SF(Flame\_on\_s) \wedge SF(Flame\_off\_s)$$
$$\wedge SF(Start\_s) \wedge SF(Ign\_off\_s) \wedge SF(Stop\_s) \wedge SF(Close\_s) \ ,$$

$$F^w \overset{\Delta}{=} T \ ,$$

where action Req_on_s, for instance, is

$$
\begin{aligned}
Req\_on\_s \overset{\Delta}{=}\ & req\_e = \text{true} \\
\wedge\ & req\_s \neq \text{true} \\
\wedge\ & req\_e' = req\_e \\
\wedge\ & flam\_e' = flam\_e \\
\wedge\ & flow\_e' = flow\_e \\
\wedge\ & ign\_e' = ign\_e \\
\wedge\ & req\_s' = \text{true} \\
\wedge\ & flam\_s' = flam\_s \\
\wedge\ & flow\_s' = flow\_s \\
\wedge\ & ign\_s' = ign\_s \ .
\end{aligned}
$$

In general, in transforming an action language action $A_i$ into a corresponding TLA action $A_i$, conjuncts in both the guard and the body are conjoined. However, whereas it is a default in the action language for a variable $x \in X$ to stay unchanged if no new value is assigned to it, this has to be made explicit in TLA by an additional conjunct $x' = x$. In other respects the mapping into TLA actions is straightforward.

From the viewpoint of TLA, several conventions in the action language can be seen as simplifications that have been adopted in order to make the execution of action systems more natural:

- The guards of actions are given as explicit expressions, which simplifies the evaluation of enabling conditions Enabled $A_i$.
- Action bodies are given as multiple assignments, which simplifies the idea of their execution.
- Fairness requirements are given only with respect to those actions that are given as actions to be executed.

With parameterization of actions, to be introduced in Chap. 5, the first two of these simplifications do not constrain the expressiveness of the language. Discussing the effect of the third simplification will be left as an exercise to the reader (Exercise 3.5.3).

### 3.5.6 Erroneous Action Systems

An important difference between models given as action systems on one hand, and specifications given as canonical TLA expressions on the other hand, concerns 'run-time errors'.

An action system may involve expressions that are undefined in some situations, in which case an execution may detect an error in the model. We then say that the action system is *erroneous*. In TLA, on the other hand, all state functions and enabling conditions have, by definition, unique values in all states, which means that no 'run-time errors' may occur in their operational interpretation.

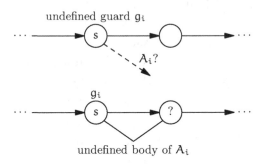

**Fig. 3.8.** Illustration of erroneous executions and their exclusion

The problems with erroneous action systems are illustrated in Fig. 3.8. In the upper part of the figure, the guard $g_i$ of action $A_i$ is undefined in state s, which leaves the enabling of $A_i$ also undefined. In the lower part, the guard $g_i$ is true and action $A_i$ is selected for execution, but its effects are undefined. Still, in TLA an action $A_i$ and its enabling condition $\mathsf{Enabled}\ A_i$ are assumed always to be well defined. Therefore, the translation of action systems to TLA would not seem to be well defined if such situations can arise.

As suggested in Sect. 3.1.3 (p.59), we can assume that all expressions always have some unique values. This means that the above mapping of action systems always leads to a TLA formula, but, in the presence of 'undefined' expressions, we may be unable to analyze this expression for the properties that we are interested in. As a solution it was suggested to ensure that expressions never need to be evaluated in situations where their values cannot be determined. Intuitively, we then need to impose an invariant that guarantees that such states are not reachable where 'undefined' values would be needed.

This idea can be made precise by associating two state predicates with each action $A_i$ in the action system: $P_i$ that ensures that the guard $g_i$ of action $A_i$ can be evaluated, and $Q_i$ that ensures that all expressions in the body of $A_i$ can be evaluated whenever $P_i$ and the guard $g_i$ are true. If the TLA actions $A_i$ that are obtained by the above translation procedure are replaced by $P_i \wedge Q_i \wedge A_i$, we get a canonical TLA expression S where an action is always false in situations where its enabling or effects would be undefined without the additional conjuncts $P_i$ and $Q_i$.

With these notations we get the proof obligation that the well-defined TLA expression S implies the state invariant

$$\bigwedge_i \Box(P_i \wedge (g_i \Rightarrow Q_i)) \,. \tag{3.85}$$

Obviously, when this *non-erroneousness condition* holds, predicates $P_i$ and $Q_i$ are superfluous in the actions of S and can therefore be omitted.

Further reasons for an action system to be erroneous will follow from the constructions to be introduced in Chap. 5, and associated further proof obligations will be discussed there.

We have left it unspecified, by purpose, when the value of an expression cannot be uniquely evaluated. The reason for this is that this also depends on the evaluation strategy that is used for expressions – for instance, whether one can be sure that the evaluation of state predicate $1/x = 1/x$ gives value **T** also when $x = 0$ – and no assumptions on an evaluation strategy seem universally acceptable. Therefore, for the correctness of an implementation it is always crucial to check that the assumed predicates $P_i$ and $Q_i$ are, in fact, sufficient to guarantee error-free evaluation of all action guards and bodies in that implementation.

### 3.5.7 Action Identity

Another difference between logic and an operational view of executions is whether the identities of actions have any significance.

The actions in an action system constitute a set $\{A_1, \ldots, A_n\}$, where each action has a unique name, and fairness requirements can be associated only with these named actions. Even when the effects of an execution step may have been caused by several alternative actions, it is reasonable to think that exactly one of them has been executed. In some sense this resembles event-based approaches, where execution steps are labeled by event names.

In contrast, no notion of individually identifiable actions is associated with a TLA expression in the canonical form (3.84) on p. 89. It is just a TLA expression, even though the step invariant [A] in it may have been constructed from actions in the action language as a disjunction $[A_1 \vee \cdots \vee A_n]$. The identities of actions $A_i$ in the action system have been lost in this mapping, and expression (3.84) could be replaced by any other TLA expression that is equivalent to it. Also, if $A_i$ and $A_j$ are non-disjoint, i.e., $A_i \wedge A_j$ is not identically false, it makes no sense in TLA to try to distinguish whether a step that satisfies $A_i \wedge A_j$ is an 'execution' of $A_i$ or $A_j$.

As far as those behaviors are concerned that correspond to fair executions, it does not matter, however, whether steps are considered as executions of individually identified actions or not (see Exercise 3.5.4).

Although the structure that is imposed by the set of actions in an action system is irrelevant for its meaning in TLA, it is important for a design method that is based on action systems. Therefore, when discussing canonical TLA specifications of the form (3.84), we will always assume a set of individual TLA actions $\{A_1, \ldots, A_n\}$ such that

$$A \Leftrightarrow A_1 \vee \cdots \vee A_n \ .$$

For simplicity, we will denote this set by the same symbol, i.e.,

$$A = \{A_1, \ldots, A_n\} \ ,$$

since it will always be clear from context whether $A$ denotes a disjunction or a set of TLA actions.

Similarly, notations $F^s$ and $F^w$ will be used both for the TLA expressions in (3.83) on p. 88 and for the associated sets of (strongly and weakly) *fair* actions,

$$F^s = \{B_1^s, \ldots\} \ ,$$
$$F^w = \{B_1^w, \ldots\} \ .$$

### 3.5.8 Specification vs. Modeling

Some explanation is now given about a few terms that have no precisely defined meanings in the literature.

The word *executable specifications* is commonly used about specification models that can be run on a computer. Here we use the attribute 'operational' in a somewhat more general meaning. An *operational specification* is assumed to be based on an abstract execution model, but this model may utilize possibilities that cannot be effectively translated into executable or simulatable code, or are outright impossible to implement. In canonical TLA expressions and action systems such possibilities are offered by nondeterminism and by the generality of state predicates and actions.

In fact, it is easy to see that, unless some constraints are imposed on state predicates, the power of action-system specifications goes beyond the limits of effective computability. Consider, for instance, an algorithmically computable function $f : \mathbb{N} \to \mathbb{N}$ for which the set $\{f(0), f(1), \ldots\}$ is undecidable. That is, no effective algorithm is possible that would determine for an arbitrary $x \in \mathbb{N}$ whether there exists an $n \in \mathbb{N}$ such that $x = f(n)$. Still, a solution to this undecidable problem would be needed to evaluate the predicate

$$\exists n \in \mathbb{N} : x = f(n) \ ,$$

which could appear in the guard of an action.

For the proponents of executable specifications – or any specifications for which automatic implementation can be provided – this is, of course, far too general. There are, however, good reasons to argue that the expressive power of a specification language is too limited if it cannot also describe unimplementable systems. This is analogous to considering an algorithmic language too limited if its expressive power is restricted to effective computations that are guaranteed to terminate.

In providing executable models, executable specifications describe *how* one could implement the desired system. In the other end of the spectrum are *property-oriented specifications*, which can be said to describe only *what* to implement. Whereas executable specifications usually means *overspecification* in the sense that implementations are restricted more severely than what would be necessary, property-oriented specifications easily lead to *underspecification*, which also allows behaviors that do not satisfy the intended requirements, or to logically contradictory specifications that are impossible to satisfy.

Operational specifications provide a compromise between the two ends. On one hand, they are not property-oriented but *model-oriented*, in the sense that they provide *operational models*. These models are based on an abstract notion of executions and are therefore close to software engineers' intuitive understanding of programs. On the other hand, they allow an essentially higher level of abstraction than what is possible with outright executability. Logically impossible models can only arise when the initial condition is unsatisfiable.

As model-oriented specifications, action systems make no distinction between variables that are essential in the specification and those that have an auxiliary role only, or between variables and actions that model the system to be implemented and those that model the environment. Although we will give these distinctions separately whenever they are important for us, one can argue that the action language is not a specification language but a *modeling language*. The line between operational specification and operational modeling is, however, fine and often debatable.

### 3.5.9 Non-canonical Requirements

Canonical TLA expressions are only the 'tip of the iceberg' of all TLA expressions (see Fig. 1.6, p. 15). Although this 'tip' corresponds to those expressions that have a natural operational interpretation, it is mathematically simpler to have access to the whole iceberg. Therefore, it is an advantage to have the full power of TLA available in expressing properties of behaviors and in proving them.

In *requirements specification* it is often desirable to express properties in a non-operational form. For instance, canonical TLA expressions do not allow direct expression of simple state invariants $\Box P$, or simple 'leads to', 'unless', and 'until' properties, which are quite useful in the formulation of requirements. The additional freedom given by such property-oriented use of TLA leads, however, to the same dangers as any other kinds of property-oriented specifications.

Of course, it is possible to give also mixed specifications, where an operational basis is combined with property-oriented formulation of additional requirements. For instance, if one does not want to construct a detailed enough operational model of the environment, one can give a 'liberal' operational approximation of it, and conjoin it with additional non-canonical safety and/or liveness requirements. For instance, the restrictions of the action language in expressing arbitrary fairness properties can be compensated in this manner by giving additional liveness assumptions as TLA formulas.

### 3.5.10 Example: Mutual Exclusion

As an example of non-canonical requirements, consider possible requirements for an operating system kernel to implement mutual exclusion for $n$ processes. The purpose is to protect the $n$ processes from interfering with each other, by allowing at most one of them to be in its 'critical region' at any time.

Let the communication between the $n$ processes and the kernel take place through binary variables $\mathsf{request}_i$ and $\mathsf{grant}_i$, $i = 1,\ldots,n$, of which only process $i$ is allowed to change the value of $\mathsf{request}_i$, and only the kernel is allowed to change the value of any $\mathsf{grant}_i$.

These variables are assumed to be used as follows:

- In the initial state we assume that $\mathsf{request}_i = \mathsf{grant}_i = 0$ for all $i$.
- When process $i$ becomes ready to enter its critical region, it sets $\mathsf{request}_i$ to 1.
- When the kernel gives process $i$ permission to enter its critical region, it sets $\mathsf{grant}_i$ to 1.
- When process $i$ exits its critical region, it resets $\mathsf{request}_i$ to 0.
- When the kernel notices that process $i$ has exited its critical region, it acknowledges this by resetting $\mathsf{grant}_i$ to 0.

### Safety Requirements for the Kernel

In analyzing safety requirements in this example, we first notice that the values of $\mathsf{grant}_i$ must always remain within the specified range, and at most one of them can be 1 at a time. This gives the following state invariants:

$$\Box(\mathsf{grant}_i \in \{0, 1\}) , \quad i = 1,\ldots,n ,$$

$$\Box(\sum_{i=1}^{n} \mathsf{grant}_i \leq 1) .$$

As for state changes, it is reasonable to require that permission to enter a critical region is never given to a process that has not requested it. Correspondingly, $\mathsf{grant}_i$ should not be reset before process $i$ has exited its critical region. This gives us requirement

$$\textbf{steady } \mathsf{grant}_i \textbf{ unless } \langle \mathsf{grant}_i' = \mathsf{request}_i \rangle , \quad i = 1,\ldots,n .$$

### Safety Requirements for the Processes

Also, the values of $\mathsf{request}_i$ must always remain within the specified range, which gives us state invariants

$$\Box(\text{request}_i \in \{0, 1\}) , \quad i = 1, \dots, n .$$

In its operation, the kernel needs to rely on the processes to behave in a reasonable manner. Problems could arise, for instance, if a process would withdraw its request before it has been granted permission for an entry. Similarly, a process should not request another entry until the previous exit has been acknowledged. This leads to requirement

**steady** $\text{request}_i$ **unless** $\langle \text{request}_i' = 1 - \text{grant}_i \rangle , \quad i = 1, \dots, n .$

## Liveness Requirements

As for liveness requirements for the kernel, it seems reasonable to require that, whenever a process is willing to enter its critical region, it will eventually be granted permission to do this. Similarly, an exit from a critical region should always eventually be acknowledged. This gives us

$$\text{request}_i \neq \text{grant}_i \rightsquigarrow \langle \text{grant}_i' = \text{request}_i \rangle , \quad i = 1, \dots, n .$$

However, the former of these requirements cannot be satisfied if some process remains indefinitely in its critical region. Therefore, we also need liveness requirements for the $n$ processes:

$$\text{request}_i = \text{grant}_i = 1 \rightsquigarrow \langle \text{request}_i' = 0 \rangle , \quad i = 1, \dots, n .$$

### 3.5.11 Enforcing Causal Relations

By causality we understand that some steps are in some sense 'caused' by the earlier history in behaviors. As an example, let A and B be two disjoint and non-stuttering actions, and consider the property $\phi$ that A and B steps strictly alternate, so that each B step is 'caused' by a preceding A step, and no intervening A steps can appear.

Obviously, $\phi$ holds if $\langle A \rangle \rightsquigarrow \langle B \rangle$ and, in addition, the specification has been constructed so that there is a state predicate P that is initially false, and is turned on and off by A and B as follows:

$$\Box[A \Leftrightarrow \neg P \wedge P'] \wedge \Box[B \Leftrightarrow P \wedge \neg P'] .$$

In designing a specification one can explicitly construct such a state predicate P, for instance by introducing an auxiliary Boolean variable b, initialized as true, and using its value to control the enabling of actions A and B so that

$$A \Rightarrow b = \text{true} \wedge b' = \text{false} ,$$
$$B \Rightarrow b = \text{false} \wedge b' = \text{true} ,$$
$$\Box[b' \neq b \Rightarrow A \vee B] .$$

In general, auxiliary variables provide a powerful but programming-like way to keep track of the history, and to enforce causal relations between the steps that are taken.

### 3.5.12 Possibility Properties

As a linear-time logic, TLA cannot directly express requirements of the form 'for each initial prefix of a behavior it is always possible that action B will be executed in the future'. Notice that this does not imply that B would need to be executed at all. The situation is illustrated in Fig. 3.9, where the behavior $\langle s_0, s_1, \ldots \rangle$ does not contain B steps, but there is infinitely often a possibility for another branch of execution where B could appear. In fact, the given requirement implies that there would always be a possibility for an infinite number of B steps.

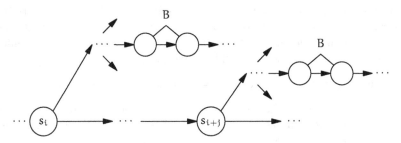

**Fig. 3.9.** Illustration of a possibility property

Properties of this kind are called *possibility properties*. Obviously, possibility properties are not properties of individual behaviors, but of trees of possible behaviors.

Since we are usually interested only in what really happens in behaviors, possibility properties are less important for us. In Chap. 10 on real-time specifications a special need for them will, however, arise.

If the safety part of a specification is $S$,

$$S \Leftrightarrow P \wedge \Box[A] ,$$

the above possibility property holds if one can find a stronger step invariant $\Box[A_1]$, i.e., one for which $A_1 \Rightarrow A$, and a conjunction of fairness formulas $F$, for which $S$ implies

$$\Diamond\Box[A_1] \wedge F \Rightarrow \Box\Diamond\langle B \rangle . \tag{3.86}$$

We will not prove this, but the intuition behind it can be explained as follows. If it is always possible to execute B in the future, it must be possible to 'guide' any execution after any arbitrary initial part into a direction where infinitely many B steps will appear. Such 'guidance' can be given by eventually restricting actions to $A_1$ and by applying suitable fairness assumptions $F$.

Verifying a possibility property with the aid of (3.86) needs, of course, the invention of appropriate $A_1$ and $F$.

### 3.5.13 Parameterization

Existentially quantified rigid variables can be used in state functions and also in actions. Their use in actions gives the possibility for parameterized actions, which will be incorporated in the action language in Chap. 5.

In addition, rigid variables can be used to construct *parameterized specifications*. Parameterized specifications have *free* (non-quantified) rigid variables, which are assumed to have some fixed but unknown values in all state functions and actions. Being rigid they are not part of the state, and cannot appear primed in actions. In programming terminology they would be called 'constants'.

### Review Questions

QUESTION 3.5.1 When is a liveness requirement feasible for a safety specification?

QUESTION 3.5.2 What is meant by strong feasibility, and why are strongly feasible liveness requirements useful in specifications?

QUESTION 3.5.3 In which respects are canonical TLA expressions more general than TLA expressions resulting from action systems?

QUESTION 3.5.4 Discuss how an operational view of action systems may differ from a logical view of the corresponding canonical TLA expressions.

QUESTION 3.5.5 What is meant by erroneous action systems, and why does a similar phenomenon not arise in canonical TLA formulas?

QUESTION 3.5.6 Why do we say that canonical TLA expressions are operational but not executable?

QUESTION 3.5.7 What is the contrast between property-oriented and model-oriented specifications?

QUESTION 3.5.8 What is understood by overspecification and underspecification?

QUESTION 3.5.9 What is understood by possibility properties, and why are they not directly expressible in TLA?

**Exercises**

EXERCISE 3.5.1 Give an example of a situation where liveness properties $L_1$ and $L_2$ are feasible for a safety property S, but their conjunction $L_1 \wedge L_2$ is not. Hint: see Exercise 3.4.2 on p. 84.

EXERCISE 3.5.2 Let S be a safety property of the form (3.81) on p. 86, and let $B_1, B_2, \ldots$ be a countably infinite collection of actions such that, for each i, fairness with respect to $B_i$ is strongly feasible for S. Show that any finite prefix of a behavior that satisfies S can be completed into an infinite behavior that satisfies $S \wedge SF(B_1) \wedge SF(B_2) \wedge \cdots$. Hint: introduce counters that indicate for how long each action $B_i$ has not been executed, and use these counters in selecting the next action to be executed. Since an infinite number of counters cannot be maintained, increase gradually the number of actions considered.

EXERCISE 3.5.3 Consider the modification of an action system to impose an arbitrary strongly feasible fairness requirement.

EXERCISE 3.5.4 Show that a nondeterministic execution model that achieves fairness by treating each step as an execution of a specific action $A_i$ does not exclude any behaviors that satisfy the TLA expression in question.

EXERCISE 3.5.5 Show that the requirements given in Sect. 3.5.10 (p. 96) imply that variables $\mathsf{request}_i$ and $\mathsf{grant}_i$ cannot be modified in the same action.

EXERCISE 3.5.6 Show that the requirements given in Sect. 3.5.10 (p. 96) imply the following mixed properties:

**stable** $\mathsf{request}_i \neq \mathsf{grant}_i$ **until** $\langle \mathsf{grant}'_i = \mathsf{request}_i \rangle$ ,   $i = 1, \ldots, n$ ,

**stable** $\mathsf{request}_i = \mathsf{grant}_i = 1$ **until** $\langle \mathsf{request}'_i = 0 \rangle$ ,   $i = 1, \ldots, n$ .

EXERCISE 3.5.7 Construct an action system for the mutual exclusion example in Sect. 3.5.10 (p. 96). Show that the corresponding TLA formula implies the safety and liveness properties formulated there.

EXERCISE 3.5.8 Impose a first-come-first-serve policy on the specification constructed in Exercise 3.5.7.

EXERCISE 3.5.9 Discuss how the specification constructed in Exercise 3.5.7 implements the required causality relations between actions.

# Bibliographic Notes

*Temporal logic* was introduced to computer science by Pnueli [170, 171]. For a comprehensive treatment of using temporal logic for the specification and verification of reactive systems, the reader is referred to textbooks by Manna and Pnueli [152, 153].

One of the basic operators in usual presentations of temporal logic is the 'next state' operator ($\bigcirc$), with which $\bigcirc$P expresses that state predicate P holds in the next state. To obtain a weaker logic that is insensitive to stuttering, Lamport developed TLA, where the need for this operator has been removed by the notion of actions [141]. His first article on using TLA for specifications was [138]. Most of the treatment of TLA in this chapter follows Lamport's work. The assumption that X in $[A]_X$ consists of all variables involved in a specification is a convention introduced for the purposes of this book. Another difference is that stuttering executions of an action are not counted as its executions in Lamport's definitions of fairness properties.

Chandy and Misra have developed another version of linear-time temporal logic, which is dedicated to their UNITY language [36]. The approach in this book is similar to theirs in the sense that both a specification language and an associated logic are used. Rather than designing a dedicated logic, we have, however, taken a language-independent logic. The selection of TLA was based on its suitability for our execution model, and on its insensitivity to stuttering, which is important for the design methodology to be introduced in the later chapters.

Instead of using a separate specification language, Lamport advocates the use of only logic in specifications, and has designed a structured language TLA$^+$ [144, 145] for writing specifications in TLA.

The formalization of safety and liveness properties in terms of closures is due to Alpern and Schneider [11].

Possibility properties can be directly expressed in branching-time logics, where expressions are interpreted over execution trees, not sequences. The idea of using TLA in proving possibility properties is due to Lamport [143]. For the relationship between linear-time and branching-time temporal logics, the interested reader is referred to [137].

The mutual exclusion example of Sect. 3.5.10 was adapted from [172].

# 4

## Proving Behavioral Properties

The design method to be discussed in this book is intended to support 'correctness by design'. Still, no matter how carefully specification models are constructed and reviewed, design errors do occur, and some reasoning is always needed in order to be convinced of the satisfaction of the required properties. Depending on the application and the criticality of the crucial properties of a system, different degrees of formality can be used. In addition to informal reasoning with mathematical argumentation (as is done in the examples of this book), complemented in various ways by testing and debugging of designs, a specification formalism should also support formal proof techniques that are mechanizable.

For this purpose we discuss in this chapter how logical deductions in TLA can be carried out in detail, although this is not essential for understanding the rest of this book. The chapter should not be read as a formal treatise of logic, since its viewpoint is not that of logics. Instead, its aim is to give a software designer a basis for understanding the arguments that can be used in proving behavioral properties. The reader is warned, however, that even 'obvious' properties may lead to long and complicated proofs, when carried out in all detail. Fortunately, less detailed proofs in English – ultimately based on essentially the same kinds of arguments – are perfectly adequate for most practical purposes.

A large collection of proof rules will be given, which are useful for detailed manual proofs. No attention is paid to their redundancy or mathematical elegance. Since quantification of state variables in TLA is only of secondary importance for us, it will be ignored.

The structure of the chapter is as follows:

- Section 4.1 gives a brief introduction to proof systems, and how proofs in TLA are based on non-temporal proofs for state predicates and actions.
- Section 4.2 discusses proof rules for invariants and other safety properties.
- Section 4.3 gives proof rules for liveness properties, for which fairness assumptions are essential.

## 4.1 Introduction

We start by briefly examining the role of formal proofs, and explaining the non-temporal basis of temporal proofs.

### 4.1.1 Logical Proofs in System Design

When TLA is used, the situation where proofs are of concern is typically as follows: we have two concrete TLA expressions $E$ and $F$, and we need to prove that every behavior satisfying $E$ does also satisfy $F$. Obviously, this is the case when $E \Rightarrow F$ is a tautology.

For instance, when $E$ is an operational specification, given as a canonical TLA expression, and $F$ is a required property of the system, then the tautology $E \Rightarrow F$ shows that this property does indeed hold for the specification. The situation is the same when $F$ is a specification and $E$ is a TLA description of a proposed implementation. Then the tautology $E \Rightarrow F$ shows that (the description of) the implementation satisfies the specification.

More generally, the specification and design of a system may proceed in incremental steps, where each step corresponds to refining a TLA expression $E_i$ into $E_{i+1}$, with the correctness criterion $E_{i+1} \Rightarrow E_i$. Similarly to programs, complex specifications cannot be given in one step. Therefore, this process may involve steps where $E_i$ is an incomplete specification in which some of the required properties have not yet been addressed, and $E_{i+1}$ is a slightly more refined version of it. On the other hand, $E_{i+1}$ might also describe an operational model with some more detailed design decisions than those incorporated in $E_i$.

Ultimately, reliable reasoning on reactive systems can only be achieved by using computer assistance in the generation and checking of proofs. When the required degree of confidence in system correctness is very high, as it is in life-critical applications, disciplined informal approaches and extensive testing are no substitute for formal machine-checked proofs. All of these are then important and they all complement each other.

Unfortunately, the current state-of-the-art and the available tools are not yet sufficiently ripe for using formal methods as widely as would be desirable. However, even when reactive systems are designed with a modest degree of formality, the designer should be able to think in terms of the formal arguments that would be crucial in formal proofs. Although proofs are then not expected to be carried out in detail, it is the same kind of arguments that the designer should use in convincing himself and the rest of the design review team of the correctness of a design.

### 4.1.2 Logical Deductions

When $E \Rightarrow F$ is proved to be a tautology, we say that $F$ is logically *deduced* from $E$.

In the semantic interpretation of temporal formulas, an expression of the form $E \Rightarrow F$ can be proved to be a tautology by showing that every behavior that satisfies $E$ also satisfies $F$. Reasoning in terms of behaviors is, however, complicated and error-prone. Therefore, it is preferable to use an abstract logical calculus for deductions.

*Axioms* in a logical system are formulas that are known to be identically true, i.e., can be deduced from any assumptions. For our purposes we can take as axioms all the laws given in Sects. 3.3 and 3.4. For instance, (3.48) on p. 79, which is a law by definition, gives an axiom

$$\Diamond E \Leftrightarrow \neg \Box \neg E \,,$$

where $E$ stands for an arbitrary temporal predicate.

For deductions, a logical system has *deduction rules* or *proof rules*, by which true formulas can be deduced from what is already known or assumed to be true. In fact, every law of the form

$$E_1 \wedge \cdots \wedge E_k \Rightarrow E \tag{4.1}$$

gives a rule by which one can deduce $E$, if all $E_i$, $i = 1, \ldots, k$, are either axioms or assumptions, or have already been deduced from these. Such a rule can be written in the form given in Table 4.1, where the *premises* $E_i$ are written above the horizontal line, and the *conclusion* $E$ is written below it. This form is obviously more convenient than writing out laws in the form (4.1), which may easily be confused with expressions of the same form that are not identically true.

**Table 4.1.** The format of a proof rule

$$
\begin{array}{c}
E_1 \\
\cdots \\
\underline{E_k} \\
E
\end{array}
$$

### 4.1.3 Non-temporal Basis

Although temporal operators require special proof rules, the proofs of temporal properties are ultimately based on non-temporal rules. There are two reasons for this:

- Non-temporal logical connectives have the same meaning in temporal and non-temporal expressions. Therefore, proof rules for them can be taken as such from non-temporal logics.

- Non-temporal rules are needed in proving that a state predicate or an action is identically true, i.e., is satisfied for any state or step, respectively.

A well-known example of non-temporal rules is the *modus ponens* rule for implication ($\Rightarrow$), given in Table 4.2. Since all laws have the form $E \Rightarrow F$ (or $E \Leftrightarrow E$), the *modus ponens* rule formalizes how arbitrary laws can be utilized in deductions.

**Table 4.2.** The *modus ponens* rule

$$\frac{\begin{array}{c} E \\ E \Rightarrow F \end{array}}{F}$$

Since we want to concentrate on temporal deductions, non-temporal rules will be taken here as granted and will not be discussed any further.

The proofs of all interesting temporal properties are ultimately based on proving that some concrete state predicates or actions are identically true. The connection of this to temporal logic is that an identically true state predicate (action) is satisfied by all states (steps) in any behavior. This is formalized by the two *tautology rules* given in Table 4.3. Deducing that the premises of these rules hold takes place by non-temporal reasoning, which is omitted here.

**Table 4.3.** Tautology rules

| P is identically true | A is identically true |
|---|---|
| $\Box P$ | $\Box[A]$ |

### Review Questions

QUESTION 4.1.1 What is the difference between an expression $E \Rightarrow F$ and a proof rule with premise $E$ and conclusion $F$?

QUESTION 4.1.2 What is the non-temporal basis of temporal proofs?

### Exercises

EXERCISE 4.1.1 Take a few temporal laws in Chap. 3, and write them out as proof rules.

EXERCISE 4.1.2 Why can the premises of the two tautology rules in Table 4.3 not be written simply as P and [A], respectively?

## 4.2 Deduction of Invariants

The discussion of temporal proof rules is started with those for state invariants and step invariants.

### 4.2.1 State Invariants

As a simple special case, consider the situation where $P$ and $P \Rightarrow Q$ are not tautologies, but both $\Box P$ and $\Box(P \Rightarrow Q)$ can be deduced from the given assumptions. Obviously, $\Box Q$ then also holds. Although such a deduction resembles *modus ponens*, it is not an application of it.

The first rule in Table 4.4 formalizes this *temporal weakening* of a state invariant.

More generally, to deduce that state predicate $P$ is invariantly true, it suffices to show that the initial state satisfies $P$, and that any allowed action preserves it. This *state invariant rule* is given as the second rule in Table 4.4.

**Table 4.4.** State invariant rules

| | | $P$ |
|---|---|---|
| | $P$ | $\Box I$ |
| $\Box P$ | $\Box[A]$ | $\Box[A]$ |
| $\Box(P \Rightarrow Q)$ | $\Box[P \wedge A \Rightarrow P']$ | $\Box[P \wedge I \wedge I' \wedge A \Rightarrow P']$ |
| $\Box Q$ | $\Box P$ | $\Box P$ |

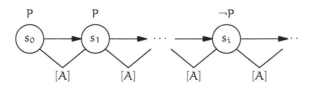

**Fig. 4.1.** Checking the state invariant rule

The validity of this rule can be shown by considering an arbitrary behavior $\sigma = \langle s_0, s_1, \ldots \rangle$ that satisfies the second premise but violates the conclusion $\Box P$, as illustrated in Fig. 4.1. If $s_i$ is the first state where $P$ is not true, then either $i = 0$, in which case the first premise does not hold, or $i > 0$, in which case the third premise is violated by step $(s_{i-1}, s_i)$. This means that the conclusion must hold in each case. Notice, however, that for this reasoning to hold it is essential that $P$ and $A$ contain no variables outside of set $X$, which is the (omitted) subscript of the brackets.

In order to show that the third premise in this rule is satisfied in a given situation, one only needs to consider states and steps that are reachable from a legal initial state. A way to rule out (some) non-reachable states is to use another invariant for characterizing those states that are (or may be) reachable. The third rule in Table 4.4 captures such a use of an auxiliary invariant I.

### 4.2.2 Step Invariants

Step invariants appear in stability and steadiness conditions for state predicates and state functions, respectively (see Sect. 3.3.10, p. 76). They are also needed in deducing state invariants, as is evident from the state invariant rules.

Analogously to temporal weakening of state invariants, the first rule in Table 4.5 formalizes *temporal weakening* of step invariants. A more generally applicable *step invariant rule*, which makes use of an auxiliary state invariant, is given as the second rule in the same table.

**Table 4.5.** Step invariant rules

| | |
|---|---|
| | $\Box I$ |
| $\Box[A]$ | $\Box[A]$ |
| $\Box[A \Rightarrow B]$ | $\Box[I \wedge I' \wedge A \Rightarrow B]$ |
| $\Box[B]$ | $\Box[B]$ |

### 4.2.3 Simple Examples

Two small examples will be discussed on using the above invariant rules.

### State Invariant Rule

As an example of formally deducing a state invariant, consider the assertion

$$\Box(\mathsf{flam\_s} = \mathsf{true} \vee \mathsf{flam\_s} = \mathsf{false})$$

for the gas-burner example of Chap. 2. Its deduction from the specification is given in Table 4.6. The proof in this table is organized in a top-down fashion. The formula to be deduced is first given as a goal, and then an instantiation of a proof rule is given for its deduction.[1] The validity of each premise is

---

[1]Local names will be introduced for expressions so that they are always the same as those used in the proof rules referred to. The same names may therefore be used for several different purposes, but indentation shows their scopes.

**Table 4.6.** Proof of a simple state invariant

---

$\square(\mathsf{flam\_s} = \mathsf{true} \vee \mathsf{flam\_s} = \mathsf{false})$ – goal

To prove this goal, use the second state invariant rule (Table 4.4, p. 107) for
$P : \mathsf{flam\_s} = \mathsf{true} \vee \mathsf{flam\_s} = \mathsf{false}$
$A : \mathsf{Req\_on\_e} \vee \mathsf{Req\_off\_e} \vee \mathsf{Flame\_on\_e} \vee \mathsf{Flame\_off\_e}$
$\quad \vee \mathsf{Req\_on\_s} \vee \mathsf{Req\_off\_s} \vee \mathsf{Flame\_on\_s} \vee \mathsf{Flame\_off\_s}$
$\quad \vee \mathsf{Start\_s} \vee \mathsf{Stop\_s} \vee \mathsf{Ign\_off\_s} \vee \mathsf{Close\_s}$
with premises:

| | |
|---|---|
| 1 $P$ | – from assumptions |
| 2 $\square[A]$ | – from assumptions |

3 $\square[P \wedge A \Rightarrow P']$
   Written out, this subgoal is
   $\square[(\mathsf{flam\_s} = \mathsf{true} \vee \mathsf{flam\_s} = \mathsf{false}) \wedge$
      $(\mathsf{Req\_on\_e} \vee \mathsf{Req\_off\_e} \vee \mathsf{Flame\_on\_e} \vee \mathsf{Flame\_off\_e}$
      $\vee \mathsf{Req\_on\_s} \vee \mathsf{Req\_off\_s} \vee \mathsf{Flame\_on\_s} \vee \mathsf{Flame\_off\_s}$
      $\vee \mathsf{Start\_s} \vee \mathsf{Stop\_s} \vee \mathsf{Ign\_off\_s} \vee \mathsf{Close\_s})$
   $\Rightarrow \mathsf{flam\_s}' = \mathsf{true} \vee \mathsf{flam\_s}' = \mathsf{false}]$

To prove this subgoal, use action tautology rule (Table 4.3, p. 106) for
$A : (\mathsf{flam\_s} = \mathsf{true} \vee \mathsf{flam\_s} = \mathsf{false}) \wedge$
   $(\mathsf{Req\_on\_e} \vee \mathsf{Req\_off\_e} \vee \mathsf{Flame\_on\_e} \vee \mathsf{Flame\_off\_e}$
   $\vee \mathsf{Req\_on\_s} \vee \mathsf{Req\_off\_s} \vee \mathsf{Flame\_on\_s} \vee \mathsf{Flame\_off\_s}$
   $\vee \mathsf{Start\_s} \vee \mathsf{Stop\_s} \vee \mathsf{Ign\_off\_s} \vee \mathsf{Close\_s})$
   $\Rightarrow \mathsf{flam\_s}' = \mathsf{true} \vee \mathsf{flam\_s}' = \mathsf{false}$
with premise:

| | |
|---|---|
| 1 $A$ is identically true | – by non-temporal deduction |

---

checked, either by non-temporal deduction, or by taking it as a subgoal to be proved in the same manner. Once all premises have been checked, the proof is complete.

The last non-temporal step in this proof is to check that

$$(\mathsf{flam\_s} = \mathsf{true} \vee \mathsf{flam\_s} = \mathsf{false}) \wedge (\mathsf{Req\_on\_e} \vee \cdots) \Rightarrow$$
$$\mathsf{flam\_s}' = \mathsf{true} \vee \mathsf{flam\_s}' = \mathsf{false}$$

is an identically true action. This reduces to checking separately for all actions of the specification that expressions

$$(\mathsf{flam\_s} = \mathsf{true} \vee \mathsf{flam\_s} = \mathsf{false}) \wedge \mathsf{Req\_on\_e} \Rightarrow$$
$$\mathsf{flam\_s}' = \mathsf{true} \vee \mathsf{flam\_s}' = \mathsf{false} \,,$$

$$\cdots$$

$$(\mathsf{flam\_s} = \mathsf{true} \vee \mathsf{flam\_s} = \mathsf{false}) \wedge \mathsf{Close\_s} \Rightarrow$$
$$\mathsf{flam\_s}' = \mathsf{true} \vee \mathsf{flam\_s}' = \mathsf{false}$$

are identically true. This is obviously trivial, since there are only three choices for the value of flam_s' in the actions, and these are flam_s, true, and false.

**Step Invariant Rule**

As an example of using step invariant rules, consider the invariant

$$\Box[\neg\text{flow\_s} \land \text{flow\_s}' \Rightarrow \text{ign\_s}'] \,.$$

Deduction steps for this are given in Table 4.7, and they are very similar to the ones in the previous example. Again, the proof involves a non-temporal step, where an action expression is shown to be identically true.

**Table 4.7.** Proof of a simple step invariant

---

$\Box[\neg\text{flow\_s} \land \text{flow\_s}' \Rightarrow \text{ign\_s}']$ – goal

To prove this goal, use the first step invariant rule (Table 4.5, p. 108) for
A : Req_on_e ∨ Req_off_e ∨ Flame_on_e ∨ Flame_off_e
  ∨ Req_on_s ∨ Req_off_s ∨ Flame_on_s ∨ Flame_off_s
  ∨ Start_s ∨ Stop_s ∨ Ign_off_s ∨ Close_s
B : ¬flow_s ∧ flow_s' ⇒ ign_s'
with premises:
1 □[A]                                        – from assumptions
2 □[A ⇒ B]
  Written out, this subgoal is
    □[Req_on_e ∨ Req_off_e ∨ Flame_on_e ∨ Flame_off_e
    ∨ Req_on_s ∨ Req_off_s ∨ Flame_on_s ∨ Flame_off_s
    ∨ Start_s ∨ Stop_s ∨ Ign_off_s ∨ Close_s
    ⇒ (¬flow_s ∧ flow_s' ⇒ ign_s')]

To prove this subgoal, use action tautology rule (Table 4.3, p. 106) for
A : Req_on_e ∨ Req_off_e ∨ Flame_on_e ∨ Flame_off_e
  ∨ Req_on_s ∨ Req_off_s ∨ Flame_on_s ∨ Flame_off_s
  ∨ Start_s ∨ Stop_s ∨ Ign_off_s ∨ Close_s
  ⇒ (¬flow_s ∧ flow_s' ⇒ ign_s')
with premise:
1 A is identically true          – by non-temporal deduction

---

**Exercises**

EXERCISE 4.2.1 Show that it is essential for the state invariant rules (Table 4.4 on p. 107) that P and A contain only state variables in X.

EXERCISE 4.2.2 Use the laws given in Chap. 3 to show that the temporal weakening rule for invariants (first rule in Table 4.4 on p. 107) is valid.

EXERCISE 4.2.3 Show how the third state invariant rule in Table 4.4 (p. 107) can be derived from the other rules in this table.

EXERCISE 4.2.4 Show that the second step invariant rule in Table 4.5 (p. 108) can be derived from the simple rule in the same table.

EXERCISE 4.2.5 Deduce the property

$$\Box[\text{ign\_s}' \Rightarrow \text{flow\_s}']$$

for the gas-burner example by utilizing law (3.41) on p. 75, and using a state invariant rule.

EXERCISE 4.2.6 Prove formally that your construction in Exercise 3.5.7 (p. 100) for the semaphore example satisfies the given safety requirements.

EXERCISE 4.2.7 Deduce state invariant $\Box(x \geq 0)$ for an action system with initial condition $x = 0$ and actions

$$A : x \geq 0 \qquad\qquad B : x \bmod 3 = 1 \qquad C : x \bmod 2 = 1$$
$$\rightarrow x' = x + 2 , \qquad \rightarrow x' = x - 1 , \qquad \rightarrow x' = x - 3 .$$

## 4.3 Deduction of Eventualities

In general, liveness properties lead to more complex deductions than safety properties. In this section we give a number of useful proof rules for them.

### 4.3.1 Temporal Weakening of Eventualities

Similarly to temporal weakening of invariants, *temporal weakening* of eventualities can be described by the intuitively simple rules in Table 4.8.

Table 4.8. Temporal weakening of eventualities

|  |  | $P \rightsquigarrow Q$ | $P \rightsquigarrow \langle A \rangle$ | $\langle A \rangle \rightsquigarrow \langle B \rangle$ |
|---|---|---|---|---|
| $\Diamond P$ | $\Diamond \langle A \rangle$ | $\Box(R \Rightarrow P)$ | $\Box(Q \Rightarrow P)$ | $\Box[C \Rightarrow A]$ |
| $\Box(P \Rightarrow Q)$ | $\Box[A \Rightarrow B]$ | $\Box(Q \Rightarrow S)$ | $\Box[A \Rightarrow B]$ | $\Box[B \Rightarrow D]$ |
| $\Diamond Q$ | $\Diamond \langle B \rangle$ | $R \rightsquigarrow S$ | $Q \rightsquigarrow \langle B \rangle$ | $\langle C \rangle \rightsquigarrow \langle D \rangle$ |

Since $\Box(P \Rightarrow P \wedge I)$ always holds when I is an invariant, these temporal weakening rules also allow us to weaken preconditions in 'leads to' properties by invariants, as shown by the rules in Table 4.9. Of course, by weakening the preconditions the 'leads to' properties themselves are strengthened.

**Table 4.9.** Strengthening of 'leads to' properties

$$
\frac{P \wedge I \rightsquigarrow Q}{\square I} \qquad \frac{P \wedge I \rightsquigarrow \langle A \rangle}{\square I}
$$
$$
\frac{}{P \rightsquigarrow Q} \qquad \frac{}{P \rightsquigarrow \langle A \rangle}
$$

### 4.3.2 Deduction of Fairness Properties

Eventualities and 'leads to' properties are usually proved utilizing some fairness properties. Therefore, it is useful to have rules for also deducing such fairness properties that have not been given as assumptions.

For weak fairness, law (3.75) on p. 83 expresses its deduction directly from an associated 'leads to' property. For strong fairness no equally simple law can be given. However, if the enabling of A either leads to its execution or to a state from which point onwards A will be continually disabled, then we obviously have strong fairness with respect to A. Continual disabling of A can be guaranteed by a suitable stable state predicate P. This can be formalized as the rule given in Table 4.10. To avoid the use of too many kinds of operators, stability is expressed here and in other proof rules of this chapter in terms of explicit step invariants.

**Table 4.10.** Rule for deducing strong fairness

$$
\frac{\begin{array}{l} \mathsf{Enabled}\,A^+ \rightsquigarrow \langle A \vee \mathsf{Enabled}'\,A^0 \vee P' \rangle \\ \square(P \Rightarrow \neg \mathsf{Enabled}\,A^+) \\ \square[P \Rightarrow P'] \end{array}}{\mathrm{SF}(A)}
$$

Further rules for deducing weak and strong fairness properties were given as laws in Sects. 3.4.9 (p. 83) and 3.4.10 (p. 84).

### 4.3.3 Utilizing Weak Fairness

If a weakly fair action A can be disabled only by its own execution, then its enabling will eventually force its execution. Such a situation is illustrated in the left-hand part of Figure 4.2, which shows the kinds of transitions that are then possible in those reachable states that satisfy $\mathsf{Enabled}\,A^+$, and which either preserve this enabling or make it false.

This situation is generalized in the right-hand part of Fig. 4.2 to a situation where weak fairness with respect to action A forces an eventual execution of action B. Here P is assumed to be stable unless B is executed, and P is also assumed to ensure the enabling of $A^+$ and that A implies B. With these

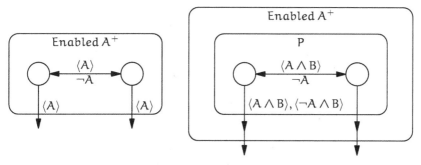

**Fig. 4.2.** Transitions in the situation of the weak fairness rule

assumptions, if P has become true, then A will stay enabled until either it is executed (which implies execution of B), or P becomes false (which can only take place by executing B).

To make this precise, the deduction of $P \rightsquigarrow \langle B \rangle$ in this situation is formulated as the *weak fairness rule* in Table 4.11. Because of the third premise, the conclusion in the rule could also be replaced by **stable** P **until** $\langle B \rangle$.

**Table 4.11.** Weak fairness rule

$$
\begin{array}{l}
\text{WF}(A) \\
\Box(P \Rightarrow \text{Enabled } A^+) \\
\Box[P \Rightarrow P' \vee B] \\
\underline{\Box[P \wedge A \Rightarrow B]} \\
P \rightsquigarrow \langle B \rangle
\end{array}
$$

To check that this rule is, indeed, valid, consider an arbitrary behavior that satisfies the premises of the rule but violates the conclusion. As shown in Fig. 4.3, such a behavior has a state $s_i$ that satisfies P, but there are no subsequent $\langle B \rangle$ steps. On account of the third premise, P is permanently true from state $s_i$ on. As a consequence, the fourth premise then requires that there is no subsequent $\langle A \rangle$ step either. Since the second premise requires $A^+$ to stay continually enabled (which means that there can be no stuttering A steps, either), we reach a contradiction with the first premise.

### 4.3.4 Utilizing Strong Fairness

Since a strong fairness property always implies the corresponding weak fairness property, the above weak fairness rule is directly applicable also with strong fairness assumptions. When this is not sufficient, we need to use a stronger rule that is specific to strong fairness.

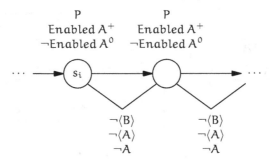

**Fig. 4.3.** Checking the weak fairness rule

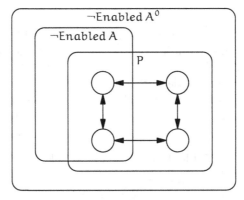

**Fig. 4.4.** Transitions that preserve P in the situation of the strong fairness rule

Analogously to the situation in the weak fairness rule, Fig. 4.4 illustrates state transitions in the following situation, where strong fairness with respect to action A forces eventual execution of action B. State predicate P is again assumed to be stable unless action B is executed, and P is also assumed to ensure that A implies B. Instead of implying the enabledness of $A^+$, P is now assumed to imply only that $A^0$ is not enabled. In addition, an auxiliary liveness assumption is made that the predicate $P \wedge \neg Enabled\, A$ cannot stay true indefinitely. Under these assumptions, once P has become true, either it becomes false in the execution of B, or action A is repeatedly enabled, forcing its eventual execution (which then is also an execution of B). For simplicity, transitions in which P turns false are omitted from Fig. 4.4.

The rule for deducing $P \rightsquigarrow \langle B \rangle$ in this situation is made precise as the *strong fairness rule* given in Table 4.12.

To check the validity of this rule, consider an arbitrary behavior that satisfies its premises but violates the conclusion. As shown in Fig. 4.5, it has a state $s_i$ that satisfies P but has no subsequent $\langle B \rangle$ step. The third premise then implies that P stays true in all subsequent states. The second premise guarantees that $A^0$ is not enabled in any of these states. Because of the fifth

**Table 4.12.** Strong fairness rule

$$SF(A)$$
$$\Box(P \Rightarrow \neg Enabled\ A^0)$$
$$\Box[P \Rightarrow P' \vee B]$$
$$P \wedge \neg Enabled\ A \rightsquigarrow \langle \neg P' \vee Enabled'\ A \rangle$$
$$\Box[P \wedge A \Rightarrow B]$$

---

$$P \rightsquigarrow \langle B \rangle$$

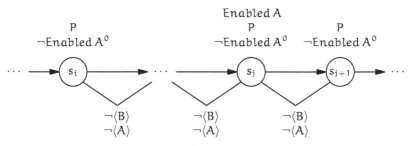

**Fig. 4.5.** Checking the strong fairness rule

premise, none of the steps can now be $\langle A \rangle$ steps, either. On account of the fourth premise, A must be enabled either in state $s_i$ or in one of the subsequent states $s_j$. Repeating the reasoning from the next state after that leads to an infinite number of states with $A^+$ enabled without any execution of $\langle A \rangle$, and without intervening states with $A^0$ enabled, which is in contradiction with the first premise.

Notice that this rule for utilizing strong fairness requires that another eventuality has already been proved. This means that we cannot avoid using weak fairness rules even when all liveness assumptions are strong fairness assumptions.

### 4.3.5 Well-founded Ordering

The above fairness rules assume a state predicate P that stays continually true until the desired action $\langle B \rangle$ is executed. However, it is not always possible to find such a state predicate. The transitivity of $\rightsquigarrow$ may be helpful in such situations, but even this is not always sufficient. A more general solution is provided by a rule that utilizes *well-founded* (partial) *ordering*.

A binary relation $\succ$ in a non-empty set Z is *well founded* if there are no infinite descending sequences $z_1 \succ z_2 \succ \ldots$ with $z_i \in Z$. That is, starting from any $z_1 \in Z$, all descending sequences are necessarily finite.

The arithmetic 'greater than' relation in the set of non-negative integers is obviously well founded. Another example of frequently used well-founded relations is the 'lexicographic greater than' relation between n-tuples of non-negative integers, for which $(x_1, \ldots, x_n) > (y_1, \ldots, y_n)$ when we have $x_j > y_j$ for some $j$, $1 \leq j \leq n$, but $x_i = y_i$ for all $i$, $1 \leq i < j$. A very simple well-founded ordering of non-negative integers is the one where $i \succ 0$ for all $i > 0$, and $\succ$ is undefined for all other pairs.

Let $f$ now denote a state function whose value is guaranteed to be in some set $Z$ when the state satisfies state predicate $P$, and let $\succ$ be a well-founded relation in $Z$. If we can show that, starting from any state where $P$ is satisfied, eventually either $\langle A \rangle$ is executed, or a state is entered where $P$ again holds but the value of $f$ has been decreased, then $\langle A \rangle$ must eventually be executed. The basis for this reasoning is that $f$ can be decremented only finitely many times.

This reasoning is formalized in Table 4.13 as the *well-founded ordering rule*, where $z$ denotes an arbitrary element of $Z$.

**Table 4.13.** Well-founded ordering rule

$$P \Rightarrow f \in Z \ \text{ is identically true}$$
$$\frac{P \wedge (f = z) \rightsquigarrow \langle A \vee P' \wedge z \succ f' \rangle}{P \rightsquigarrow \langle A \rangle}$$

The second premise in the well-founded ordering rule may require case analysis, where this premise is checked for the possible values of $f$. In fact, the simple *case rule* in Table 4.14 can be derived trivially from the well-founded ordering rule by replacing $P$ by $P \vee Q$ and defining the state function $f$, for instance, as

$$s[\![f]\!] = \begin{cases} 1 & \text{if } s[\![P]\!] \,, \\ 0 & \text{if } s[\![\neg P \wedge Q]\!] \,. \end{cases}$$

The ordering $\succ$ is even irrelevant here, since both cases lead to the execution of action $\langle A \rangle$.

**Table 4.14.** Case rule for 'leads to'

$$P \rightsquigarrow \langle A \rangle$$
$$Q \rightsquigarrow \langle A \rangle$$
$$\frac{}{P \vee Q \rightsquigarrow \langle A \rangle}$$

### 4.3.6 Example

As an example we consider proofs about exiting states $\mathsf{Starting}$ and $\mathsf{Ignited}$ in the gas-burner example of Chap. 2 (see Fig. 2.5, p. 38).

**Table 4.15.** Proof of exiting state Starting

---

Starting $\rightsquigarrow \langle$Stop_s $\vee$ Ign_off_s$\rangle$ – goal

To prove this goal, use weak fairness rule (Table 4.11, p. 113) for
A, B : Stop_s $\vee$ Ign_off_s
P : Starting
with premises:
1 WF(A)
  By (3.78) this is implied by SF(A); written out as
  SF(Stop_s $\vee$ Ign_off_s)        – by assumptions and (3.79), p. 84

2 $\square$(P $\Rightarrow$ Enabled A$^+$)
  Written out, this subgoal is
  $\square$(Starting $\Rightarrow$ Enabled(Stop_s $\vee$ Ign_off_s))

  To prove this subgoal, use the first tautology rule (Table 4.3, p. 106) for
  P : Starting $\Rightarrow$ Enabled(Stop_s $\vee$ Ign_off_s)
  with premise:
  1 P is identically true
    Written out, this subgoal is
    Starting $\Rightarrow$ Starting $\wedge$ ($\neg$flam_s $\vee$ flam_s) is identically true
                                – nontemporal tautology
3 $\square$[P $\Rightarrow$ P$'$ $\vee$ B]
  Written out, this subgoal is
  $\square$[Starting $\Rightarrow$ Starting$'$ $\vee$ Stop_s $\vee$ Ign_off_s]

  To prove this subgoal, use the first step invariant rule (Table 4.5, p. 108) for
  A : Req_on_e $\vee$ Req_off_e $\vee$ Flame_on_e $\vee$ Flame_off_e
     $\vee$ Req_on_s $\vee$ Req_off_s $\vee$ Flame_on_s $\vee$ Flame_off_s
     $\vee$ Start_s $\vee$ Stop_s $\vee$ Ign_off_s $\vee$ Close_s
  B : Starting $\Rightarrow$ Starting$'$ $\vee$ Stop_s $\vee$ Ign_off_s
  with premises:
  1 $\square$[A]                    – from assumptions
  2 $\square$[A $\Rightarrow$ B]
    Written out, this subgoal is
    $\square$[Req_on_e $\vee$ Req_off_e $\vee$ Flame_on_e $\vee$ Flame_off_e
    $\vee$ Req_on_s $\vee$ Req_off_s $\vee$ Flame_on_s $\vee$ Flame_off_s
    $\vee$ Start_s $\vee$ Stop_s $\vee$ Ign_off_s $\vee$ Close_s
    $\Rightarrow$ (Starting $\Rightarrow$ Starting$'$ $\vee$ Stop_s $\vee$ Ign_off_s)]
                                – by action tautology rule (Table 4.3, p. 106)
4 $\square$[P $\wedge$ A $\Rightarrow$ B]               – by action tautology rule (Table 4.3, p. 106)
                                – since A and B are the same

---

## Exit from Starting

Intuitively it is clear that state Starting is always eventually exited either by
action Stop_s or by action Ign_off_s:

$$\text{Starting} \rightsquigarrow \langle \text{Stop\_s} \vee \text{Ign\_off\_s} \rangle .$$

The justification for this is that always either Stop_s or Ign_off_s is enabled in
state Starting, and both of these actions have a strong fairness requirement.

A formal proof of this is given in Table 4.15. The crucial step is the use
of the weak fairness rule. Since the enabling condition of Stop_s ∨ Ign_off_s
is Starting, this step gives the desired result directly. The first premise of
this step, WF(A), follows directly from the fairness assumptions in the specification. The second premise needs only non-temporal proofs and a tautology
rule, whereas the third premise also needs a simple use of a step invariant
rule.

## Exit from Ignited

Obviously, state Ignited need not be exited ever, if the heat request and
the flame indicator are never turned off. Therefore, let us make the additional
fairness assumption that continual burning of gas will always eventually result
in variable req_e being set off, i.e.,

$$\text{WF}(\text{flam\_e} \wedge \text{Req\_off\_e}) . \tag{4.2}$$

Notice that this does not prevent the request from being repeatedly turned
off and on while the flame is burning.

With this additional assumption we can prove that action Close_s is always eventually executed in state Ignited, i.e., that

$$\text{Ignited} \rightsquigarrow \langle \text{Close} \rangle$$

is true.

The idea of the proof is illustrated in Fig. 4.6. In state Ignited, either
req_s and flam_s are both true, or one of them is false (state 3). In the
former case, either req_e and flam_e are both true (state 1), or one of them
is false (state 2). The weak fairness assumption (4.2) ensures that state 1 is
always eventually exited to state 2, although it can still be re-entered from
there. Strong fairness on both Req_s and Flame_off_s guarantees, however,
that state 2 will always eventually be exited to state 3, although state 2 can
still be re-entered from there. Finally, strong fairness on Close_s guarantees
that this action will eventually be executed in state 3. This reasoning is made
more precise in Table 4.16.

## Review Questions

QUESTION 4.3.1 What is meant by well-founded ordering?

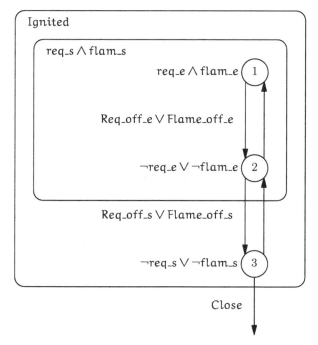

**Fig. 4.6.** Illustration of proving Ignited $\rightsquigarrow$ $\langle$Close_s$\rangle$

## Exercises

EXERCISE 4.3.1 Complete the deductions in Tables 4.15 (p. 117) and 4.16 (p. 120).

EXERCISE 4.3.2 Prove that $\Box\Diamond$Idle holds in the gas-burner example under the additional fairness assumption (4.2) on p. 118.

EXERCISE 4.3.3 Prove formally that your construction in Exercise 3.5.7 (p. 100) for the mutual exclusion example satisfies the given liveness requirements.

EXERCISE 4.3.4 Prove that $x = 0 \rightsquigarrow x = 1$ holds for an action system with initial condition $y = 0$ and actions

$$^{SF}A : y \bmod 5 = 0 \qquad ^{WF}B : \mathbf{T}$$
$$\rightarrow x' = x + 1 , \qquad \rightarrow y' = y + 1 .$$

EXERCISE 4.3.5 How do you prove for the action system of Exercise 4.3.4 that $x = 0 \rightsquigarrow x > n$ for any integer $n > 0$?

**Table 4.16.** Proof of exiting state Ignited

---

Ignited $\rightsquigarrow$ ⟨Close_s⟩        – goal

To prove this goal, use strong fairness rule (Table 4.12, p. 115) for
A, B : Close_s
P : Ignited
with premises:
1 SF(A)                    – from assumptions
2 □(P ⇒ ¬Enabled A⁰)        – trivial for non-stuttering A
3 □[P ⇒ P′ ∨ B]            – by step invariant (Table 4.5, p. 108) and
                           – action tautology rules (Table 4.3, p. 106)
4 P ∧ ¬Enabled A $\rightsquigarrow$ ⟨¬P′ ∨ Enabled′ A⟩
  This subgoal is implied by
  Ignited ∧ req_s ∧ flam_s $\rightsquigarrow$ ⟨Req_off_s ∨ Flame_off_s⟩

  To prove this subgoal, use strong fairness rule (Table 4.12, p. 115) for
  A, B : Req_off_s ∨ Flame_off_s
  P : Ignited ∧ req_s ∧ flam_s
  with premises:
  1 SF(A)                  – from assumptions by (3.79) and (3.80), p. 84
  2 □(P ⇒ ¬Enabled A⁰)      – trivial for non-stuttering A
  3 □[P ⇒ P′ ∨ B]          – by step invariant (Table 4.5, p. 108) and
                           – action tautology rules (Table 4.3, p. 106)
  4 P ∧ ¬Enabled A $\rightsquigarrow$ ⟨¬P′ ∨ Enabled′ A⟩
    This subgoal is implied by
    Ignited ∧ req_s ∧ flam_s ∧ req_e ∧ flam_e $\rightsquigarrow$
      ⟨Req_off_e ∨ Flame_off_e⟩

    To prove this subgoal, use weak fairness rule for
    A : flam_e ∧ Req_off_e
    B : Req_off_e ∨ Flame_off_e
    P : Ignited ∧ req_s ∧ flam_s ∧ req_e ∧ flam_e
    with premises:
    1 WF(A)                – the additional assumption
    2 □(P ⇒ Enabled A⁺)     – by first tautology rule (Table 4.3, p. 106)
    3 □[P ⇒ P′ ∨ B]        – by step invariant (Table 4.5, p. 108) and
                           – action tautology rules (Table 4.3, p. 106)
    4 □[P ∧ A ⇒ B]         – since A implies B

  5 □[P ∧ A ⇒ B]          – since A and B are the same

5 □[P ∧ A ⇒ B]            – since A and B are the same

---

EXERCISE 4.3.6 Assuming that the initial values of $i$ and $j$ are positive integers, that function $n(i)$ always yields a positive integer, and that $S$ does not change the values of $i$ and $j$, the following actions model a double loop around statement $S$:

$$^{\mathrm{WF}}A : i > 0 \wedge j > 0 \qquad ^{\mathrm{WF}}B : i > 0 \wedge j = 0$$
$$\rightarrow S \qquad\qquad\qquad \rightarrow i' = i - 1$$
$$\wedge\, j' = j - 1, \qquad\qquad \wedge\, j' = n(i).$$

Prove that these actions will lead to a state in which $i = j = 0$.

## Bibliographic Notes

In the domain of transformational input–output computations, state invariants correspond to *inductive assertions* – assertions that should hold at given points of program execution. With these, partial correctness proofs are essentially inductive.

Some indication of the inductive-assertions method can be found even in some early papers by Goldstine and von Neumann [68] and by Turing [190]. Later, Naur elaborated on this idea [163], and Floyd's work [57] brought it to the general attention of the computer science community. An extensive survey of this early history of formal reasoning on programs can be found in [97].

The idea of using properties of well-founded sets to prove program termination (i.e., liveness properties) was also presented by Floyd [57].

The first machine implementation of a verification system was constructed in 1969 by King in connection with his PhD thesis; see [116]. Currently used proof systems include the *Larch prover* [66], which relies on the user to provide an outline of a proof, and *HOL* [69], *Isabelle* [167], and *PVS* [166], which are based on higher-order logics.

An early presentation of temporal proof systems for programming languages was given by Manna and Pnueli [151]. As the basic TLA reference, Lamport's paper [141] also introduced proof rules for TLA. For references to TLA-related tools and papers, including a Larch-based proof checker and a formulation of TLA in Isabelle, the reader is referred to Lamport's web page on TLA [135].

In connection with the DisCo project, Kellomäki has studied the use of PVS for proving temporal properties of DisCo specifications [107, 108, 112].

# Part III

# Building a Practical Theory

# 5

# Basic Language Facilities

Basically, only an execution model for an action language was given in Chap. 2, and anybody who is used to high-level programming languages will miss the conveniences that have been developed for them. In this chapter the action language will therefore be extended with some basic language facilities.

The main purpose of these facilities is to make it easier for the specifier to express his or her intentions. On the other hand, with precise definition of their meanings, the possibilities for formal reasoning are not weakened. The formalization reveals, however, some complexities that the specifier has to be aware of.

The intention of this chapter – and this book as a whole – is not to develop a complete specification language with precise syntax, but to explore the basic concepts needed in such a language, and the consequences of their introduction. To make the presentation more concrete, notation and conventions will be introduced for expressing these concepts in the action language, even though detailed language-design issues are avoided by purpose.

The plan for the chapter is as follows:

- *Finite-state structures* are introduced in Sect. 5.1 for the modeling of control flow. Instead of using only flat state structures, where all states are on the same level, hierarchical structuring is imposed on them by using the ideas of *statecharts* to express both parallel and nested states.
- In Sect. 5.2 we explore the effects of variable declarations with *types*, *scopes*, and *initial* or *default* values.
- The modeling facilities of action systems are extended in Sect. 5.3 with the notions of *objects*, *classes*, and *relations* between objects. More advanced aspects of object orientation will be postponed to Chap. 7.
- The idea of *multi-object actions* is introduced in Sect. 5.4. Technically this leads to parameterized actions where the parameters denote objects. Intuitively, an action is then executed jointly by its 'participant' objects, and the capability to participate in actions replaces the conventional notion of encapsulated 'methods'.

- The logical meaning of multi-object actions is analyzed in Sect. 5.5. In particular, this leads to more refined needs in expressing fairness requirements in the action language.
- In logic, action parameters correspond to existentially quantified rigid variables. The use of rigid variables and their effect on logical reasoning is therefore discussed in Sect. 5.6.

## 5.1 Finite-state Structures

As programming abstractions, finite-state structures are useful for the modeling of control flow. In this section we extend the action language with facilities for their utilization.

### 5.1.1 Motivation for Finite-state Structures

Finite-state structures are not available as a programming facility in conventional high-level languages, in which explicit state transitions are avoided by the implicit control flow of structured programming. In some areas, like the design of embedded systems and communication protocols, modeling in terms of finite-state structures is, however, standard practice.

Compared to implicit control with high-level statement structures, explicit states and state transitions seem to correspond better to human intuition in situations where events are atomic, and the control flow between them does not obey the simple patterns of structured programming. Natural possibilities for graphical illustration are also an advantage.

Since action systems have no implicit variables for control threads, and no distinction is made between variables that are used for storing data and those used for controling the enabling of actions, finite-state structures add an important facility for providing intuition about this difference.

### 5.1.2 Mutually Exclusive States

In the following, *finite-state structures* are introduced in the action language by *state declarations* of the form

$$\text{state } \text{State}_1, \ldots, \text{State}_m \,, \tag{5.1}$$

where each $\text{State}_i$, $i = 1, \ldots, m$, is a *state name*.

State names in a state declaration (5.1) are understood as mutually exclusive state predicates, whose truth values satisfy

$$\Box(\text{State}_1 \vee \cdots \vee \text{State}_m) \,, \tag{5.2}$$

$$\Box(\text{State}_i \Rightarrow \neg \text{State}_j) \qquad \text{for } i \neq j \tag{5.3}$$

in all executions.

In terms of TLA, a finite-state structure can be understood to correspond to an implicit variable, whose value always directly indicates which of the alternative state predicates is currently true. In an implementation such an implicit state variable might correspond to the program counter of a control thread.

In action systems we adopt the convention that a primed state name in an action body indicates an entry to that state. Since the associated implicit state variable cannot be directly modified, no explicit proofs are then needed for checking that the value of this variable always indicates one of the alternative states, assuming that it initially indicates one.

It is also convenient to have a simple notation for the initial state in a finite-state structure, i.e., for the associated state predicate that is assumed to be initially true. We adopt the convention that marking a state name in a state declaration (5.1) with an asterisk denotes such an initial state. In the absence of such a marking, a state declaration gives no constraints for the initial state, except that condition (5.2) needs to be satisfied.

### 5.1.3 Example: Gas-burner States

In the gas-burner example of Chap. 2, state names Idle, Starting, and Ignited were used as shorthand for certain state predicates that depend on variables flow_s and ign_s (see Sect. 2.2.9, p. 37). Another possibility would be to introduce these mutually exclusive states by a state declaration

$$\textbf{state } \text{Idle}^*, \text{Starting}, \text{Ignited} ,$$

and to change those system actions that control the actuators into

$$^{\text{SF}}\text{Start\_s} : \text{Idle} \wedge \text{req\_s} \wedge \neg\text{flam\_s}$$
$$\rightarrow \text{ flow\_s}' = \text{true}$$
$$\wedge \text{ ign\_s}' = \text{true}$$
$$\wedge \text{Starting}' ,$$

$$^{\text{SF}}\text{Ign\_off\_s} : \text{Starting} \wedge \text{flam\_s}$$
$$\rightarrow \text{ ign\_s}' = \text{false}$$
$$\wedge \text{Ignited}' ,$$

$$^{\text{SF}}\text{Stop\_s} : \text{Starting} \wedge \neg\text{flam\_s}$$
$$\rightarrow \text{ flow\_s}' = \text{false}$$
$$\wedge \text{ ign\_s}' = \text{false}$$
$$\wedge \text{Idle}' ,$$

$$^{\text{SF}}\text{Close\_s} : \text{Ignited} \wedge (\neg\text{req\_s} \vee \neg\text{flam\_s})$$
$$\rightarrow \text{ flow\_s}' = \text{false}$$
$$\wedge \text{ Idle}' \,.$$

Invariants

$$\square(\text{Idle} \Leftrightarrow \text{flow} \neq \text{true} \wedge \text{ignition} \neq \text{true}),$$
$$\square(\text{Starting} \Leftrightarrow \text{flow} = \text{true} \wedge \text{ignition} = \text{true}),$$
$$\square(\text{Ignited} \Leftrightarrow \text{flow} = \text{true} \wedge \text{ignition} \neq \text{true})$$

would then not be satisfied as tautologies, by the definition of the state predicates involved, but they could easily be proved as state invariants for the behaviors of the system.

It is a matter of taste whether the specification is easier to understand in this form or not. On one hand, this form introduces another (implicit) state variable, which is superfluous, but, on the other hand, this variable is useful in describing the control flow, which was represented in the Ada implementation by the program counter of the main program.

### 5.1.4 Parallel State Structures

Single finite-state structures are often insufficient for practical use. In particular, the number of states may become too large to be managed easily, and a multitude of often similar state transitions may complicate their graphical illustration.

This leads to a need for multiple state declarations of the form (5.1) on p. 126, each giving rise to a finite-state structure of its own. We then say that these finite-state structures are *parallel* to each other.

In principle, each of the parallel finite-state structures can be in any of its states independently of the others. Therefore, in the presence of k parallel state structures, each with $m_i$ different states, $i = 1, \ldots, k$, the total number of state combinations is $m_1 \times \cdots \times m_k$. In graphical illustrations, where each finite-state structure is given separately, only $m_1 + \cdots + m_k$ nodes are needed to visualize the states.

With parallel finite-state structures, invariants (5.2) and (5.3) hold separately for each of them.

### 5.1.5 Nested State Structures

It is often desirable to group several states into superstates, which gives the possibility for a hierarchical view of the state structure. This leads to the idea of *nested* finite-state structures, where states may be defined to contain internal substate structures.

Let State be a state name, and let

$$\textbf{state } Sub_1, \dots, Sub_n$$

declare another finite-state structure immediately within State. States $Sub_i$ are then called (immediate) *substates* of State, which in turn is their (immediate) *superstate*. In the presence of intermediate levels of substates or superstates the word 'immediate' is left out.

For substate structures, invariant (5.2) on p. 126 changes into

$$\Box(\mathsf{State} \Leftrightarrow \mathsf{Sub}_1 \lor \cdots \lor \mathsf{Sub}_n) , \tag{5.4}$$

whereas (5.3) stays as

$$\Box(\mathsf{Sub}_i \Rightarrow \neg\mathsf{Sub}_j) \qquad \text{for } i \neq j . \tag{5.5}$$

Obviously, (5.2) is a special case of (5.4), where the predicate for the immediate superstate is the identically true state predicate **T**.

In terms of TLA, state invariant (5.4) means that the implicit variable that corresponds to a substate structure also needs an $(n+1)$st alternative value for the situation where the superstate predicate State is false.

For clarity and unique identification of state names, it is often convenient to prefix a substate name by the name(s) of its superstate(s), as for instance in $\mathsf{State.Sub}_i$.

With nested finite-state structures the role of marked states extends in a natural way to denote *default substates* with the following meaning. If the system is initially in a named state that has substates, and one of these substates is marked, then this marked substate predicate will be initially true. Also, when a state is entered by a primed state name in an action body, and this state has a marked substate, then this marked substate is entered by default, unless explicitly specified otherwise.

### 5.1.6 Example

As an example, consider modeling an interface between user requests and system services, as illustrated in Fig. 5.1. At the highest level of abstraction, this interface is either Free to be used by a user process, or Engaged with some user. When Engaged, it shows two faces, one towards the user and one towards the system, represented as two parallel substate structures separated in Fig. 5.1 by a dashed horizontal line.

Towards the user, the interface is either Live, i.e., still capable of communication, or Dead. Similarly, it is either Active or Finished towards the system. When Live, the interface is either Listening to the user or Responding to some request. From the viewpoint of the system, when the interface is Active, it is either Idle or Requesting a service.

To illustrate the notation that will be used for textual representation of nested and parallel finite-state structures, the state structure in Fig. 5.1 can be given in the form

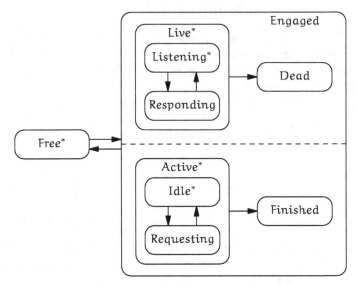

**Fig. 5.1.** Example of nested and parallel states

state Free*, Engaged
    **where** Engaged = {**state** Live*, Dead;
                **state** Active*, Finished}
      **where** Live = {**state** Listening*, Responding};
        Active = {**state** Idle*, Requesting} ,

where state declarations are followed by **where** clauses, in which the internal substate structures are specified.

### 5.1.7 On the Role of Graphical Illustrations

The action language will not be designed as a visual language. Therefore, state-transition diagrams, like the one in Fig. 5.1, will not be given a primary role in specifications. They have to be taken only as illustrations that are intended to provide better intuitive understanding.

In fact, it can be argued that the power of graphical illustrations is in providing abstractions, in which only selected properties are displayed. For instance, Fig. 5.1 shows that graphical illustrations may have arrows that do not enter or exit elementary states, but some intermediate structures of parallel and/or nested states. This means that there may be several alternatives for the exact source and/or target substates of such transitions, and one may by purpose omit visualizing these more precisely.

Also, action systems could not, in general, be easily edited in the graphical form of state-transition diagrams. The reason for this is that one action may give rise to several arrows in such a diagram, and several actions may also give rise to multiple arrows between the same states.

### 5.1.8 Interpreting Substate Structures in TLA

When language facilities are introduced, it is important that they are well defined in terms of the basic concepts that are used. Although the idea of nested and parallel finite-state structures looks quite harmless, its incorporation in a specification language may lead to some complexities. The purpose of this subsection is to analyze these complexities in the light of translating action systems into TLA.

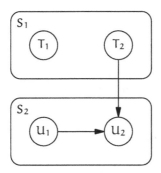

**Fig. 5.2.** Different kinds of transitions between substates

As an example, consider the situation illustrated in Fig. 5.2. If the target state of a transition is $S_2.U_2$, for instance, this can be indicated in an action simply by $S_2.U_2'$. This can, however, affect all three implicit variables that correspond to the three finite-state structures, as is illustrated by the transition from state $S_1.T_2$ to $S_2.U_2$.

Another point to notice is that, if the new state given in an action is one that has substates, say $S_2$, then the actual target state must be the default substate within $S_2$, even if the current state already is some substate of $S_2$. If no default substate is given, this is an error that can be found by static analysis.

In the presence of parallel finite-state structures, an action body may need to have several primed state names. In the situation of Fig. 5.1, for instance, $Dead' \wedge Finished'$ would indicate target states in both of the two parallel substate structures within Engaged. On the other hand, if the current state already is Engaged, and one wishes to change the state in only one of the substate structures, then $Dead'$, for instance, would be sufficient. However, if the current state is Free, then this is not sufficient as such, and automatic completion with the default $Live.Listening'$ also seems suspicious in this case.

Since our purpose is not to design a complete action language in this book, we do not need to adopt a complete solution to these problems. Therefore, we do not constrain the action language so that multiple primed state names could always be statically checked to be both consistent with each other and sufficient to uniquely indicate the target state. We will, however, use the language so that this will always be the case.

For the reasons discussed above, finite-state structures introduce, in general, proof obligations for action systems, and further possibilities for action systems to be *erroneous*. These proof obligations are associated with state invariants that ensure that all actions are well defined also with respect to transitions in finite-state structures, in all those reachable states in which the actions are enabled. Such proof obligations strengthen those discussed in Sect. 3.5.6 (p. 91).

**Review Questions**

QUESTION 5.1.1 What are the advantages of parallel and nested finite-state structures over ordinary flat finite-state structures?

QUESTION 5.1.2 How do the actions of the action language correspond to arrows in state-transition diagrams?

QUESTION 5.1.3 Why would it not be a good idea to make the action language a visual language, based on parallel and nested state structures?

QUESTION 5.1.4 Why can parallel finite-state structures make an action system erroneous?

## 5.2 Typing of State Variables

Declaration of variables, as used in high-level programming languages, associates variables with types and scopes, and possibly also with initial values. A variable may also be declared to be immutable in the sense that its value cannot be changed by assignments.

In this section we discuss the introduction of these kinds of facilities into the action language. Although this makes the language more convenient for a specifier, the discussion shows that there are also some drawbacks in the complexity behind the seeming simplicity of these features.

### 5.2.1 Types as Sets of Values

Basically, the *type* of a variable determines the set of values that can be assigned to the variable. For a human reader typing provides intuition about how the variables are intended to be used. Typing is also helpful in resolving the overloading of operator symbols, and it makes it possible to use static checks to reveal errors that lead to type inconsistency in expressions and assignments.

A type brings with it a collection of operations that are defined for it. One has, however, to be aware of exceptional situations where the result of an operation is undefined, as it is in division by zero for instance, or falls otherwise outside of the range of values specified for the type.

No fixed collection of types will be given here, but, corresponding to the sets of values included in $\mathsf{Val}$ (see Sect. 3.1.1, p. 58), at least the availability of *Booleans* ($\mathbb{B}$), *enumeration types*, *natural numbers* ($\mathbb{N}$), *integers* ($\mathbb{Z}$), *characters* ($\mathbb{C}$), *strings* ($\mathbb{S}$), and *reals* ($\mathbb{R}$) will be assumed as primitive types. Obviously, declarations of finite-state structures can be understood as a variant of using enumeration types.

When no type constraints are given for the values of a variable, it is said to be *untyped*, and its 'type' will be denoted by $\mathbb{U}$.

In addition to primitive types, *structured* and *aggregated* types like *lists* (**list**), *records*, *sequences* (**sequence**), *sets* (**set**), and *multisets* will be assumed. Cartesian products of primitive values and other self-explanatory notations will be used for values of these types.

### 5.2.2 Type Invariants

Given a type $\mathsf{T}$, a variable declaration $x : \mathsf{T}$ is understood to introduce the intended *type invariant* that the value of $x$ always belongs to the set of values of type $\mathsf{T}$,

$$\Box(x \in \mathsf{T}) . \tag{5.6}$$

As a state invariant this cannot be explicitly expressed in a canonical TLA expression. It is also unreasonable to assume that type invariants could, in general, be effectively enforced just by declaring variables to be typed.

For this reason, type invariants (5.6) are assumed to be *assertions* about the intentions of the specifier. Conditions $x \in \mathsf{T}$ are then assumed to be included in the initial conditions, and their preservation as state invariants gives additional proof obligations. Such proof obligations strengthen those discussed in Sect. 3.5.6 (p. 91) even further, so that expressions are required to be not only well defined but also type-correct in all reachable states. If type invariants are violated, an action system is *erroneous*.

### 5.2.3 Scopes of Variables

In programming languages, the *scope* of a variable is usually restricted to a given syntactic unit. For a human reader this indicates that the variable does not 'exist' outside its scope in the sense that it could be accessed, or that its value would have any other relevance. Scopes also make it easier to manage large name spaces.

Such aspects are also relevant in specifications. Statements in action bodies have no block structure in the action language, but the individual states in hierarchical finite-state structures determine natural scopes for variables. We therefore allow variables to be declared 'within' given named states, in which case they are said to be *local* to those states, and can be accessed only when the system is in those states.

Syntactically, if an integer variable x, for instance, is local to state State, its declaration will be included in the definition of state State as follows:

$$\mathsf{State} = \{\ldots\ \mathsf{x} : \mathbb{Z}\ \ldots\}\,.$$

For clarity and unique identification of variables we adopt the convention that a variable name can be prefixed by the state for which it is defined, as for instance in State.x.

Within actions, a variable should not be referenced unless the system is in the state for which the variable is local, and new values should be given only to those variables that are local to the new state. Such constraints can be expressed as further state invariants, which are understood as further assertions about the specification. An action system where these state invariants do not hold is *erroneous*. For a specifier they give additional proof obligations.

### 5.2.4 Initial and Default Values

As another facility to be adopted from programming languages, variable declarations are allowed to contain expressions for *initial* and *default values*, as shown by the value 0 in

$$\mathsf{State} = \{\ldots\ \mathsf{x} : \mathbb{Z}(0)\ \ldots\}\,.$$

For variables that 'exist' in the initial state, these expressions determine their initial values. Non-initialized variables can have arbitrary initial values of the associated types, provided that all other initial conditions are satisfied. Prefixing by keyword **const** will indicate that the initial value is immutable, or constant, in the sense that it cannot be changed in any action.

When a substate is entered,[1] its local variables are not assumed to retain the values they had when the state was last exited. Instead, the values of the default expressions are then taken, unless explicitly specified otherwise in the action. In the absence of default values, arbitrary values of the associated types are taken in this situation. For these reasons, the effects of an action cannot, in general, be seen just from the action body, without also considering the types and default values of variables.

---

[1] Whenever a primed state name appears in an action body, this is interpreted to denote an entry to that state, independently of whether this differs from the current state or not.

For simplicity, the variables that are local to a state are assumed to retain their values when the state is exited, even though these values can no longer be referenced in actions.

## 5.2.5 Discussion

Finite-state structures and declaration of variables extend the action language with facilities that a programmer would probably expect a specification and design language to possess. Of course, the conventions could have been designed differently from what we have done here, without sacrificing the main ideas of the approach. Some of the more complex possibilities could also have been left out. In any case, it would have been misleading not to show the kinds of problems that are encountered when the core of a formally defined specification language is extended with convenient programming facilities that have 'obvious' meanings.

As in programming languages, interactions between the different facilities – like state transitions and default values, for instance – often lead to complicated situations. Mechanical tools can, of course, cope with such complications, but for humans they involve potential dangers.

Technically, these extensions have led to different kinds of possibilities for *erroneous* action systems. In Chap. 3 we already discussed errors that arise if state functions or state predicates are used in situations where their values are not well defined. The facilities introduced here have increased essentially the possibilities for such 'run-time errors'.

To some degree, such errors can be revealed by static inspection, i.e., by means traditionally used in compilers, but, in general, they are inherently dynamic in nature, and their absence can be shown only by formal proofs or fully exhaustive testing (when this is possible).

Comparing programs to specifications, we notice that an executable program can be incomplete in the sense that it may lead to unpredictable results or run-time errors if some assumptions are not satisfied during its execution, whereas a specification does not have this possibility. In contrast, a specification is expected to give explicit conditions under which it is well defined. In a way, *assertions* are a bridge between these two worlds. When an operational specification is simulated, assertions can be used to detect 'run-time errors', whereas for a formal treatment they should be understood as state invariants to be proved.

The main justification for introducing these kinds of facilities into a specification language is that they make it easier for the specifier to express some intended properties of the specification. In many situations the associated proof obligations are also trivial. This involves, however, a potential trap, especially because 'trivial' proof obligations are usually left implicit, unless mechanical proofs are systematically carried out. The trap is that, if an operational specification does not satisfy the associated assertions – and is therefore erroneous – a human reader may still be misled to trust in these intended properties.

**Review Questions**

QUESTION 5.2.1 What is meant by assertions?

QUESTION 5.2.2 Is it possible to check type invariants by static inspection?

QUESTION 5.2.3 What are the situations in which an action system is erroneous?

QUESTION 5.2.4 Why may types and other convenient programming facilities be misleading for a human reader?

**Exercises**

EXERCISE 5.2.1 Elaborate on the complexities caused by default values and default substates in connection with entries to nested states.

## 5.3 Objects and Relations

Experience with object-oriented programming and design has convinced the software-engineering community about the usefulness of the notions of *objects*, *classes*, and *relations* between objects. They seem to reflect in a natural manner the ways in which we tend to organize our understanding of the world.

In this section we will introduce these notions to the action language in a way that is suitable for specifications.

### 5.3.1 The State of an Object

As a first approximation, we understand an *object* as a collection of state variables, possibly including ones implicitly introduced by state declarations (i.e., finite-state structures). From this viewpoint, the notion of objects provides a facility for partitioning the state of a system into smaller parts that consist of variables in individual objects.

Each object c has a unique *identity*, which will be denoted by **c.id**. These identities, together with a special value **none**, which denotes (the identity of) a non-existing object, are assumed to be values that are contained in the universal set $\mathsf{Val}$ of values, and the subset formed by them will be denoted by $\mathbb{ID}$, $\mathbb{ID} \subseteq \mathsf{Val}$.

The variables constituting an object are its *local variables*, also called its *attributes*. The values of these variables determine the *local state* of an object. As for notation, variable a within object c will be denoted by a prefixed name c.a. Multiple prefixing can also be used. For instance, variable x that is local to a named state S within object c could be denoted by c.S.a.

The set of all state variables used in a specification consists of the local variables of all objects, and of *global variables* that do not belong to any object. To distinguish between the different uses of the word 'state', the state that involves all state variables in a specification will be called the *global state*.[2]

### 5.3.2 Classes

The possibility for an arbitrary number of similar objects is one aspect of *scalability* in specifications. This is made possible by the notion of a class.

In the following, a *class* is understood to be a set of objects with some common characteristics. Each object belongs to some class, and – following common programming parlance – is also said to be an *instance* of that class.[3] The declaration of a class gives the attributes (local variables) that are available for all objects of the class. In agreement with the general philosophy of state variables in TLA, we can assume that objects also have an infinite number of other variables that are not of interest to us. Similarly, we can assume an infinite number of other classes that are not referred to in a specification.

As an example, class declaration

$$\textbf{class } C = \{a : \mathbb{Z}; \textbf{ state } S_1^*, S_2\}$$

would declare that each object $c \in C$ has a local integer variable $c.a$, and local state predicates $c.S_1$ and $c.S_2$. Knowing only that object $c$ is in class $C$ would not allow us to access any other variables that $c$ may have.

The set of identities of objects in class $C$ will be denoted by $\mathbb{ID}_C$. This allows us to use typed variables that are intended to 'refer' to objects of a given class only.

Ignoring multiple inheritance, we will assume in this chapter that different classes are disjoint sets of objects, i.e., $C \neq D$ implies $C \cap D = \emptyset$ for any two classes $C$ and $D$. With the more advanced aspects of object orientation to be discussed in Chap. 7, this assumption will be removed.

### 5.3.3 The Size of a Class

In programming languages, variables need to be 'created' by declarations or dynamic generation, whereas in TLA they are assumed to 'exist' throughout all behaviors. Similarly, in object-oriented programming languages, objects

---

[2]Notice the heavily overloaded use of the word 'state'. In TLA, *state* includes the values of all possible state variables; the state variables used in a specification determine the *global state* of a system; the state variables of an object determine its *local state*; state declarations introduce finite-state structures with *named states*. The word 'state' is also used synonymously to the states that satisfy given *state predicates*.

[3]When multiple inheritance is used, an object may be an instance of several classes.

'exist' only after being created, and they can be destroyed when no longer needed, whereas specifications need no such implementation-oriented facilities. All classes and all objects can simply be assumed to exist throughout all behaviors.

We adopt the convention that the number of objects in a class can be given in the class declaration within parentheses after keyword **class**. Finite sizes can be indicated in terms of integers and rigid variables. The possibility for (countably) infinite classes is needed in specifications where unbounded numbers of objects may be required during execution. This can be indicated by specifying the size to be $\infty$.

With access to the local variables of an arbitrary object in a given class, an infinite class gives, in some sense, simultaneous access to an infinite number of variables. As an unimplementable facility this also gives possibilities that go beyond effective computability. Consider, for instance, a function $f : \mathbb{N} \to \mathbb{N}$ discussed in Sect. 3.5.8 (p. 94), for which no effective algorithm can determine for an arbitrary $x \in \mathbb{N}$ whether there exists an $n \in \mathbb{N}$ such that $x = f(n)$. However, an infinite class C with local variables $i$ and $j$ can be specified so that, for each $n \in \mathbb{N}$, there is an object $c \in C$ with $c.i = n$ and $c.j = f(c.i)$ in the initial state. The algorithmically unsolvable problem could then be solved for an arbitrary $x \in \mathbb{N}$ by 'accessing' all objects $c \in C$ simultaneously with the enabling condition

$$\exists c \in C : c.j = x$$

of some action.

A more 'normal' way to use an infinite class C would model how a finite but unbounded class can be used in object-oriented programming. All but a finite number of objects $c \in C$ are then always assumed to have local states that are identical to each other, and can be interpreted as the state of the still 'unborn' objects in C.

### 5.3.4 Relations

Objects in a model often have various *relations* between each other. These may be *constant* or immutable relations, which cannot be changed in executions, or *dynamic* relations that can be modified in actions. In the following we will use binary relations only.

To indicate that R is a (binary) relation between objects of classes C and D, we write $R : C \times D$. In the action language we will introduce it by a declaration

**relation** $R : C \times D$ .

Constant relations that stay unchanged in all behaviors will be prefixed by an additional keyword **const**.

Mathematically, R is a subset of the Cartesian product $C \times D$ of all ordered pairs $(c, d)$, $c \in C$, $d \in D$, i.e.,

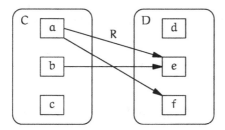

**Fig. 5.3.** Illustration of a relation R

$$R \subseteq C \times D .$$

For pairs in R we write $c \cdot R \cdot d$, that is,

$$c \cdot R \cdot d \stackrel{\Delta}{=} (c, d) \in R . \tag{5.7}$$

Figure 5.3, where the small boxes denote objects, illustrates such a relation R, which consists of pairs $(a, e)$, $(a, f)$, and $(b, e)$.

In terms of explicit state variables, a relation $R : C \times D$ can always be represented as a global variable of type

$$\textbf{set} \; (\mathbb{ID}_C \times \mathbb{ID}_D) .$$

More economical representations can often be used for special classes of relations.

### 5.3.5 Special Classes of Relations

Some specific kinds of relations are often useful in specifications, and one may also wish to combine relations with each other. To give the reader some idea about the facilities that a specification language could provide in this respect, we elaborate on this topic in this subsection.

### Mappings

Important special cases of relations can be distinguished by specifying the number of objects that can be in a given relation to the same object. For instance, by writing

$$\textbf{relation} \; (*) \cdot R \cdot (1) : C \times D$$

we can specify that for each $c \in C$ there is exactly one $d \in D$ for which $c \cdot R \cdot d$, and for each $d \in D$ there are zero or more such $c \in C$. In this connection, an asterisk $(*)$ will stand for 'zero or more', and a plus sign $(+)$ will stand for 'one or more'. In addition, lower and upper bounds for the numbers can also be given.

Mathematically, the above declaration declares R as a (total) *function* that *maps* each object in C into a unique object in D. Other important special cases are *partial functions,*

$$\textbf{relation } (*) \cdot R \cdot (0..1) : C \times D \ ,$$

which map each object in C to at most one object in D, *injections*

$$\textbf{relation } (0..1) \cdot R \cdot (1) : C \times D \ ,$$

which never map two different objects in C to the same object in D, and *bijections*

$$\textbf{relation } (1) \cdot R \cdot (1) : C \times D \ ,$$

which are *one-to-one mappings.*

When relation R is known to be (any kind of) a function, it is often convenient to use the functional notation $d = R(c)$, instead of $c \cdot R \cdot d$.

Notice that for dynamic relations the above properties should be understood as assertions, and an action system is erroneous if it does not preserve such properties in all situations.

## Derived Relations

For two relations $R_1 : C \times D$, $R_2 : D \times E$, the *combined relation* $R_1 \circ R_2$ is defined as

$$c \cdot (R_1 \circ R_2) \cdot d \ \overset{\Delta}{=} \ \exists e \in D : (c \cdot R_1 \cdot e \wedge e \cdot R_2 \cdot d) \ .$$

Obviously, if both $R_1$ and $R_2$ are functions, partial functions, injections, or bijections, then so is $R_1 \circ R_2$.

Since relations are sets of pairs, the *union* and *intersection* of two relations $R_1, R_2 : C \times D$ between the same classes can also be formed:

$$c \cdot (R_1 \cup R_2) \cdot d \ \overset{\Delta}{=} \ c \cdot R_1 \cdot d \vee c \cdot R_2 \cdot d \ ,$$

$$c \cdot (R_1 \cap R_2) \cdot d \ \overset{\Delta}{=} \ c \cdot R_1 \cdot d \wedge c \cdot R_2 \cdot d \ .$$

A relation $R : C \times C$ between objects of the same class C gives rise to *power relations* $R^i$. Using $Id_C : C \times C$ to stand for the *identity relation* in C,

$$Id_C \ \overset{\Delta}{=} \ \{(c,c) \mid c \in C\} \ ,$$

these can be defined as

$$R^0 \ \overset{\Delta}{=} \ Id_C \ ,$$

$$R^{i+1} \ \overset{\Delta}{=} \ R \circ R^i, \quad \text{for } i \geq 0 \ ,$$

$$R^+ \ \overset{\Delta}{=} \ \bigcup_{i>0} R^i \ ,$$

$$R^* \ \overset{\Delta}{=} \ R^0 \cup R^+ \ .$$

Relations $R^+$ and $R^*$ are called the *transitive closure* and the *reflexive transitive closure* of R, respectively.

Each relation $R : C \times D$ also gives rise to an *inverse relation* $R^{-1} : D \times C$ defined as

$$d \cdot R^{-1} \cdot c \overset{\Delta}{=} c \cdot R \cdot d .$$

### Topological Relations

Relations $R : C \times C$ can be used to define topological structures among objects $x \in C$. For simplicity, we assume here that C is finite.

Given a relation $R : C \times C$, an object $c \in C$ is a *root* of R if it satisfies the condition

$$\mathsf{Root}_R(c) \overset{\Delta}{=} \neg \exists d \in C : d \cdot R \cdot c .$$

Correspondingly, c is a *leaf* of R if it satisfies

$$\mathsf{Leaf}_R(c) \overset{\Delta}{=} \neg \exists d \in C : c \cdot R \cdot d .$$

For an illustration, see Fig. 5.4.

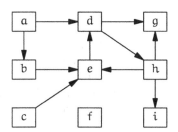

**Fig. 5.4.** Relation with roots $a$, $c$, and $f$, and leaves $f$, $g$, and $i$

The following conditions on $R : C \times C$ now define some useful topologies for a finite class C:

- Relation R is a *dag* relation[4] if it is *acyclic*, i.e.,

$$\forall c \in C : \neg \, c \cdot R^+ \cdot c .$$

- A dag relation R is a *tree* relation if $R^{-1}$ is a partial function and R has exactly one root.
- A tree relation R is a *sequence* relation if it has exactly one leaf.
- Relation R is a *ring* relation if it is a bijection satisfying

$$\forall c, d \in C : c \cdot R^+ \cdot d .$$

A ring has no leaves and no roots.

---

[4]The word 'dag' comes from 'directed acyclic graph'.

When a relation is assumed to generate one of these topologies, we will prefix its declaration with the corresponding attribute. Obviously, for dynamic relations these topological properties generate assertions that are not satisfied by erroneous specifications.

**Review Questions**

QUESTION 5.3.1 Review the different uses for the word 'state'.

QUESTION 5.3.2 Why do we need to deal with infinite classes?

QUESTION 5.3.3 What are objects and relations from the viewpoint of state variables in behaviors?

QUESTION 5.3.4 What kinds of assertions may be associated with relations?

## 5.4 Parameterized and Multi-object Actions

For objects of the same class it is natural to assume that the actions that are relevant for them are also similar. In object-oriented programming such actions are given as 'methods' defined for all objects of a class. For the specification of collective behaviors in object systems, a more appropriate level of abstraction is provided by the notion of multi-object actions.

Technically this leads to parameterization of actions by the objects that are needed for their execution. Without fixed class sizes, specifications then also become generic *patterns* of object systems, which can be instantiated in different ways. Effective use of such patterns requires, however, additional support for object orientation, which will be the topics of Chap. 7.

### 5.4.1 Action Parameters

Actions in the action language can be *parameterized*. For instance, an action with an integer parameter x would be written in the format

$$A(x : \mathbb{Z}) : g(x)$$
$$\rightarrow b(x) \, ,$$

where both the guard $g(x)$ and the body $b(x)$ could depend on the parameter x. Such an action would be enabled for any parameter value x for which the guard is true, and its execution would then execute the body for such a parameter value x.

When a parameterized action is executed, the selection between different parameter values, for which the action is enabled, is nondeterministic.

Parameters therefore provide a mechanism for nondeterminism within individual actions, without a need to relax the convention that action bodies are given as deterministic 'assignments'. In addition, parameters also give convenient 'handles' to control such nondeterminism by constraints that can be appended to action guards at later stages.

A natural application for action parameters is in the modeling of input and output. When the environment, for instance, gives input to the system, nondeterministic selection of parameter values corresponds to lack of information about the values to be chosen by the environment for input.

### 5.4.2 Action Participants

Since object identities are also values in $\mathsf{Val}$, actions can also be parameterized by them. The values chosen for such parameters will be called action *participants*.

This provides a convenient mechanism to define similar actions for all objects of the same class. With more than one object parameter, an action is a *multi-object action*. As an example, consider an action

$$A(c, d : C) : g(c, d)$$
$$\rightarrow b(c, d)$$

with two participants, $c$ and $d$, of class $C$.[5] To make a distinction between the formal parameters in an action and the actual participant objects for which the action is executed, the term *role* will be used for the former. That is, the above action has two participant roles, for which actual participant objects are chosen nondeterministically from among those that satisfy the guard $g(c, d)$.

To avoid problems in aliasing, no object is allowed to take more than one role in an action at the same time. Therefore, the guard $g(c, d)$ in the above example is assumed also to contain an implicit conjunct $c \neq d$, which we take as an abbreviation for $c.\mathbf{id} \neq d.\mathbf{id}$.

Encapsulation of 'methods' is an important principle in object orientation, meaning that the local state of an object can be modified only by the object itself. For multi-object actions this generalizes in a natural manner into the requirement that the local state of an object can be modified only in actions in which the object is a participant. Syntactic checks are sufficient to enforce this requirement.

### 5.4.3 Intuition for Action Execution

Intuitively, there are two extreme possibilities to think about the execution of multi-object actions.

---

[5]For simplicity, we introduce notation only for a fixed number of participants, although variable numbers of participants would be useful in some situations.

On one hand, one can think of a global scheduler, which selects actions that are enabled for some participants and other parameter values, and then invokes their execution. In this interpretation objects are treated as *passive* data structures.

Intuitively, a more appealing possibility is to think of objects as *active* execution agents, and that actions are executed jointly by their participant objects. Obviously, an intermediate interpretation with both active and passive objects is also possible.

When objects are considered to be active agents, some communication and handshaking mechanism has to be postulated by which objects can establish that an action is enabled for them, agree on the possibly required parameter values, and get committed to its execution. During action execution, the participants may still continue communicating with each other, in order for each of them to change its own local state as specified by the action body, but other objects can no longer affect this in any way.

Execution by active objects will be discussed in more detail in Chap. 9 on distributed action systems.

### 5.4.4 Multi-object Actions in Specifications

When objects are understood as active execution agents, multi-object actions provide an implicit communication mechanism for them. Therefore, explicit communication mechanisms are not needed, as is the case in conventional approaches to object orientation.

In contrast to a conventional 'individualistic' view of objects, multi-object actions provide an inherently collective view of a system, which is suitable for the specification of collective behaviors in closed-system models. Single-object 'methods', on the other hand, are suited for describing objects as independent open systems, which supports the idea of reusable object implementations. The difference is illustrated in Fig. 5.5.[6]

With multi-object actions, object-oriented specifications can be given in an operational form but still at a high level of abstraction. This makes it possible to specify *what* the objects should do together (action bodies), and in *which* situations (action guards), without telling *how* they should make the required decisions, or *how* they should communicate with each other in doing this. Obviously, the *how* questions have also to be addressed at some point during the design, but implementation-oriented design decisions should not be made too early, and a specification language needs to be designed with this in mind.

---

[6]In graphical illustrations we adopt the convention that rectangles denote objects or classes, and ellipses denote actions.

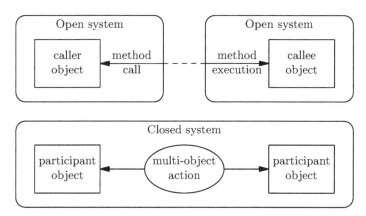

**Fig. 5.5.** Single-object methods in open systems vs. multi-object actions in closed-system models

### 5.4.5 Absence of Object Names

For simplicity, no global naming system will be assumed for objects. That is, objects will not be given names by which they could be referenced. Whenever an object needs to be accessed (in an action), it needs to be selected from its class by the values of its attributes, or by the relations in which it stands to other objects. If several objects satisfy the selection criteria, then any of them can be chosen.

Within an action, the formal names (roles) given to its participants are local to this action. Two actions can be ensured to have the same object as a participant only by making sure that it can be uniquely identified by its attributes and relations.

### 5.4.6 Quantification and Relations in Actions

In addition to referencing local variables of participants, an action can also involve global expressions, i.e., global variables and expressions that are quantified over all objects in given classes. In particular, quantification over classes makes it easy to specify enabling conditions in an implicit form. For instance, if a participant $c \in C$ is needed with the smallest value in attribute $c.a$, a quantified expression

$$\forall d \in C : d.a \geq c.a$$

can be used to select it.

This kind of global expressions makes an action also depend on other objects besides its participants. To support the intuition that only participant objects (and global variables) are needed during action execution, the use of such expressions will be limited to action guards only.

Interpreted as global variables, relations can also be used in actions, both in guards and in bodies. When a relation R is modified in an action, we will indicate $(c, d) \in R'$ by writing

$$c \cdot R' \cdot d .$$

The assumption is that only those changes are made in R that are explicitly indicated in this way. To avoid conflicts, and to keep the operational interpretation clear, derived relations cannot appear primed in actions.

As an example, if R is a relation, removing the pair $(c, d)$ from it and adding $(c, e)$ to it can be expressed as

$$
\begin{aligned}
&\cdots \\
&\wedge c \cdot R \cdot d \\
&\rightarrow \ \neg(c \cdot R' \cdot d) \\
&\wedge c \cdot R' \cdot e \\
&\cdots
\end{aligned}
$$

In order to use c, d, and e in this manner, they must all be participants in the action. Quantification makes it, however, possible to modify relations also for other objects than participants, for instance by writing a conjunct

$$\forall c, d \in C : \neg(c \cdot R' \cdot d)$$

in the body. Notice that this does not make an action depend on all objects in C, since this modifies only the value of a global variable where relation R is assumed to be represented.

## Review Questions

QUESTION 5.4.1 Explain the intuition behind multi-object actions when the participants are considered as active execution agents.

QUESTION 5.4.2 What are the advantages of multi-object actions in specifications?

QUESTION 5.4.3 How can one make sure that two actions have the same object as participant?

## Exercises

EXERCISE 5.4.1 Discuss the problems that would arise if an object could participate in an action in multiple roles at the same time.

## 5.5 Formalization of Multi-object Actions

Multi-object actions were introduced above with the execution model of action systems in mind. In this section we analyze their logical meaning. This also leads to more refined needs in expressing fairness requirements in the action language.

### 5.5.1 Quantified Action Expressions

Let $A(x)$ be an action expression that contains a rigid variable $x$, and let $A$ denote the expression obtained from it by existential quantification,

$$A \stackrel{\Delta}{=} \exists x : A(x) .$$

Action $A$ can then be understood as a parameterized action, where the parameter $x$ can be selected arbitrarily.

Substituting $x$ in $A(x)$ by some value $a \in \mathsf{Val}$ gives an *instance* $A(a)$ of $A$, also called an instantiation of $A$. Every $A$ step in a behavior is then an $A(a)$ step for some instance $A(a)$.

Action $A$ being the disjunction of all its instantiations, its enabling condition is the disjunction of the enabling conditions of these instantiations,

$$\mathsf{Enabled}\,A \stackrel{\Delta}{=} \exists x : \mathsf{Enabled}\,A(x) .$$

### 5.5.2 Mapping Between Actions

Parameterized actions in the action language can now be mapped into existentially quantified action expressions. For instance, action

$$\begin{aligned} A(x : \mathbb{Z}) : \ & g(x) \\ \rightarrow \ & b(x) \end{aligned}$$

would correspond to expression

$$A \stackrel{\Delta}{=} \exists x \in \mathbb{Z} : (g(x) \wedge b(x) \wedge \mathsf{Stutter}_Y) ,$$

where $Y$ denotes the set of those variables of the specification that are not modified in $A$. The enabling condition of this action would be

$$\mathsf{Enabled}\,A \stackrel{\Delta}{=} \exists x \in \mathbb{Z} : g(x) .$$

With participant objects, i.e., with parameterization by objects, this correspondence also needs to honor the requirement that no object is allowed to take more than one role in an action at the same time. Therefore, if $C$ is a class, then action

$$A(c, d : C) : g(c, d)$$
$$\rightarrow b(c, d)$$

would correspond to expression

$$\exists c, d \in C : (c \neq d \land g(c, d) \land b(c, d) \land \text{Stutter}_Y) \,,$$

where Y again denotes those variables of the specification that are not modified in the action. This time, Y consists of

- those global variables that are not modified,
- those local variables in the actual participants c and d that are not modified,
- all local variables of all other objects in class C, and
- all local variables of objects in other classes than C.

### 5.5.3 Fairness for Multi-object Actions

A parameterized action with participants and other parameters can be understood as a pattern for different instances of an action, one instance for each selection of participants and other parameter values. As a consequence, there are several possibilities to associate meaningful fairness requirements with respect to a parameterized action in the action language.

As an example, let $A(c : C; d : D)$ be an action in the action language, with two participant roles c and d, and let $\exists c, d : A(c, d)$ be the corresponding logical action. There are now different kinds of fairness requirements that one may wish to associate with A. Already with strong fairness we have the following alternatives:

- If no distinction needs to be made between executing different instances of A, a natural strong fairness requirement would be

$$\text{SF}(\exists c, d : A(c, d)) \,. \tag{5.8}$$

Under this requirement, if A is repeatedly enabled for any combination of participants, it will eventually be executed for some participants.

- If distinction needs to be made between different participants in role c, we may require strong fairness separately with respect to each object $c \in C$ in this role:

$$\forall c : \text{SF}(\exists d : A(c, d)) \,. \tag{5.9}$$

Under this requirement, if A is repeatedly enabled for the same object in role c, it will eventually be executed for this object in role c.

- Analogously, if distinction needs to be made between the cases where the second participant is different, we may require strong fairness with respect to objects $d \in D$ in the second role:

$$\forall d : SF(\exists c : A(c, d)) \, . \tag{5.10}$$

Then, if A is repeatedly enabled for the same object in role d, it will eventually be executed for this object in role d.

- Finally, making a distinction between all instances of A would lead to strong fairness with respect to object pairs $c \in C, d \in D$,

$$\forall c, d : SF(A(c, d)) \, . \tag{5.11}$$

Then, if A is repeatedly enabled for the same pair of objects, it will eventually be executed for this pair.

Obviously, similar alternatives would also be obtained for weak fairness properties.

### 5.5.4 The Effect of Infinite Classes

In the above example, fairness requirements (5.9)–(5.11) generate conjunctions of several fairness formulas. With finite classes their numbers are also finite. In the finite case the situation is also such that each of (5.9) and (5.10) implies (5.8), and (5.11) implies both (5.9) and (5.10). Similar implications do not, however, hold for the corresponding weak fairness properties.

With infinite classes the situation is slightly different. Firstly, the above implications between strong fairness properties (5.8)–(5.11) no longer hold in general (see Exercise 5.5.2). Secondly, (5.9)–(5.11) now generate conjunctions of (countably) infinite numbers of fairness formulas. However, as shown in Exercise 3.5.2 (p. 100), the resulting fairness conditions are still feasible.

The parameters for which fairness is required can also be non-participant parameters. To ensure the feasibility of the conjuncted fairness conditions it is, however, essential to require that the ranges of such parameters are either finite or countably infinite.

### 5.5.5 Expressing Fairness Requirements

As is evident from the above, prefixing action names with $^{SF}$ or $^{WF}$ is no longer sufficient for expressing the variety of fairness requirements that we would like to express. A natural solution is to allow fairness prefixes also on participants, in order to express fairness requirements with respect to them. Some care is, however, needed in defining what this exactly means, in order to maintain the property that adding of prefixes cannot change any unfair behaviors into fair behaviors.

The convention that we adopt is first explained in terms of the above example. For simplicity, let XF stand for X-fairness, i.e., either strong or weak fairness, depending on whether X is replaced by S or W.

Prefixing the action name itself,

$$^{XF}A(c : C; \; d : D) \, ,$$

will require X-fairness for action A, that is

$$XF(\exists c, d : A(c, d)) \, .$$

Prefixing a participant, say c,

$$A(^{XF}c : C; \; d : D) \, ,$$

will require X-fairness for this participant, that is

$$\forall c : XF(\exists d : A(c, d)) \, .$$

Prefixes on both participants will impose separate fairness requirements for each of them and, in addition, X-fairness for all participant pairs,

$$\forall c, d : XF(A(c, d)) \, ,$$

where X is now either S or W, depending on whether both prefixes are $^{SF}$ or not.

More generally, if $(x, y)$ denotes an arbitrary partitioning of all parameters (i.e., both participant and non-participant parameters) in action A into two subsets $x$ and $y$, such that all parameters in $x$ are prefixed by either $^{SF}$ or $^{WF}$, and those in $y$ may or may not have such prefixes, then the fairness requirement

$$\forall x : XF(\exists y : A(x, y)) \tag{5.12}$$

is assumed in the following situations:

- $x$ is empty, and the action name is prefixed by $^{XF}$,
- $x$ contains only parameters prefixed by $^{SF}$, and X is S,
- some of the parameters in $x$ are prefixed by $^{WF}$, and X is W.

### Review Questions

QUESTION 5.5.1 Why did we need to reconsider how fairness requirements are expressed in the action language?

### Exercises

EXERCISE 5.5.1 What is the difference between the meanings of $^{SF}A(c : C)$, $A(^{SF}c : C)$, and $^{SF}A(^{SF}c : C)$? Does any of them imply any other of them?

EXERCISE 5.5.2 Prove the implications and non-implications between fairness properties discussed in Sect. 5.5.4 (p. 149).

EXERCISE 5.5.3 Explain the meaning of fairness markings with the assumption that only strong fairness is used, and all classes are finite.

## 5.6 Dealing with Quantification

A price that we have to pay for the way we use classes in action systems is an extensive need for quantified expressions in TLA, with quantification carried over classes. This means that quantified rigid variables play an important role in formal treatment of action systems. Therefore, we discuss the use of rigid variables in more detail in this section.

### 5.6.1 Free Variables

A rigid variable $x$ that occurs in an expression $E(x)$ and is not bound in it by a quantifier is said to be a *free* variable in $E(x)$. Substituting all free variables in an expression by some values in $Val$ gives an expression that is an *instance* (or instantiation) of that expression.

An intended type $T$ may be given for a free variable, as in

$$x \in T : E(x) .$$

Intuitively, this constrains the values by which $x$ can be substituted into those that belong to $T$. For completeness it is assumed, however, that any substitution is possible, but it will be irrelevant what the resulting expression means for 'type-incorrect' substitutions. Since object identities are also values in $Val$, an intended type may also be a class.

### 5.6.2 Quantifiers

An expression can be quantified over the type of a free variable in it. *Universal quantification* is denoted by $\forall$ (for all), and *existential quantification* by $\exists$ (there exists).

For instance, if $P(x)$ is a state predicate with a free variable $x \in C$, then

$$\forall x \in C : P(x)$$

and

$$\exists x \in C : P(x)$$

are quantified state predicates with their obvious meanings. These are, in fact, considered to be the same as

$$\forall x : (x \in C \Rightarrow P(x))$$

and

$$\exists x : (x \in C \wedge P(x)) ,$$

respectively, which means that typing of rigid variables is just a 'decoration' indicating intended types.

When the intended types can be understood from context, they will be omitted from expressions in the following, abbreviating the above expressions, for instance, into $\forall x : P(x)$ and $\exists x : P(x)$.

Quantification can appear in all kinds of temporal expressions. In particular, quantified action expressions were utilized in Sect. 5.5 in defining actions as patterns that are applicable to all objects of the same class(es).

As was already mentioned in Chap. 3, existential and universal quantifiers are each other's duals,

$$\exists x : E(x) \Leftrightarrow \neg\forall x : \neg E(x) \ .$$

It can easily be checked that this also holds for the above interpretation of typing:

$$\begin{aligned}
\exists x \in C : E(x) &\Leftrightarrow \exists x : (x \in C \wedge E(x)) \\
&\Leftrightarrow \neg\forall x : \neg(x \in C \wedge E(x)) \\
&\Leftrightarrow \neg\forall x : (x \notin C \vee \neg E(x)) \\
&\Leftrightarrow \neg\forall x : (x \in C \Rightarrow \neg E(x)) \\
&\Leftrightarrow \neg\forall x \in C : \neg E(x) \ .
\end{aligned}$$

For simplicity, a single quantifier symbol will be used to stand for any number of successive quantifications of the same kind, as for instance in

$$\exists x, n : x.a = n \ .$$

Variables that are quantified in an expression are said to be *bound* by the quantifier. For instance, variable $x$ that is free in $P(x)$ is bound by the quantifier $\forall$ in $\forall x : P(x)$.

An expression may have a nested structure with several levels of quantification. Analogously to conventions with block structure in programming languages, a variable is always understood to be bound by the closest enclosing quantification with the same variable name.

Obviously, the meaning of an expression is independent of the names that are used for its bound variables, provided that no name clashes arise with free variables or with other bound variables.

### 5.6.3 Quantified Operators

In predicates, $\forall x$ and $\exists x$ correspond to quantified conjunction $\bigwedge_x$ and quantified disjunction $\bigvee_x$, respectively. When rigid variables occur in state functions, quantified operators can also be used. For instance, if $x \in C : f(x)$ is a state function, then

$$\sum_{x \in C} f(x)$$

denotes the sum of $f(x)$ over all objects $x \in C$, and

$$\max_{x \in C} f(x) \,, \qquad \min_{x \in C} f(x)$$

denote the maximum and the minimum value of $f(x)$, respectively, over all objects $x \in C$.

For such quantification to make sense, the quantified operator needs to be a binary operator that is both associative and commutative. In order to be defined for an empty class, there must also be a unique zero element for the operator. For conjunction, disjunction, addition, and multiplication, such zero elements are $\mathbf{T}$, $\mathbf{F}$, $0$, and $1$, respectively. Since max and min have no natural zero elements in $\mathbb{R}$, they are undefined for empty classes.

A special case of a quantified operation is the size of a class $C$, which will be denoted by $|C|$, and is defined as

$$|C| \stackrel{\Delta}{=} \sum_{x \in C} 1 \,.$$

Correspondingly, the number of objects $x \in C$ satisfying a given condition $P(x)$ will be denoted by $|\{x \in C \mid P(x)\}|$:

$$|\{x \in C \mid P(x)\}| \stackrel{\Delta}{=} \sum_{x \in C} (\text{if } P(x) \text{ then } 1 \text{ else } 0) \,.$$

In connection with infinite or empty classes, quantified state functions must be used with care, in order to avoid situations where their values could be infinite or undefined. For universal and existential quantification such problems do not arise.

### 5.6.4 Proof Rules for Quantification

The proof rules of Chap. 4 are all still valid. Whenever a free variable is involved in the premises and the conclusion, its intended type has, however, to be the same in all of them.

Similarly to non-temporal logical connectives, proof rules for quantifiers can be taken from non-temporal logic. Only one additional rule for the 'leads to' operator will be introduced here, but, for completeness, other quantifier rules will also be briefly discussed in this subsection.[7] It will be assumed that the intended types of the quantified variables are always given although, for simplicity, they will be omitted from these rules. Also, although only a single quantified variable $x$ is written, it may stand for several, and the intended classes of these may be different.

---

[7] A reader who has skipped Chap. 3 may wish to skip this subsection also.

**Basic Laws**

Assuming that no naming clashes will arise, quantifiers can be pushed to the outside of conjunctions and disjunctions. That is, we have laws

$$E \wedge \forall x : F(x) \Leftrightarrow \forall x : (E \wedge F(x)) \;, \qquad (5.13)$$

$$E \vee \forall x : F(x) \Leftrightarrow \forall x : (E \vee F(x)) \;, \qquad (5.14)$$

$$E \wedge \exists x : F(x) \Leftrightarrow \exists x : (E \wedge F(x)) \;, \qquad (5.15)$$

$$E \vee \exists x : F(x) \Leftrightarrow \exists x : (E \vee F(x)) \;, \qquad (5.16)$$

where $x$ is assumed not to occur free in $E$.

The order of universal quantification and the box operator ($\square$) can always be exchanged,

$$\square \forall x : E(x) \Leftrightarrow \forall x : \square E(x) \;, \qquad (5.17)$$

which also gives the dual law for existential quantification and the diamond operator ($\Diamond$):

$$\Diamond \exists x : E(x) \Leftrightarrow \exists x : \Diamond E(x) \;. \qquad (5.18)$$

Table 5.1 gives rules for *introduction* and *elimination of quantifiers*. The first of them simply states that, if $E(x)$ is true for an arbitrary $x$, then it is true for all $x$, and the second rule is the converse of this. The third rule states that, if $E(x)$ is true for an arbitrary $x$, then there must exist such an $x$, unless the class of $x$ is empty. In the fourth rule, the second premise is that, for an arbitrary $x$, $E(x)$ would imply $F$. Conclusion $F$ can be made if such an $x$ exists.

**Table 5.1.** Quantifier rules

| $\dfrac{E(x)}{\forall x : E(x)}$ | $\dfrac{\forall x : E(x)}{E(x)}$ | $\dfrac{\exists x : \mathbf{T} \quad E(x)}{\exists x : E(x)}$ | $\dfrac{\exists x : E(x) \quad E(x) \Rightarrow F,\ \ x \text{ not free in } F}{F}$ |
|---|---|---|---|

The second and third rules can be slightly generalized, but this needs a notation for substitution for free variables to be given below.

**Notation for Substitution**

A notation is needed to express that a free variable $x$ in a formula $E(x)$ is replaced by another variable, say $y$.

No problems arise if it is known that $y$ does not occur free in $E(x)$. For instance, if $E(x)$ is defined as

$$E(x) \stackrel{\Delta}{=} x \in C : x.a = 0 ,$$

then we can simply write $E(y)$ to stand for $y \in C : y.a = 0$. Replacing $y$ again by $x$ would then obviously give the original $E(x)$.

The situation is, however, different if $E(x)$ also contains $y$ as a free variable, as for instance in

$$E(x) \stackrel{\Delta}{=} x, y \in C : x.a = y.a .$$

Obviously, replacing $x$ first by $y$, and then $y$ by $x$, would no longer give the original $E(x)$.

To avoid misleading expressions, we therefore write $E(x)[y/x]$ to express that all free occurrences of $x$ in $E(x)$ are replaced by $y$. When this notation is used, we will always assume that no naming conflicts will arise, i.e., that the new occurrences of $y$ in $E(x)[y/x]$ are also free, and not bound by a quantification of $y$ within the expression.

With this notation, the second and third rules of Table 5.1 can be generalized into those given in Table 5.2. In the first of these rules, for instance, expression $\exists x : E(x)$ can now contain free occurrences of $y$. For instance, if $E(x)$ is defined as

$$E(x) \stackrel{\Delta}{=} x.a = y.b ,$$

the rule allows us to conclude from $\forall x : x.a = y.b$ that $y.a = y.b$.

**Table 5.2.** Quantifier rules with substitution

|  |  |
|---|---|
|  | $\exists x : \mathbf{T}$ |
| $\dfrac{\forall x : E(x)}{E(x)[y/x]}$ | $\dfrac{E(x)[y/x]}{\exists x : E(x)}$ |

## Case Rules

If $P_1 \vee \cdots \vee P_n$ is known to be true, and $P_i \Rightarrow Q$ holds for each $i$, then ordinary non-temporal rules allow us to make the conclusion that $Q$ is true. In other words, if there are $n$ possible cases, and $Q$ is true for each of these, then $Q$ must be true.

The rule for eliminating existential quantifiers (fourth rule in Table 5.1) can be understood as a variant of this, where the cases $P_i$ are replaced by $E(x)$ for arbitrary $x \in C$, and $Q$ is replaced by $F$. Reformulated as the first rule in Table 5.3, we call it a *case rule* for implication.

Similar reasoning also applies to the 'leads to' operator ($\rightsquigarrow$). The case rule in Table 4.14 (p. 116) allows the deduction that, if $P_i \rightsquigarrow \langle A \rangle$ is true for each $i$, then also $P_1 \vee \cdots \vee P_n \rightsquigarrow \langle A \rangle$ is true. Analogously to the case rule for implication, we now have a similar rule for the 'leads to' operator, given as the second rule in Table 5.3.

**Table 5.3.** Case rules for implication and 'leads to'

| $\dfrac{E(x) \Rightarrow F,\quad x \text{ not free in } F}{(\exists x : E(x)) \Rightarrow F}$ | $\dfrac{P(x) \leadsto \langle A \rangle,\quad x \text{ not free in } A}{(\exists x : P(x)) \leadsto \langle A \rangle}$ |
| --- | --- |

### 5.6.5 Example: Simple Exchange Sort

Finally, a simple example is discussed to illustrate parameterized actions and their effect on reasoning.

**Problem and its Solution**

Consider a sequence of processes $p_1, \ldots, p_n$, $n \geq 1$, connected to each other as shown in Fig. 5.6, so that process $p_i$ can execute actions together with either one of its immediate neighbors $p_{i-1}$ (when $i > 1$) and $p_{i+1}$ (when $i < n$) only. Each $p_i$ has an integer variable $x_i$, and the numbers in these variables should be rearranged into a non-descending order $x_1 \leq \cdots \leq x_n$.

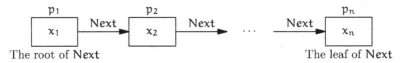

Fig. 5.6. A sequence of processes

Processes $p_i$ can be modeled as objects of class P, with a sequence relation Next, declared by

$$\textbf{class } (n)\ P = \{x : \mathbb{Z}\},\quad n > 1,$$
$$\textbf{const sequence relation } (0..1) \cdot \text{Next} \cdot (0..1) : P \times P.$$

The root of the sequence now corresponds to process $p_1$, and the leaf to $p_n$.

To allow the exchange of neighboring numbers that are in the wrong mutual order, the following action is introduced, with two neighboring processes as its participants:

$$^{WF}\text{Exchange}(p, q : P) : p \cdot \text{Next} \cdot q$$
$$\wedge\ p.x > q.x$$
$$\rightarrow\ p.x' = \min(p.x, q.x)$$
$$\wedge\ q.x' = \max(p.x, q.x).$$

Since this is the only action, its fairness assumption reflects mere fundamental liveness, which is obviously sufficient to get the numbers eventually sorted.

**Safety Properties**

Three crucial safety properties can be formulated for this system.

Firstly, the topological structure must remain unchanged,

$$\textbf{steady } \mathsf{Next} \ . \tag{5.19}$$

Being enforced by the keyword **const** for the relation $\mathsf{Next}$, a static check is sufficient to verify this. Therefore, no proof technique is needed for this property.

Secondly, the collection of numbers $\mathsf{r.x}$, $\mathsf{r} \in \mathsf{P}$, stays unchanged. Defining state function $\mathsf{N}$ as

$$\mathsf{N} \overset{\Delta}{=} \sum_{\mathsf{r} \in \mathsf{P}} \{\mathsf{r.x}\} \ ,$$

where summation denotes multiset union, this can be expressed as

$$\textbf{steady } \mathsf{N} \ . \tag{5.20}$$

This would also imply that all $\mathsf{p.x}$ are always integers, as asserted by the associated type invariant. Intuitively the satisfaction of (5.20) is obvious, since each exchange only exchanges two numbers in $\mathsf{N}$.

Thirdly, each execution of an action decreases the 'unsortedness' of the numbers. The disorder of the numbers can be measured by the following integer-valued state function $\mathsf{f}$, which counts the number of process pairs whose numbers are in the wrong mutual order:

$$\mathsf{f} \overset{\Delta}{=} \sum_{\mathsf{r} \in \mathsf{P}} |\{\mathsf{s} \in \mathsf{P} \mid \mathsf{r \cdot Next^+ \cdot s} \wedge \mathsf{r.x} > \mathsf{s.x}\}| \ .$$

Obviously, $\mathsf{f} \in \mathbb{N}$ by definition, the numbers are sorted if $\mathsf{f} = 0$, and the desired safety property is

$$\square[\mathsf{f'} < \mathsf{f}] \ . \tag{5.21}$$

The satisfaction of this property is also obvious, since each execution of action **Exchange** improves the order.

**Proving Safety Properties**

Although these safety properties are all obvious, we use them as an example to see how multi-object actions affect formal proofs.

In proving (5.20) with the step invariant rule, the crucial step is to show that action expression

$$\exists \mathsf{p}, \mathsf{q} : \mathsf{Exchange}(\mathsf{p}, \mathsf{q}) \Rightarrow \mathsf{N'} = \mathsf{N}$$

is an identically true action that is satisfied by any step. By the case rule for implication (Table 5.3 on p. 156), it is now sufficient to prove that

$$\text{Exchange}(p, q) \Rightarrow N' = N$$

is satisfied by any step.

To show this we notice that the multiset union $N$ is quantified over the class to which both $p$ and $q$ belong, and $N$ can therefore be expressed as

$$N = \{p.x\} + \{q.x\} + \sum_{r \in P \setminus \{p,q\}} \{r.x\} \, .$$

Since an action can modify the local states of its participants only, the third term necessarily has the same value in $N$ and $N'$, and we only need to show that

$$\text{Exchange}(p, q) \Rightarrow \{p.x\} + \{q.x\} = \{p.x'\} + \{q.x'\} \, ,$$

which can easily be checked.

Checking of (5.21) is left as an exercise to the reader (Exercise 5.6.4).

### Liveness Property and its Proof

The crucial liveness property in this example is that the unsortedness (if there is any) will always decrease, i.e.,

$$f = a > 0 \leadsto \langle f' < a \rangle \, . \tag{5.22}$$

Since $f \in \mathbb{N}$, the well-founded ordering rule (Table 4.13, p. 116) then gives

$$f > 0 \leadsto \langle f' = 0 \rangle \, ,$$

which means that

$$\mathbf{T} \leadsto f = 0 \, ,$$

i.e., that the numbers will eventually be sorted. On account of (5.21) they will then also continually stay sorted.

The weak fairness rule (Table 4.11, p. 113) can be used to prove (5.22), by choosing $A$, $P$, and $B$ in it as follows:

$$A : \exists p, q : \text{Exchange}(p, q) \, ,$$
$$P : f = a > 0 \, ,$$
$$B : f' < a \, .$$

### Review Questions

QUESTION 5.6.1 What is the meaning of the 'type decorations' in quantified expressions $\forall x \in C : E(x)$ and $\exists x \in C : E(x)$?

**Exercises**

EXERCISE 5.6.1 Applying the first rule in Table 5.2 on p. 155 (elimination of $\forall$) with $E(x)$ as

$$\exists z : z.a = x.a + y.a \ ,$$

what is the premise and what is the conclusion?

EXERCISE 5.6.2 Discuss the application of the second rule in Table 5.2 on p. 155 (introduction of $\exists$) with $E(x)$ as

$$x.a = y.a \ .$$

EXERCISE 5.6.3 If condition $p.x > q.x$ were changed into $p.x \geq q.x$ in the guard of action **Exchange** in Sect. 5.6.5 (p. 156), would this have any effect on the crucial properties?

EXERCISE 5.6.4 Prove invariant (5.21) in Sect. 5.6.5 (p. 157).

EXERCISE 5.6.5 Prove property (5.22) in Sect. 5.6.5 (p. 158).

EXERCISE 5.6.6 Modify the example in Sect. 5.6.5 (p. 156) so that each $p_i$ enters a special final state when it is no longer needed for sorting.

# Bibliographic Notes

Graphical illustrations of designs, including finite-state structures, have a long history in software engineering. The *Unified Modeling Language (UML)* [177, 191] is a recent and widely accepted approach to unify graphical notation in a form that is suited for object-oriented design.

Hierarchical finite-state structures with concurrent and nested states were introduced by Harel in a formally defined graphical language for the specification of reactive systems, which he called *statecharts* [76]. This language also includes a broadcast communication mechanism, which is not used in this book, since multi-object actions provide a higher-level notion for communication.

The advantages and disadvantages of typed variables in specification languages have been analyzed by Lamport and Paulson [146].

The idea of multi-partner actions was introduced for distributed systems by Back and Kurki-Suonio [20]. A similar approach was introduced independently by Ramesh and Mehndiratta [175]. Multi-party interactions were also incorporated by Forman and Attie in the *Raddle* language for distributed programming [59, 14]. For later development of this research, see [63]. As pointed out in [20], multi-party actions can also be explained in a natural manner in terms of *high-level Petri nets* [94].

In the specification language DisCo [93, 92], multi-object actions were taken as the basis of its execution model. The language features discussed in this chapter were added to this basis by Järvinen [91], defining their semantics in TLA. For the current state of DisCo-related research, the reader is referred to the DisCo home page [49].

The idea of multi-object actions has also been promoted in the UML-related design method *Catalysis* [50] by D'Souza and Wills.

In object-oriented programming languages, interactions usually involve only two partners, and are asymmetric with respect to the callers and callees. An exception is the Lisp-based language *CLOS* [25], which allows several objects to be in a symmetric position with respect to each other in generic function invocations.

# 6

# Fundamentals of Design Methodology

Non-trivial specifications cannot be derived or understood in one piece: they have to be constructed incrementally, possibly from several component modules that can be inspected separately. Also, there is no logically clear borderline between specification and design: similar design steps can be used both in *incremental specification*, where specifications are formulated in incremental steps, and in *stepwise refinement*, where implementation-oriented decisions are imposed on an implementation-independent specification.

This chapter focuses on the theoretical basis for incremental design of closed-system specifications, and on the kind of modularity supported by this basis. It is characteristic to this approach that we are not only interested in the action system that results from an incremental design process, but also in the intermediate levels involved. The resulting specifications therefore have a *layered structure*, where each level adds another layer to the specification. For simplicity, we will use the term *layer* to refer not only to the properties added in a step, but also to the whole action system produced by the step.

When a new layer $T$ is constructed, some earlier layers $S_1, \ldots, S_k$ can be utilized as its basis by *importing* them to $T$. Such a step will usually be required to produce a *refinement* of each imported layer $S_i$, by which we mean logical implication[1]

$$T \Rightarrow S_i$$

in terms of TLA.

The resulting layered structure is in some sense orthogonal to conventional modularity. Since each layer is a closed-system model of global behaviors, structuring in terms of them supports *aspect-oriented* specification, where an individual step addresses *crosscutting concerns*, which cut across several components in an eventual implementation.

---

[1]We continue using different fonts for action-language specifications and the corresponding TLA expressions. The strict refinement relation, i.e., logical implication, will be relaxed in Sect. 6.4 in ways that make it possible to analyze the relevance of those properties that are not preserved.

The plan for this chapter is as follows:

- Section 6.1 introduces *superposition*, by which a new layer of properties can be added to a closed-system specification in an intuitively natural manner.
- When different aspects of a specification are addressed in independent refinement paths, the views provided by them need to be synthesized or composed. In Sect. 6.2, *composition* of specification layers is introduced as simultaneous superposition on each of them.
- The resulting superposition-based design method is discussed in more detail in Sect. 6.3.
- Since pure superposition has its limitations, some possibilities to relax the associated requirements are introduced and analyzed in Sect. 6.4.
- Finally, the techniques introduced in this chapter are illustrated by two non-trivial examples in Sects. 6.5 and 6.6.

## 6.1 Refinement by Superposition

The basic facility for refinement steps is *superposition*, which is a technique for adding or superposing new properties on imported specification layers.

### 6.1.1 Refinement of Actions

In terms of logic, an action $B$ is a *refinement* of action $A$ if every $B$ step is also an $A$ step, i.e., if action implication

$$B \Rightarrow A \tag{6.1}$$

is identically true.

**Example**

Suppose $A$,

$$A(c : C; \, x : \mathbb{Z}) : c.a > 0$$
$$\rightarrow c.a' = c.a + x \,,$$

is an action given in layer $S$, and $T$ is a layer that imports $S$, extending the class $C$ with another local variable $b$. By writing in layer $T$

$$B(c : C) : S.A(c, 5)$$
$$\wedge c.b = c.a$$
$$\rightarrow c.b' = 0 \,,$$

we understand that action A of layer S is refined in layer T into action B, where the parameter x has been fixed as 5, the guard has been strengthened with condition c.b = c.a, and another assignment c.b' = 0 has been appended to the body. As a result, we have then obtained the following action B in layer T:

$$B(c : C) : c.a > 0$$
$$\wedge \, c.b = c.a$$
$$\rightarrow \; c.a' = c.a + 5$$
$$\wedge \, c.b' = 0 \, .$$

This action clearly implies the original action A of layer S, i.e.,

$$\exists c \in C : B(c) \Rightarrow \exists c \in C, x \in \mathbb{Z} : A(c, x) \, .$$

## Discussion

More generally, if $A(x)$ is an action in specification layer S, and x stands for its participants and other parameters, a refinement of $A(x)$ can be given in the form

$$B(y) : S.A(z)$$
$$\wedge \, \cdots$$
$$\rightarrow \; \cdots \, ,$$

where y stands for the participants and other parameters of B, $S.A(z)$ is an instance of action $A(x)$, where the formal parameter list x has been replaced by a list z of actual participants and parameter values, and the rest gives additional guarding conditions as well as assignments to such variables that were not involved in layer S. The guard (body) of the resulting action B consists of the guarding conditions (assignments) in $S.A(z)$, together with those given in the refinement. Since the new assignments are restricted to the newly introduced variables, no conflicting assignments can arise, and implication

$$\exists y : B(y) \Rightarrow \exists x : A(x)$$

is guaranteed to hold.

Since there is no global naming system for objects, the only objects that can be given in the actual parameter list z in the 'applied occurrence' $S.A(z)$ are the participants of B. Therefore, the participant roles in the refined action $B(y)$ must be a superset of those in $A(x)$ (with possible renaming).

Notice that the applied occurrence $S.A(z)$ is analogous to subroutine invocation: executing action $B(y)$ will always involve executing $A(z)$. The situation is, however, different in the sense that an execution of $B(y)$ cannot even start unless the guarding condition of $S.A(z)$ is also true.

In addition to explicitly given actions, a specification layer S with variables X can be understood to contain also an implicit stuttering action $\text{Stutter}_X$.

Refinements of this stuttering action are not allowed to modify any variables in X and are therefore called *new actions* in T, indicating that they are 'new' with respect to layer S.

### 6.1.2 Superposition

Let S and T be two action systems with actions $A_i$, $i = 1, \ldots, m$, $m \geq 0$, and $B_j$, $j = 1, \ldots, n$, $n \geq 0$, respectively, and let the associated canonical TLA expressions be[2]

$$S \triangleq P \wedge \square[A_1 \vee \cdots \vee A_m]_X \wedge F, \tag{6.2}$$

$$T \triangleq Q \wedge \square[B_1 \vee \cdots \vee B_n]_Y \wedge G. \tag{6.3}$$

Suppose now that T has been obtained from S by a construction where

- the set of variables may have been extended, i.e., $X \subseteq Y$,
- the initial condition may have been strengthened, i.e., $Q \Rightarrow P$,
- each action $B_j$ is either a new action (with respect to S) or a refinement of some action $A_i$ in S, and
- fairness requirements G may be given arbitrarily in T.

We then say that T has been obtained from S by *superposition*.

Superposition determines an *ancestor* relation between actions in the two systems, so that each action $B_j$ in T has a unique ancestor action in S, which is either some $A_i$ such that $B_j \Rightarrow A_i$ or $\text{Stutter}_X$.[3] For completeness we say that the ancestor of the (implicit) stuttering action $\text{Stutter}_Y$ in T is $\text{Stutter}_X$ in S.

Obviously, the superposition relationship between action systems is transitive, and the liveness properties F and G have no effect in its definition.

### 6.1.3 Preservation of Properties

Basically, superposition is a relation between safety specifications, since the fairness formulas F and G in (6.2) and (6.3) are irrelevant in its definition. Also, for a given safety part in (6.3) there need not exist any feasible fairness formula G that would make T imply the liveness property F in (6.2), i.e., would make T a refinement of S (see Exercise 6.1.2).

The ancestor relation between actions means, however, that implication

$$[B_1 \vee \cdots \vee B_n]_Y \Rightarrow [A_1 \vee \cdots \vee A_m]_X \tag{6.4}$$

---

[2]Since disjunction of zero actions is understood as an identically false action, $m = 0$ ($n = 0$) would mean that only stuttering steps are allowed by S (T).

[3]Although a TLA action $B_j$ could imply several different actions $A_i$ of layer S, only one $A_i$ can be specified as the ancestor of $B_j$.

is identically true (Exercise 6.1.1). An important property of superposition therefore is that all safety properties are preserved, i.e., $Cl(T) \Rightarrow Cl(S)$, or

$$Q \wedge \square[B_1 \vee \cdots \vee B_n]_Y \Rightarrow P \wedge \square[A_1 \vee \cdots \vee A_m]_X .$$

Unfortunately, preservation of liveness properties cannot be guaranteed in superposition by any generally applicable and mechanically enforceable constraints. Additional proofs are therefore needed, in general, to show that a given superposition step also preserves liveness properties and is therefore a refinement. This will be discussed in more detail below in Sects. 6.1.7–6.1.9.

## 6.1.4 Supporting Superposition

An import mechanism and language conventions support superposition in the action language as follows.

Let $T$ be a specification layer that imports $S$, and let (6.3) and (6.2) be the associated canonical TLA expressions. Condition $X \subseteq Y$ is then enforced by the following conventions:

- All global variables of layer $S$ are taken into $T$, and further global variables can also be introduced.
- All classes of layer $S$ are taken into $T$, and these can also be extended in $T$ with further attributes, as for example in

$$\textbf{class } C = \{\ldots z : \mathbb{Z}\} .$$

- New class declarations can also be introduced in $T$.
- All relations of layer $S$ are taken into $T$, and further relations can also be introduced.

Condition $Q \Rightarrow P$ is enforced by the following convention:

- All initial conditions of layer $S$ are taken into $T$, and further initial conditions can also be introduced.

Notice, however, that the satisfiability of $Q$ cannot be mechanically checked, in general.

The required ancestor relation between actions is established by the following conventions:

- No action definition in layer $T$ is allowed to introduce new modifications to any state variables in $X$.
- Each refinement of an action $A_i$ in layer $S$ is given either by a definition that uses an explicit instance of $A_i$, or as the *default refinement* of $A_i$, which corresponds to

$$A_i \wedge Stutter_{Y \setminus X} .$$

As for fairness requirements for actions, these will be explicitly indicated for all explicit refinements and all new actions. For default refinements they will be taken as such from S.[4]

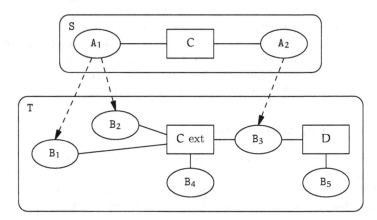

**Fig. 6.1.** Illustration of superposition

Figure 6.1 illustrates a situation where layer T, to which layer S has been imported, extends class C with new attributes and introduces a new class D. Actions $B_1$ and $B_2$ in T refine action $A_1$, action $B_3$ refines $A_2$ adding another participant of class D to it, and $B_4$ and $B_5$ are new actions in T. The dashed arrows indicate the ancestor relation between the actions of the two layers.

### 6.1.5 Example: Refining a Stack

As a simple example, consider an initial layer of specification, Stack, where a stack is modeled as a list of natural numbers, initialized as an empty list $\langle\rangle$,

$$s : \mathbf{list} \ \mathbb{N} \ (\langle\rangle) \ ,$$

with two actions for pushing and popping numbers $x$,

$$\mathrm{Push}(x : \mathbb{N}) : \mathbf{T}$$
$$\rightarrow \ s' = \langle x \rangle \circ s \ ,$$

$$\mathrm{Pop}(x : \mathbb{N}) : \mathrm{length}(s) > 0$$
$$\wedge \ x = \mathrm{first}(s)$$
$$\rightarrow \ s' = \mathrm{rest}(s) \ .$$

---

[4]Default refinements can therefore be directly taken in their textual forms from layer S.

Functions length(s), first(s), and rest(s) are here assumed to give the length of a list, its first element, and the rest of the list, respectively, and 'o' denotes list concatenation.

Wishing to extend this initial specification with a display, through which numbers can be entered to the stack, and to which numbers can be popped from it, we can import it to a new layer Refined_Stack with a new variable

$$\text{display} : \mathbb{N} \ (0) \ .$$

As for new actions in this refined specification, the display can be cleared at any time by an action

$$\text{Clear} : \text{Stack.Stutter}$$
$$\rightarrow \ \text{display}' = 0 \ ,$$

and a new number, consisting of at most N digits, can be entered to it digit by digit by another new action

$$\text{Digit}(\text{d} : \mathbb{N}) : \text{Stack.Stutter}$$
$$\wedge \ 0 \leq \text{d} \leq 9$$
$$\wedge \ \text{display} < 10^{N-1}$$
$$\rightarrow \ \text{display}' = 10 \times \text{display} + \text{d} \ .$$

Refining action Push into

$$\text{Enter} : \text{Stack.Push}(\text{display}) \ ,$$

only numbers in display can be pushed to the stack, and refining action Pop into

$$\text{Pop}(\text{x} : \mathbb{N}) : \text{Stack.Pop}(\text{x})$$
$$\rightarrow \ \text{display}' = \text{x} \ ,$$

the popped number is always shown in the display.

### 6.1.6 Example on Liveness Preservation

As stated above, preservation of liveness properties needs to be checked in superposition. As an example consider non-preemptive allocation of a single resource to concurrently running processes.

In the initial layer of specification, Basis, each process $p \in P$ is assumed to have Boolean variables *need* and *use* to indicate whether the process needs or is currently using the resource, respectively:

$$\textbf{class } P = \{\text{need}, \text{use} : \mathbb{B} \ (\text{false})\} \ .$$

Requesting the resource, granting it to a process, and releasing the resource can then be expressed by the following actions:

$$\texttt{Request}(p : P) : p.use = p.need = \mathsf{false}$$
$$\rightarrow\ p.need' = \mathsf{true}\ ,$$

$$\texttt{Grant}(^{SF}p : P) : p.need = \mathsf{true}$$
$$\wedge\ \forall q \in P : q.use = \mathsf{false}$$
$$\rightarrow\ p.need' = \mathsf{false}$$
$$\wedge\ p.use' = \mathsf{true}\ ,$$

$$\texttt{Release}(^{WF}p : P) : p.use = \mathsf{true}$$
$$\rightarrow\ p.use' = \mathsf{false}\ .$$

Obviously, the given fairness assumptions guarantee that, once a process has requested the resource (by action **Request**), it will eventually obtain it (by **Grant**) and also release it (by **Release**).

A first-come-first-serve policy can be superposed on this layer by importing it to a new layer **Simple_Policy** and introducing the following refinements. For identification of processes, class P is extended with unique identification numbers,[5]

$$\textbf{class } P = \{\ldots id : \mathbb{N}\}\ , \quad \forall p, q \in P : p \neq q \Rightarrow p.id \neq q.id\ ,$$

a queue is introduced for pending requests,

$$queue : \textbf{list } \mathbb{N}\ (\langle\rangle)\ ,$$

actions **Request** and **Grant** are refined to use this queue as follows,

$$\texttt{Request}(p : P) : \texttt{Basis.Request}(p)$$
$$\rightarrow\ queue' = queue \circ \langle p.id \rangle\ ,$$

$$\texttt{Grant}(^{WF}p : P) : \texttt{Basis.Grant}(p)$$
$$\wedge\ \mathrm{first}(queue) = p.id$$
$$\rightarrow\ queue' = \mathrm{rest}(queue)\ ,$$

and action **Release** is kept as its default refinement. Obviously, when several pending requests exist, the resource will now always be given to the process that has waited longest.

The liveness property expressed by the fairness marking in **Basis.Release** is obviously preserved in this superposition, since the default refinement

---

[5]These numbers p.**id** are identification attributes to be used in the application, not the postulated object identities p.**id** (see Sect. 5.3.1, p. 136).

Simple_Policy.Release is enabled whenever the guard of Basis.Release is true, and the fairness marking is not changed in default refinement. As for the fairness requirement in Basis.Grant, we have to show that, if the guard of this action is repeatedly true for process p in the refined system, the refined action Simple_Policy.Grant will eventually be executed for it. Whenever the (non-refined) guard is true, the fairness marking in the refined action forces its execution for the process that has waited longest. Therefore, process p will eventually be the one that has waited longest, and Simple_Policy.Grant will then be executed for it.

### 6.1.7 Proof Obligations for Liveness Preservation

In terms of the notation in (6.2) and (6.3) on p. 164, preservation of liveness properties in superposition requires that implication $T \Rightarrow F$ holds. Since $F$ is a conjunction of some strong and weak fairness conditions $F_i$, we get proof obligations

$$T \Rightarrow F_i \qquad (6.5)$$

for each $F_i$. If $G \Rightarrow F_i$ holds for each $i$, we have a simple situation where the fairness conditions of $T$ are as such sufficient to prove (6.5), but, in general, a proof requires us to utilize safety properties of $T$ also.

To look into this in more detail, let

$$A \stackrel{\Delta}{=} \exists x, y : A(x, y)$$

be the TLA expression for an action $A$ in layer $S$, where $x$ and $y$ denote an arbitrary partitioning of parameters, such that at least those in $x$ have fairness markings. According to Sect. 5.5.5 (p. 149), $F$ then includes a fairness requirement of the form (5.12) on p. 150, and the proof obligations for (6.5) therefore have the form

$$T \Rightarrow \forall x : \mathrm{XF}(\exists y : A(x, y)) , \qquad (6.6)$$

where XF stands for either SF or WF.

### 6.1.8 Liveness Preservation: Special Case

It is often the case that the refinements of an action $A$ are such that (at least) those participants and other parameters that have fairness markings in $A$ also appear as parameters in these refinements. In that case it is natural to transfer the fairness markings of $A$ as such to these refinements also. For instance, fairness marking on role $c$ in action $A(^{\mathrm{SF}}c : C \ldots)$ could then be taken as such in each of its refinements $B$,

$$B(\ldots {}^{\mathrm{SF}}c : C \ldots) : S.A(c \ldots)$$

$$\cdots .$$

In this subsection we discuss some conditions that are sufficient for (6.6) in this special situation. First we also make some additional simplifying assumptions.

### Default Refinements

Default refinements obviously satisfy the above assumptions, since all parameters then remain the same, and all fairness markings are also retained.

In terms of logic, default refinement of an action $\exists x, y : A(x, y)$ gives an action $\exists x, y : B(x, y)$, where the enabling guard is the same, and $B(x, y)$ implies $A(x, y)$. Therefore, $XF(\exists y : B(x, y))$ always implies $XF(\exists y : A(x, y))$. This means that preserving fairness markings also preserves all associated fairness properties.

### Single Non-disabling Refinements

Default refinements can be understood as a special case of a more general situation, where action A has only one refinement B in layer T, and its guard is not strengthened for such participant combinations that are critical for the preservation of liveness properties.

Let $A(x, y)$ therefore be an action in layer S, where x stands for all those participants and other parameters that have fairness markings, and y stands for all other parameters, and let $g_A^+(x, y)$ be the enabling condition for the stutter-excluding part of $A(x, y)$.[6] Furthermore, let action $B(x, z)$, whose enabling guard is $g_B(x, z)$, be the only refinement of action A, and let all parameters x of A be present in B as such.

If all fairness markings of A (on participants and other parameters in list x) are also included as such in B, then the condition

$$\exists y : g_A^+(x, y) \Rightarrow \exists z : g_B(x, z) \tag{6.7}$$

is sufficient to ensure that for each fairness condition $F_i$ on action A in S there is a corresponding fairness condition $G_j$ on action B in T such that $G_j \Rightarrow F_i$ (Exercise 6.1.3). In other words, all fairness properties with respect to action A in layer S are then also satisfied in layer T.

### Multiple, Possibly Disabling Refinements

Let $A(x, y)$ and $g_A^+(x, y)$ be as above, but let T have multiple refinements $B_i(x, z_i)$, $i = 1, \ldots, k$, of action A, with enabling guards $g_{B_i}(x, z_i)$. If condition

$$\exists y : g_A^+(x, y) \rightsquigarrow \exists z_1 : g_{B_1}(x, z_1) \vee \cdots \vee \exists z_k : g_{B_k}(x, z_k) \tag{6.8}$$

---

[6] For the stutter-excluding part, see Sect. 3.4.8, p. 83. Since $g_A^+$ implies the enabling of A, the guard of A can be used here instead of $g_A^+$, whenever this is sufficient for the conditions to be given in this subsection.

holds in T, then the fairness properties of action A are preserved in T if the fairness markings of A are taken to all $B_i$ so that weak markings are replaced by strong markings (Exercise 6.1.4).

Notice that weak markings cannot, in general, be kept weak here, even if the 'leads to' operator in (6.8) is replaced by implication, since the guard of A could stay continually true without any $B_i$ being continually enabled. This shows that strong fairness properties are, in general, more stable in superposition than their weak counterparts.

### 6.1.9 Liveness Preservation: General Case

To discuss proof obligations (6.6) for arbitrary situations, let $g(x,y)$, $g^+(x,y)$, and $g^0(x,y)$ be the enabling guards of A, $A^+$, and $A^0$, respectively.

When XF stands for SF, proving (6.6) requires us to prove that, for any x, a state satisfying

$$\exists y : g^+(x,y) \tag{6.9}$$

always eventually leads to one of the following situations in T:

- state predicate $\exists y : g^0(x,y)$ holds, i.e., a stuttering execution of $A(x,y)$ is encountered,
- state predicate $\neg\exists y : g^+(x,y)$ holds permanently, or
- a non-stuttering step is taken that implies $A^+(x,y)$ for some y.

Notice that, in the case of non-disjoint actions in S, executing an action B in T may give an A step even when A is not the ancestor of B.

Correspondingly, when XF stands for WF, any state satisfying (6.9) must always lead to one of the following situations in T:

- state predicate $\neg\exists y : g^+(x,y)$ holds, or
- a non-stuttering step is taken that implies $A^+(x,y)$ for some y.

### Review Questions

QUESTION 6.1.1 What is understood here by a specification layer?

QUESTION 6.1.2 What is the criterion for an action system to be a refinement of another action system?

QUESTION 6.1.3 Why is it crucial in superposition not to introduce any new assignments to old variables?

QUESTION 6.1.4 Is superposition defined as a relation between TLA expressions or between specifications in the action language?

QUESTION 6.1.5 What is understood by the ancestor relation?

QUESTION 6.1.6 Why is it so that there need not exist any fairness properties that would make a given superposition step a refinement?

QUESTION 6.1.7 Is there a difference in the stability of weak and strong fairness properties under superposition?

**Exercises**

EXERCISE 6.1.1 Show that implication (6.4) on p. 164 is identically true in superposition.

EXERCISE 6.1.2 Give an example of a superposition step that cannot be made a refinement by any fairness markings. Hint: consider the simple situation where $n = 0$ in (6.3) on p. 164, i.e., there are no actions in T.

EXERCISE 6.1.3 Show that condition (6.7) on p. 170 is sufficient for the situation discussed there.

EXERCISE 6.1.4 Show that condition (6.8) on p. 170 is sufficient for the situation discussed there.

EXERCISE 6.1.5 Check that the proof obligations given in Sect. 6.1.9 (p. 171) are correct.

EXERCISE 6.1.6 Discuss the special cases of Sect. 6.1.8 (p. 169) in the light of the general discussion in Sect. 6.1.9 (p. 171).

EXERCISE 6.1.7 Let $T_1$ and $T_2$ be obtained from layer S by two consecutive superposition steps, so that $T_1$ is obtained from S, and $T_2$ from $T_1$ by superposition. Is it possible that $T_2$ is a refinement of S, but $T_1$ is not?

## 6.2 Composition and Layered Specifications

Different closed-system models can be given to model the same system from different (possibly overlapping) viewpoints. By *composition* we then understand their *synthesis* into a single closed-system model.

Formally, composition of two or more specification layers is defined as simultaneous superposition on all of them. In particular, the initial condition of a composed layer then implies the initial conditions of all components, and each of its actions is a refinement of one (possibly stuttering) action in each of them.

With this definition, composition is not a uniquely defined operation between layers, and it need not preserve their liveness properties.

Composition is expressed in the action language by importing the component layers (which imports all associated global variables, classes, relations, and initial conditions), and giving the additional global variables, classes, class extensions, relations, and initial conditions, as well as the actions of the composition and their fairness assumptions.

Since composition is superposition on all component layers, the safety properties of all components are preserved. In order to be a refinement of its components, their liveness properties must also be preserved, which can be shown in the same way as for superposition on a single layer.

Before going to technical details of composition, we explain how superposition and composition are intended to be used for layered specifications.

### 6.2.1 Layered Specifications

Superposition and composition are transformations that are used to obtain *layered specifications*, in which each layer is obtained from some previous layers by these constructions. For completeness, an empty initial layer can be assumed, from which all other layers are derived.

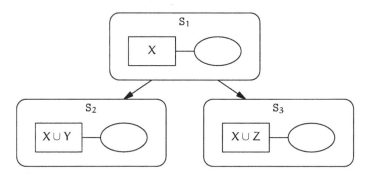

**Fig. 6.2.** Illustration of independent superposition steps on the same layer

Entities that are introduced in a layer are always considered to be different from those introduced in any other layer.[7] Therefore, when several different superposition steps are applied to the same layer, the new variables introduced in these steps are different. Figure 6.2 illustrates this for two independent superposition steps on layer $S_1$. The associated sets of new variables, $Y$ and $Z$, are therefore disjoint. The resulting layers $S_2$ and $S_3$ are non-independent, since the variables $X$ of layer $S_1$ are included in both.

In general, the layered structure obtained by superposition and composition has the form of a directed, acyclic graph, as illustrated in Fig. 6.3. In this structure, a layer is called a *predecessor* of another layer if the latter has

---

[7]Introducing the same name in two different layers causes a name clash, which can always be resolved by renaming.

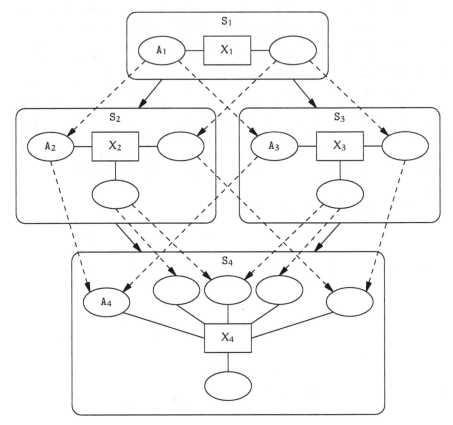

**Fig. 6.3.** Illustration of a layered structure

been obtained from the former by a sequence of superposition and composition steps. Layer $S_1$ in Fig. 6.3 is a common predecessor of layers $S_2$ and $S_3$, which in turn are predecessors of layer $S_4$. As for variables, $X_4$ includes both $X_2$ and $X_3$, which in turn include $X_1$.

Extending the *ancestor* relation between actions to its transitive closure, composition will be defined so that each action of any layer has unique ancestor actions in all predecessor layers. More precisely, each execution of an action will have a unique interpretation as an action execution in each predecessor layer.

The predecessor relation between layers and the ancestor relation between (non-stuttering) actions are shown in Fig. 6.3 by solid and dashed arrows, respectively. For instance, action $A_1$ in layer $S_1$ is a common ancestor of actions $A_2$, $A_3$, and $A_4$ in the other layers. Notice that layer $S_4$ could not have an action whose ancestors would be $A_2$ and $\text{Stutter}_{X_3}$, for instance, since then it would have two different ancestors, $A_1$ and $\text{Stutter}_{X_1}$, in $S_1$.

Obviously, if all superposition and composition steps in the layered structure are refinements, then each layer is a refinement of all its predecessor layers. Conversely, we can then understand each layer as a correct *abstraction* of those derived from it.

### 6.2.2 Composition of Independent Layers

In the following we consider composition of only two layers. The discussion can, however, be immediately generalized to any number of them.

Let $S$ and $T$ be two specification layers with actions $A_i(x_i)$, $i = 1, \ldots, m$, and $B_j(y_j)$, $j = 1, \ldots, n$, respectively, and let the associated TLA formulas be

$$S \triangleq P \wedge \Box[A]_X \wedge F ,$$

$$T \triangleq Q \wedge \Box[B]_Y \wedge G ,$$

where

$$A \triangleq \exists x_1 : A_1(x_1) \vee \cdots \vee \exists x_m : A_m(x_m) ,$$

$$B \triangleq \exists y_1 : B_1(y_1) \vee \cdots \vee \exists y_n : B_n(y_n) .$$

To simplify the presentation we will assume in the following that the stuttering actions $\mathsf{Stutter}_X$ and $\mathsf{Stutter}_Y$ also appear explicitly among actions $A_i(x_i)$ and $B_j(y_j)$, respectively.

Layers $S$ and $T$ are said to be *independent* if $X$ and $Y$ are disjoint, i.e., $X \cap Y = \emptyset$. In this case the situation is simplified by the facts that $P \wedge Q$ is satisfiable if both $P$ and $Q$ are satisfiable, and that no pair of actions $(A_i(x_i), B_j(y_j))$ can have conflicting assignments. The latter property makes it possible for a composition to have actions with any two actions $A_i$ and $B_j$ as their ancestors.

Analogously to superposition on a single layer, actions of a composition will be expressed in the action language in a form that first gives (the instantiations of) the ancestors explicitly, and then the added guarding conditions and assignments to the new variables:

$$\begin{aligned}
C(x) : {}& S.A_i(y) \\
& \wedge\ T.B_j(z) \\
& \wedge\ \cdots \\
\rightarrow{}& \cdots .
\end{aligned}$$

Such an action is called a *synchronization* of the given ancestors. In an operational interpretation, its execution implies executing these ancestors at the same time. When both ancestors are stuttering actions, an action is called a *new action*.

By *default synchronization* we mean synchronization where no additional strengthening is added to the synchronized actions, and the participants and other parameters (together with their fairness markings) are taken as such from both. In terms of TLA this means plain conjunction of the synchronized actions.

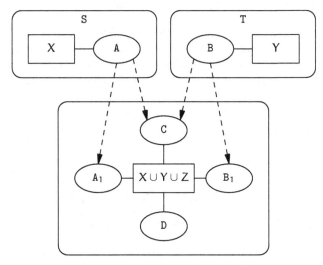

**Fig. 6.4.** Illustration of composition of independent layers

Composition of two independent layers may now have three kinds of actions, as illustrated in Fig. 6.4: synchronizations of non-stuttering actions (C), actions in which variables of only one component are modified ($A_1$ and $B_1$), and new actions (D).

### 6.2.3 Unification of Action Instances

When layers S and T are non-independent, they have common variables, which must have been introduced in the common predecessor layers. If arbitrary (instances of) actions in S and T were allowed to be synchronized in composition, the implied (instances of) actions in those common predecessors might be different. This is the case, in particular, if the ancestors of the synchronized actions are different, but even common ancestors do not prevent this, as is shown by the following example.

### Example

Let actions A and B in layers S and T be defined as refinements of action $A_0(c : C; x : \mathbb{Z})$ in a common predecessor layer $S_0$ (see Fig. 6.5) as follows:

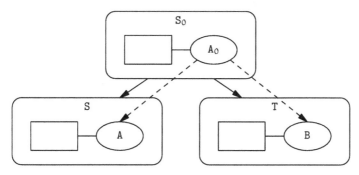

**Fig. 6.5.** Actions with a common ancestor

$$A(c : C; \ x : \mathbb{Z}) : \ S_0.A_0(c, x + 2)$$

$$\cdots \ ,$$

$$B(c : C) : \ S_0.A_0(c, 5)$$

$$\cdots \ .$$

Consider now arbitrary instances $S.A(c, z)$ and $T.B(d)$ of these actions. The instances of action $A_0$ that these would imply in layer $S_0$ are $S_0.A_0(c, z + 2)$ and $S_0.A_0(d, 5)$, respectively. These implied instances are the same only when the condition

$$c = d \wedge z + 2 = 5 \tag{6.10}$$

is satisfied.

### Unification Condition

Condition (6.10) is called the *unification condition* for the above instantiations $S.A(c, z)$ and $T.B(d)$. More generally, given instances of two actions with common ancestors in all common predecessor layers, their unification condition is defined to express that all participants and other parameters are the same in the implied instances of these common ancestors. (For actions with different ancestors in a common predecessor layer the unification condition is defined to be identically false.)

As a special case, the unification condition is identically true for actions with only stuttering ancestors in their common predecessor layers. In particular, for actions in independent layers it is always true.

The unification condition can always be constructed by tracing the ancestors in the common predecessor layers and their implied instances. When not identically false, its form is such that some participants are equated ($c = d$ in the above example), and some equations are given to constrain the values of other parameters ($z + 2 = 5$ above).

### 6.2.4 Composition of Layers: General Case

Composition, as discussed above, can now be generalized to arbitrary layers in a natural manner. Compared to independent layers, the only constraint is that the unification condition must always be true for the synchronized action instances. For the participants in these instances this can be mechanically checked; for the other parameters this can be ensured by the guarding conditions.

In the following we will always use action synchronization in such a way that the unification conditions are trivially true.

Finally, we give a few concluding remarks on layered specifications and composition:

- The preservation of all safety properties of the preceding layers is always guaranteed by construction.
- Each action execution can always be projected to a unique action execution (possibly stuttering) in all preceding layers.
- Composition depends on the derivation history of layers; a specification therefore always consists of the whole layered structure of this history.
- Sometimes there is a need to compose several *copies* of the same specification. In this case deep copies are assumed, i.e., copies of the whole layered structure involved.
- In non-independent layers, initial conditions may be conflicting in the sense that their satisfaction need not be possible in composition (Exercise 6.2.1).
- In non-independent layers, their liveness properties may be conflicting in the sense that their preservation need not be possible in composition (Exercise 6.2.2).

### 6.2.5 Example: Simple Component Composition

As an example of composing independent layers, consider a simple situation of independently specified 'producer' and 'consumer' objects. The producer objects $p \in P$ are defined in layer $S$ with action

$$\texttt{Give}(p : P;\ x : \mathbb{Z}) : g_p(p, x)$$
$$\rightarrow \cdots ,$$

where the guard $g_p(p, x)$ determines when $p$ is ready to deliver the next piece of data $x$ and what the value of $x$ then is. Correspondingly, layer $T$ contains consumer objects $c \in C$ with action

$$\texttt{Take}(c : C;\ y : \mathbb{Z}) : g_c(c, y)$$
$$\rightarrow \cdots ,$$

where the guard $g_c(c, y)$ determines when $c$ is ready to receive the next piece of data $y$, possibly with constraints on acceptable values of $y$.

Layers S and T can now be composed so that actions Give and Take are synchronized to model their concurrent execution with the same piece of data:

$$\text{Transfer}(p : P; \ c : C; \ z : \mathbb{Z}) : \text{S.Give}(p, z)$$
$$\wedge \text{ T.Take}(c, z) \ .$$

Notice that the action language makes no distinction between 'input parameters' and 'output parameters'. For instance, both Give and Take may impose constraints in a similar manner on the values of x and y, respectively. If these constraints are contradictory, action Transfer is identically false.

### Review Questions

QUESTION 6.2.1 Why is composition, as defined here, not a uniquely defined operation between specifications, and why does it depend on their derivation histories?

QUESTION 6.2.2 What are the characteristic properties of layered specifications, obtained by superposition and composition?

QUESTION 6.2.3 What is meant by the unification condition of action instances?

### Exercises

EXERCISE 6.2.1 Give an example of non-independent layers, whose initial conditions cannot be satisfied in their composition.

EXERCISE 6.2.2 Give an example of non-independent layers, whose liveness properties cannot be preserved in composition.

EXERCISE 6.2.3 Give an example where the unification condition is false, but the implied instances of the common ancestor actions are still equivalent.

## 6.3 Superposition-based Design

The techniques discussed above lead to a superposition-based design method to derive specifications incrementally. As discussed in Sect. 6.2.1 (p. 173), we can start from an empty initial layer and construct further layers as refinements, so that a layered structure of superpositions is created. In this section we take a closer look at some general properties of this method.

### 6.3.1 Closed-system Modularity

In conventional object-oriented programming and design, objects are often taken as natural units for modularity. The aim then is to design entities whose implementations are reusable components. Since individual components cannot enforce constraints on their environments, they are described as 'open' systems with given interfaces. Formulation of behavioral properties then requires *assume–guarantee* pairs of properties, where the system guarantees a property assuming that a given assumption is true of the environment.

Since "it takes two to tango," objects do not produce behaviors in isolation from their environments. Also, the properties that are relevant in system specification are not, in general, properties of individual objects (or classes), but collective properties that arise from possible interactions between them. The closed-system principle makes it possible to consider such collective properties without the need to compose them from the individual assume–guarantee pairs of open components.

For the approach of this book the natural units of modularity are therefore not individual objects, but 'closed' action systems with class declarations, definitions of multi-object actions, constraints for initial conditions, etc. Such systems are, in fact, generic *patterns*, of which different kinds of concrete instantiations are possible.

In general, layers of specification are *logical modules*, which introduce logically coherent layers of collective properties. They also use each other by logical implication – actions imply their ancestors, and layers imply their predecessors – whereas conventional software modules produce behaviors only when put together by explicit communication and invocation mechanisms.

As shown by the simple example in Sect. 6.2.5 (p. 178) it is, however, also possible to use independent layers to specify individual *implementation modules*. In such a case the environment of a component is only implicit in the model – but still involved in the actions – and the distinction between an open and a closed system is therefore more or less in the eye of the beholder.

### 6.3.2 Development Strategies

In this subsection we take a brief look at different development strategies (or design methods) that are possible with superposition-based techniques.

The notion of state was defined so that all possible variables have unique values in each state. Each behavior therefore contains a complete description of how 'the whole world' behaves during a single execution. Each specification layer $S_i$ focuses, however, on a given set of variables $X_i$ only, and nothing is said about other variables. If one observes only how variables in this set $X_i$ behave in an intended world, then one should obtain only such observation sequences that satisfy $S_i$. This means that layer $S_i$ is a correct *abstraction* of the intended world, where the focus is on $X_i$, and everything else is ignored.

Another way to put this is that each layer $S_i$ is a *projection* of the intended world to the variables in $X_i$.

The word 'abstraction' is often associated with a *design-oriented view*, where higher-level abstractions are utilized in order to achieve 'correctness by design', whereas the word 'projection' associates more with a *verification-oriented* view, where one verifies properties of a system by utilizing suitable projections of it.

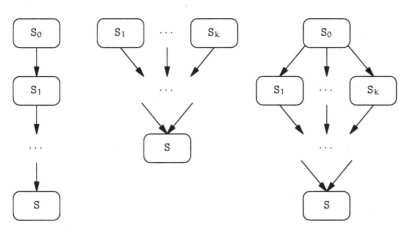

**Fig. 6.6.** Layered structures resulting from top-down (left), bottom-up (center), and aspect-oriented development (right)

These two views also relate to the design approaches that are used. In *top-down development* one starts with an overall idea of the whole system, and proceeds stepwise, making the design more and more concrete by filling in the details. This can be done in a natural manner by superposition steps, as illustrated in the left-hand part of Fig. 6.6. When the emphasis is on logical rather than architectural properties, the design process then starts from a very abstract level $S_0$, and the *level of abstraction* is lowered stepwise by widening the focus with further variables and incorporating more detailed design decisions, until all necessary aspects have been included and an implementable model $S$ has been reached. The unique ancestor relation between actions at different levels then guarantees *traceability* of actions to all higher levels of abstraction.

In contrast, *bottom-up development* starts from the specifications of parts (components) of a system, and composes a total solution from them. The center part of Fig. 6.6 is a schematic illustration of how this can be done by composition steps, in which independent specification layers $S_i$ are composed into a specification $S$ of the total system. In this case, each layer in the specification is a temporally complete *projection* of the total system to some part of it. The ancestor relation between actions then projects actions in the final specification to actions in those components that are involved in them.

In bottom-up development the intended logical properties of the total system are present only in the final stage S, whereas in pure top-down development they are included already in the initial layer $S_0$, although perhaps in an abstract form that may not be directly implementable. Neither of these extremes is, in general, recommendable in its pure form. Even when the linear path of the left-hand part of Fig. 6.6 is followed, *incremental development* also needs steps in which new required properties are added to the specification. Therefore, the structure of the resulting layered specification does not directly indicate the associated development process.

The rightmost part in Fig. 6.6 illustrates the result of another form of development process, *aspect-oriented development*, for which the layered structure of specifications is eminently suited. In it, layers that address different *aspects* of the specification have a common predecessor layer $S_0$, but they are specified in otherwise independent branches $S_i$, which are in the end composed to the final specification S. The role of the root $S_0$ is to provide a common framework for which all aspects $S_i$ should be designed (bottom-up concern), and it can also give an abstract specification of those properties for which the aspects are intended to provide implementable refinements (top-down concern).

For separation of concerns, aspect-oriented development gives more powerful possibilities than bottom-up development, since aspects are, in general, independent of the intended architectural components. Typically, aspects correspond to groups of logical properties that cut across several components in an implementation (crosscutting concerns). In that case the components are not complete in the specification until all aspects $S_i$ have been composed into S.

The two examples in Sects. 6.5 and 6.6 will demonstrate different kinds of uses for this kind of a pattern for layered specifications.

No matter which development strategy is used, it is important that the first layers try to address the most stable properties of a system, i.e., those that are the most likely not to change during the specification and design process, or during the evolution of an implemented system. In the case of a product family, these layers should also address properties that will be common to the whole family. The layered structure can then provide a valuable basis for maintaining the specifications of evolving systems, and for estimating how deeply some proposed changes will affect the system.

### 6.3.3 Note on Variables and Associated Actions

In connection with conventional design methods it may be recommended to start with 'static' aspects of the system, by first analyzing in detail the required state variables (i.e., objects and their local states), and to postpone the consideration of 'dynamic' properties.

This is in obvious conflict with the principles of superposition-based design. If a state variable x has been introduced in layer S without any actions to modify its value, then x would stay unchanged in S. No later layer T could introduce such actions, either, without violating the implication T ⇒ S.

This may at first sound like an undesirable restriction. It is, however, intuitively quite natural, since variables without associated actions are meaningless in a specification – except for immutable constants, which describe some fixed parameters of the problem. An 'ordinary variable' is given a meaning only by the behaviors in which its value is utilized, i.e., by the actions that access and/or modify its value. If the values to be assigned to a variable are not available at the stage where the variable is introduced, nondeterministic actions should be used, as will be discussed below.

A useful way to describe the purpose of a variable is to give invariants that are intended to be maintained for it. These invariants are obviously intimately tied to the actions by which the variable can be modified.

### 6.3.4 Nondeterminism and Refinement Steps

Extending the focus of a specification with further variables can be understood as a step that decreases the nondeterminism that is allowed by a specification layer. Obviously, the assumed empty initial layer is the most nondeterministic specification that is possible, since it allows all possible behaviors. Each nontrivial design step, on the other hand, decreases the nondeterminism that is allowed by the layers imported to it.

In addition to completely unrestricted nondeterminism with respect to those variables that are not talked about in a specification, there is also nondeterminism in selecting the next action, and also in the effects of action bodies.

As an example of the former, consider modeling of the environment in the gas-burner example of Chap. 2. Obviously, the model that was given was more nondeterministic than the reality. With a wider focus one could extend the model, for instance, to describe how heating, changes in weather, etc., would affect the enabling of environment actions.

Nondeterministic effects of actions, on the other hand, can be achieved by action parameters, whose values are selected nondeterministically but may be constrained by the guards. This provides an effective way to introduce explicit nondeterminism without nondeterministic bodies, and also to control this nondeterminism in later refinement steps.

For instance, when a variable has been introduced at a stage where it is impossible to give the exact values that are assigned to it in actions, these values can be given as nondeterministic parameters. When more information becomes available in later refinement steps, these parameter values can be determined more precisely.

### 6.3.5 Notes on Encapsulation

Modularity usually involves encapsulation, by which internal details of a module can be hidden from the modules in which it will be utilized. The need for this may also arise when specification layers are imported. State variables and actions that have been introduced in a layer may only serve a local purpose within the layer itself, and would not need to be visible for access or refinement in importing layers.

On the other hand, starting with a closed-system model at a high level of abstraction, one may wish to partition further work into subprojects in which different aspects of the model are refined independently. This may require that different variables and actions are made visible to different subprojects only. In order not to complicate the presentation, we shall not, however, introduce any special hiding mechanisms for such purposes.

Compared to programming languages, the situation is simplified by the rules for superposition, which guarantee that an importing layer cannot introduce accidental changes in state variables. Non-modifying use of imported variables may, however, also be harmful, since this introduces superfluous dependences on predecessor layers, which complicates their later modification.

Action parameters provide a useful mechanism to avoid such dependences. For instance, if the value of variable $a$ is expected to be relevant for future refinements of an action, then convenient access to this value can be provided by adding a parameter $x$ and a guarding condition $x = a$ to the action. Refinements of $A$ can then access the value of $a$ through this parameter, without explicit reference to the variable itself.

## Review Questions

QUESTION 6.3.1 Why are objects not the natural units of modularity in closed-system specifications?

QUESTION 6.3.2 What is the difference in modeling an individual component as an open system or as a closed system?

QUESTION 6.3.3 In which sense is every layer in a layered specification a correct abstraction of the intended 'world'?

QUESTION 6.3.4 What is characteristic to aspect-oriented development?

QUESTION 6.3.5 Why is it not possible to introduce further changes to a variable in later layers of specification, and why is this not an essential restriction?

QUESTION 6.3.6 In which ways is nondeterminism decreased in superposition steps?

# 6.4 Beyond Superposition

Superposition – by itself or in connection with composition – is a powerful technique that fits the basic philosophy of our approach in a most natural way. A pure superposition relationship is not, however, sufficient for all transformations that may be needed in practice. In this section we therefore discuss some natural possibilities to relax this relationship in a carefully constrained manner.

Basically, these relaxations have three kinds of effects:

- They allow simplification of specifications in manners that are not possible by pure superposition.
- Some of the relaxations weaken the role of predecessor layers as abstractions. In particular, the unique ancestor relation between actions may be violated for some actions.
- Some logical properties cannot be preserved in some of the relaxed transformations. Such transformations are still useful in situations where these properties concern only auxiliary variables (i.e., quantified state variables in terms of TLA), or the weakened properties have been unnecessarily strong due to overspecified models.

### 6.4.1 Simplification of Actions

Action refinement was defined in Sect. 6.1.1 (p. 162) so that action B in T refines action A in S if implication $B \Rightarrow A$ is identically true. Relaxing this into the weaker requirement that this implication is true for all reachable steps, i.e., that

$$\Box[B \Rightarrow A] \tag{6.11}$$

holds in T, the essential properties of superposition are still retained: safety properties of S are preserved, and a unique ancestor relation is established between actions.

The same effect can be achieved conveniently by combining an ordinary superposition step with *simplification* of the resulting actions. To be more precise, if I is a state invariant in a system, and

$$I \wedge A \Leftrightarrow I \wedge B \tag{6.12}$$

is identically true, then action A can be replaced by B without affecting the behaviors that are generated by the system. If B is in some sense simpler than A, then the specification has been simplified.

The main use of this kind of action simplification is in the simplification of action guards. For instance, if action A has guard $g \wedge h$, and we can show that $g \Rightarrow h$ is true in all reachable states, then we can remove conjunct h from the guard.

Other kinds of action transformations that satisfy (6.12) also include ones that involve addition and/or deletion of action parameters. For instance, action simplification may lead to a situation where some of its participants are no longer needed. In deleting such a participant one has, however, to remember that the guard implicitly also contains the condition that such an object exists. An instance of such a situation will appear in the example of Sect. 6.6.

### 6.4.2 Data Refinement

As far as state variables are concerned, superposition allows us only to introduce new variables, not to remove old ones. It is often the case, however, that one wishes to change the representation of state functions by replacing previously introduced variables by new ones. Such a transformation is called *data refinement*.

To illustrate the situation, let $x$ be a state variable that should be replaced by new variable(s) $y$. The technique that can be used is to introduce $y$ in a superposition step, and to prove that

$$\Box(x = f(y))$$

then holds for some state function $f(y)$ that does not depend on $x$. After that, all applied occurrences of $x$ can be replaced by $f(y)$, and variable $x$ then turns into a non-primitive state function (or 'ghost' variable) that can be omitted. In other words, $x$ has then been changed into an *abstraction* that needs no explicit representation as such, and $f(y)$ provides the associated *abstraction mapping*. As a byproduct, this may also lead to elimination of participants that have become superfluous for some actions.

When used in combination, superposition and data refinement provide a very powerful technique for the refinement of specifications, and none of the essential characteristics of superposition-based design are then violated.

### 6.4.3 Refinement of Atomicity

In principle, the atomicity of an action cannot be refined in superposition. If an action has an effect on two variables $x$ and $y$, these effects cannot be split into separate actions without affecting some safety properties. Such refinement of atomicity would, however, often be useful in practice.

The associated problems can often be circumvented by introducing another variable $z$ that mimics one of the variables, say $y$, but is modified separately from $x$. Obviously, this means that in some states the values of $y$ and $z$ do not agree, but if $y$ is not accessed in such states (which needs to be proved with the aid of suitable invariants), all its applied occurrences can be replaced by $z$. Variable $y$ has then, in fact, become an abstraction that need not be explicitly present, and the splitting of an action has also been effectively accomplished.

This technique is especially useful in refining centralized algorithms into a form for which distributed implementation is possible. Some variables of the centralized algorithm are then turned into abstractions that are not explicitly accessed in distributed implementations. Examples of using the technique for this purpose will be given in later chapters of this book.

### 6.4.4 Disjunctive Actions

Ignoring fairness requirements, a set of actions $A_1, \ldots, A_k$ could be replaced by one that corresponds to their disjunction $A_1 \vee \cdots \vee A_k$. In action refinement one might therefore wish to relax condition (6.11) further into

$$\Box[B \Rightarrow A_1 \vee \cdots \vee A_k] . \tag{6.13}$$

An important special case of such *disjunctive actions* is that of *stuttering relaxation* of an action $A$, by which we mean the situation where (6.13) has the form

$$\Box[B \Rightarrow A \vee \mathsf{Stutter}_X] . \tag{6.14}$$

Obviously, introduction of disjunctive actions does not violate any safety properties. There are, however, two things to be noticed in connection with them.

Firstly, it may not be possible to preserve fairness properties for the individual actions if they are replaced by corresponding disjunctive actions or stuttering relaxations. Therefore, such replacements are not always possible.

Secondly, a disjunctive action or stuttering relaxation no longer has unique ancestors in the predecessor layers, which weakens the abstractions provided by these layers, and also complicates (or prevents) composition with other branches of refinement. When these restrictions are not considered important (and fairness properties can be preserved), disjunctive actions provide a useful mechanism for refining specifications.

### 6.4.5 Concatenated Actions

As the opposite of refining the atomicity of actions, one may also wish to combine actions of the same layer into larger atomic actions. Semantically, such *concatenated actions* can be defined as

$$s[\![A(x) \circ B(y)]\!]t \stackrel{\Delta}{=} \exists u : (s[\![A(x)]\!]u \wedge u[\![B(y)]\!]t) ,$$

where '$\circ$' is the concatenation operator. The effect of such an action is executing $A(x)$ and $B(y)$ sequentially, but only in situations where $B(y)$ is enabled after executing $A(x)$.

Similarly to disjunctive actions, concatenated actions also weaken the abstractions provided by the predecessor layers, and complicate (or prevent) composition with other branches of refinement.

Two special cases of action concatenation will be used in this book. These and the associated effects on preservation of logical properties will be discussed below.

### Simple Concatenation

Concatenation $A(x) \circ B(y)$ seems especially natural in situations where $B(y)$ is always enabled after executing $A(x)$, i.e., when

$$\Box[A(x) \Rightarrow Enabled' B(y)] \tag{6.15}$$

holds in the imported layer in question.[8] Under this condition we will use the special notation

$$A(x) ; B(y)$$

for concatenation. In terms of the action language, the guard of B can then be totally omitted from the resulting action.

### Combined Actions

When the participants in the two instances $A(x)$ and $B(y)$ are different, and the global variables used in them are also different, it would seem natural to 'synchronize' them by combining their guards and their bodies. Although similar to action synchronization in terms of the action language, this is not real synchronization, since the implicit stuttering assignments in the actions would make their logical conjunction identically false, in general.

If the guard of B is denoted by $g_B$, this construction corresponds to the simple concatenation

$$(g_B(y) \wedge A(x)) ; B(y) ,$$

with condition (6.15) trivially satisfied. A special notation

$$A(x) \& B(y)$$

is introduced for this construction, and the resulting action is called a *combined action*. The use of this construction will be restricted to the symmetric situations described above, and $A(x) \& B(y)$ is then identical to $B(y) \& A(x)$.

### Effects on Preservation of Properties

Concatenation of actions removes the intermediate states between their execution. As a consequence, safety properties are then also violated, in general, but only in a restricted manner. All state invariants, for instance, are preserved.

---

[8]If $y$ contains non-participant parameters, their values are assumed to be evaluated *before* executing $A(x)$, not after it.

As discussed in Chap. 2, state variables are divided into essential variables and auxiliary variables, of which the latter correspond to hidden or quantified state variables in TLA. Although this distinction is not indicated in the action language, we say that a safety property is *essential* if it involves only variables that are considered essential.

If at most one of $A(x)$ and $B(y)$ modifies essential state variables, then all essential safety properties are preserved by the introduction of their concatenation. When action concatenation is utilized, one therefore has to check that this condition is satisfied.

As for liveness properties, two things have to be noticed. Firstly, removing intermediate states may remove states in which some fair actions would be enabled. Therefore, preservation of such fairness properties has to be checked.

Secondly, if there are fairness requirements on the actions that are concatenated, then it may be impossible to preserve the associated liveness properties as such, since concatenated actions are not refinements of their components. It has to be noted, however, that the fairness properties in question may involve overspecification, in which case their weakening need not be harmful. In considering liveness properties it may therefore be reasonable to consider that an execution of a concatenated action is not a single step in a behavior but a sequence of individual steps. If the liveness properties of the imported layer are satisfied by such modified behaviors, then it is in most cases reasonable to consider that the intended liveness properties are satisfied.

## Review Questions

QUESTION 6.4.1 How can guards be simplified?

QUESTION 6.4.2 How can variables be effectively removed in superposition?

QUESTION 6.4.3 What is meant by ghost variables, and what is their role in specifications?

QUESTION 6.4.4 What is the problem in refining the atomicity of actions in superposition?

QUESTION 6.4.5 Why is a combined action not equivalent to logical conjunction?

QUESTION 6.4.6 What are the precautions in using concatenated actions?

## Exercises

EXERCISE 6.4.1 Elaborate on the difference between the stuttering closure (defined in Sect. 3.3.6, p. 72) and the stuttering relaxation of actions (defined in Sect. 6.4.4, p. 187).

EXERCISE 6.4.2 How could a concatenated action be constructed from its components in the action language in the general case?

EXERCISE 6.4.3 Give an example of a safety property that is violated by combining two actions.

EXERCISE 6.4.4 Give a simple example where an action with a fairness requirement is replaced by a concatenated action, and elaborate on the non-preservation/preservation of the associated liveness properties.

## 6.5 Example: Pocket Calculator

Finally, the use of superposition and composition will be illustrated by two examples of developing layered specifications. The first example is a simplified stack-based pocket calculator. Its purpose is to demonstrate how different aspects of a specification can be addressed in independent branches of refinement in an aspect-oriented manner and then composed.

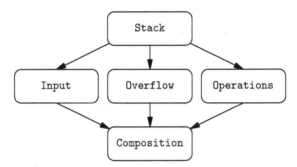

**Fig. 6.7.** Layered structure of a pocket-calculator specification

### 6.5.1 Overall Plan

The overall plan of the specification is illustrated in Fig. 6.7. The initial layer, Stack, specifies the common framework – an operand stack – for the different aspects, which deal with entering of numbers, implementing the operations, and handling of overflow, respectively. The final specification is obtained by composing the layers in which these three aspects are addressed separately.

The development follows the idea of bottom-up development in the sense that the initial layer gives no formal requirements for the total system.

## 6.5.2 Operand Stack

The first layer, **Stack**, is given as a slight modification of the initial layer in Sect. 6.1.5 (p. 166). The operand stack s is specified as a list of real numbers, initialized as an empty list $\langle \rangle$,

$$s : \mathbf{list}\ \mathbb{R}\ (\langle \rangle)\ .$$

Using the type $\mathbb{R}$ means only that the values in the stack are real numbers, not that arbitrary real numbers should be representable in it. As for standard functions on lists, we now assume that first(s) gives either the first element of list s or 0, depending on whether s is nonempty or not, and that rest(s) gives either the rest of s as a list, or an empty list if s has less than two elements.

Push and pop actions for the stack can now be given as

$$\text{Push}(x : \mathbb{R}) : \mathbf{T}$$
$$\rightarrow\ s' = \langle x \rangle \circ s\ ,$$

$$\text{Pop}(x : \mathbb{R}) : x = \text{first}(s)$$
$$\rightarrow\ s' = \text{rest}(s)\ .$$

Since arithmetic operations will also modify the stack, they have also to be introduced in some form at this level. We give them as generic monadic and dyadic operations for the topmost value(s) in the stack as follows:

$$\text{Monadic}(x, z : \mathbb{R}) : x = \text{first}(s)$$
$$\rightarrow\ s' = \langle \text{round}(z) \rangle \circ \text{rest}(s)\ ,$$

$$\text{Dyadic}(x, y, z : \mathbb{R}) : x = \text{first}(s)$$
$$\wedge\ y = \text{first}(\text{rest}(s))$$
$$\rightarrow\ s' = \langle \text{round}(z) \rangle \circ \text{rest}(\text{rest}(s))\ .$$

Operands (x and y) and the result (z) are given here as parameters, which makes it easier to access them in later refinements. The value of the result (z) is left open at this stage, but its rounded value, assumed to be obtained by function round(z), is stored in the stack. Overflow situations will be addressed separately below.

## 6.5.3 Entering Numbers

One aspect that can be addressed independently of other aspects is how numbers are keyed in. Modifying again the example in Sect. 6.1.5 (p. 166), we introduce layer **Input**, which imports **Stack** and has a new variable temp,

$$\text{temp} : \mathbb{N}\ (0)\ ,$$

and new actions

$$\text{Clear} : \text{Stack.Stutter}$$
$$\rightarrow \text{temp}' = 0 \ ,$$

$$\text{Digit}(d : \mathbb{N}) : \text{Stack.Stutter}$$
$$\wedge \, 0 \le d \le 9$$
$$\wedge \, \text{temp} < 10^{N-1}$$
$$\rightarrow \text{temp}' = 10 \times \text{temp} + d \ ,$$

$$\text{Cancel} : \text{Stack.Stutter}$$
$$\rightarrow \text{temp}' = (\text{temp} - \text{temp} \ \mathbf{mod} \ 10)/10 \ .$$

Of these, action **Clear** clears temp, **Digit** models entering a number of at most $N$ digits to temp, and **Cancel** cancels the last digit entered. For simplicity, we allow entering of natural numbers only, and omit specifying the display of numbers.

The number entered into temp can now be pushed to the stack by a refinement of action **Push**,

$$\text{Enter} : \text{Stack.Push}(\text{temp}) \ .$$

In addition, two other refinements of **Push** are included, one that pushes another copy of the top element to the stack, and the other that can be used for further refinements, if found necessary in later design steps:

$$\text{Push\_top} : \text{Stack.Push}(\text{first}(s)) \ ,$$

$$\text{Push}(x : \mathbb{R}) : \text{Stack.Push}(x) \ .$$

Default refinements are assumed for actions **Pop**, **Monadic**, and **Dyadic**.

### 6.5.4 Operations

In layer **Operations**, arithmetic operations are defined as refinements of actions **Monadic** and **Dyadic**.

As the only monadic operation we take **Neg**, which negates a number:[9]

$$\text{Neg}(x : \mathbb{R}) : \text{Stack.Monadic}(x, -x) \ .$$

As dyadic operations we take the four usual arithmetic operations:

$$\text{Plus}(x, y : \mathbb{R}) : \text{Stack.Dyadic}(x, y, x + y) \ ,$$

---

[9]Notice that the values of parameters $x$ and $y$ in these actions have been uniquely determined already in layer **Stack**. Here these parameters are reintroduced only for the purpose of defining how the result values depend on them.

$$\text{Minus}(x, y : \mathbb{R}) : \text{Stack.Dyadic}(x, y, x - y) \,,$$

$$\text{Times}(x, y : \mathbb{R}) : \text{Stack.Dyadic}(x, y, x \times y) \,,$$

$$\text{Divide}(x, y : \mathbb{R}) : \text{Stack.Dyadic}(x, y, x/y) \,.$$

When these are given as the only refinements of Monadic and Dyadic, no other operations can be introduced for the stack in later design steps.

Other actions of layer Stack are taken into Operations as their default refinements.

### 6.5.5 Overflow

To record overflow situations in layer Overflow, two exclusive states are introduced,

**state** $\text{Normal}^*, \text{Ofl}$ .

Checking of overflow and prevention of further calculations when an overflow has occurred can then be included in actions Monadic and Dyadic by refining them into

$$\text{Monadic}(x, z : \mathbb{R}) : \text{Stack.Monadic}(x, z)$$
$$\wedge \, \text{Normal}$$
$$\rightarrow \text{ if } |z| > \text{Max then Ofl}' \text{ else Normal}' \,,$$

$$\text{Dyadic}(x, y, z : \mathbb{R}) : \text{Stack.Dyadic}(x, y, z)$$
$$\wedge \, \text{Normal}$$
$$\rightarrow \text{ if } |z| > \text{Max then Ofl}' \text{ else Normal}' \,,$$

where Max is the limit that numbers are assumed not to exceed without causing overflow.

A refinement of action Pop can now reset the overflow indication, and remove the overflow value from the top of the stack:

$$\text{Reset} : \text{Stack.Pop}(\text{first}(s))$$
$$\wedge \, \text{Ofl}$$
$$\rightarrow \text{Normal}' \,.$$

Another refinement will keep Pop available for other purposes, including later refinements of it,

$$\text{Pop}(x : \mathbb{R}) : \text{Stack.Pop}(x)$$
$$\wedge \, \text{Normal} \,,$$

and a refinement of Push makes sure that overflow values are not pushed deeper into the stack,

$$\text{Push}(x : \mathbb{R}) : \text{Stack.Push}(x)$$
$$\wedge \, \text{Normal} \,.$$

### 6.5.6 Composition

In layer Composition the three independent refinements are brought together. In this case we can use a simple composition, where no new variables or initial conditions are introduced, and all possible action synchronizations are included without any further refinements. (The unification condition obviously requires the parameters to be the same in the action instances that are synchronized.)

The ancestor histories of the resulting actions are shown in Fig. 6.8. For simplicity some related actions have been grouped together, and those ancestors have been omitted that are either stuttering actions or default refinements of their ancestors. The names for actions in Composition have been chosen from suitable ancestors.

Notice that the new actions introduced in layer Input cannot be synchronized with any non-stuttering actions in the other layers. Action Push has been given three refinements in Input and one in Overflow. In the composition this leads to three pairwise combinations, where the overflow checking, which was given in Overflow.Push, is added to each of the refinements given in Input.

Synchronizing the refinements of Monadic and Dyadic leads to the arithmetic operations specified in Operations, combined with the overflow checking added to them in Overflow.

### 6.5.7 Discussion

The purpose of this example was to illustrate how different aspects of a specification can be addressed independently in different paths of refinement. In this case we started from a crude initial model, where only the very basic decisions were made, and other design decisions were then superposed on this initial model.

Each layer in the resulting specification is a correct but restricted view of behaviors in the final specification. Therefore, properties that relate only to a given aspect can be inspected from a layer where other aspects are not visible and therefore do not confuse this inspection. Obviously, when the interplay of different aspects is concerned, one has to look at the layer where these aspects are brought together.

The example also illustrates how the rigor of the specification process may prevent subsequent addition of new features without revising some earlier layers of specification. For instance, if a need for additional arithmetic operations arises in later steps, this would require revision of layer Operations. On the other hand, the purpose of leaving actions Push and Pop also as such in layer Composition is to allow later refinements where the stack may communicate with variables that have not yet been included in the specification.

No fairness requirements were relevant for this specification. Therefore, preservation of liveness properties was not an issue, and each step was trivially guaranteed to produce a refinement of the preceding layers.

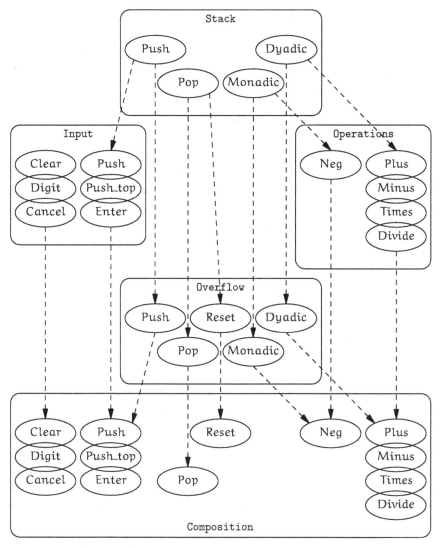

**Fig. 6.8.** Ancestor relations for pocket-calculator actions

**Exercises**

EXERCISE 6.5.1 Write out the final actions in the pocket-calculator example in their complete forms, and simplify them, if possible.

EXERCISE 6.5.2 Augment the pocket-calculator specification with read and write operations for memory cells.

EXERCISE 6.5.3 Discuss augmenting the pocket-calculator specification with a display. At which place would you put this in the layered structure?

EXERCISE 6.5.4 An unbounded stack was assumed in the pocket-calculator specification. Consider different ways to modify it to use a bounded stack.

## 6.6 Example: Resource Allocation

The second example of this chapter concerns non-preemptive resource allocation for distributed processes in a situation where each resource $r \in R$ can be assigned to at most one process $p \in P$ at a time. In addition to illustrating a somewhat different use of superposition-based design techniques than the pocket-calculator example above, it also provides an example of using some of the techniques introduced in Sect. 6.4 (p. 185) for overcoming the limitations of pure superposition.

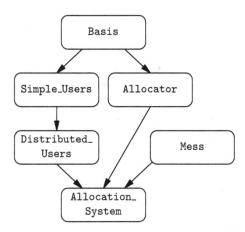

**Fig. 6.9.** Layers in a specification of resource allocation

### 6.6.1 Overall Plan

The overall plan for this specification is illustrated in Fig. 6.9. We start with layer Basis, where classes P and R are introduced for the processes and the resources, respectively, and which specifies the basic requirement that each resource $r \in R$ can be used by at most one process $p \in P$ at any time. Since formulating this leads to quantification over all processes $p \in P$ in an action guard, this high-level specification does not describe a solution that would be directly implementable for distributed processes.

The two aspects that are then elaborated in independent branches of refinement correspond to the views of the distributed processes p ∈ P (layers `Simple_Users` and `Distributed_Users`) and of the allocator (layer `Allocator`), respectively. In the former, the initial layer `Basis` is refined so that the requirement is also included that a process will eventually obtain a requested resource, unless it cancels the request before this has happened. The allocator's view, on the other hand, expresses fair treatment of allocation requests.

An auxiliary, independent layer `Mess` models process communication by asynchronous messages, to be used in composing the two aspects into layer `Allocation_System`. Finally, the actions of the composed specification will be simplified in order to show their distributed implementability.

The development follows the idea of top-down development in the sense that the root layer `Basis` already specifies the most crucial overall requirement, which is then made implementable in a distributed fashion by the subsequent steps. The requirement for fair access to resources is, however, not yet introduced in the initial layer.

The use of an independent layer `Mess` for process communication adds the use of an independent specification component to this development process.

### 6.6.2 Basis

In the initial layer `Basis`, let P and R stand for the classes of user processes p ∈ P and resources r ∈ R, respectively. For simplicity we assume each of these to have a unique identification attribute p.id (r.id), which is a natural number,

$$\textbf{class } P = \{\textbf{const } id : \mathbb{N}\}, \quad \forall p, q \in P : (p \neq q \Rightarrow p.id \neq q.id),$$
$$\textbf{class } R = \{\textbf{const } id : \mathbb{N}\}, \quad \forall r, s \in R : (r \neq s \Rightarrow r.id \neq s.id).$$

Relation $\mathsf{Using}$ is introduced at this level for indicating that a user process is currently using a resource,

$$\textbf{relation } (0..1) \cdot \mathsf{Using} \cdot (*) : P \times R\ (\emptyset),$$

and its declaration also expresses the intended property that no resource is used by more than one process at any time.

The actions of this basic layer will just model how processes take resources into use, and how they will release them:

$$\mathsf{Take}(p : P;\ r : R) : \neg \exists q \in P : (q \cdot \mathsf{Using} \cdot r)$$
$$\rightarrow p \cdot \mathsf{Using}' \cdot r,$$

$$\mathsf{Release}(^{\mathrm{WF}}p : P;\ ^{\mathrm{WF}}r : R) : p \cdot \mathsf{Using} \cdot r$$
$$\rightarrow \neg p \cdot \mathsf{Using}' \cdot r.$$

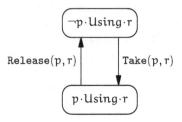

**Fig. 6.10.** State transitions in the basic layer

Obviously, the guard in `Take` ensures the intended safety property for the relation `Using`, and the fairness requirement on `Release` guarantees that each user process will eventually release any process that it is using. Figure 6.10 illustrates the associated transitions for an arbitrary pair $p \in P$, $r \in R$.

### 6.6.3 Simple User Processes

In layer `Simple_Users` we start elaborating the specification from the viewpoint of user processes.

In order to distinguish the state when process $p \in P$ needs a resource $r \in R$, which need not be immediately available, class $P$ is extended with a set-valued attribute $need$ to indicate those resources that are needed by $p$ but not yet obtained by it. Another attribute, $use$, is also added for representing locally that part of relation `Using` that concerns process $p$. This gives us extensions:

$$\textbf{class } P = \{\ldots need, use : \text{set } \mathbb{N} \ (\emptyset)\} \, .$$

The intended invariants for these attributes are that, for each $p \in P$, the values of $p.need$ and $p.use$ are disjoint sets that contain only identification numbers of existing resources, and that variables $p.use$ provide a representation for the relation `Using`:

$$\Box(n \in (p.need \cup p.use) \Rightarrow \exists r \in R : (r.id = n)) \, , \qquad (6.16)$$

$$\Box(p.need \cap p.use = \emptyset) \, , \qquad (6.17)$$

$$\Box(r.id \in p.use \Leftrightarrow p \cdot \text{Using} \cdot r) \, . \qquad (6.18)$$

The actions of layer `Simple_Users` can now be given as

$$\text{Request}(p : P; \ r : R) : \text{Basis.Stutter}$$
$$\wedge \ r.id \notin (p.need \cup p.use)$$
$$\rightarrow \ p.need' = p.need \cup \{r.id\} \, ,$$

$$\text{Take}(p : P; \ r : R) : \text{Basis.Take}(p, r)$$
$$\wedge \ r.id \in p.need$$
$$\rightarrow \ p.need' = p.need \setminus \{r.id\}$$
$$\wedge \ p.use' = p.use \cup \{r.id\} \, ,$$

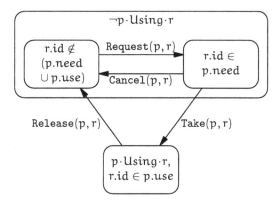

**Fig. 6.11.** A simple view of user processes

$$Cancel(p : P; \ r : R) : Basis.Stutter$$
$$\wedge \ r.id \in p.need$$
$$\rightarrow \ p.need' = p.need \setminus \{r.id\} \,,$$

$$Release(^{WF}p : P; \ ^{WF}r : R) : Basis.Release(p, r)$$
$$\rightarrow \ p.use' = p.use \setminus \{r.id\} \,.$$

As a result, the transitions of Fig. 6.10 have been refined as illustrated in Fig. 6.11.

For these actions it is easy to check that the intended invariants (6.16)–(6.18) are, indeed, satisfied, and that the liveness properties of the basic layer are also preserved.

It would be tempting to add a strong fairness assumption to action Take, to ensure that processes $p \in P$ have fair access to resources $r \in R$, when these eventually become available. The possibility to cancel a need by action Cancel complicates the situation, however, since we do not wish to exclude the possibility that a process always cancels a need for a resource, if this is never obtained soon enough, for instance.

The liveness property that should be satisfied but cannot be properly achieved with fairness requirements on these actions is

$$WF(Take(p, r) \vee Cancel(p, r)) \,. \tag{6.19}$$

Being symmetric with respect to actions Take and Cancel, this would not, however, prevent an implementation where action Take is not implemented at all, and therefore does not properly describe the intended liveness property.

Although proper modeling of the intended liveness property would be possible already at this level (see Exercise 6.6.6), we postpone further discussion of it to the stage where the complete specification is formed.

### 6.6.4 Distributed Users

Layer `Distributed_Users` is a refinement of `Simple_Users`. In it we anticipate a distributed implementation, where communication between processes takes place by asynchronous messages. Therefore, user processes cannot proceed freely after actions `Cancel` and `Release`, as was the case in layer `Simple_Users`. Instead, they have to wait until an anticipated allocator has been able to recognize these transitions.

To model such a refined view, class P is extended with two additional set-valued attributes,

$$\textbf{class } P = \{\ldots cncl, rel : \textbf{set } \mathbb{N}(\emptyset)\}\,,$$

which indicate the resources for which the process is canceling its requests before obtaining them, and those that it is releasing after using them, respectively.

As intended invariants, p.cncl and p.rel are assumed to contain identification numbers of existing resources, and they are assumed to be disjoint from each other and also from p.need and p.use:

$$\Box(n \in (p.cncl \cup p.rel) \Rightarrow \exists r \in R : (r.id = n))\,, \qquad (6.20)$$

$$\Box(p.cncl \cap p.rel = \emptyset)\,, \qquad (6.21)$$

$$\Box((p.cncl \cup p.rel) \cap (p.need \cup p.use) = \emptyset)\,. \qquad (6.22)$$

Figure 6.12 shows the intended refinement of Fig. 6.11. Actions `Cont_1` and `Cont_2` are new actions that have been inserted for the purpose described above. The reason why a canceled request leads to two consecutive stages of waiting is that the anticipated allocator is expected to react separately both to a request and to its cancelation.

Weak fairness on actions `Cont_1` and `Cont_2` is obviously sufficient to ensure that the associated waitings will eventually terminate. In the case when a resource is obtained, it is action `Take` that models the termination of the associated waiting. However, for reasons that were explained above, no fairness assumption on it is directly suitable for modeling its eventual execution.

Actions of this layer can now be given as follows:

$$\text{Request}(p : P;\ r : R) : \text{Simple\_Users.Request}(p, r)$$
$$\wedge\, r.id \notin (p.cncl \cup p.rel)\,,$$

$$\text{Take}(p : P;\ r : R) : \text{Simple\_Users.Take}(p, r)\,,$$

$$\text{Release}(^{WF}p : P;\ ^{WF}r : R) : \text{Simple\_Users.Release}(p, r)$$
$$\rightarrow\ p.rel' = p.rel \cup \{r.id\}\,,$$

$$\text{Cancel}(p : P;\ r : R) : \text{Simple\_Users.Cancel}(p, r)$$
$$\rightarrow\ p.cncl' = p.cncl \cup \{r.id\}\,,$$

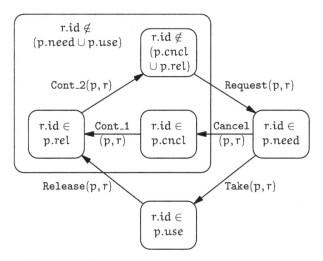

**Fig. 6.12.** Transitions in layer Distributed_Users

$\text{Cont\_1}(^{\text{WF}}p : P; \; ^{\text{WF}}r : R) : \text{Simple\_Users.Stutter}$
$$\wedge \, r.id \in p.cncl$$
$$\rightarrow \; p.cncl' = p.cncl \setminus \{r.id\}$$
$$\wedge \, p.rel' = p.rel \cup \{r.id\} \, ,$$

$\text{Cont\_2}(^{\text{WF}}p : P; \; ^{\text{WF}}r : R) : \text{Simple\_Users.Stutter}$
$$\wedge \, r.id \in p.rel$$
$$\rightarrow \; p.rel' = p.rel \setminus \{r.id\} \, .$$

It is easy to check that the intended invariants that were given above are, indeed, satisfied, and that the fairness properties of the previous layer are also preserved. Fair access to resources $r \in R$ has not yet been modeled, however.

### 6.6.5 Allocator

As the next step we elaborate how the initial layer Basis can be refined from the viewpoint of the allocator process. In layer Allocator we introduce a singleton allocator class A with two set-valued attributes, req, which for each allocation request of resource r by process p will contain a pair (p.id, r.id), and alloc, which will contain similar pairs for all allocations performed:

$$\textbf{class } (1) \, A = \{req, alloc : \textbf{set } \mathbb{N} \times \mathbb{N}(\emptyset)\} \, .$$

The intended invariants for these attributes are that the pairs identify existing processes and resources, the two sets are disjoint, no resource has been allocated to more than one process, and that a process p cannot be using a resource r unless this has been allocated to it:

$$\Box((x, y) \in (a.\mathsf{req} \cup a.\mathsf{alloc}) \Rightarrow \exists p \in P, r \in R : (p.\mathsf{id} = x \wedge r.\mathsf{id} = y)) , \tag{6.23}$$

$$\Box(a.\mathsf{req} \cap a.\mathsf{alloc} = \emptyset) , \tag{6.24}$$

$$\Box((p.\mathsf{id}, r.\mathsf{id}) \in a.\mathsf{alloc} \wedge (q.\mathsf{id}, r.\mathsf{id}) \in a.\mathsf{alloc} \Rightarrow p = q) , \tag{6.25}$$

$$\Box(p \cdot \mathsf{Using} \cdot r \Rightarrow (p.\mathsf{id}, r.\mathsf{id}) \in a.\mathsf{alloc}) . \tag{6.26}$$

Enqueuing and dequeuing of allocation requests and decisions can now be added to the system in terms of the following actions:

$$\mathsf{Enq}(p : P; \; r : R; \; a : A) : \mathsf{Basis.Stutter}$$
$$\wedge (p.\mathsf{id}, r.\mathsf{id}) \notin (a.\mathsf{req} \cup a.\mathsf{alloc})$$
$$\rightarrow a.\mathsf{req}' = a.\mathsf{req} \cup \{(p.\mathsf{id}, r.\mathsf{id})\} ,$$

$$\mathsf{Deq}(p : P; \; r : R; \; a : A) : \mathsf{Basis.Stutter}$$
$$\wedge (p.\mathsf{id}, r.\mathsf{id}) \in a.\mathsf{req}$$
$$\rightarrow a.\mathsf{req}' = a.\mathsf{req} \setminus \{(p.\mathsf{id}, r.\mathsf{id})\} ,$$

$$\mathsf{Alloc}(^{\mathrm{SF}}p : P; \; ^{\mathrm{SF}}r : R; \; a : A) : \mathsf{Basis.Stutter}$$
$$\wedge (p.\mathsf{id}, r.\mathsf{id}) \in a.\mathsf{req}$$
$$\wedge \neg \exists q \in P : (q.\mathsf{id}, r.\mathsf{id}) \in a.\mathsf{alloc}$$
$$\rightarrow a.\mathsf{req}' = a.\mathsf{req} \setminus \{(p.\mathsf{id}, r.\mathsf{id})\}$$
$$\wedge a.\mathsf{alloc}' = a.\mathsf{alloc} \cup \{(p.\mathsf{id}, r.\mathsf{id})\} ,$$

$$\mathsf{Take}(p : P; \; r : R; \; a : A) : \mathsf{Basis.Take}(p, r)$$
$$\wedge (p.\mathsf{id}, r.\mathsf{id}) \in a.\mathsf{alloc} ,$$

$$\mathsf{Release}(^{\mathrm{WF}}p : P; \; ^{\mathrm{WF}}r : R) : \mathsf{Basis.Release}(p, r) ,$$

$$\mathsf{Dealloc}(^{\mathrm{SF}}p : P; \; ^{\mathrm{SF}}r : R; \; a : A) : \mathsf{Basis.Stutter}$$
$$\wedge (p.\mathsf{id}, r.\mathsf{id}) \in a.\mathsf{alloc}$$
$$\wedge \neg p \cdot \mathsf{Using} \cdot r$$
$$\rightarrow a.\mathsf{alloc}' = a.\mathsf{alloc} \setminus \{(p.\mathsf{id}, r.\mathsf{id})\} .$$

The fairness properties of layer Basis are obviously preserved, and the fairness requirements on actions Alloc and Dealloc ensure fulfilling of allocation requests in a fair manner. The refinement of action Take also guarantees that only allocated resources are taken into use by the processes.

Figure 6.13 now illustrates how the transitions in Fig. 6.10 (p. 198) have been refined in this layer. Notice the possibility to deallocate a resource without actions Take and Release taking place, which is needed (only) for the

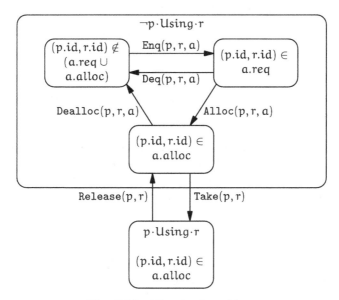

**Fig. 6.13.** Allocator transitions

situation where the request has been canceled. At this level it is also possible for a process to retake a resource if it has not yet been deallocated from it. This possibility will, however, be removed in the composed system.

### 6.6.6 Messages

In a distributed situation, communication between remote user processes and an allocator takes place by messages. Facilities for this are introduced here in a separate layer Mess.

Messages will be represented as objects of a non-empty class $M$, where the local state indicates whether the message is an 'unused frame for a message' or 'in use' and, if it is in use, then it also contains message type and contents:

$$\text{class } M = \{\text{state Unused}^*, \text{In\_use};$$
$$\textbf{where } \text{In\_use} = \{\text{type}, \text{cont} : U\}\}\,.$$

Two actions are given at this level to model sending and receiving of a message with given type and contents:

$$\text{Send}(m : M; \ t, c : U) : m.\text{Unused}$$
$$\rightarrow m.\text{In\_use}'$$
$$\wedge m.\text{type}' = t$$
$$\wedge m.\text{cont}' = c\,,$$

$$\text{Rec}(^{WF}m : M; \; t, c : U) : m.\text{In\_use}$$
$$\wedge \; m.\text{type} = t$$
$$\wedge \; m.\text{cont} = c$$
$$\rightarrow \; m.\text{Unused}' \, .$$

Weak fairness in Rec expresses the reliability requirement that each message that has been sent will also eventually be received. Messages that have been sent may, however, be received in any order.

For simplicity we will assume in the following that class M is infinite. This means that there is no bound for the number of messages that have been sent but not yet received. The minimum size of M that is sufficient for this example is considered in Exercise 6.6.3.

### 6.6.7 Composed System

The idea of the final specification Allocation_System is to compose layers Distributed_Users, Allocator, and Mess so that asynchronous messages are used for the communication between user processes $p \in P$ and the allocator $a \in A$. Only two message types will be used: type req will indicate a message from user processes to the allocator, and type ack will indicate a response message from the allocator. The message contents will always be a pair $(p.\text{id}, r.\text{id})$.

This gives us the following intended message invariants for all $m \in M$:

$$\Box(m.\text{In\_use} \Rightarrow m.\text{type} = \text{req} \vee m.\text{type} = \text{ack}) \, , \tag{6.27}$$

$$\Box(m.\text{In\_use} \Rightarrow \exists p \in P, r \in R : m.\text{cont} = (p.\text{id}, r.\text{id})) \, . \tag{6.28}$$

The intended use of messages is the following:

- Each of actions Request, Cancel, and Release sends a req message to the allocator, which will then receive them in actions Enq, Deq, and Dealloc.
- Actions Alloc and Dealloc send an ack message to a user process, and action Deq sends two such messages. These messages will be received in actions Take, Cont_1, and Cont_2.[10]

Notice that, since messages may be received in an arbitrary order, the req message received in action Enq may also be one that was sent in action Cancel, in which case the one sent in Request has not yet been received. Similarly, the ack message received in action Cont_1 may have been sent either by action Deq or by action Alloc. This is the reason why a single ack message is not sufficient when action Deq responds to a canceling request.

---

[10]Each execution of action Take(p, r) then requires a preceding execution of Alloc(p, r, a), which removes the possibility for repeating Take(p, r) without an intervening execution of Dealloc(p, r, a), which was possible in layer Allocator.

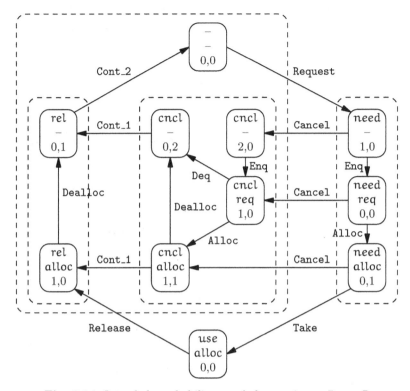

**Fig. 6.14.** Intended reachability graph for a pair $p \in P$, $r \in R$

The intended invariants expressing the states that are concurrently possible for a user process and the allocator, as well as for the messages that have been sent but not yet received, can be formulated as the reachability graph given in Fig. 6.14 for an arbitrary pair $p \in P$, $r \in R$. The first line in each node indicates whether $r.id$ is in $p.need$, $p.use$, $p.cncl$, $p.rel$, or in none of them; the second line indicates whether $(p.id, r.id)$ is in $a.req$, $a.alloc$, or in none of these; the third line indicates the numbers of non-received $req$ and $ack$ messages with contents $(p.id, r.id)$. Obviously, the graph, which has been drawn in the shape of Fig. 6.12 (p. 201), is a refinement of those given in Figs. 6.12 and 6.13.

The actions of the composed system can now be given as follows:

$$\text{Request}(p : P; \ r : R; \ m : M) : \text{Distributed\_Users.Request}(p, r)$$
$$\wedge \text{Mess.Send}(m, req, (p.id, r.id))$$
$$\wedge \text{Allocator.Stutter},$$

$\text{Enq}(p : P; r : R; a : A; {}^{WF}m : M) : \text{Distributed\_Users.Stutter}$
$\wedge \text{Mess.Rec}(m, req, (p.id, r.id))$
$\wedge \text{Allocator.Enq}(p, r, a)$ ,

$\text{Deq}(p : P; r : R; a : A; {}^{WF}m_1, m_2 : M) : \text{Distributed\_Users.Stutter}$
$\wedge (\text{Mess.Rec}(m_1, req, (p.id, r.id));$
$\text{Mess.Send}(m_1, ack, (p.id, r.id)))$
$\& \text{Mess.Send}(m_2, ack, (p.id, r.id))$
$\wedge \text{Allocator.Deq}(p, r, a)$ ,

$\text{Alloc}({}^{SF}p : P; {}^{SF}r : R; a : A; m : M) : \text{Distributed\_Users.Stutter}$
$\wedge \text{Mess.Send}(m, ack, (p.id, r.id))$
$\wedge \text{Allocator.Alloc}(p, r, a)$ ,

$\text{Take}(p : P; r : R; a : A; {}^{WF}m : M) : \text{Distributed\_Users.Take}(p, r)$
$\wedge \text{Mess.Rec}(m, ack, (p.id, r.id))$
$\wedge \text{Allocator.Take}(p, r, a)$ ,

$\text{Release}({}^{WF}p : P; {}^{WF}r : R; m : M) : \text{Distributed\_Users.Release}(p, r)$
$\wedge \text{Mess.Send}(m, req, (p.id, r.id))$
$\wedge \text{Allocator.Release}(p, r)$ ,

$\text{Dealloc}(p : P; r : R; a : A; {}^{WF}m : M) : \text{Distributed\_Users.Stutter}$
$\wedge \text{Mess.Rec}(m, req, (p.id, r.id));$
$\text{Mess.Send}(m, ack, (p.id, r.id))$
$\wedge \text{Allocator.Dealloc}(p, r, a)$ ,

$\text{Cancel}(p : P; r : R; m : M) : \text{Distributed\_Users.Cancel}(p, r)$
$\wedge \text{Mess.Send}(m, req, (p.id, r.id))$
$\wedge \text{Allocator.Stutter}$ ,

$\text{Cont\_1}(p : P; r : R; {}^{WF}m : M) : \text{Distributed\_Users.Cont\_1}(p, r)$
$\wedge \text{Mess.Rec}(m, ack, (p.id, r.id))$
$\wedge \text{Allocator.Stutter}$ ,

$\text{Cont\_2}(p : P; r : R; {}^{WF}m : M) : \text{Distributed\_Users.Cont\_2}(p, r)$
$\wedge \text{Mess.Rec}(m, ack, (p.id, r.id))$
$\wedge \text{Allocator.Stutter}$ .

Actions of layer Mess have been concatenated (see Sect. 6.4.1, p. 185) here in two cases (actions Deq and Dealloc). The assumption of an infinite number of message objects makes it easy to check that condition (6.15) on p. 188 for simple concatenation is satisfied in these cases. Since message objects have an auxiliary role only, no essential safety properties are violated by having the intermediate states removed in these cases. It is easy to see that fairness requirements with respect to any other actions are not violated by this, either (see discussion of preservation of properties in concatenation, p. 188).

Action concatenation has, however, the effect that the fairness requirement that was given in layer Mess for action Mess.Rec is no longer satisfied. This requirement can, however, be understood as overspecification, the intended liveness property being only that each message that has been sent will eventually be received. If the executions of these concatenated actions are understood as sequences of steps, instead of single steps (see discussion of preservation of properties in concatenation, p. 188), then the associated fairness properties would be preserved. This can be taken as justification for concluding that the intended liveness properties are still satisfied. For further consideration of this issue, see Exercise 6.6.4.

The satisfaction of the intended safety properties (6.27) and (6.28) can be immediately checked. Those given in terms of the reachability graph of Fig. 6.14 can also be easily shown by checking that the graph describes correctly the possible effects of all actions.

As for the crucial liveness property (6.19) on p. 199, it would now be satisfied even if action Cancel were removed from the system, which prevents the trivial implementation where action Take is omitted. The satisfaction of (6.19) can be checked by the following lines of reasoning, based on the fairness assumptions and on the safety properties expressed in the reachability graph of Fig. 6.14:

- If action Request$(p, r, m)$ has been executed and $r.id \in p.need$ stays persistently true (i.e., the need is not canceled), weak fairness for Enq guarantees that the request $(p.id, r.id)$ will eventually enter $a.req$ and stay there until either Cancel or Alloc is executed for it.
- If the resource has been allocated to some other process, i.e., action Alloc is not enabled for $p$ and $r$, fairness on actions Deq, Take, Release, Dealloc, Cont_1, and Cont_2 guarantees that $\neg \exists q \in P : (q.id, r.id) \in a.alloc$ will be repeatedly true, enabling action Alloc for $p$ and $r$ (unless action Cancel is executed for $p$ and $r$).
- Strong fairness on Alloc with respect to the pair $(p, r)$ will then ensure its eventual execution for this pair (unless action Cancel is executed for it before this).
- Action Take will then stay enabled for $p$ and $r$ until either it or Cancel is executed for the pair. Weak fairness on Take therefore guarantees that one of these actions is eventually executed.

### 6.6.8 Simplification for Distributed Implementation

Although the composed system satisfies all the required logical properties, its distributed implementability, which was the whole purpose of the specification, is not yet obvious, since processes $p \in P$, resources $r \in R$, and the allocator $a \in A$ all appear as participants in many of the actions. Therefore, the specification needs to be simplified so that a process $p$ and the allocator $a$ are not both involved in any action, and that resources $r$ are also removed from being participants.

As an example, consider action **Take** of the final specification. It can be mechanically written out from the implied actions as follows:

$$\textsf{Take}(p : P;\ r : R;\ a : A;\ {}^{WF}m : M) : \neg\exists q \in P : (q \cdot Using \cdot r)$$
$$\wedge\ r.id \in p.need$$
$$\wedge\ m.In\_use$$
$$\wedge\ m.type = ack$$
$$\wedge\ m.cont = (p.id, r.id)$$
$$\wedge\ (p.id, r.id) \in a.alloc$$
$$\rightarrow\ p \cdot Using' \cdot r$$
$$\wedge\ p.need' = p.need \setminus \{r.id\}$$
$$\wedge\ p.use' = p.use \cup \{r.id\}$$
$$\wedge\ m.Unused' .$$

To simplify this, we notice the following:

- On account of (6.18) on p. 198, relation $Using$ has been turned into a ghost variable and can be removed (see Sect. 6.4.2, p. 186). When its occurrences in guards are replaced by the use of variables $p.use$, $p \in P$, its modifications in bodies can also therefore be omitted. In particular, the first conjunct in the above guard is then replaced by $\neg\exists q :\in P : r.id \in p.use$, and assignment $p \cdot Using' \cdot r$ is removed.
- By invariants (6.17) and (6.18) on p. 198, and (6.25) and (6.26) on p. 202, implication

$$r.id \in p.need \wedge (p.id, r.id) \in a.alloc \Rightarrow \neg\exists q \in P : r.id \in q.use$$

holds in all reachable states, which makes the first conjunct in the guard redundant (see Sect. 6.4.1, p. 185).
- On account of the safety properties expressed in the graph of Fig. 6.14, implication

$$r.id \in p.need \wedge m.In\_use \wedge m.type = ack \Rightarrow (p.id, r.id) \in a.alloc$$

holds in all reachable states, which also makes conjunct $(p.id, r.id) \in a.alloc$ in the guard redundant.

- Since $a$ is no longer needed in the action, it can be omitted as a participant (see Sect. 6.4.1, p. 185). The required existence of an object $a \in A$ cannot obviously be violated in this case.
- Resource $r$ can be omitted as a participant by taking $r.id$ as a new parameter $x$ (see Sect. 6.4.1, p. 185). The required existence of a resource $r \in R$ with $r.id = x$ is guaranteed by $x \in p.need$ and invariant (6.16) on p. 198.

This leads to a simplified action

$$
\begin{aligned}
\texttt{Take}(p : P;\ {}^{WF}m : M;\ x : \mathbb{N}) :\ & m.\text{In\_use} \\
& \wedge\ m.\text{type} = ack \\
& \wedge\ m.\text{cont} = (p.id, x) \\
& \wedge\ x \in p.need \\
& \rightarrow\ p.need' = p.need \setminus \{x\} \\
& \wedge\ p.use' = p.use \cup \{x\} \\
& \wedge\ m.\text{Unused}',
\end{aligned}
$$

which can be executed by process $p$ alone, when it receives message $m$ in a state where $x \in p.need$.

Similar simplification gives us the following further actions to be executed by the processes $p \in P$:

$$
\begin{aligned}
\texttt{Request}(p : P;\ m : M;\ x : \mathbb{N}) :\ & \exists r \in R : (r.id = x) \\
& \wedge\ x \notin (p.need \cup p.use \cup p.cncl \cup p.rel) \\
& \wedge\ m.\text{Unused} \\
& \rightarrow\ p.need' = p.need \cup \{x\} \\
& \wedge\ m.\text{In\_use}' \\
& \wedge\ m.\text{type}' = req \\
& \wedge\ m.\text{cont}' = (p.id, x),
\end{aligned}
$$

$$
\begin{aligned}
\texttt{Release}({}^{WF}p : P;\ m : M;\ {}^{WF}x : \mathbb{N}) :\ & x \in p.use \\
& \wedge\ m.\text{Unused} \\
& \rightarrow\ p.use' = p.use \setminus \{x\} \\
& \wedge\ p.rel' = p.rel \cup \{x\} \\
& \wedge\ m.\text{In\_use}' \\
& \wedge\ m.\text{type}' = req \\
& \wedge\ m.\text{cont}' = (p.id, x),
\end{aligned}
$$

$$
\begin{aligned}
\text{Cancel}(p : P;\ m : M;\ x : \mathbb{N}) : \ &x \in p.\text{need} \\
&\wedge\ m.\text{Unused} \\
\rightarrow\ &p.\text{need}' = p.\text{need} \setminus \{x\} \\
\wedge\ &p.\text{cncl}' = p.\text{cncl} \cup \{x\} \\
\wedge\ &m.\text{In\_use}' \\
\wedge\ &m.\text{type}' = \text{req} \\
\wedge\ &m.\text{cont}' = (p.\text{id}, x)\ ,
\end{aligned}
$$

$$
\begin{aligned}
\text{Cont\_1}(p : P;\ {}^{\text{WF}}m : M;\ x : \mathbb{N}) : \ &m.\text{In\_use} \\
&\wedge\ m.\text{type} = \text{ack} \\
&\wedge\ m.\text{cont} = (p.\text{id}, x) \\
&\wedge\ x \in p.\text{cncl} \\
\rightarrow\ &p.\text{cncl}' = p.\text{cncl} \setminus \{x\} \\
\wedge\ &p.\text{rel}' = p.\text{rel} \cup \{x\} \\
\wedge\ &m.\text{Unused}'\ ,
\end{aligned}
$$

$$
\begin{aligned}
\text{Cont\_2}(p : P;\ {}^{\text{WF}}m : M;\ x : \mathbb{N}) : \ &m.\text{In\_use} \\
&\wedge\ m.\text{type} = \text{ack} \\
&\wedge\ m.\text{cont} = (p.\text{id}, x) \\
&\wedge\ x \in p.\text{rel} \\
\rightarrow\ &p.\text{rel}' = p.\text{rel} \setminus \{x\} \\
\wedge\ &m.\text{Unused}'\ ,
\end{aligned}
$$

and the following actions to be executed by the allocator:

$$
\begin{aligned}
\text{Enq}(a : A;\ {}^{\text{WF}}m : M) : \ &m.\text{In\_use} \\
&\wedge\ m.\text{type} = \text{req} \\
&\wedge\ m.\text{cont} \notin (a.\text{req} \cup a.\text{alloc}) \\
\rightarrow\ &a.\text{req}' = a.\text{req} \cup \{m.\text{cont}\} \\
\wedge\ &m.\text{Unused}'\ ,
\end{aligned}
$$

$$
\begin{aligned}
\text{Deq}(a : A;\ {}^{\text{WF}}m_1, m_2 : M) : \ &m_1.\text{In\_use} \\
&\wedge\ m_1.\text{type} = \text{req} \\
&\wedge\ m_1.\text{cont} \in a.\text{req} \\
&\wedge\ m_2.\text{Unused}
\end{aligned}
$$

$$\rightarrow a.req' = a.req \setminus \{m_1.cont\}$$
$$\wedge\, m_1.type' = ack$$
$$\wedge\, m_2.In\_use'$$
$$\wedge\, m_2.type' = ack$$
$$\wedge\, m_2.cont' = m_1.cont\,,$$

$\texttt{Alloc}(a : A;\ m : M;\ {}^{SF}x, {}^{SF}y : \mathbb{N}) : (x, y) \in a.req$
$$\wedge\, \neg\exists z \in \mathbb{N} : (z, y) \in a.alloc$$
$$\wedge\, m.Unused$$
$$\rightarrow a.req' = a.req \setminus \{(x, y)\}$$
$$\wedge\, a.alloc' = a.alloc \cup \{(x, y)\}$$
$$\wedge\, m.In\_use'$$
$$\wedge\, m.type' = ack$$
$$\wedge\, m.cont' = (x, y)\,,$$

$\texttt{Dealloc}(a : A;\ {}^{WF}m : M) : m.In\_use$
$$\wedge\, m.type = req$$
$$\wedge\, m.cont \in a.alloc$$
$$\rightarrow a.alloc' = a.alloc \setminus \{m.cont\}$$
$$\wedge\, m.type' = ack\,.$$

As a result, the specification has been shown to be implementable in a distributed fashion.

### 6.6.9 Discussion

Pure bottom-up development is usually applied in this kind of a situation. The behaviors of the distributed processes and the allocator would then be specified independently, including their use of the available communication mechanisms. This would mean that the crucial properties of the total system would emerge only when the components are composed. Verifying that the requirements are, indeed, satisfied by the resulting system would then be done in the end, and the reachability graph of Fig. 6.14 (p. 205) would play an essential role in this.

In contrast, we have by purpose adopted here the design-oriented approach, where the logical correctness of the composed system is ensured by its construction. In particular, the satisfaction of the required safety properties is here straightforward, but, on the other hand, the distributed implementability of the resulting actions is not. It can therefore be said that we have traded the verification effort of a verification-oriented approach into the effort of simplifying the resulting actions into a form that can be implemented in a distributed fashion.

For the role of the reachability graph, this change of viewpoint means that this graph is not considered as something to be constructed from the final system, but as the intended safety properties in its construction.

### Exercises

EXERCISE 6.6.1 Check that the intended safety properties are, indeed, satisfied in the specification layers of this section.

EXERCISE 6.6.2 Modify layer Mess (Sect. 6.6.6, p. 203) so that transmission delays are also modeled. Would this affect the specification of distributed resource allocation in any way?

EXERCISE 6.6.3 If the size of the message class M in layer Mess (Sect. 6.6.6, p. 203) is 2, is it always possible for the processes to get messages sent? Modify the solution so that even size 1 is sufficient. How would this affect the reachability graph of Fig. 6.14 (p. 205)?

EXERCISE 6.6.4 Modify layer Mess (Sect. 6.6.6, p. 203) so that the intended liveness property 'every message that has been sent will eventually be received' can be formulated in TLA so that it will be also preserved when combined actions are introduced in the composed system. Hint: introduce auxiliary variables that help in expressing this property.

EXERCISE 6.6.5 Check that the actions of the final specification layer have been simplified correctly in Sect. 6.6.8 (p. 208).

EXERCISE 6.6.6 Give a slight refinement of layer Simple_Users (Sect. 6.6.3, p. 198), where the intended liveness property is properly modeled. Hint: split the state where r.id ∈ p.need into two consecutive substates so that action Cancel is enabled only in the first. How would this affect synchronized actions in the final composition?

## Bibliographic Notes

An early use of the superposition technique, along with the term 'superimpose', can be found in the termination-detection algorithm of Dijkstra and Scholten [48]. A superposition-based method for the design of distributed systems was described by Back and Kurki-Suonio in 1983 [20]. The abbreviated term *superposition* was coined by Chandy and Misra in UNITY [36], where it was introduced as a mechanism for modularity in specification languages. As a control structure for distributed programming it has been discussed by Bougé and Francez [28] and by Katz [105].

Instead of treating superposition steps individually, as was done here, one could support generic superposition steps as suggested by Katz [105, 182] and also investigated in connection with the DisCo language by Kellomäki [113, 110, 111]. This would make it possible to have libraries of verified superpositions.

As analyzed in [127] and [63], for instance, several different varieties of superposition can be used. In our terminology, the variety adopted in UNITY does not allow strengthening of guards. This means that liveness properties are also then preserved, but its use as a basis for design methods is therefore more restricted. On the other hand, instead of using superposition for module composition also, UNITY has a separate 'union' mechanism. This provides a very liberal way to combine specifications textually, but even safety properties are then not preserved, in general.

The preservation of safety properties in our versions of superposition and composition has advantages in formal verification also, as discussed by Kellomäki [107, 108, 112]. In particular, [112] demonstrates how superposition-based decomposition can simplify formal verification of complex specifications.

Related ideas of program derivation have also appeared elsewhere in various contexts. In connection with the LOTOS language, Bolognesi and Brinksma have introduced a 'constraint-oriented specification style' [26], which can in our terminology be interpreted as composition of independent layers. Herrmann and Krumm have applied similar ideas of compositionality to TLA-based specifications in *cTLA* [81, 82].

In the form presented here, superposition and composition of closed systems and the resulting layered specifications were first proposed in connection with the DisCo language [127, 93]. At a more informal level, composition of parallel refinement paths was also suggested for specifications by Feather [55]. The use of layered specifications to manage evolving systems has been discussed by Mikkonen et al. [156, 157, 5].

At the level of programming languages, the need to manage concerns that cut across several objects has led to *aspect-oriented programming*, which imposes an auxiliary structure of 'aspects' on object-oriented programs [115, 51, 183]. The relationship between superposition and aspects was first noted by Katz and Gil [106].

The process of deriving a specification by superposition can also be reversed, yielding a verification method by projections, as presented by Lam and Shankar [134]. Program slicing, as suggested by Weiser [194], is an analogous approach to program testing.

For a theoretical treatment of refinement and composition of TLA specifications, the reader is referred to Abadi's and Lamport's papers [6, 8]. Composition of TLA$^+$ specifications is also discussed extensively in [145].

Data refinement, which is essential to all systematic methods for program refinement, was first given formal treatment by Hoare [84].

# 7

# Object Orientation Elaborated

The notion of a *class* has been introduced in this book for sets of objects that have similar local states and actions. So far, different classes have been treated as if they were disjoint sets of objects. This no longer stays true with the notions of *subclasses* and *inheritance*, which lead to a subset relation between classes. With *multiple inheritance* the resulting class system is not even hierarchical.

Another notion that needs further discussion is that of *relations*. As introduced in Chap. 5, relations provide a general facility to express arbitrary dependences between objects. As such this facility is too general to be practical for certain specific relationships that are important in object-oriented modeling. Such specific needs appear in *aggregation*, i.e., when *composite objects* are constructed of *subobjects*.

Facilities to be included in the action language for these purposes will be discussed and analyzed in this chapter. The plan for the chapter is as follows:

- Section 7.1 is an introduction to the idea of subclasses in closed-system specifications.
- In Sect. 7.2 we discuss the general structure of a class system, and how superposition and composition of specification layers affect this structure.
- The role of subclasses in the superposition-based design method is illustrated by an example in Sect. 7.3.
- The notion of aggregated objects and the associated subobject relations are introduced and analyzed in Sect. 7.4. Unlike in programming languages, this leads to considering subobjects to form special subclasses of those classes to which they belong.
- Although the intuitions behind aggregation and inheritance are different, they provide technically somewhat similar mechanisms. Another mechanism that can serve for similar purposes is *copying* of specification layers. Section 7.5 is devoted to the analysis of the relationship between these three mechanisms. The possibilities that are offered by combining subclassing and aggregation of the same class are also studied.

# 7.1 General Principles

The notions of subclasses and inheritance are of fundamental significance in object orientation. In programming languages they are usually treated like any other mechanisms, whose meanings are ultimately explained in terms of their implementation. Since such an attitude is unsatisfactory in specification, we start with a brief informal analysis of the meaning of object orientation in closed-system specifications.

### 7.1.1 Specification vs. Implementation Concerns

Object orientation is often described to offer two kinds of advantages: *reusability* of designs (and also implementations), and intuitively natural concepts for *modeling*. The needs in specification and design are, however, somewhat different from those in implementation (programming). Therefore, reuse in specification need not concern the same kinds of entities as in programming, and intuitively natural specification concepts are not obtained simply by adopting the mechanisms of object-oriented programming languages.

For the purposes of this book it is therefore important to understand the significance of the following differences between the aims of specification languages and programming languages:

- The level of abstraction should be higher in specification than in programming. Whereas programming languages need mechanisms by which the desired properties can be implemented, specification formalisms can use facilities that are not directly implementable, in general.
- Support for rigorous reasoning is important for specifications. Modeling concepts in specification formalisms should therefore be evaluated not only by the constructive possibilities they provide, but especially by their support for reasoning on logical properties.
- Specifications should be as simple to understand as possible. Therefore, the execution model for object-oriented specifications should not be obscured by those non-trivial problems that arise in execution models for object-oriented programming languages.
- Specification modules are logical modules, which need not correspond to implementation modules.

### 7.1.2 Intuitive Meaning of Subclasses

Subclasses are usually explained in terms of an *'is-a' relationship*, where each object of a *subclass* is at the same time also an object of the *base class* from which the subclass has been derived. Even the intuitive meaning of this may, however, vary.

One interpretation, which is important in specification, is that a subclass models a possible *implementation* or *refinement* of its base class. In that case the base class can be viewed as an *abstraction* of the subclass. In the presence of several subclasses of the same base class, the latter provides a common abstraction of all of them.

This view is also used in object-oriented programming. There the term 'abstract class' usually refers to a class of which no instantiations can be made as such. That is, each object of an abstract class then has to belong also to one of its 'concrete' subclasses.

Another possible interpretation is that a subclass models a special case or *specialization* of the base class. Usually a special case has to satisfy the properties defined at the more general level, but, in addition, it may also exhibit constraints of and extensions to these general possibilities.

A more liberal interpretation is that there is some similarity between the base class and a subclass, which makes it practical to construct the latter as a *modification* of the former. In particular, this similarity may concern the interface of objects to the rest of the world, independently of what the effects of the 'methods' will actually be.

It should be noted that in object-oriented programming the possibilities for specialization and modification can be much more liberal than what is useful in formal specification. To serve a useful purpose in specifications, the subclass relationship has to be helpful in proving formal properties. Similarity of interfaces, for instance, guarantees nothing about the behavioral properties of an object. Also, if all properties of the base class could be modified for a subclass at will, then any class could be defined as a subclass of any other class, and the subclass relationship would therefore offer no support for formal reasoning.

### 7.1.3 Formal Requirements for Subclasses

The formal properties that are considered in our specifications give a formal interpretation for the 'is-a' relation between subclasses and their base classes: a behavior is not allowed for a subclass if it is not allowed for the base class. As a consequence, an action for a subclass must logically imply the corresponding action for the base class. For instance, an action for a subclass may have a stronger guard – strengthening the guard to be identically false removes an action – but a specialized action may also provide additional functionality that is not in conflict with the corresponding action for the base class.

In contrast to this, conventional object-oriented programming languages lack a precise semantic definition of an 'is-a' relation. Therefore, the similarity or compatibility between subclasses and their base classes is usually considered at the level of static semantics only, and semantically arbitrary replacements of methods may be allowed for subclasses.

### 7.1.4 Classes vs. Layers as Basic Units

Replacing conventional single-object methods of object-oriented programming by multi-object actions raises the level of abstraction so that behavioral properties can be considered rigorously even in early stages of specification. Luckily, inheritance of methods generalizes in a natural way to inheritance of capabilities to participate in multi-object actions.

Multi-object actions allow the description of collective behaviors in a natural manner. As already discussed in Sect. 6.3.1 (p. 180), this has the consequence that objects (or classes) are no longer the natural basic units for modularity. Instead, this role is taken by specification layers, which contain definitions of cooperating classes and their actions. The notions of classes and specification layers are, in fact, orthogonal to each other in the sense that classes and the associated actions can be defined incrementally in several subsequent layers.

In object-oriented programming it is essential that an object encapsulates its local variables and has full control of access to them. As discussed in Sect. 6.3.5 (p. 183), this role of objects (or classes) has been taken here by layers: a variable can be modified only within the layer in which it is introduced. Furthermore, an action can modify the local states of its participant objects only.

In principle, layers would also be suitable entities for constraining the visibility of variables for non-modifying access. No facilities have, however, been introduced for this purpose here, since this is not considered to be a fundamental issue for the purposes of this book.

### 7.1.5 Specifications as Patterns

Describing collective behaviors of objects is associated with the *closed-system principle* used in this book. According to this principle, objects are not specified in isolation, but in the context where they will be used. Instead of specifying how an arbitrary single object of a given class behaves, a closed-system specification describes how an arbitrary collection of objects in the given classes behave in cooperation with each other.

The notion of *instances*, or *instantiations*, then extends from classes to specification layers, which therefore are generic *patterns* for all possible instantiations of them. In particular, an instantiation of a layer determines the objects (i.e., instantiations of classes) that are involved in it.

In the absence of global naming of objects, all objects in a class are treated in a uniform manner as members of this class. Even if a class has been defined as a singleton class with only one object, this object is referred to as a member of its class. With uniform treatment, more specific behaviors can still be specified for some objects of a class in one of two ways: either a specialized subclass is introduced for them, or an identification attribute is provided by which these objects can be distinguished from other objects of the same class.

To see some of the consequences of this, consider the situation where an object appears as a component (i.e., subobject) in an aggregate. In conventional approaches the component could be considered just as a specific instantiation of its class. Since the behaviors of such component objects have common characteristics that are more specialized than the general possibilities offered by the class in question, it is natural in our approach to consider such components always to form a subclass of their own. This will be discussed in more detail in Sect. 7.4.

### 7.1.6 Incremental Definition of Classes

The crux of the design methodology in this book is that the focus of a specification is extended incrementally by superposition. As has been shown, this mechanism can also be used for incremental *class extension* and for the associated refinement of actions.

In object-oriented terminology, an extended class with associated actions can be understood as a subclass that has inherited from the original class all its attributes and all its capabilities to participate in actions. Addition of new attributes and actions, and refinement of inherited actions, are then considered as specialization.

The extension facility of superposition provides, however, only a restricted form of subclassing, since the base class does not remain available as such, or for the derivation of further subclasses. A more general class system is therefore needed for flexible reuse of previously defined classes.

In terms of our incremental design methodology, the purpose of introducing subclasses can now be formulated as follows: when the focus of a specification is extended at a lower level of abstraction, a homogeneous class may be split into several subclasses, which share all properties of the base class but have, in addition, more specialized properties.

### 7.1.7 Effects of the Execution Model

Some well-known intricacies in dealing with subclasses can be attributed to the low-level execution model of programming languages. In specifications, such problems can be made non-issues by raising the level of abstraction. The action-oriented execution model, where single-object 'methods' have been replaced by multi-object actions, has this kind of an effect. This is evident, for instance, for the problems that arise with 'dynamic binding' and concurrent objects at the level of programming languages.

### Dynamic Binding

Dynamic binding means that the exact (sub)class of a referenced object may vary at run time, and cannot therefore be determined statically. For instance, when methods are invoked by messages (or method calls) between objects, the sender (or caller) need not be aware of the exact subclass to which the receiver (or callee) belongs. Therefore, the same message may lead to different kinds of effects, depending on the receiver. Dynamic aspects of (sub)class membership also lead to a need for run-time tests, when references to objects are used in assignments.

At the level of programming, these possibilities are important, and dynamic binding is therefore often considered essential for object orientation. Dynamic binding is not, however, needed with the action-oriented execution model, where the associated problems can therefore also be avoided.

The reason for this is that, unlike conventional methods, actions are not triggered by explicit calls, and their names therefore have no significance. Each action definition gives all the necessary information on the (sub)classes of the participants, and the execution of an action can be triggered implicitly, whenever it is enabled for some participants. When subclasses are introduced for a base class, the associated actions may be split into corresponding alternatives, but objects of each subclass may still participate in non-specialized inherited actions without any complications.

## Concurrent Objects

The idea of concurrently executing objects, which can call each other's methods, sounds intuitively natural and simple. The simplicity is, however, lost with the possibilities for interference between concurrently active methods of the same object. This also obscures the role that methods have for reasoning on object-oriented programs.[1]

The most natural approach in concurrent object-oriented programming is to coordinate concurrent execution of methods by those mechanisms that have been developed in other concurrent programming languages. Combining such mechanisms with object-oriented inheritance leads, however, to additional problems that have been investigated under the name 'inheritance anomaly'.

As already discussed in Sect. 5.4.4 (p. 144), explicit communication mechanisms are not needed in operational specifications, when multi-object actions are used, and the associated problems are therefore also avoided. Modeling of concurrent and distributed objects will be discussed in more detail in Chap. 9.

## Review Questions

QUESTION 7.1.1 What is the relationship between subclasses and class extension in superposition?

QUESTION 7.1.2 What is the purpose of introducing subclasses from the viewpoint of incremental design?

---

[1]The role that methods may have for reasoning is not clear even in the absence of concurrency, since an object cannot control nested execution of its methods, when these issue calls to methods in other objects. Agent-oriented techniques have been proposed as a solution to this problem.

QUESTION 7.1.3 In what sense are our specifications generic?

QUESTION 7.1.4 Why is 'dynamic binding' not an issue in the action-oriented execution model?

QUESTION 7.1.5 Why are concurrency control mechanisms not needed in the action-oriented execution model?

## 7.2 Class System

Basically, classes are sets of objects with certain common characteristics. Class membership is static in the sense that it cannot be dynamically changed by the execution of actions.

So far, classes have been assumed in this book to be disjoint sets of objects. With the notion of subclasses this assumption has to be relaxed. In particular, a subclass is a subset of its base class.

In this section we analyze in more detail the set-theoretic relations between classes, and how actions can be specialized for subclasses.

### 7.2.1 Subclasses

For two different classes $C$ and $D$, set inclusion $D \subseteq C$ means that all objects of class $D$ are also objects of class $C$. We then say that $D$ is a *subclass* of $C$, and that $C$ is a *superclass* of $D$.[2]

For completeness, a dummy *root class* $C_0$ is assumed, which is a superclass of all classes. At the other end of the class hierarchy, classes for which no subclasses have been introduced are called *leaf classes*.

When class $D$ is constructed as a subclass of another class $C$, $D \subseteq C$, then $C$ is called the *base class* of $D$. As a consequence, the complement subclass $C \setminus D$ then also arises, which consists of all those objects in $C$ that do not belong to $D$. In the absence of this subclass, $C$ and $D$ would actually be the same. This complement subclass is also necessary for the possibility to introduce further subclasses of $C$ (which are not subclasses of $D$) in later stages of refinement.

Discussion of classes is mathematically simplified by adopting the view that the class system is closed under set-theoretic operations. That is, if $C$ and $D$ are classes, then so also are $C \cap D$, $C \setminus D$, and $C \cup D$. Some of these classes are explicitly constructed and named in a specification; some arise implicitly and can only be referred to by set-valued expressions.

A simple hierarchical class system is illustrated in Fig. 7.1. The leaf classes in it are not only $D$ and $C_2$, which have explicit names, but also $C_1 \setminus D$,

---

[2]Technically it is possible to define a class to have exactly the same objects as the superclass of which it is derived. In this case the classes are actually the same, and no proper subclass relationship then exists between them.

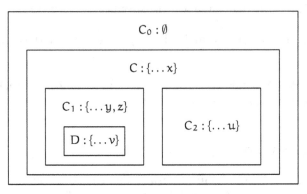

**Fig. 7.1.** Illustration of a simple class system

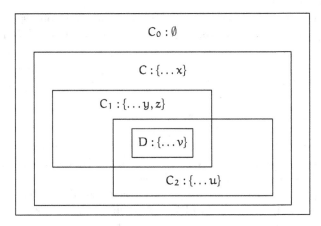

**Fig. 7.2.** Illustration of non-disjoint classes

$C \setminus (C_1 \cup C_2)$, and $C_0 \setminus C$, which have arisen as a result of the set-theoretic closure.

A subclass $D$ can also be constructed as a subclass of several base classes $C_1, \ldots, C_k$, $k > 1$, at the same time. Since we then have $D \subseteq C_i$ for all $i$, this is possible only if $C_1 \cap \cdots \cap C_k \neq \emptyset$. The situation is illustrated for $k = 2$ in Fig. 7.2, where the leaf classes are $D$, $(C_1 \cap C_2) \setminus D$, $C_1 \setminus C_2$, $C_2 \setminus C_1$, $C \setminus (C_1 \cup C_2)$, and $C_0 \setminus C$.

Introduction of subclasses essentially means refinement of a specification. For simplicity it will be allowed in the action language only in superposition and composition steps, and only for imported base classes. Although new subclasses are usually leaf classes, this need not be true, in general.

## 7.2.2 Local Variables of Subclasses

Each class determines the *local variables* that are available in all objects of that class. If class D is a subclass of C, $D \subseteq C$, then the local variables for D include all those for C, and we say that D has *inherited* them from C.

In addition to inherited variables, a subclass may have *class-specific local variables*, which are not available for its superclasses. Figure 7.1 illustrates this by showing the class-specific variables for the named classes in it. For instance, the local variables for class D are the inherited variables x, y, and z, and a class-specific variable v.

As already mentioned in Sect. 7.1.6 (p. 219), the notion of a subclass is, in fact, a generalization of *class extension*. Class extension can be understood as the special case of a subclass D, $D \subseteq C$, where $C \setminus D = \emptyset$, in which case the two classes are actually the same, and no new name is therefore needed for the subclass.

When the superclasses of a class do not form a strict hierarchy, the term *multiple inheritance* is used. In Fig. 7.2, class D inherits local variables from both $C_1$ and $C_2$, so that its local variables are all the variables shown in this figure.

Any class C can be extended in a superposition step by extending the associated set of class-specific local variables. This implicitly extends the set of local variables in all subclasses of C also.

## 7.2.3 Explicit Subclasses

Subclasses can be introduced explicitly by (sub)class definitions. In object-oriented programming languages this is the standard way to create subclasses.

To define a new class D as a subclass of an existing base class C, we use the format

$$\textbf{class } D = C + \{\ldots\} \, ,$$

where the class-specific local variables of subclass D are given within the braces. When no base class C is given, the dummy root class $C_0$ is implicitly assumed. In each case, the base class must be an imported class.

Because of the 'preexistence' of all possible variables, introducing a subclass should not be understood as creating something new that did not 'exist' before, but as a more detailed description of a class, which makes it possible to recognize distinctions that were not recognizable before. In other words, all objects of a subclass D were treated as objects of its base class C at those higher levels of abstraction where no information was available about D.

The base class C can be any class in the class system. For instance, when classes $C_1$ and $C_2$ overlap, their intersection $C_1 \cap C_2$ can be used as a base class for a subclass D,

$$\textbf{class } D = C_1 \cap C_2 + \{\ldots\} \, ,$$

which then inherits local variables and actions from both of them. In this situation of *multiple inheritance* it is important to notice that objects in the intersection $C_1 \cap C_2$ needed to exist already before the introduction of D. That is, the possibility for $C_1 \cap C_2 \neq \emptyset$ cannot be introduced, unless this was understood to be possible already when $C_1$ and $C_2$ were introduced.

Since multiple inheritance is an exception rather than the rule, the default assumption will be that explicitly introduced classes are disjoint, as was also assumed in the earlier chapters of this book.

### 7.2.4 Actions for a Subclass

A participant c in an action A is always specified to belong to some class C in the class system. We then say that action A is available for class C. The local variables of participant c that can be accessed in A are those that are local to class C. All other local variables of participant c stay unchanged in A independently of whether c is known to belong to some subclass of C or not.

Let D be a subclass introduced in a superposition step where a specification layer S is refined into T, and let $A(c : C \ldots)$ be an action that is available in layer S for the base class C of D. If action A is not replaced by explicit refinements in layer T, objects in D can also take the role c in the default refinement of A, since $D \subseteq C$. We therefore say that objects in subclass D *inherit* action A, or the capability to participate in action A.

If an action is replaced by explicit refinements in a superposition step, such a refinement may also constrain the (sub)classes of the participants. For instance, a refinement of the form

$$B(d : D \ldots) : S.A(d \ldots)$$
$$\wedge \cdots$$

could be given for the above action $A(c : C \ldots)$, in which case the class-specific local variables of participant $d \in D$ could also be accessed and modified in the refined action B.

An alternative way to refine action $A(c : C \ldots)$ is to *specialize* it for a given subclass of C, with the idea that the original action A then remains available for other subclasses of C. Although this is analogous to specialization of single-object methods in object-oriented programming languages, the situation is complicated by the possibility of specializing multi-object actions for multiple participant roles.

For simplicity, specializations for subclass D will be allowed in the action language only in the same superposition step where subclass D itself is introduced. Below, we explain some conventions that seem natural and will be followed in the rest of this book.

### Specialization for a Single Role

Action $A(c : C...)$ can be specialized in layer $T$ for subclass $D$, $D \subseteq C$, by giving for it one or more *specializations* of the form

$$B(d : D...) : S.A(^*d...)$$
$$\wedge \cdots .$$

The subclass for which a specialization is valid is that of the participant marked with an asterisk (*) in the applied occurrence of the inherited action $A$.

Syntactically this differs from the corresponding ordinary action refinement

$$B(d : D...) : S.A(d...)$$
$$\wedge \cdots$$

only by the marking of the role for which the specialization is introduced. The semantic difference is that, in specialization, the original action $A$ is kept available for the complement subclass $C \setminus D$, as illustrated in Fig. 7.3.

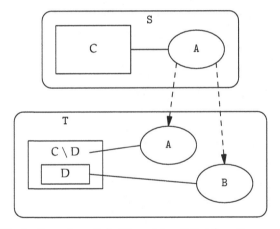

**Fig. 7.3.** Illustration of explicit ($B$) and implicit ($A$) action specializations

Several specializations of an action can also be given, for the same or for different subclasses. If an action $A(c : C...)$ has been specialized separately for subclasses $D_1, \ldots, D_k$, $D_i \subseteq C$, in role $c$, then the original action $A$ is kept available for all other objects in $C$ except those in $D_1 \cup \cdots \cup D_k$. This means that a default specialization is implicitly assumed, which corresponds to the refinement

$$A(c : C \setminus (D_1 \cup \cdots \cup D_k)...) : S.A(c...),$$

with fairness markings taken as such from $A$. As a result, action $S.A$ has then been split in layer $T$ into its explicitly specialized variants for $c \in D_i$, $i = 1, \ldots, k$, and the implicit default variant for $c \in C \setminus (D_1 \cup \cdots \cup D_k)$.

**General Case**

An action with several participants can be specialized for several participants at the same time. For instance, if $D_1 \subseteq C_1$ and $D_2 \subseteq C_2$, then action $A(c_1 : C_1; c_2 : C_2)$ could be specialized for two participants by

$$B(d_1 : D_1; d_2 : D_2) : S.A(^*d_1, ^*d_2)$$
$$\wedge \cdots ,$$

which would give an implicit specialization that corresponds to refinement

$$A(c_1 : C_1 \setminus D_1; c_2 : C_2 \setminus D_2) : S.A(c_1, c_2) .$$

In general, if there are specializations for different combinations of roles and subclasses, it is a reasonable convention to assume only one implicit specialization, where for each participant role all those subclasses have been subtracted for which specializations have been given.

Action concatenation can also be used in connection with specialization, with the precautions that are also otherwise associated with it, as discussed in Sect. 6.4.5 (p. 188). For instance, if $D_1 \subseteq C_1$ and $D_2 \subseteq C_2$, and $A_1(c : C_1)$ and $A_2(c : C_2)$ are two actions in layer $S$, then the simple concatenation

$$B(d_1 : D_1; d_2 : D_2) : (S.A_1(^*d_1); S.A_2(^*d_2))$$
$$\wedge \cdots$$

would yield two implicit specializations that correspond to refinements

$$A_1(c : C_1 \setminus D_1) : S.A_1(c) ,$$
$$A_2(c : C_2 \setminus D_2) : S.A_2(c) .$$

**7.2.5 Composition in the Presence of Subclasses**

As a default, classes that are introduced in independent refinement paths will be considered to be disjoint. For instance, if two refinement paths of a common predecessor layer would lead to the two class systems shown in Fig. 7.4, then the default class system for the composition would be the one shown in Fig. 7.1 (p. 222).

In composition it is reasonable, however, to allow also the possibility that the classes defined in independent refinement paths are not disjoint, which would make their multiple inheritance possible. For instance, in the above

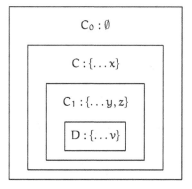 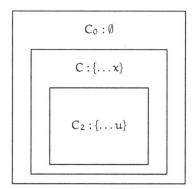

**Fig. 7.4.** Classes in two refinement paths of a common predecessor layer

situation a composition could also be defined to yield the class system of Fig. 7.2 (p. 222).

Actions for a composed system can be given as described in Sect. 6.2 (p. 172). For simplicity, we omit examining here what could be considered as reasonable conventions for implicit action specializations, when specializations are introduced in composition.

As an example of composition in the presence of subclasses, let C be a class with action $A(c : C)$ in layer S, and let $D_1$ and $D_2$ be two subclasses of C defined in independently refined layers $T_1$ and $T_2$, respectively. Furthermore, let

$$B_1(c : D_1) : S.A(^*c)$$
$$\wedge \cdots$$

and

$$B_2(c : D_2) : S.A(^*c)$$
$$\wedge \cdots$$

be explicit specializations of S.A introduced in $T_1$ and $T_2$, respectively (see illustration in Fig. 7.5). When layers $T_1$ and $T_2$ are composed, it is important to know whether classes $D_1$ and $D_2$ are assumed to be disjoint or not. If not, intersection $D_1 \cap D_2$ provides a possibility for their multiple inheritance. Four different subclasses of C then arise in composition, and different action synchronizations are available for each, as shown in Fig. 7.5.

### 7.2.6 Subclasses and Preservation of Properties

From the viewpoint of logic, subclasses introduce only language conventions. In superposition they affect the conventions for extending the set of available

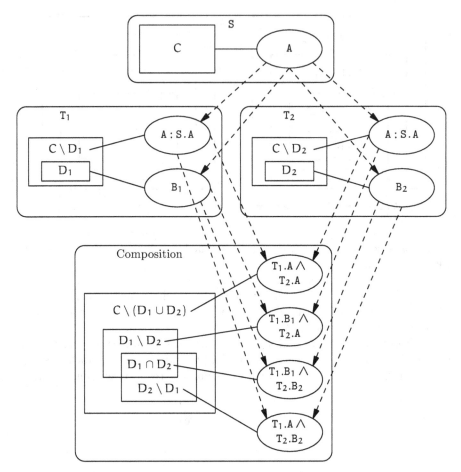

**Fig. 7.5.** Illustration of subclasses and multiple inheritance in composition

variables and for refining actions. Composition also remains as superposition on the layers that are composed. Therefore, all safety properties of predecessor layers are also preserved in the presence of subclasses.

As for liveness properties, similar proof obligations are obtained as those discussed in Sect. 6.1.7 (p. 169). Separate proofs may, however, be required for all new subclasses. For instance, if $B(^{SF}d : D)$ is the only specialization of action $A(^{SF}c : C)$ for subclass $D$, $D \subseteq C$, and the enabling conditions for their stutter-excluding parts are $g_B^+(d)$ and $g_A^+(c)$, respectively, then the following class-specific proof obligation is obtained for $D$:

$$\forall d \in D : (\Box\Diamond g_A^+(d) \Rightarrow \Box\Diamond g_B^+(d)) .$$

Since the possibility for multiple inheritance introduces intersection subclasses even when these are not explicitly used, it leads to proof obligations that would not appear in its absence.

For each class C, a specification determines the TLA properties $E(c)$ that are satisfied by objects $c \in C$. If D is a subclass of C, $D \subseteq C$, preservation of logical properties implies that properties $E(d)$ are then also satisfied by all objects $d \in D$. This gives a precise formal meaning for the 'is-a' relation between subclasses and their superclasses.

This interpretation of the 'is-a' relation is intuitively natural for specifications, since reasoning on logical properties is then important. It is, however, an essentially stronger interpretation than any of those that have been proposed in more traditional literature on object-oriented modeling, where the mechanisms of object orientation receive more attention than the formal properties that can be achieved by them, and at least liveness properties are usually ignored.

**Review Questions**

QUESTION 7.2.1 Why is it reasonable to consider the class system to be closed under set-theoretic operations?

QUESTION 7.2.2 Why is it necessary to know about the possibility for multiple inheritance of two classes even when this possibility has not been explicitly utilized?

QUESTION 7.2.3 What is the meaning of the 'is-a' relation between a subclass and its superclass(es) in this approach?

**Exercises**

EXERCISE 7.2.1 Give an example of composition, where the unification condition for synchronized action instances equates participants in different subclasses of the same superclass. (For the condition to be satisfied, the equated participant in question must then, of course, be defined to belong to the intersection class.)

## 7.3 Example: Doctors' Office

As an example of explicit subclasses we consider the modeling of a world where people go to a doctors' office when they get ill, receptionists organize patients to meet doctors, and the doctors then cure the patients, who finally settle their bills with the receptionists.

In practice, in designing such a system one would probably pay more attention to queuing and waiting aspects than to logical properties. Here we ignore, however, real time and efficiency, and use the example to illustrate the notions of modularity and specialization introduced so far. There are also some lessons to be learnt about the design methodology that these notions are intended to support.

### 7.3.1 First Layer: Illness

We do not start the design by analyzing what kinds of objects the final system would involve, what kinds of relationships there would exist between them, and what kind of information should be contained in their local states. Instead, we try to find the simplest possible focus for a meaningful projection of the intended world. Since variables have no significance in isolation from the actions that affect them, even the first approximation of the world to be modeled must contain both.

In principle, there are several possibilities for where to start. Perhaps the most natural candidate for the first focus is the 'illness bit' in the potential patients, together with the events of getting ill and well.

Focusing on this single aspect we design the first layer **Illness** to contain patient objects $p \in \mathsf{Pat}$ with the structure

$$\textbf{class } \mathsf{Pat} = \{\textbf{state } \mathsf{Well}^*, \mathsf{Ill}\}$$

and actions

$$\mathtt{Get\_ill}(p : \mathsf{Pat}) : p.\mathsf{Well}$$
$$\rightarrow p.\mathsf{Ill}',$$

$$\mathtt{Get\_well}(^{\mathrm{WF}}p : \mathsf{Pat}) : p.\mathsf{Ill}$$
$$\rightarrow p.\mathsf{Well}'.$$

In its simplicity this model is straightforward, but it allows us to get started. In the initial state we assume all patients to be well, and the fairness assumption in **Get_well** ensures that every patient that gets ill will eventually also get well:

$$p.\mathsf{Ill} \rightsquigarrow p.\mathsf{Well}. \tag{7.1}$$

### 7.3.2 An Independent Initial Layer: Work

Having written down the most important requirement that all ill patients do get well, we have to decide how this will take place.

From the very beginning we do know that we will need doctors and receptionists for this purpose. The next logical question might be to ask what the most essential behavioral properties are for these people. From their viewpoint, involvement in the doctors' office may primarily look like going to work and returning home after work.

This leads to another view that is independent of the previous layer, and where doctors and receptionists are both seen as employees (class Emp). This layer, called Work, is also quite primitive and almost isomorphic to the previous one, containing the following definitions:

$$\textbf{class } \textsf{Emp} = \{\textbf{state } \textsf{Off}^*, \textsf{On}\} \,,$$

$$\textsf{Go\_to\_work}(^{\textsf{WF}}e : \textsf{Emp}) : e.\textsf{Off}$$
$$\rightarrow \ e.\textsf{On}' \,,$$

$$\textsf{Go\_home}(e : \textsf{Emp}) : e.\textsf{On}$$
$$\rightarrow \ e.\textsf{Off}' \,.$$

All employees are assumed to be initially in state Off, i.e., off from work, but eventually they will all go to work by the fairness requirement on Go_to_work. For simplicity, we have minimized the liveness properties to be preserved in the development, by not requiring similar fairness for actions Go_home.

### 7.3.3 Combining the Two Views

Next we want to compose the two simple views by importing them both to a new layer People. In this layer people may get ill and then get well, and some people are employees that go to work and from work to home. Multiple inheritance of the two classes is permitted to allow employees to be patients also. The resulting leaf subclasses are illustrated in Fig. 7.6.

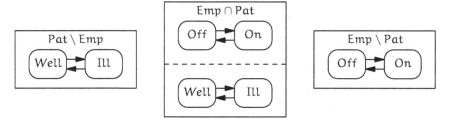

**Fig. 7.6.** Illustration of state transitions in patient and employee objects

The newly arising subclass $\textsf{Emp} \cap \textsf{Pat}$ raises the question of whether some dependences are required between the two views of the employees that are patients also. In particular, problems might be foreseen in allowing someone to appear both as a working doctor and as an ill patient at the same time. Therefore, we wish to maintain the invariant that nobody is working when ill:

$$e \in \textsf{Emp} \cap \textsf{Pat} : \Box(e.\textsf{Ill} \Rightarrow e.\textsf{Off}) \,.$$

Having formulated this invariance, we can avoid its violations by specializing actions `Work.Go_to_work` and `Illness.Get_ill` (i.e., their synchronizations with a stuttering action) as follows:

$$P\_go\_to\_work(^{SF}e : Emp \cap Pat) : Illness.Stutter$$
$$\wedge Work.Go\_to\_work(^*e)$$
$$\wedge e.Well ,$$

$$E\_get\_ill(p : Emp \cap Pat) : Illness.Get\_ill(^*p)$$
$$\wedge Work.Stutter$$
$$\wedge p.Off .$$

This obviously prevents employees from going to work when they are ill, and from getting ill when they are at work. The use of specialization for subclass $Emp \cap Pat$ (indicated by asterisks in the applied occurrences of the inherited actions) keeps the nonrefined versions of these two synchronizations available for the complement subclasses $Emp \setminus Pat$ and $Pat \setminus Emp$, respectively.

Actions `Get_well` and `Go_home` are taken into the composition 'as such', i.e., as default synchronizations with stuttering actions.

Also, non-stuttering pairs of actions could be synchronized in the composition, both for the case when the patient and the employee are different objects and for the case when they are the same. Since there is no need for this, no such synchronizations are introduced.

It is easy to check that the liveness properties of both imported layers have been preserved in this construction. Notice, however, that a weak fairness marking in `P_go_to_work` would not have been sufficient for this, since getting ill could repeatedly disable this action for an employee.

### 7.3.4 Next Layer: Doctors

For the next refinement step (layer `Doctors`) we extend the view of how patients get well, and require that a doctor must participate in that action.

For the purposes of this modeling exercise, doctors (class $Doc$) are a special case of employees. When at work, they are assumed to be either idle or busy healing some patient. To reflect this, we define doctors as employees with two additional states, and introduce a relation $Curing$ to indicate that a doctor is currently taking care of a given patient:

$$\textbf{class } Doc = Emp + \{state\ Idle^*, Busy\} ,$$
$$\textbf{relation } (0..1) \cdot Curing \cdot (0..1) : Doc \times Pat\ (\emptyset) .$$

Since employees may or may not be patients, we can now have two kinds of doctors also, as illustrated in Fig. 7.7.

In addition to the intended invariants introduced by the relation $Curing$, the following further invariants (for $d \in Doc$, $p \in Pat$) describe the intended meaning of the new state variables:

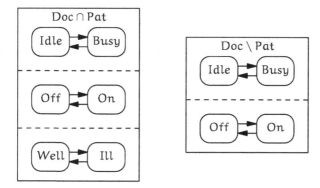

**Fig. 7.7.** Illustration of doctors

$$\Box(\text{d.Off} \Rightarrow \text{d.Idle}) \,,$$
$$\Box(\text{d·Curing·p} \Rightarrow \text{d.Busy} \land \text{p.Ill}) \,,$$
$$\Box(\text{d.Busy} \Rightarrow \exists \text{p} : \text{d·Curing·p}) \,.$$

Initially these conditions are satisfied if all doctors are Idle and Curing is empty.

Starting the treatment of a patient by a doctor is modeled by a new action Start_curing that establishes the association Curing between a doctor and a patient. The treatment ends by a refinement of Get_well, which removes this association:

$$\begin{aligned}
\text{Start\_curing}(\text{d} : \text{Doc}; \,^{SF}\text{p} : \text{Pat}) : \text{People.Stutter} \\
\land \, \neg \exists \text{d} \in \text{Doc} : \text{d·Curing·p} \\
\land \, \text{d.On} \\
\land \, \text{d.Idle} \\
\land \, \text{p.Ill} \\
\rightarrow \, \text{d.Busy}' \\
\land \, \text{d·Curing}'\text{·p} \,,
\end{aligned}$$

$$\begin{aligned}
\text{Get\_well}(^{WF}\text{p} : \text{Pat}; \, \text{d} : \text{Doc}) : \text{People.Get\_well}(\text{p}) \\
\land \, \text{d·Curing·p} \\
\rightarrow \, \text{d.Idle}' \\
\land \, \neg \text{d·Curing}'\text{·p} \,.
\end{aligned}$$

The intended invariants given above also require that a doctor cannot go home in the middle of treating a patient, which is achieved by specializing action Go_home for doctors as follows:

$$D\_go\_home(d : Doc) : People.Go\_home(^*d)$$
$$\land\, d.Idle\,.$$

Other actions of the imported layer are taken into Doctors as their default refinements.

The required liveness property (7.1) on p. 230 is no longer valid, however, without some further assumptions about the system. Even when the set of doctors is non-empty, there is the possibility that all doctors get ill, in which case nobody can get healed.

To avoid this problem we make the simple assumption that there are doctors who never get ill,

$$Doc \setminus Pat \neq \emptyset\,,$$

which is sufficient to guarantee that the liveness property (7.1) is preserved.

### 7.3.5 Final Layer: Receptionists

In the final refinement step we introduce receptionists to the system. The layered structure of the resulting specification is shown in Fig. 7.8, where the final layer is called Office.

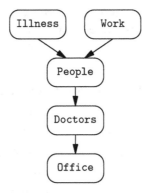

**Fig. 7.8.** Specification layers in the example

Receptionists (class Rec) are introduced as employees who have the task to organize waiting patients to meet doctors. As a subclass of $Emp \setminus Doc$, class Rec may overlap with both Pat and $Emp \setminus Pat$, as shown in Fig. 7.9. The leaf class $Rec \cap Pat$ then inherits from both Emp and Pat. As with doctors, we assume that there are receptionists who are not patients, i.e.,

$$Rec \setminus Pat \neq \emptyset\,.$$

Each patient is assumed to register at one of the receptionists, who also keeps a list of those idle doctors to whom she can send patients. Assuming

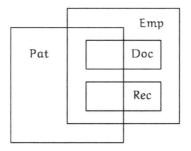

**Fig. 7.9.** Final class system

that each waiting patient and each idle doctor can be the responsibility of at most one receptionist, the two associations can be introduced by partial functions

$$\textbf{relation } (*) \cdot Waiting\_at \cdot (0..1) : Pat \times Rec\ (\emptyset)\ ,$$
$$\textbf{relation } (*) \cdot Idle\_at \cdot (0..1) : Doc \times Rec\ (\emptyset)\ ,$$

with the following intended invariants (in addition to those introduced by the partial functions themselves):

$$\Box(p \cdot Waiting\_at \cdot r \Rightarrow p.Ill \wedge r.On \wedge \neg \exists d : d \cdot Curing \cdot p)\ ,$$
$$\Box(d \cdot Idle\_at \cdot r \Rightarrow d.On \wedge d.Idle \wedge r.On)\ .$$

In order to meet each other, a patient and a doctor have to get registered at the same receptionist, and this receptionist then also becomes another participant in action Start_curing:

$$Register\_patient(^{SF}p : Pat;\ r : Rec) : Doctors.Stutter$$
$$\wedge\ p.Ill$$
$$\wedge\ \neg \exists d : d \cdot Curing \cdot p$$
$$\wedge\ \neg \exists r : p \cdot Waiting\_at \cdot r$$
$$\wedge\ r.On$$
$$\rightarrow\ p \cdot Waiting\_at' \cdot r\ ,$$

$$Register\_doctor(d : Doc;\ ^{SF}r : Rec) : Doctors.Stutter$$
$$\wedge\ d.On$$
$$\wedge\ d.Idle$$
$$\wedge\ \neg \exists r : d \cdot Idle\_at \cdot r$$
$$\wedge\ r.On$$
$$\rightarrow\ d \cdot Idle\_at' \cdot r\ ,$$

$$\text{Start\_curing}(d : \text{Doc}; {}^{\text{SF}}p : \text{Pat}; r : \text{Rec}) : \text{Doctors.Start\_curing}(d, p)$$
$$\wedge\ p \cdot Waiting\_at \cdot r$$
$$\wedge\ d \cdot Idle\_at \cdot r$$
$$\rightarrow\ \neg p \cdot Waiting\_at' \cdot r$$
$$\wedge\ \neg d \cdot Idle\_at' \cdot r\ .$$

To model that a patient also has to pay his bill, state p.$Well$ needs to be partitioned into two substates, $Paying$ and $Released$, the latter being the initial state:

$$\textbf{class } Pat = \{\dots\} \textbf{ where } Well = \{\textbf{state } Released^*, Paying\}\ .$$

Notice that this extension also applies to all subclasses of patients.

In the $\texttt{Get\_well}$ action, a patient now needs to enter substate $Paying$, and a separate action with a receptionist is required to release him from the office. This would, however, introduce problems for patients that get ill again before being released. Therefore, we make such events impossible by refining those actions where a patient gets ill. As a result, we arrive at the following actions:

$$\texttt{Get\_well}({}^{\text{WF}}p : \text{Pat}; d : \text{Doc}) : \text{Doctors.Get\_well}(p, d)$$
$$\rightarrow\ p.Well.Paying'\ ,$$

$$\texttt{Release}({}^{\text{SF}}p : \text{Pat}; r : \text{Rec}) : \text{Doctors.Stutter}$$
$$\wedge\ p.Well.Paying$$
$$\wedge\ r.On$$
$$\rightarrow\ p.Well.Released'\ ,$$

$$\texttt{Get\_ill}(p : \text{Pat} \setminus \text{Emp}) : \text{Doctors.Get\_ill}(p)$$
$$\wedge\ p.Well.Released\ ,$$

$$\texttt{E\_get\_ill}(p : \text{Emp} \cap \text{Pat}) : \text{Doctors.E\_get\_ill}(p)$$
$$\wedge\ p.Well.Released\ .$$

Finally, we need some policy to restrict when receptionists and doctors can go home when there are waiting patients. The following reflects the decisions that a receptionist with waiting patients is not allowed to go home, and a doctor cannot go home when registered at a receptionist:

$$\texttt{D\_go\_home}(d : \text{Doc}) : \text{Doctors.D\_go\_home}(d)$$
$$\wedge\ \neg\exists r : d \cdot Idle\_at \cdot r\ ,$$

$$\texttt{R\_go\_home}(r : \text{Rec}) : \text{Doctors.Go\_home}(^*r)$$
$$\wedge\ \neg\exists p : p \cdot Waiting\_at \cdot r$$
$$\rightarrow\ \forall d : \neg d \cdot Idle\_at' \cdot r\ .$$

Since R_go_home is a specialization for receptionists, the default specialization of Go_home is implicitly kept available for the complement subclass, which is (Emp \ Doc) \ Rec.

The remaining actions of layer Doctors are taken as their default refinements. Inspection of liveness properties, and of possible unwanted situations, is left to the reader (Exercises 7.3.3–7.3.5).

**Exercises**

EXERCISE 7.3.1 List all actions of the final layer Office.

EXERCISE 7.3.2 Check that the intended safety properties are satisfied by each layer of this specification.

EXERCISE 7.3.3 Check that each step also preserves all liveness properties, implying that the main requirement (7.1) on p. 230 is also satisfied by the final layer Office.

EXERCISE 7.3.4 Modify the design so that each employee will always eventually go home from work.

EXERCISE 7.3.5 Discuss further aspects that you would like to change in the model, and consider whether these changes would affect any of its crucial properties.

## 7.4 Composite Objects and Subobject Classes

*Aggregation* is a facility to form *composite objects* or *aggregates* that contain one or more *subobjects* as their *components*.

Although aggregation adds nothing to the expressive power of a specification language, it is an intuitively natural concept for expressing certain kinds of relations between objects. It affects the class system in two ways that will be discussed below: aggregate objects belong to *aggregate classes*, and their subobjects introduce implicit *subobject classes*.

### 7.4.1 Aggregate Classes

Consider the situation illustrated on the left-hand side of Fig. 7.10: for each object $d \in D$ there is a unique object $c \in C$, such that a permanent relation s exists between them. If it is intuitively natural to interpret relation s as a 'part of' or 'has-a' relation, we may wish to illustrate the situation by drawing c inside d, as illustrated on the right-hand side of the figure. Object d is then understood to be an *aggregate* or *composite object*, which has a *component* or

**Fig. 7.10.** A permanent relation between objects (left), and its representation as a subobject relation (right)

*subobject* c. Instead of using the functional notation s(d) for c, we denote it as d.s.

Each composite object belongs to an *aggregate class*. The class definition for the aggregate class D in Fig. 7.10 could be given in the form

$$\textbf{class } D = \{\dots s : C\},$$

where s is an identifier for component selection, and C is the class of the component object. Since a subobject in class C gives rise to a corresponding subclass of C (to be discussed below), class C is required to be an imported class.

Besides one or more components, the definition of an aggregate class D may also introduce class-specific local variables and finite-state structures for D, similarly to other class definitions. In addition to introducing subobjects individually, collections of subobjects could also be easily introduced as components. Such facilities will not, however, be utilized in the following.

### 7.4.2 Identity of Aggregates and Subobjects

Since subobject relations are just a special form of relations between objects, an aggregate object and its subobjects all have different identities as objects. As reflected in graphical illustrations, shared subobjects will not be allowed. The converse of selecting a component s, denoted by $s^{-1}$, is therefore unique. If $c = d.s$, we write $d = c.s^{-1}$. We then have $d.s.s^{-1} = d$ and $c.s^{-1}.s = c$.

When an aggregate object participates in an action, its components are often also needed in it. Similarly, an action for a component object may need the whole aggregate to which it belongs. Instead of writing all these objects explicitly as participants and giving the associated subobject relations in the guard, we simplify notation by giving only one of them as a participant, and referring to the others by component selectors. To avoid problems of aliasing, we will therefore not allow an object and its subobject, or several subobjects of the same aggregate, to participate in the same action as different explicit participants.[3]

---

[3] The arising of such situations should also be avoided in connection with implicit specialization of actions.

### 7.4.3 Subobject Classes

In object-oriented programming languages, a method of a composite object may invoke the methods of its subobjects. In the action-oriented execution model invocation of methods has been replaced by action refinement. It is therefore natural that aggregate classes may have actions that refine actions for their subobjects.

Considering the example of Fig. 7.10, to specialize an action $A(c : C)$ for the situation where $c$ is a subobject $d.s$ in an aggregate $d \in D$, a specific subclass of $C$ is needed for such subobjects. Therefore, the subobject selector $s$ is assumed to introduce another subclass, denoted by $D.s$, which is a subclass of $C$, i.e., $D.s \subseteq C$. Subclasses introduced implicitly in this way will be called *subobject classes*.

If an ordinary relation $s$ were used instead of a subobject relation (see the left-hand side of Fig. 7.10), the same effect would require two refinements of action $A(c : C)$ for explicit participants $c \in C$ and $d \in D$, one for the case where $d \cdot s \cdot c$, and the other for the case $\neg d \cdot s \cdot c$.

A subobject class $D.s$ is a simple special case of subclasses in the sense that it does not have any class-specific variables. The need for them is removed by the possibility for class-specific variables in the associated aggregate class $D$.

### 7.4.4 Subobject Relations

The relationship between an aggregate object and its subobject is a specific *subobject relation*, often called a 'has-a' relation. In contrast to subobject relations, explicitly introduced relations will be called *associations*.

In order to be useful for modeling purposes, subobject relations need to possess some inherent constraints in comparison to general associations. Although it can be debated which constraints would most truthfully reflect the intuitive notion of aggregation, it is important to make decisions that leave no mathematical ambiguity. The main criterion for useful constraints is that they are helpful for reasoning.

The following general assumptions will be made in this book:

- Subobject relations are constant relations that cannot be modified by actions.
- A subobject may itself be an aggregate, and an aggregate may itself be a subobject of another aggregate, but no infinite chains are allowed in either direction.
- No object can be an immediate subobject of more than one aggregate.

In particular, these constraints imply that subobject relations are constant bijections between aggregate classes and subobject classes.

The first of the above constraints captures the intuition that subobject relations are used only to express permanent structures in an instantiation of a specification. Since the classes to which an object belongs cannot be changed in actions, this assumption was, in fact, already utilized in the above discussion of subobject classes and action specialization for component objects.

On intuitive grounds one might argue for removing this constraint. As far as reasoning is concerned, removing this constraint would, however, also remove the advantages that subobject relations have as a special case of associations.

The second constraint simply excludes infinite structures, including those that would result from circularity, like defining an aggregate class with a component in this aggregate class itself. Together with the first constraint it even excludes structures that would be potentially infinite, like binary trees where the structure could grow and shrink as needed.

The third constraint, which was also already assumed above, is perhaps the most debatable. Notice, however, that sharing of subobjects would require multiple inheritance from all associated subobject classes. Therefore, disallowing this possibility simplifies the situation as far as proof obligations for liveness properties are concerned.

### 7.4.5 Example: Putting Buffers Together

Let class B1 model a single-element buffer, defined in specification layer S as follows:

$$\textbf{class } B1 = \{y : \mathbb{Z};\ \mathsf{empty} : \mathbb{B}\ (\mathsf{true})\}\,,$$

$$\mathsf{Put1}(b : B1;\ x : \mathbb{Z}) : b.\mathsf{empty}$$
$$\rightarrow\ b.\mathsf{empty}' = \mathsf{false}$$
$$\wedge\ b.y' = x\,,$$

$$\mathsf{Get1}(b : B1;\ x : \mathbb{Z}) : \neg b.\mathsf{empty}$$
$$\wedge\ x = b.y$$
$$\rightarrow\ b.\mathsf{empty}' = \mathsf{true}\,.$$

The Boolean variable $\mathsf{empty}$, initialized as $\mathsf{true}$, is intended to indicate whether a buffer is empty or full.

Two-element buffers can now be constructed in a subsequent specification layer as aggregates that consist of two one-element buffers (see Fig. 7.11),

$$\textbf{class } B2 = \{b_1, b_2 : B1\}\,.$$

This introduces implicitly two subclasses of B1, namely $B2.b_1$ and $B2.b_2$, for which the actions for B1 can be specialized as follows:

$$\mathsf{Put2}(c : B2;\ x : \mathbb{Z}) : \mathsf{S.Put1}(^*c.b_1, x)\,,$$

$$\mathsf{Transfer}(^{\mathrm{WF}}c : B2;\ x : \mathbb{Z}) : \mathsf{S.Get1}(^*c.b_1, x)\ \&$$
$$\mathsf{S.Put1}(^*c.b_2, x)\,,$$

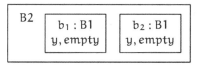

**Fig. 7.11.** Two-element buffer as an aggregate of two one-element buffers

$$\text{Get2}(c : B2;\ x : \mathbb{Z}) : S.\text{Get1}(^*c.b_2, x)\ .$$

Of these, action Put2 specializes Put1 for subclass $B2.b_1$, putting a data value to the first component $c.b_1$ of $c \in B2$. Action Transfer is a combined action (see Sect. 6.4.5, p. 188) that specializes action Get1 for subclass $B2.b_1$ and action Put1 for subclass $B2.b_2$. The fairness requirement on it guarantees that a data value cannot remain indefinitely in the first component when the second component is empty. Finally, action Get2 gets a data value from the second component as a specialization of Get1 for subclass $B2.b_2$.

### 7.4.6 Data Refinement by Aggregation

Given an abstract specification of a class, data refinement (see Sect. 6.4.2, p. 186) can be used in deriving more concrete 'implementations' of it. The class is then extended with new variables that are needed for the implementation, and some of the original variables are turned into non-primitive state functions, which can be omitted as state variables.

Aggregation is often useful in the class extensions that are used in such constructions. As an example we consider another derivation of two-element buffers.

#### Abstract Specification of Two-element Buffers

Let length(x), first(x), rest(x), and 'o' denote the length of list x, its first element, the rest of the list, and list concatenation, respectively. An abstract specification of class B2b, which corresponds to B2 given above, could now be given directly as

$$\textbf{class } B2b = \{q : \textbf{list } \mathbb{U}\ (\langle \rangle)\}\ ,$$

where q is a list, initialized as an empty list, representing the contents of the buffer, with an intended invariant $0 \leq \text{length}(q) \leq 2$, and with actions

$$\text{Put}(b : B2b;\ x : \mathbb{Z}) : \text{length}(b.q) < 2$$
$$\rightarrow\ b.q' = b.q \circ \langle x \rangle\ ,$$

$$\text{Get}(b : B2b;\ x : \mathbb{Z}) : \text{length}(b.q) > 0$$
$$\wedge\ x = \text{first}(b.q)$$
$$\rightarrow\ b.q' = \text{rest}(b.q)\ .$$

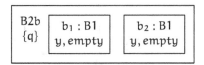

**Fig. 7.12.** Implementation of an abstract two-element buffer

## Implementation as an Aggregate

Suppose that buffer classes B1 and B2b have been defined in layers S and T, respectively. When these layers are composed, class B2b can be extended with two single-element buffers, yielding

$$\textbf{class } B2b = \{\ldots\ b_1, b_2 : B1\}$$

as illustrated in Fig. 7.12, with the intended invariant that $b.q$ for $b \in B2b$ always consists of the elements in the two single-element buffers $b.b_1$ and $b.b_2$,

$$\Box(b.q = (\text{if } b.b_2.\text{empty then } \langle\rangle \text{ else } \langle b.b_2.y\rangle) \circ$$
$$(\text{if } b.b_1.\text{empty then } \langle\rangle \text{ else } \langle b.b_1.y\rangle))\ .$$

This would allow us to take $b.q$ as a non-primitive state function, indicated by enclosing it in braces in Fig. 7.12.

Actions

$$\text{Put2}(b : B2b;\ x : \mathbb{Z}) : \text{T.Put}(b, x)$$
$$\wedge \text{S.Put1}(^*b.b_1, x)\ ,$$

$$\text{Transfer}(^{\text{WF}}b : B2b;\ x : \mathbb{Z}) : \text{T.Stutter}$$
$$\wedge \text{S.Get1}(^*b.b_1, x) \&$$
$$\text{S.Put1}(^*b.b_2, x)\ ,$$

$$\text{Get2}(b : B2b;\ x : \mathbb{Z}) : \text{T.Get}(b, x)$$
$$\wedge \text{S.Get1}(^*b.b_2, x)$$

now preserve the invariant, and therefore allow us to omit $b.q$ from an implementation.

Class B2b now has the same structure as the directly constructed B2, but its derivation guarantees that it satisfies the properties given to it at the more abstract level T. In Chap. 8 we will analyze the conditions that have to be satisfied in order that B2b be applicable in all contexts where the original B2 is applicable.

## Review Questions

QUESTION 7.4.1 When a composite object participates in an action, do its subobjects also have roles in it?

QUESTION 7.4.2 What are the conditions that a subobject relation is assumed to satisfy?

QUESTION 7.4.3 What is a natural criterion in judging whether a given form of aggregation is a useful facility in modeling, even though it can always be replaced by ordinary association relations between objects?

QUESTION 7.4.4 Why is it natural in this approach that subobjects introduce subclasses?

## Exercises

EXERCISE 7.4.1 Give examples of situations where constant bijections between two classes do not satisfy the constraints given for subobject relations.

EXERCISE 7.4.2 Consider the consequences that removing the different constraints for subobject relations would have.

EXERCISE 7.4.3 Instead of using aggregation, consider the two-element buffer example of Sect. 7.4.5 (p. 240) in terms of association relations. Write down the essential assumptions on these relations, and rewrite actions Put2, Transfer, and Get2 as needed.

# 7.5 Aggregation vs. Inheritance vs. Copying

The intuitions behind aggregation and explicit subclasses are different. As technical facilities they are, however, often interchangeable. A third mechanism that can serve similar purposes is copying (see Sect. 6.2.4, p. 178), which we restrict, however, to entire layered specifications.

To understand these facilities better, the limits of their technical interchangeability are analyzed in this section. The possibilities offered by the combined use of aggregation and inheritance will also be presented.

## 7.5.1 Similarity of Aggregation and Inheritance

At an intuitive level, aggregation and explicit subclasses are suitable for modeling 'has-a' and 'is-a' relations, respectively. Their distinction is, however, rather subtle, and the choice between them often reflects a selection of viewpoint rather than inherent characteristics of the problem.

For instance, it may seem natural to consider Man and Woman to be subclasses of Person, since the associated relationships are intuitively understood as 'is-a' relations. One could, however, also defend the somewhat counterintuitive view that there is an asexual Person component within each Man and Woman object, and one may not find any logical contradictions in modeling the world in this way. As for the class system, this choice would also lead to two subclasses of Person, to those that are components in Man, and to those that are components in Woman.

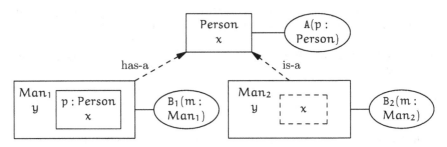

**Fig. 7.13.** Illustration of the similarity between aggregation and inheritance

Technically, both modeling possibilities lead to the same sets of local variables in the classes, and to similar specializations of actions that have been defined for Person. To see this in more detail, let the class-specific variables of Person be denoted by $x$, and those that are specific to Man by $y$. Figure 7.13 then illustrates the situation where $Man_1$ is an aggregate class that gives rise to subobject class $Man_1.p$, whereas $Man_2$ is an explicitly defined subclass of Person. To emphasize the similarity, inherited local variables $x$ have been given in the figure in a dashed box within $Man_2$.

As for actions, any action A for Person can be specialized in both cases so that their effects are identical. In the situation illustrated in Fig. 7.13 such specializations could be written as

$$B_1(m : Man_1) : A(^*m.p)$$

$$\cdots ,$$

$$B_2(m : Man_2) : A(^*m)$$

$$\cdots ,$$

and attributes $x$ could be accessed in them as $m.p.x$ and $m.x$, respectively.

### 7.5.2 Non-equivalence of Aggregation and Inheritance

In the above situation, aggregation and explicit subclasses exhibit no essential differences. The situation remains the same when aggregation of multiple

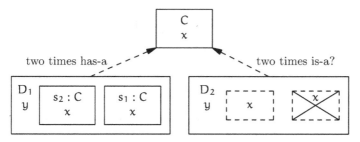

**Fig. 7.14.** Two subobjects of the same class is possible (left), whereas two sets of inherited variables is not (right)

components (belonging to disjoint classes) is compared to an explicit subclass with multiple base classes.

There are, however, situations where the equivalence of the two facilities breaks down:

- Several subobjects of the same class can be introduced in aggregation, whereas an object of a subclass is always just one object of its base class(es) (see Fig. 7.14).
- When two components of an aggregate belong to different subclasses of a common superclass, the local variables of this superclass appear separately in each subobject. In contrast, in multiple inheritance of such subclasses the local variables of the common superclass are inherited only once (see Fig. 7.15).
- Combined use of aggregation and explicit subclasses allows the definition of recursive structures in a manner that is not possible with either facility alone.

The first situation, illustrated in Fig. 7.14, is one where aggregation is more powerful than explicit subclasses.

The second situation is illustrated in Fig. 7.15, where $D_1$ is an aggregate class containing components in $C_1$ and $C_2$, whereas $D_2$ is an explicit subclass that inherits them both. If one were to try to use aggregation to achieve the effects of $D_2$, then the two subobjects $d.s_1$ and $d.s_2$ of an object $d \in D_1$ would need to have a common subobject with variable x. That is, one would need to relax the requirement that a subobject can be an immediate subobject in at most one aggregate. This shows that explicit subclasses with multiple inheritance provide restricted means to overcome this intended limitation of aggregation, without resorting to the full generality of associations.

The third situation of recursive structures will be discussed separately below, starting in Sect. 7.5.7.

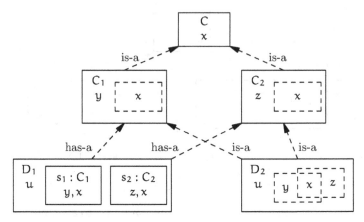

**Fig. 7.15.** Each subobject has separate local variables (left), whereas all inherited variables are included only once (right)

### 7.5.3 Copying and the 'Uses' Relation

As mentioned in Sect. 6.2.4 (p. 178), it is sometimes useful to utilize copies of a specification layer, with different names for their global variables, classes, and relations. Although copying could be defined in several ways, we restrict it to 'deep copying' of specification layers. That is, copying is applied to entire layered specifications only, and there is no sharing between the original specification and its copies.

Let $S$ be a specification layer with copies $S_i$, $i = 1,\ldots$. When a copy, say $S_1$, is imported to layer $T$, we can say that relation 'uses' is established between $T$ and $S$; specification $T$ is not a refinement of $S$, but it makes use of it. There is an analogy to aggregation in the sense that specification $T$ may at the same time use several independent copies $S_i$.

Copying can also be used with effects that are similar to subclassing. To see this, consider the simple situation illustrated in the left-hand part of Fig. 7.16, where layer $S$ with no global variables specifies a single class $C$ with action $A$. Layer $S$ is then imported to $T$, which introduces a subclass $C_1$ of $C$ with a specialization $B$ of action $A$.

Effectively the same is done in the right-hand part of Fig. 7.16 by importing to $T$ both layer $S$ and a copy $S_1$ of it, where class $C$ is called $C_1$. Class $C_1$ is then extended and the associated action $A_1$ is refined similarly to how the corresponding subclass and specialized action were formed on the left.

The main difference between the two constructions is that, in the right-hand part, classes $C_1$ and $C$ are disjoint, corresponding to classes $C_1$ and $C \setminus C_1$ in the left-hand part, respectively. Intuitively, an 'is-a' relation holds between $C_1$ and $C$ in the left-hand part, whereas in the right-hand part one can say that class $C_1$ uses $C$ (as defined in layer $S$), i.e., a 'uses' relation holds between them. As a consequence of this difference, any subsequent additions

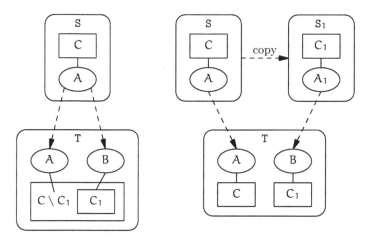

**Fig. 7.16.** Similar effects achieved by a subclass (left) and by copying (right)

to class C will also affect $C_1$ in the construction on the left, but not in the one on the right.

### 7.5.4 Simple Use of Multiple Inheritance

In discussing object-oriented design methods it has often been debated whether multiple inheritance offers any real advantages, and what proper multiple inheritance does, in fact, mean. In many situations where the use of multiple inheritance has been suggested, one can indeed argue whether a true 'is-a' relationship holds to more than one of the base classes. The relationship to the others might be more natural to express by aggregation, or by an association that expresses some kind of clientship.

In specification the situation is not, however, the same as in programming, and examples can easily be provided where multiple inheritance corresponds intuitively to a multiple 'is-a' relationship. Usually this results from providing several independent views of some objects, and from a subsequent need to synthesize these views. When multiple inheritance is used for classes without a common superclass (except for the trivial root class $C_0$), aggregation could technically be used instead, as was explained above. Multiple 'is-a' relationship may, however, be more truthful to intuition in this case also, as is shown by multiple inheritance of classes Pat and Emp in the doctors' office example discussed in Sect. 7.3.

### 7.5.5 Multiple Inheritance with a Common Superclass

Multiple inheritance of classes with a common superclass is analogous to combining independent extensions of a class. Together with composition of layers, the mechanism of class extension allows us to express independent refinements independently. Multiple inheritance allows us, in addition, to combine such independent refinements at will. The situation is then the one illustrated above in Fig. 7.5 (p. 228).

As an example, let us consider a generic class definition for random-number generators and two independent subclasses that one might wish to combine by multiple inheritance.

### Example: Generic Random-number Generator

Let class

$$\textbf{class } G\_rand = \{y : \mathbb{R}\} \, ,$$

defined in layer G, model random-number generators with a local seed variable y, and let actions for it be

$$\texttt{Initialize}(r : G\_rand; \, x : \mathbb{R}) : \textbf{T}$$
$$\rightarrow \, r.y' = x \, ,$$

$$\texttt{Next}(r : G\_rand; \, z, x : \mathbb{R}) : z = r.y$$
$$\rightarrow \, r.y' = x \, ,$$

where Initialize initializes y with a seed number x, and Next gives the current value of y as output z and updates y with another value x.

### Subclass that Determines the Algorithm

A concrete random-number generator could be obtained from G_rand in another layer C by determining the function f by which y is updated, and restricting initialization to take place only once:

$$\textbf{class } C\_rand = G\_rand + \{\texttt{initialized} : \mathbb{B} \, (\texttt{false})\} \, ,$$

$$\texttt{C\_initialize}(c : C\_rand; \, x : \mathbb{R}) : G.\texttt{Initialize}(^*c, x)$$
$$\wedge \, \neg c.\texttt{initialized}$$
$$\rightarrow \, c.\texttt{initialized}' = \texttt{true} \, ,$$

$$\texttt{C\_next}(c : C\_rand; \, z : \mathbb{R}) : G.\texttt{Next}(^*c, z, f(c.y))$$
$$\wedge \, c.\texttt{initialized} \, .$$

### Subclass that Adds Functionality

Independently of C_rand, we could add functionality to G_rand, for instance by keeping a log of all numbers generated, and outputting this log when requested. This could be achieved in layer L as follows:

$$\textbf{class } \mathsf{L\_rand} = \mathsf{G\_rand} + \{\log : \mathbb{R} \, (\langle\rangle)\} \, ,$$

$$\mathsf{L\_initialize}(l : \mathsf{L\_rand}; \; x : \mathbb{R}) : \mathsf{G.Initialize}({}^{*}l, x)$$
$$\rightarrow \; l.\log' = \langle\rangle \, ,$$

$$\mathsf{L\_next}(l : \mathsf{L\_rand}; \; z, x : \mathbb{R}) : \mathsf{G.Next}({}^{*}l, z, x)$$
$$\rightarrow \; l.\log' = l.\log \circ \langle z\rangle \, ,$$

$$\mathsf{Output\_log}(l : \mathsf{L\_rand}; \; u : \mathbb{R}) : \mathsf{G.Stutter}$$
$$\wedge u = l.\log$$
$$\rightarrow \; l.\log' = \langle\rangle \, .$$

## Combination by Multiple Inheritance

The properties of C_rand and L_rand could now be combined by multiple inheritance. In particular, the actions for the intersection C_rand ∩ L_rand would imply the corresponding actions for both base classes, as shown in the generic illustration in Fig. 7.5 (p. 228).

### 7.5.6 Combining Explicit Subclasses and Aggregation

In Sect. 7.4.6 (p. 241) it was shown how class extension can be used to refine an abstract class specification into an implementation that utilizes a collection of other objects. The same idea is also applicable so that subclasses are used instead of class extension, and this provides a systematic approach to deriving implementations of abstract classes.[4]

Given an abstract base class C, an implementation of C can be derived as an aggregate subclass D, $D \subseteq C$, which contains as subobjects those objects that will constitute the implementation. The situation is illustrated in Fig. 7.17, where the braces around the inherited variable $x_2$ in D indicate that it has been effectively removed by data refinement.

The *abstraction mapping* between the implementation subclass D and the abstract class C is provided by invariants that show how (some of) the inherited variables are represented in terms of variables in the subobjects. The purpose of these invariants is to turn these inherited variables into non-primitive state functions that can be omitted from an implementation. In the situation of Fig. 7.17 such an invariant for $d \in D$ would have the form

$$\Box(d.x_2 = f(d.s_1.y, d.s_2.z)) \, .$$

---

[4]In object-oriented programming languages the term 'abstract class' has a technical meaning. Here it just denotes a class whose specification is at a high level of abstraction. Correspondingly, an 'implementation' denotes here a specification that is at a lower level of abstraction, and is therefore closer to a concrete implementation.

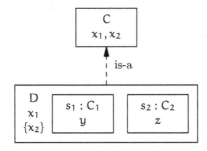

**Fig. 7.17.** Implementation of a class as an aggregate

Actions for subclass D must then be either new actions or specializations of those for C, $C_1$, and $C_2$. Action combination or concatenation may also be needed, as was shown in the example in Sect. 7.4.6 (p. 241).

### 7.5.7 Recursive Aggregates

The above idea of implementing an abstract class C as an aggregate class D, $D \subseteq C$, can also be utilized in such a way that D contains subobjects that belong to C. This situation is illustrated in Fig. 7.18, which corresponds to a class definition of the form

$$\textbf{class } D = C + \{\ldots\, s : C\}\,.$$

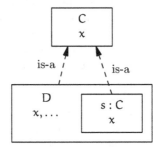

**Fig. 7.18.** Recursive implementation of a class

At first sight this might seem to be useless, or to be in conflict with the general restrictions on subclasses and subobject relations. However, although some kind of recursion is involved, this does not mean that some class would be a proper subclass of its own. Also, the constraints given in Sect. 7.4.4 (p. 239) for subobject relations are not violated either, since the situation does not imply the existence of infinite subobject chains, or that some subobject would be an immediate subobject in more than one aggregate object.

What is special in this situation is that two subclasses of C are introduced at the same time: $D \subseteq C$ and $D.s \subseteq C$. If these are disjoint, i.e., $D \cap D.s = \emptyset$, the situation is similar to what has already been discussed. New possibilities arise, however, if multiple inheritance of D and D.s is permitted, i.e., $D \cap D.s \neq \emptyset$. For instance, we can then have an object $d \in D$ illustrated in Fig. 7.19, where d.s is in $D \cap D.s$ and therefore has a further subobject d.s.s, which then belongs to subclass $(D \cap D.s).s$.

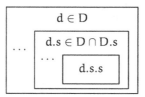

**Fig. 7.19.** Multiple inheritance of a subobject class and an explicit aggregate subclass

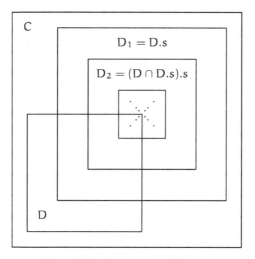

**Fig. 7.20.** Recursive subclasses

For the class system the situation $D \cap D.s \neq \emptyset$ means that there is an infinite sequence of nested subclasses

$$D_1 = D.s , \quad D_2 = (D \cap D.s).s , \quad \dots , \quad D_{i+1} = (D \cap D_i).s , \quad \dots \tag{7.2}$$

as illustrated in Fig. 7.20. Objects $d \in D_i$ are those that are at least on the ith level of nested subobjects, and objects $d \in (D_i \setminus D_{i+1}) \setminus D$ are those that are at level i and have no further subobjects d.s.

Notice that the non-existence of infinite subobject chains requires each object $d \in D$ to have a maximal depth for which a sub...subobject d.s...s exists. Because of the assumption that subobject relations are constant relations, this depth must also be constant for each $d \in D$.

Recursive aggregates exhibit situations that cannot be represented in terms of only aggregation or inheritance. Combined use of these facilities therefore offers restricted possibilities to overcome their limitations, without resorting to the full generality of associations. In the following such possibilities will be analyzed in more detail in the light of a simple example.

### 7.5.8 Example: Nested Stacks

A simple example of a stack is used to illustrate the idea of recursive aggregates.

### Basic Stack

Let C be a class definition for a stack, defined in layer S. A list-valued local variable u, initialized as empty, is used in C to store the contents of a stack, with 'length', 'first', 'rest', and '∘' as used before in this book. For simplicity, an additional redundant variable n will be used to indicate the current length of u, i.e.,

$$\Box(c.n = \text{length}(c.u))$$

is an intended invariant for all $c \in C$.

This leads to class definition

$$\textbf{class } C = \{u : \textbf{list } \mathbb{U} \ (\langle\rangle); \ n : \mathbb{N} \ (0)\}$$

and actions

$$\begin{aligned}
\textbf{Push}(c : C; \ x : \mathbb{U}) &: \textbf{T} \\
&\rightarrow \ c.u' = \langle x \rangle \circ c.u \\
&\wedge c.n' = c.n + 1 \ ,
\end{aligned}$$

$$\begin{aligned}
\textbf{Pop}(c : C; \ x : \mathbb{U}) &: c.n > 0 \\
&\rightarrow \ x = \text{first}(c.u) \\
&\wedge c.u' = \text{rest}(c.u) \\
&\wedge c.n' = c.n - 1 \ .
\end{aligned}$$

Notice that, since there is no fairness requirement in Push, class C can also have subclasses with finite capacity. The specialization of action Push would be disabled for objects of such a subclass, when the stack is full.

**Stack within Stack**

Consider an implementation of the stack class C that stores separately the top element of the stack and uses an internal stack for the rest of it. Although this does not sound very useful in itself, it offers a basis for a recursive structure where each level – except the innermost one – stores just one stack element.

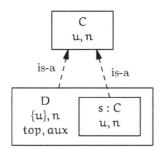

**Fig. 7.21.** Stack within a stack

Introducing further state variables to indicate whether a push or pop operation is pending for the internal stack, and using an auxiliary variable $aux$ to store an additional value, we get subclass $D \subseteq C$,

**class** $D = C + \{top, aux : \mathbb{U};$ **state** $Ready^*, Pushing, Popping; s : C\}$,

illustrated in Fig. 7.21, with an intended invariant

$$\Box(d.Ready \wedge d.n = d.s.n = 0 \vee$$
$$d.Ready \wedge d.u = \langle d.top \rangle \circ d.s.u \vee$$
$$d.Pushing \wedge d.u = \langle d.top, d.aux \rangle \circ d.s.u \vee$$
$$d.Popping \wedge d.u = d.s.u) \tag{7.3}$$

for $d \in D$. Obviously, $d.n \geq d.s.n$ is then also invariantly true and, if $d$ is $Ready$ and $d.n > 0$, then $d.top$ contains the first element of the stack, $d.top = first(d.u)$.

The purpose of invariant (7.3) is to make variable $d.u$ into a non-primitive state function that need not be present. Since D contains a subobject in C, and infinite subobject chains are not possible, the construction will not, however, remove the need for implementing class C either directly or as another subclass.

Assuming that the two subclasses D and D.s are disjoint, actions Push and Pop can now be specialized for them as

$$Push\_first(d : D; x : \mathbb{U}) : S.Push(^*d, x)$$
$$\wedge d.Ready$$
$$\wedge d.n = 0$$
$$\rightarrow d.top' = x,$$

$$\text{Push\_rest}(d:D;\ x:\mathbb{U}):\texttt{S.Push}(^*d,x)$$
$$\wedge\ d.\text{Ready}$$
$$\wedge\ d.n>0$$
$$\rightarrow\ d.\text{aux}'=d.\text{top}$$
$$\wedge\ d.\text{top}'=x$$
$$\wedge\ d.\text{Pushing}'\,,$$

$$\text{Push\_internal}(^{\text{WF}}d:D):\texttt{S.Push}(^*d.s,d.\text{aux})$$
$$\wedge\ d.\text{Pushing}$$
$$\rightarrow\ d.\text{Ready}'\,,$$

$$\text{Pop\_last}(d:D;\ x:\mathbb{U}):\texttt{S.Pop}(^*d,x)$$
$$\wedge\ d.\text{Ready}$$
$$\wedge\ d.n=1$$
$$\wedge\ x=d.\text{top}\,,$$

$$\text{Pop\_rest}(d:D;\ x:\mathbb{U}):\texttt{S.Pop}(^*d,x)$$
$$\wedge\ d.\text{Ready}$$
$$\wedge\ d.n>1$$
$$\wedge\ x=d.\text{top}$$
$$\rightarrow\ d.\text{Popping}'\,,$$

$$\text{Pop\_internal}(^{\text{WF}}d:D):\texttt{S.Pop}(^*d.s,x)$$
$$\wedge\ d.\text{Popping}$$
$$\rightarrow\ d.\text{top}'=x$$
$$\wedge\ d.\text{Ready}'\,,$$

and the satisfaction of invariant (7.3) can then be immediately verified.

Since no liveness requirements were given in layer S for class C, the fairness assumptions given here for subclass D may seem superfluous. However, by preventing objects $d\in D$ from staying permanently in state d.Pushing or d.Popping, in which external push and pop actions are disabled, the given fairness assumptions allow the use of subclass D to replace C in connections where fairness assumptions have also been added to push and pop actions. This question will be discussed in a more general setting in Chap. 8.

### Recursive Stack

Consider now the situation $D\cap D.s\neq\emptyset$. There are then objects d that are subobjects of $d.s^{-1}$ but also themselves have subobjects d.s, as illustrated in Fig. 7.22. Since infinite chains of subobjects are not allowed, this nesting

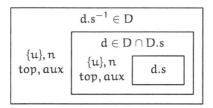

**Fig. 7.22.** Object d that belongs to both D and D.s

must, however, end at some point. That is, there is an innermost stack d.s...s, which does not belong to D.

The situation is exceptional in the sense that two levels of subclasses have then been introduced in the same layer – a situation that we have not allowed to arise so far. It is now reasonable to consider the specialized actions given above to be applicable only to subclasses D \ D.s and D.s \ D. Their combinations are, however, sufficient to determine the reasonable specializations for D ∩ D.s also.

To see this, consider push actions for subclass D∩D.s, and let $d \in D \cap D.s$ be as illustrated in Fig. 7.22. To be a specialization for subclass D.s, a push action for d needs to have the characteristics of `Push_internal`$(d.s^{-1})$, which implies `S.Push`$(d, d.s^{-1}.aux)$. On the other hand, to be a specialization for D, it also needs to have the characteristics of either `Push_first`$(d, x)$ or `Push_rest`$(d, x)$, both of which imply `S.Push`$(d, x)$. Unifying the implied instances of action `S.Push` therefore determines x in both cases as $x = d.s^{-1}.aux$. Combining the guards and effects of `Push_internal`$(d.s^{-1})$ with those of `Push_first`$(d, d.s^{-1}.aux)$ and `Push_rest`$(d, s^{-1}.aux)$, respectively, then gives us actions

$$\text{Push\_nested\_first}(^{\text{WF}}d : D \cap D.s) : \text{S.Push}(^*d, d.s^{-1}.aux)$$
$$\wedge\ d.s^{-1}.\text{Pushing}$$
$$\wedge\ d.\text{Ready}$$
$$\wedge\ d.n = 0$$
$$\rightarrow\ d.s^{-1}.\text{Ready}'$$
$$\wedge\ d.\text{top}' = d.s^{-1}.aux\ ,$$

$$\text{Push\_nested\_rest}(^{WF}d : D \cap D.s) : S.\text{Push}(^*d, d.s^{-1}.aux)$$
$$\wedge d.s^{-1}.\text{Pushing}$$
$$\wedge d.\text{Ready}$$
$$\wedge d.n > 0$$
$$\rightarrow d.s^{-1}.\text{Ready}'$$
$$\wedge d.aux' = d.\text{top}$$
$$\wedge d.\text{top}' = d.s^{-1}.aux$$
$$\wedge d.\text{Pushing}' ,$$

where the fairness requirements are needed to satisfy the fairness requirements associated with subclass D.s.

The corresponding specializations of S.Pop can be derived similarly.

### Discussion

As already stated, the above specializations for $D \cap D.s$ are determined by those for $D$ and $D.s$. The following general observations are sufficient to show that the resulting specializations do not lead to conflicting 'assignments' in this kind of situation:

- Unification ensures that the implied actions for base class C are the same.
- The specializations for D and D.s that are combined update class-specific variables in different objects of class D.

Multiple inheritance of D and D.s also gives proof obligations for the liveness properties of the intersection class $D \cap D.s$. To be more specific, a non-empty stack $d \in D \cap D.s$ should always eventually become Ready. Since recursive structures are finite, such a proof is basically inductive. For the innermost pair of subobjects $(d.s^{-1}, d)$ we have $d \notin D$, and this property for $d.s^{-1}$ depends on the fairness assumption in Push_internal, which is the default specialization of this action for subclass $D.s \setminus D$. For non-innermost pairs $(d.s^{-1}, d)$, where $d \in D \cap D.s$, this property for $d.s^{-1}$ depends on the induction assumption for d and the fairness assumption in Push_nested_rest.

As for the actual behavior of a recursive stack, each push and pop operation may give rise to a cascade of internal push and pop actions, and several such cascades may be proceeding concurrently at different depths. In spite of this concurrency, the safety properties of the basic stack are satisfied by construction, and only liveness properties need a proof.

### 7.5.9 Synchronous Aggregates

Actions for an aggregate and its components were synchronized in the example of Sect. 7.4.6 (p. 241). This idea can also be applied in connection with recursive aggregates.

## Synchronized Stack within Stack

As an example consider a synchronous version of the stack example, where subclass $E \subseteq C$ is defined as

$$\textbf{class } E = C + \{top : \mathbb{U}; \; s : C\} \, ,$$

with the following intended invariant for $e \in E$:

$$\Box(e.u = e.s.u = \langle\rangle \vee e.u = \langle e.top\rangle \circ e.s.u) \, .$$

Obviously, then always either $e.n = e.s.n = 0$ or $e.n = e.s.n + 1 > 0$.

Assuming first that $E \cap E.s = \emptyset$, synchronous operation on objects $e \in E$ and $e.s \in E.s$ can be expressed in terms of combined actions, and we get the following specialized actions:

$$\text{Push\_sync\_first}(e : E; \; x : \mathbb{U}) : \text{S.Push}(^*e, x)$$
$$\wedge \; e.n = 0$$
$$\rightarrow \; e.top' = x \, ,$$

$$\text{Push\_sync\_rest}(e : E; \; x : \mathbb{U}) : \text{S.Push}(^*e, x) \; \&$$
$$\text{S.Push}(^*e.s, e.top)$$
$$\wedge \; e.n > 0$$
$$\rightarrow \; e.top' = x \, ,$$

$$\text{Pop\_sync\_last}(e : E; \; x : \mathbb{U}) : \text{S.Pop}(^*e, e.top)$$
$$\wedge \; e.n = 1$$
$$\wedge \; x = e.top \, ,$$

$$\text{Pop\_sync\_rest}(e : E; \; x : \mathbb{U}) : \text{S.Pop}(^*e, e.top) \; \&$$
$$\text{S.Pop}(^*e.s, \text{first}(e.s.u))$$
$$\wedge \; e.n > 1$$
$$\wedge \; x = e.top$$
$$\rightarrow \; e.top' = \text{first}(e.s.u) \, .$$

## Synchronized Recursive Stack

Finally, we investigate the consequences of permitting multiple inheritance of $E$ and $E.s$ in the above synchronous example. Instead of cascaded push and pop operations, as in the asynchronous case, this leads to operations that push and pop synchronously through all required stack levels. Since there is no bound on the number of levels, the number of resulting actions is no longer finite, although only a finite number of them is applicable to any given object $e \in E \cap E.s$.

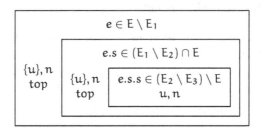

**Fig. 7.23.** Three nested and synchronous stacks

Similarly to the asynchronous case, push and pop actions for $E \cap E.s$ are again determined by the actions for the non-recursive situation. As an example, let $e$ be as illustrated in Fig. 7.23, where $e$ and $e.s$ belong to class $E$, but $e.s.s$ does not, and subclasses have been denoted analogously to the conventions in (7.2) and Fig. 7.20 (p. 251) as

$$E_1 = E.s \;,\; E_2 = (E \cap E.s).s \;,\; \dots \;,\; E_{i+1} = (E \cap E_i).s \;,\; \dots \;.$$

Consider now a push action for such an object $e$ in the situation where $e.n \geq 2$. Since the subclass of $e.s.s$ determines uniquely the subclasses of $e.s$ and $e$, we formulate it for the participant $c = e.s.s$. Similarly to the reasoning in the case of asynchronous recursive stacks, we conclude that such an action must have the characteristics of actions $\texttt{Push\_sync\_rest}(c.s^{-1}.s^{-1}, x)$, $\texttt{Push\_sync\_rest}(c.s^{-1}, y)$, and $\texttt{S.Push}(c, z)$. Unification of implied instances of actions now determines parameters $y$ and $z$ as $y = c.s^{-1}.s^{-1}.\text{top}$ and $z = c.s^{-1}.\text{top}$, which leads to a specialized action[5]

$$\texttt{Push\_sync\_f}_2(c : (E_2 \setminus E_3) \setminus E; \; x : \mathbb{U}) : \texttt{S.Push}(^*c.s^{-1}.s^{-1}, x) \;\&$$
$$\texttt{S.Push}(^*c.s^{-1}, c.s^{-1}.s^{-1}.\text{top}) \;\&$$
$$\texttt{S.Push}(^*c, c.s^{-1}.\text{top})$$
$$\wedge \; c.s^{-1}.n > 0$$
$$\rightarrow \; c.s^{-1}.s^{-1}.\text{top}' = x$$
$$\wedge \; c.s^{-1}.\text{top}' = c.s^{-1}.s^{-1}.\text{top} \;.$$

Other specialized actions for the different subclasses of $E \cap E.s$ can be derived in a similar manner.

### Review Questions

QUESTION 7.5.1 In which situations is there no essential technical difference between aggregation and inheritance?

---

[5]Suffix $f$ in the name is intended to indicate that the action operates on a 'full' stack, where all levels, except possibly the innermost stack, are already in use, and subscript 2 indicates their number.

QUESTION 7.5.2 In which situations is copying and extending a class an alternative for subclassing?

QUESTION 7.5.3 What is meant by an 'abstract class' in this book, and how can an 'implementation subclass' be introduced as an aggregate?

QUESTION 7.5.4 Why does finiteness of recursive structures simplify proofs of liveness properties?

### Exercises

EXERCISE 7.5.1 Compare multiple inheritance of two different subclasses of C and extensions of two different copies of C.

EXERCISE 7.5.2 Show that sequence (7.2) on p. 251 is, indeed, a sequence of nested subclasses, as illustrated in Fig. 7.20.

EXERCISE 7.5.3 To which leaf subclasses in Fig. 7.20 (p. 251) do objects d, d.s, and d.s.s of Fig. 7.19 (p. 251) belong, if d is not a subobject, and d.s.s is not an aggregate?

EXERCISE 7.5.4 Check that invariant (7.3) on p. 253 is maintained by the actions given in Sect. 7.5.8.

EXERCISE 7.5.5 Derive the specializations of S.Pop for subclass D ∩ D.s in Sect. 7.5.8.

EXERCISE 7.5.6 Improve the efficiency of internal stack operations for nested stacks in Sect. 7.5.8, so that push operations are also accepted in state Popping, and pop operations are also accepted in state Pushing.

EXERCISE 7.5.7 Derive all specializations of S.Push and S.Pop that are applicable to the synchronized stack object illustrated in Fig. 7.23 (p. 258).

## Bibliographic Notes

The main ideas of object orientation were discovered and investigated by Dahl et al. in developing the Algol 60-based programming language *Simula 67* [39]. After being applied in a puristic form in the *Smalltalk* language and programming environment [67], these ideas raised wider interest in programming language research and development. Finally, through *C++* [186], which was initially developed by Stroustrup as an object-oriented extension to the C language, and more recently through *Java* [70], it has become standard practice in large parts of the software industry.

From the very beginning, inheritance has been one of the characteristics of object orientation, but it has also raised a lot of discussion of its true essence, proper use, and implementation problems. The need for multiple inheritance is a specific topic that has been debated. For a discussion of such issues, the reader is referred to Sakkinen's critical analysis of inheritance in C++ [178], and to an extensive survey paper by Taivalsaari [188]. The presentation in this book has omitted those characteristics of inheritance that do not seem relevant for the logical specification of systems.

In Wegner's classification [192], a language is *object-based* if it supports objects as a language feature, and *object-oriented* if its objects belong to classes and if class hierarchies may be incrementally defined by an inheritance mechanism. Although our specification language lacks those programming level features that are often considered to be characteristic to object orientation, it clearly satisfies Wegner's criteria for object orientation.

Complement subclasses and subobject subclasses, as presented here, are notions that do not appear in object-oriented programming languages. The former is, however, a necessity for effective use of class hierarchies in the refinement of specifications, and the latter arises naturally in making a useful distinction between aggregation and more liberal associations.

In addition to programming and program design, the use of objects is also currently advocated in methods for the specification and modeling of software. A commonly used formalism, which is intended to standardize the associated concepts and graphical formalisms, is the Unified Modeling Language (UML) [191]. As for terminology, the definitive guide of UML [90] does not speak about specialization by subclasses and inheritance. Instead it uses the term 'generalization' to denote the converse of specialization. Also, the term 'composition' is used there for what is called aggregation in this book. 'Aggregation', on the other hand, denotes in UML a weaker relation, which allows a component object to be a component in several aggregates at the same time. From the viewpoint of adding useful formal properties to those of general associations, the advantages of this weaker form are, of course, also weaker.

In UML and other informal approaches, notation and graphical formalisms are introduced at an intuitive level, where precise semantics is not considered a major concern. As for attempts to add formal meaning to UML, the reader is referred to the home page of the precise UML group [173]. Although it is traditional in computing to agree on formalisms before analyzing their meanings precisely, this book tries to follow the opposite path. The reason for not having adopted the graphical notations of UML, for instance, has been the desire to use graphical diagrams to illustrate formally defined concepts, not to develop formal concepts to match informal diagrams.

The approach presented here can also be contrasted to those formal methods to which facilities have been added afterwards to cope with object-oriented features (see [147], for instance). Typically, object orientation is considered in them as a programming language mechanism, which should be modeled truthfully, whereas here the emphasis is on making the best use of object orientation in the specification process.

The modeling problem of a doctors' office is an example that has been used to compare different specification and design methods. The presentation in Sect. 7.3 has been adapted from [119].

The kind of recursive aggregates that were discussed in Sect. 7.5.7 are known in the literature on object-oriented design patterns as a pattern called 'Composite' [65].

# 8

# Components and Interfaces

As discussed in Chap. 2, a closed-system model describes how the *system* to be implemented and its *environment* behave in connection with each other. To use such a model as a basis for an implementation, the *system part* of the model should be separated from the *environment part*.[1] Similarly, the system part can itself be partitioned into *components* that communicate with each other. The purpose of this is that, once conventions for communication have been agreed on, the components could be implemented independently of each other, in either software or hardware.

This kind of partitioning and its effect on refinement is the topic of this chapter. The plan for the chapter is as follows:

- Section 8.1 introduces partitioning of the variables and actions of a closed system into components, and discusses how the components can interact through shared variables and action parameters.
- In Sect. 8.2 we discuss *non-interfering component refinements*, where actions of only one component are refined. This leads to a simple methodological guideline to start with an initial layer of specification, which basically determines only interfaces, and to refine the actions of each component independently. The resulting layers can always be composed into a refinement where all component refinements are combined.
- More liberal component refinements are considered in Sect. 8.3, in order to allow refining external interface actions also, i.e., actions that access interface variables of a component from other components. This possibility is needed, for instance, for temporary refusal of external accesses, in order to insert internal computing. Sufficient *robustness conditions* are derived in this section to ensure composability of the individual component refinements in this case also.
- In Sect. 8.4 we discuss how interfaces can be refined in component refinements.

---

[1] It should be clear from context whether the word 'system' refers to the whole closed system at hand or to the system part to be implemented.

- The chapter ends in Sect. 8.5 with an example in which a simple one-element buffer is refined in several steps into a reliable channel that uses two unreliable channels and an alternating bit protocol for communication.

## 8.1 Components in a Closed System

As discussed in Sect. 6.3 (p. 179), a closed-system model describes 'the whole world', although only those aspects of the world are made explicit that affect the variables that we are interested in. Structurally this 'whole world' can be viewed as consisting of interacting *components*, which communicate with each other through shared *interface variables*, as discussed in Sect. 2.1.3 (p. 27). In particular, the *environment* of an embedded system and the embedded *system* itself are such components, and they may also themselves consist of more elementary interacting components.

The purpose of *partitioning* a system into components can be understood as division of different *responsibilities* in an implementation to the cooperating components. Ultimately this is needed only for the final model, but usually partitioning evolves gradually in the incremental steps in which a model is constructed. To allow maximal freedom in this respect, we keep partitioning into components as an extralinguistic issue, for which no specific facilities will be provided in the action language. In this section we discuss, however, some important issues associated with it.

### 8.1.1 Partitioning of State

As discussed briefly in Sect. 2.1.3 (p. 27), the responsibilities for state variables are divided by assigning them to the different components. If $X$ is the set of variables involved in a specification (excluding possible abstract variables that need not be implemented), and there are $k$ components, we then have a partitioning of variables in $X$ into disjoint subsets $X_i$, $i = 1, \ldots, k$,

$$X = X_1 \cup \cdots \cup X_k, \quad X_i \cap X_j = \emptyset \quad \text{for} \quad i \neq j,$$

where variables in $X_i$ are assigned to component $i$ and are said to belong to it, or to be *local* to it.

As for objects, which also partition the state,

- each object is assumed to be local to some component, i.e., the local variables of an object cannot be distributed to different components,[2] and
- all objects that belong to the same leaf class are assumed to belong to the same component.

---

[2]Since the subobjects of an aggregated object are, in fact, objects in their own right, this does not prevent allocating them to different components.

Since relations between objects are understood as global variables, partitioning of variables needs to address them also.

A state predicate that depends only on local variables of one component is also called *local* to that component. State predicate P is said to be *separable* for component i if it can be expressed as a conjunction

$$P \Leftrightarrow P_i \wedge Q ,$$

where $P_i$ is local to component i and Q is independent of variables in this component.

### 8.1.2 Partitioned Action Systems

As discussed briefly in Sect. 2.2.2 (p. 30), the responsibilities for actions are also divided between the components, so that each action is assigned to a specific component. Even though an action may involve variables in several components and, intuitively speaking, then requires some cooperation from each of these, the responsibility for its execution will not be shared. However, to know which components are involved in an action, it will be assumed in the following that each participant role determines a unique component. When objects of the same leaf class belong to the same component, this is not an essential restriction.

To discuss the partitioning of actions more precisely, let

$$S \triangleq P \wedge \Box[A]_X \wedge F \tag{8.1}$$

be a canonical TLA formula that corresponds to a closed-system specification and, as before, let symbol A also stand for the set of individual actions of which the TLA action A is formed as disjunction. Similarly, let F also stand for the sets of individual (strong and weak) fairness conditions of which the TLA fairness formula F consists.

Partitioning of (8.1) for k components then means that variables in X are partitioned into sets of local variables $X_i$ as discussed above, and that actions in A are similarly partitioned into disjoint subsets of actions

$$A = A_1 \cup \cdots \cup A_k , \quad A_i \cap A_j = \emptyset \quad \text{for} \quad i \neq j ,$$

so that actions in $A_i$ are assigned to component i, and are said to be *local* to it. Obviously, such a partitioning of actions also induces partitioning of fairness conditions,

$$F = F_1 \cup \cdots \cup F_k ,$$

so that $F_i$ concerns only actions in $A_i$. Formula (8.1) then has the partitioned form

$$S \Leftrightarrow P \wedge \Box[A_1 \vee \cdots \vee A_k]_{X_1 \cup \cdots \cup X_k} \wedge F_1 \wedge \cdots \wedge F_k . \tag{8.2}$$

When an action in $A_i$ is executed, it is said to be executed by component i. For each non-stuttering step in a behavior it is important to distinguish the component that has executed the associated action. Therefore,

- the partitioning of actions is assumed to be exclusive in the sense that, for $i \neq j$,

$$A_i \wedge A_j \Rightarrow \mathsf{Stutter}_X .$$

An action system for which such a partitioning of variables and actions has been imposed is called a *partitioned action system*. Without partitioning, a specification can be understood as the special case of only one component. Partitioning of this component may, however, be imposed in refinement steps, as will be described below.

### 8.1.3 Interface Variables

In principle, each TLA action involves all variables in $X$, independently of whether it changes their values or not. In an operational interpretation, however, an action does not generally need to access all variables in $X$. A notion of *dependence* on variables is therefore needed.

Intuitively, an action $A$ *write depends* on variable $x$, $x \in X$, if it may modify the value of $x$, and it *read depends* on $x$ if its enabling condition $\mathsf{Enabled}\,A$ or its effect on state variables may depend on the value of $x$. To be more precise, we define these dependences on $x$, or *accesses* of $x$, by textual occurrences of $x'$ or $x$ in the action-language representation of action $A$, independently of whether these occurrences are semantically significant or not. Therefore, read and write dependences fall outside of TLA, and may in some situations be changed without affecting the TLA meaning of an action.

Since communication between components takes place through shared variables, the local variables in component i are subdivided further into *interface* variables ($X_i^{\mathrm{ifc}}$), which are also accessible for actions of other components, and *private* variables ($X_i^{\mathrm{pvt}}$) that are not,

$$X_i = X_i^{\mathrm{ifc}} \cup X_i^{\mathrm{pvt}} , \quad X_i^{\mathrm{ifc}} \cap X_i^{\mathrm{pvt}} = \emptyset .$$

Interface variables will be collectively denoted by $X^{\mathrm{ifc}}$,

$$X^{\mathrm{ifc}} = X_1^{\mathrm{ifc}} \cup \cdots \cup X_k^{\mathrm{ifc}} .$$

When an action of one component read or write depends on a variable in another component, this is called an *external* read or write access to it.

It is characteristic to superposition that no new write accesses can be introduced for old variables, but new read accesses can. To model situations where external read accesses are also restricted to those that have already been introduced, we define the set of *concealed* variables $X_i^{\mathrm{cnc}}$ to be a subset of $X_i^{\mathrm{ifc}}$, $X_i^{\mathrm{cnc}} \subseteq X_i^{\mathrm{ifc}}$, for which even no new external read accesses are allowed in superposition.

### 8.1.4 Interface Actions

In addition to its own variables, a component is allowed to access only interface variables in other components, as discussed in Sect. 2.2.2 (p. 30). Actions in $A_i$ may therefore depend only on variables in $X_i \cup X^{ifc}$.

An action in $A_i$ is said to be an *interface action* if it (potentially) depends on (interface) variables in other components. Otherwise it is *private* to component $i$. When this distinction is relevant, symbols $A_i^{ifc}$ and $A_i^{pvt}$ will be used to denote these sets of actions, $A_i = A_i^{ifc} \cup A_i^{pvt}$, $A_i^{ifc} \cap A_i^{pvt} = \emptyset$.

For a behavior it may be important to distinguish whether a step is associated with an interface action or not. If it is, the identity of the interface action will also be significant. Therefore, we assume that

- each individual interface action $B \in A_i^{ifc}$ is non-stuttering and disjoint from all other actions.

That is, $B \Rightarrow \neg\mathsf{Stutter}_X$ and, if $C$ is any other individual action in $A_i$, then $B \wedge C$ is identically false.

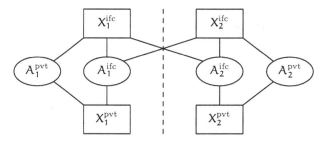

**Fig. 8.1.** Illustration of the partitioning of variables and actions

From the viewpoint of component $i$, actions in $A_i^{ifc}$ are *local interface actions*, while those in $A_j^{ifc}$, $i \neq j$, are *external* to it. The situation is illustrated for two components in Fig. 8.1.

Notice that interface actions in $A_i^{ifc}$ are said to be executed by component $i$ alone, not jointly with those other components to which they are external. About the role of the latter components we say that the execution is either *allowed* or *refused* by them.

### 8.1.5 Communication Through Action Parameters

Behaviors in a state-based approach are completely determined by the values that state variables have in consecutive states. In principle, all communication between components is therefore determined by the values that interface variables have in behaviors.

In parameterized interface actions it may, however, be the parameters that describe the values to be communicated between components. This is

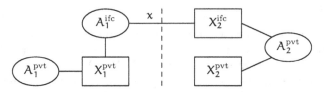

**Fig. 8.2.** Communication through an action parameter

illustrated in Fig. 8.2, where x denotes a parameter representing an input or output value transmitted between two components in action $A_1^{ifc}$. In such a situation, the values of the parameter need not only serve an auxiliary purpose in behaviors, but may be essential for them. On the other hand, the interface variables (in other components) that are affected by these parameter values may themselves be inessential in the sense that they may be quantified state variables in terms of TLA.

In such situations we implicitly assume an additional auxiliary component, which can be thought of as a *channel* between the communicating components, with a variable for intermediate storage of parameter values. A parameterized interface action is then, in fact, shorthand for two consecutive actions: one that stores the parameter value in this channel variable, and the other that immediately removes it from there.[3] With this assumption the state-based character of the approach is not violated.

In general, a parameter x in an interface action need not be a pure input or output value, which is transmitted from one component to others, but a more general *interput* value, which depends on variables in several components and may affect variables in all of them. Obviously, an implementation may then need complex communication between the components involved for the components to agree on an interput value that suits them all. Terms 'input' and 'output' now refer to the reduced situations where one of the partners gives no choice in such a negotiation.

### 8.1.6 Components and Refinement

A refinement of a partitioned system S, corresponding to TLA expression (8.2) on p. 265, should normally honor the component structure of S, i.e., either preserve or refine it. This means that the partitioning of variables and actions into components would remain compatible with their old partitionings. When partitioned systems are composed, compatible partitionings are assumed, and actions of different components will not be synchronized.

If a closed-system specification is derived in this manner, one can start with a one-component system and introduce an eventual component structure

--------

[3]Here we assume that there is no possibility for other actions to intervene. The situation is, of course, different if a channel is modeled explicitly in a specification.

stepwise. This structure is then only an add-on to the closed system, with no immediate effect on the kinds of refinement steps that can be taken. Since the whole closed system is available in each refinement step, interfaces between components – expressed in terms of interface variables and interface actions – can then be modified in an arbitrary fashion allowed by the refinement methodology. Only in the end are these interfaces important, since in the final specification they have to be implementable with those facilities that are available for implementation components.

Therefore, if the total system is allowed to be refined arbitrarily in each step, its component structure has only an intuitive role in determining the kinds of refinements that are needed to achieve modular implementability by components. This has the drawbacks that

- component structure is not utilized for guiding the division of labor in the refinement effort, and
- there is no a priori guarantee that parallel, aspect-oriented branches of refinement could be composed so that their liveness properties would also be preserved.

These considerations raise questions about the role of components in specifications. Before proceeding we therefore need to analyze this role briefly.

### 8.1.7 Modularity by Components

Components are usually understood as entities that can be described independently. This view is, however, somewhat problematic, since a description of a component always includes some assumptions about how it will be used by other components, which means modeling the component together with (some assumed properties of) its environment.

In practice, independence of components is achieved by giving assumptions on other components in interface definitions, which then have to be frozen before a description of the total system or the components is possible. The closed-system paradigm makes such assumptions explicit by always modeling a component and its environment together, and it thereby allows modeling of component interaction at a higher level of abstraction.

What is then the purpose of components? To understand their role in a (closed-system) specification process, we start from their role in implementation:

- In implementation, the purpose of components is to provide modularity, where *component implementations* are *composable* into an *implementation* of the total system.

For specification we then adopt the analogous view:

- In specification, the purpose of components is to provide modularity, where *component refinements* are *composable* into a *refined specification* of the total system.

By *composability* we mean here that the composition of component refinements is a refinement, in which the liveness properties of the individual component refinements are also preserved.

Notice that this view of specification components differs from the conventional view, where specification-level and implementation-level concerns are mixed. Starting from the idea that components are described independently, that view presumes independent implementability of component specifications, which is an unnecessarily strong requirement for the composability of specification components.

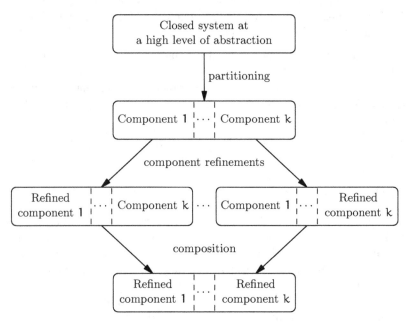

**Fig. 8.3.** Utilizing components in a closed-system specification process

The general idea of componentwise refinement of closed-system specifications is illustrated in Fig. 8.3. A crude model is first given at a high level of abstraction, with focus on cooperative behaviors. This specification is then partitioned into components, which are refined by separate (sequences of) component refinements. Each component refinement is assumed to refine only one component in the specification, and the resulting layers are composed in the end. In the following sections we will analyze such component refinements in more detail.

Technically this is a special case of aspect-oriented development (see Sect. 6.3.2, p. 180), where the aspects now correspond to components. Compared to the general case, the different branches of refinement are here restricted to concern single components, but some guarantees are needed that these branches will be composable in the end.

**Review Questions**

QUESTION 8.1.1 How does communication between components take place in a partitioned system?

QUESTION 8.1.2 What is meant by 'interput' in this book?

QUESTION 8.1.3 Why are implicit channel components sometimes assumed?

QUESTION 8.1.4 What are all the requirements for a partitioning of an action system and for the associated interface actions?

QUESTION 8.1.5 Does partitioning into components have any effect on the TLA meaning of partitioned systems?

QUESTION 8.1.6 What is the use of specification components, if they cannot be implemented independently?

## 8.2 Non-interfering Component Refinements

Utilizing component structure in the refinement of a partitioned system requires that its components can be refined independently, and that the resulting refinements are composable. A straightforward way to ensure composability of different refinements is that these refine mutually disjoint sets of actions. In this section we therefore consider component refinements where the actions of only one component are refined.

### 8.2.1 Non-interference Conditions

Given a partitioned system $S$ that corresponds to TLA expression $S$ in (8.2) on p. 265, refinement by superposition refines only component $i$ in $S$ if the following conditions are satisfied:

- The initial condition $P$ is strengthened only if it is separable for component $i$, in which case it can be strengthened by conjoining it with a state predicate $Q_i$ that is local to component $i$.
- New variables and actions are introduced only to component $i$.
- Only actions in $A_i$ are explicitly refined, and default refinements (with default fairness requirements) are taken for the actions of other components.

Let $T^i$ now be such component refinements of $S$ for all $i$, $T^i \Rightarrow S$, and let

$$T = T^1 \oplus \cdots \oplus T^k$$

denote their *weakest composition*, defined as the composition where no further variables are introduced, no further strengthening is given to the conjoined initial condition, and actions of each component i are taken 'as such' from $T^i$.

The first of the above conditions guarantees that, if S and all $T^i$ have satisfiable initial conditions, then the initial condition of T is also satisfiable. The second condition ensures that the liveness properties of all $T^i$ are also satisfied by T, i.e., $T \Rightarrow T^1 \wedge \cdots \wedge T^k \Rightarrow S$.

The two conditions are therefore sufficient to guarantee composability of component refinements. The following additional assumptions also ensure that the associated component structure is preserved:[4]

- Variables in each component remain in the same component.
- Each refined action remains in the component of its ancestor.
- Only the component that is refined may be subdivided into further components, which has to be done in a manner that satisfies the general requirements for partitioning.

When all the above conditions are satisfied, component refinements will be called *non-interfering*. Although non-interfering component refinements do not interfere with each other, they may also affect, in a restricted manner, other components than the ones being refined. For instance, the guard of a local interface action could be strengthened using additional read accesses to interface variables in other components.

Obviously, non-interfering component refinements satisfy the requirements for composability, but they have the drawback of not allowing effective interface refinement. Therefore, there is a need to relax the non-interference condition, as will be discussed below in Sect. 8.4.

### 8.2.2 Design by Non-interfering Refinements

In conventional design methods, interface definitions are usually given first, after which the different components can be designed independently. With non-interfering component refinements this approach can be adapted to closed systems as follows.

At first, a partitioned initial specification layer is given, where variables X and actions A have been partitioned into disjoint subsets associated with different components, with special focus on interface variables and on interface actions in each component. With such a partitioning, each of the components can be refined by non-interfering component refinements, with a guarantee that these are composable into a refinement of the original layer, as illustrated in Fig. 8.3 on p. 270.

Obviously, this method can also be applied recursively, so that components are partitioned into smaller components that are refined independently from each other.

---

[4]Some of these assumptions will be relaxed in Sect. 8.4.

It is often appropriate to start system specification from its external interface. The first model of an embedded system, for instance, could then be one that specifies the 'technical possibilities' of its external interface only, without telling how this interface is used in the particular application. Such an initial *interface specification layer*, denoted in the following by I, is also a closed system, which consists of two components called the *environment part* and the *system part*, respectively. Therefore, layer I contains a model of both parts, but at a generic level only, which describes how an arbitrarily behaving environment and an arbitrarily behaving system can interact through this interface.

The assumptions that can be made of environment behavior in the particular application can then be given as layer E, which is a non-interfering component refinement of the environment part in I. Correspondingly, system behavior can be specified as layer S, which is a non-interfering component refinement of the system part in I. Obviously, E and S need not be produced in single refinement steps, but can result from several parallel and consecutive steps.

**Fig. 8.4.** Illustration of independent environment and system refinements

Composing the two refinements E and S (see Fig. 8.4) now gives a model of how the system behaves when combined with an environment that behaves according to the assumptions expressed by E. Properties proved of the weakest composition E ⊕ S are then properties that will hold in a correct implementation, provided that the environment also behaves correctly.

An implementation (of the system part) can now take S as its basis. Obviously, environment variables and environment actions in S describe assumptions on the environment and will not be implemented.

In this design method it is assumed that the interface between environment and system parts, as expressed by I, is directly implementable. If I is a high-level description of interactions, this need not, however, be the case. For instance, environment actions in I, and hence also in S, may access such system variables that cannot be accessed by the environment in a realistic implementation. Different kinds of refinements are then needed, where the interface is modified so that an implementation becomes feasible. Such refinements will be discussed below in Sect. 8.4.

### 8.2.3 Dealing with Environment Errors

Although layer E in Fig. 8.4 is not needed for the implementation of the system part S, the weakest composition E ⊕ S determines the properties of the combined system. However, the real environment in which a system will be used can never be prescribed by a specification E. Instead, E should be taken as an assumption of how a 'normal' environment behaves, although real environments may also exhibit unanticipated errors and faults.

If E also models behaviors where the environment behaves erroneously, or where faults take place, then the weakest composition E ⊕ S also determines how the system part should behave in such situations. Therefore, the specification, as given in terms of the pair (E, S), also specifies how the system should react to such anticipated errors.

On the other hand, if E disallows an erroneous behavior (that is allowed in I), then the composition E ⊕ S does not allow it, either. Therefore, the specification, as given in terms of the pair (E, S), does not take any stand to what the system should do in such situations. This leaves complete freedom for the implementor to handle such situations.

In the design of fault-tolerant systems one can compose system refinements with several different environment refinements, which exhibit different degrees of faulty behaviors, and analyze the properties of these compositions. Figure 8.5 illustrates this as follows.

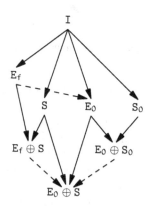

**Fig. 8.5.** Illustration of design for fault tolerance

Let $E_0$ ($S_0$) constrain only environment (system) actions in I with the assumption that both partners are 'well behaving'. Their weakest composition $E_0 \oplus S_0$ then models total behaviors with this same assumption. Suppose now that the designers also want to be prepared for those environment faults that are modeled by a weaker environment refinement $E_f$, of which $E_0$ can be understood to be a refinement.

The design of the system can now be developed as another system refinement of I, S, in which system actions are also prepared for those faulty environments that are allowed by $E_f$. If the pair $(E_0, S_0)$ is taken as the minimum requirements for correctness, then the correctness of the fault-tolerant design requires that $E_0 \oplus S \Rightarrow E_0 \oplus S_0$, whereas fault-tolerance properties can be analyzed from the composition $E_f \oplus S.^5$

### 8.2.4 Example: Database Transactions

As an example of independent refinements, consider the modeling of a serializable database system that behaves as follows.

Interactions with the system are assumed to consist of *transactions* that may contain any number of read and write requests on a database. Each transaction will either end successfully or will be aborted. Abortion takes place either as a result of an explicit request from the environment, or because the system has for some reason found it impossible to complete the transaction successfully. The latter situation will be indicated by a special return value 'abort' for the next request.

No limit will be given to the number of transactions that may proceed concurrently, but their *serializability* will be required, i.e., the total effect is required to be as if the successfully ending transactions had been executed in some sequential order. Aborted transactions therefore have no effect on the values in the database.

### Class Definitions

A generic environment is modeled as a collection of Client objects, each having a unique identification number id:

$$\textbf{class } \text{Client} = \{\textbf{const } \text{id} : \mathbb{N}\} ,$$
$$\forall c, d \in \text{Client} : (c \neq d \Rightarrow c.\text{id} \neq d.\text{id}) .$$

Client objects are assumed to communicate with the system part through Transaction objects, which are part of the interface within the system part. Figure 8.6 illustrates the intended state transitions of Transaction objects. Each $t \in$ Transaction is always either Free or Occupied with some client $c \in$ Client. When Occupied, it may be Ready for the next request, Busy when the system is processing a request, or prepared to give a response to a request (Resp).

Class Transaction can now be defined as

---

[5] If $S_0$ offers enough nondeterminism in situations where the environment behaves incorrectly, then S can be designed as a refinement of $S_0$, in which case $E_0 \oplus S \Rightarrow E_0 \oplus S_0$ is trivially true.

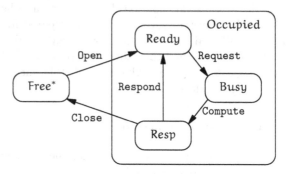

**Fig. 8.6.** State diagram for Transaction objects

**class** Transaction $= \{$**state** Free$^*$, Occupied$\}$
  **where** Occupied $= \{$id $: \mathbb{N}$; op, par, reply $: \mathbb{U}$; **state** Ready, Busy, Resp$\}$ ,

where variable id indicates the client with which a transaction is occupied, variables op and par contain the name of a requested operation and the associated parameter list, respectively, and a return value will be computed into variable reply.

    The number of concurrent transactions can be regulated by the size of class Transaction.

## Actions

A transaction is assumed to start with an environment action Open, which establishes an association between a Client and a free Transaction object:

$$\text{Open}(c : \text{Client}; \; t : \text{Transaction}) : t.\text{Free}$$
$$\rightarrow \; t.\text{Ready}'$$
$$\wedge \, t.\text{id}' = c.\text{id} \; .$$

No restrictions are given for the number of transactions opened by the same Client.

    When an associated Transaction object is Ready, a Client object can issue a request,

$$\text{Request}(c : \text{Client}; \; t : \text{Transaction}; \; \text{req}, p : \mathbb{U}) : t.\text{Ready}$$
$$\wedge \, c.\text{id} = t.\text{id}$$
$$\rightarrow \; t.\text{Busy}'$$
$$\wedge \, t.\text{op}' = \text{req}$$
$$\wedge \, t.\text{par}' = p \; ,$$

to which the system reacts by computing an appropriate return value,

$$\text{Compute}(t:\text{Transaction};\ v:\mathbb{U}):\text{t.Busy}$$
$$\rightarrow\ \text{t.Resp}'$$
$$\wedge\ \text{t.reply}' = v\,.$$

Finally, the client receives the response and possibly also closes the transaction:

$$\text{Receive}(c:\text{Client};\ t:\text{Transaction};\ v:\mathbb{U}):\text{t.Resp}$$
$$\wedge\ \text{c.id} = \text{t.id}$$
$$\wedge\ v = \text{t.reply}$$
$$\rightarrow\ \text{t.Ready}'\,,$$

$$\text{Receive\_and\_close}(c:\text{Client};\ t:\text{Transaction};\ v:\mathbb{U}):\text{t.Resp}$$
$$\wedge\ \text{c.id} = \text{t.id}$$
$$\wedge\ v = \text{t.reply}$$
$$\rightarrow\ \text{t.Free}'\,.$$

Of these actions, Request, Receive, and Receive_and_close are interface actions, and we assume that they are all assigned to the environment, whereas action Compute is a private system action.

No fairness requirements have been given at this level, where the purpose was only to give a 'technical' basis for the interaction between the system and environment parts.

## Outline for Environment and System Refinements

Taking the above as an interface specification layer I, an environment refinement E of I may restrict the requests to be only read, write, close, and abort requests that have parameter lists of appropriate lengths. Reactions to requests that violate these formal requirements can be left unspecified in E.

As for liveness properties, E can impose fairness assumptions on actions Receive and Receive_and_close, in order to ensure that each response that has been computed will also be received by the client, and to exclude nonterminating transactions with an infinite number of requests.

A system refinement S, on the other hand, can model the contents of the database, and use it for computing the return values for read requests. The range of possible data values can also be specified in this connection, and S may or may not specify how to react to requests with non-existing keys or out-of-range data values.

Instead of imposing serializability only in the most nondeterministic manner, some well-defined policy – like two-phase locking – can be specified in S for modeling the use of the database. A transaction should not be aborted in S, unless a situation is reached where serializability cannot be otherwise achieved. Of course, the trivial policy of aborting all transactions is therefore not a reasonable policy for S.

Fairness requirements should also be imposed in S on action `Compute`, in order to ensure that some response – possibly abortion – will always eventually be determined for each request.

### Notes on Liveness Properties

An important liveness property to be proved for the weakest composition $E \oplus S$ is that each request will eventually get some response. Unfortunately this cannot be guaranteed by either party alone, but only by the combination of their fairness assumptions: getting a response to a request may depend on other clients terminating their transactions, which in turn depends on the system responding to their requests.

A closed-system model avoids the difficulties that may arise in dealing with this kind of mutually recursive situations, where system liveness properties depend on environment liveness properties and vice versa. Although it is the case in the two-phase locking policy, for instance, that the system will eventually respond to each request only if each transaction will eventually terminate, and a transaction will eventually terminate only if the system eventually responds to each request, the desired liveness properties can be proved simply on the basis of the fairness assumptions specified for the closed system.

In this example we could have specified the desired liveness properties of the total system already in the interface specification layer I. In that case proving that both E and S preserve these properties would have been sufficient to guarantee that they are also satisfied by the weakest composition $E \oplus S$.

### Review Questions

QUESTION 8.2.1 Why are non-interfering component refinements always composable?

QUESTION 8.2.2 When the design method of Sect. 8.2.2 (p. 272) is used, which layer in the specification determines what to implement? What is the role of the environment refinement E?

QUESTION 8.2.3 How can different environment refinements be utilized in the design of fault-tolerant systems?

QUESTION 8.2.4 What is the advantage of closed-system specifications in proving liveness properties?

**Exercises**

EXERCISE 8.2.1 Discuss correct and faulty behaviors in the gas-burner example of Chap. 2 in the light of Sect. 8.2.3 (p. 274). If layer I generates all possible behaviors of interface variables, which of these would be excluded by $E_0$ (or by $S_0$), if it constrains only environment actions (or system actions, respectively), assuming that both partners are 'well behaving'?

EXERCISE 8.2.2 Give environment and system refinements E and S for the database example, as outlined in Sect. 8.2.4 (p. 275). Use two-phase locking in S.

EXERCISE 8.2.3 Show that $E \oplus S$ in your construction in Exercise 8.2.2 implies the required liveness properties.

EXERCISE 8.2.4 Concerning system refinement S in Exercise 8.2.2, consider the possibilities for handling environment errors in refinements of S.

# 8.3 Robust Component Refinements

A component needs to cooperate in all interface actions that concern it. Intuitively speaking, it executes of these only those that are its local interface actions, whereas external interface actions are either *allowed* or *refused* by it.

Since a non-interfering component refinement cannot refine external interface actions, it cannot, for instance, refuse them by strengthening their enabling guards. Our design methods lead, however, often to situations where this would be desirable. In this section we therefore discuss the need for relaxing the non-interference requirement, and how this can be done without violating the crucial property that component refinements remain composable.

When non-interference is relaxed, composability obviously requires some constraints on how local and external interface actions are allowed to be refined in component refinements. Since no necessary and sufficient conditions exist for this purpose, the problem is to find conditions that are sufficient but not unduly restrictive. The conditions that will be derived in the following will be called *robustness conditions*.

## 8.3.1 Need for Relaxing Non-interference

Non-interfering component refinements offer only limited possibilities to refine component interfaces, as defined by interface variables and interface actions. In particular, it is not possible for a non-interfering component refinement to refuse external interface actions even temporarily. The need for this is, however, evident in the following refinement technique.

When a refinement needs new actions that need to be executed before a given imported action, the enabling of the latter can be postponed by strengthening its guard with an additional condition that is turned true when the new actions have been executed. This technique is particularly useful in connection with distributed systems, where its purpose is to make global guards implementable in a distributed fashion.[6] Obviously, such a postponement of execution is not possible for external interface actions, unless the non-interference requirement for component refinements is relaxed.

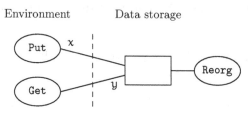

**Fig. 8.7.** Illustration of postponing the enabling of external actions

As a generic example of this technique, consider specification of a data storage with external actions Put(x) and Get(y) for storing and retrieving data values x and y, respectively. At a high level of abstraction an abstract data structure can be used for data storage, and actions Put and Get can then be enabled whenever there is room for more data, or the storage is nonempty, respectively. At a lower level of abstraction with concrete data structures, the data-storage component may, however, sometimes need internal storage reorganization. In a refined specification the need for such reorganization may therefore enable a new action Reorg and disable Put and Get temporarily, until reorganization by Reorg has taken place (see Fig. 8.7).

Although this is intuitively just a refinement of the data-storage component, external interface actions also need to be refined in it. The reason for this phenomenon is that, although external interface actions have been assigned to other components, their execution also requires cooperation from this component. When this cooperation is made more explicit at lower levels of abstraction, effective interface refinement is needed.

In this example a simple kind of interface refinement is sufficient, which makes it possible for the data-storage component to refuse external interface actions temporarily by strengthening their guards. We also notice that without a fairness requirement for Reorg such a component refinement would not be composable with environment refinements that add fairness requirements to actions Put and Get. This leads to the crucial question about the feasibility of relaxing the non-interference requirement: if other components are refined independently, how can it be ensured that all these refinements still remain composable?

---

[6]Distributed systems will be discussed in Chap. 9.

### 8.3.2 Independence of Interput Parameters

If an interput value (i.e., the value of a non-participant parameter in an interface action; see Sect. 8.1.5, p. 267) is not uniquely determined, further constraints can be imposed on it in subsequent refinement steps. If such constraints are imposed in different component refinements, they may, however, be conflicting.

To deal with this problem, which arises when interface actions can be refined both as local and as external interface actions, the responsibility for each interput parameter is assigned to one of the components involved in the action. We then say that the parameter is *local* to that component. Intuitively this determines the component that is assumed to make the final decision on the parameter value. Notice that this component need not be the one that is responsible for the action itself. For instance, the parameters in actions Put and Get in Fig. 8.7 may be determined by different components, although both actions are executed by the environment.

To avoid interference between the responsibilities of different components, we will assume that the following assumption is satisfied in interface actions:

- The values of interput parameters $x_i$ for which component $i$ is responsible are required to be independent of the values of other interput parameters.

More formally, if $\exists x_i, x : g(x_i, x)$ is the enabling guard of an interface action, where $x_i$ denotes those interput parameters that are local to component $i$, and $x$ denotes all other interput parameters, then this *independence condition* can be formulated as

$$g(x_i, x) \wedge g(y_i, y) \Rightarrow g(x_i, y) .\qquad(8.3)$$

### 8.3.3 General Assumptions

The non-interference condition is now relaxed so that external interface actions can also be refined:

- In addition to local actions, external interface actions can also be refined in a component refinement.

Before formulating the robustness conditions, under which component refinements still remain composable, a few simplifying assumptions will be made on interface actions and their refinements.

As for non-participant parameters in interface actions, we assume that they all model values to be transmitted between components. This makes it natural to make the following assumptions:

- No fairness requirements are associated with interput parameters in interface actions.
- New interput parameters can be introduced only for the component that is refined, and the independence condition (8.3) must remain satisfied in their presence.

- No interput parameters are allowed to disappear in component refinements, and only those parameters can be constrained that are assigned to the component being refined.

To make the last assumption more precise, let $\exists x_i, x : g(x_i, x)$ be the enabling guard of an interface action $A$, where $x_i$ denotes the interput parameters assigned to component $i$, and $x$ denotes all other interput parameters, and let the (disjunction of the) enabling guard(s) of the refinement(s) of $A$ be $\exists x_i, x : h_i(x_i, x)$ in a component refinement (of component $i$). We then require that

$$h_i(x_i, x) \wedge g(y_i, y) \Rightarrow h_i(x_i, y) . \tag{8.4}$$

The independence condition (8.3) is then obviously also preserved.

As for fairness requirements in interface actions, we make the following simplifying assumptions:

- A component refinement introduces no new fairness markings to external interface actions and, if an external interface action has fairness markings, it is given only one refinement.
- All fairness markings on interface actions are associated with participant roles for which the associated classes are finite.

The first of these assumptions has the effect that additional fairness properties are associated with an interface action only in the component refinement for which the action is local.[7] The second assumption simplifies essentially the conditions under which fairness properties are preserved in composition.

### 8.3.4 Robustness Conditions

Compared to the situation discussed in Sect. 8.2.1 (p. 271), the *weakest composition* of component refinements $T^i$ (of a partitioned action system $S$),

$$T = T^1 \oplus \cdots \oplus T^k ,$$

is now defined to include also synchronizations of the refined interface actions, with fairness markings taken from the component refinements for which the interface actions are local.

As far as the initial condition of $T$ is concerned, the situation is the same as with non-interfering component refinements: if the initial condition of $S$ is satisfiable, and the condition on its strengthening given in Sect. 8.2.1 (p. 271) is satisfied by each $T^i$, then the conjoined initial condition of $T$ is also satisfiable. The safety properties of all $T^i$ are obviously also preserved in $T$.

The crucial question for the composability of $T^i$, i.e., for $T \Rightarrow T^i$ to be true for all $i$, is then whether the fairness requirements of all $T^i$ for interface actions

---

[7]Notice that splitting an action with fairness requirements could also strengthen such requirements.

are also satisfied by T. Compared to S, additional fairness requirements for these actions can be introduced only in the component refinements for which these actions are local. Therefore, the purpose of *robustness conditions*, to be introduced below, is to ensure that T satisfies the fairness requirements given for local interface actions in each component refinement $T^i$. Obviously, the reason why a fairness requirement for a local interface action in $T^i$ might not be satisfied in T is that the action could be disabled when it is synchronized with corresponding action refinements in other component refinements $T^j$.

Letting $T_0^i$ denote such a reduction of $T^i$ where fairness assumptions are restricted to those local actions in component i that are not refinements of interface actions in S,[8] the following result is helpful in showing that a property is satisfied by T:

- If a property is satisfied by $T_0^i$, it is also satisfied by T.

## Notation

In the following, A will denote an interface action in S that is local to component i and external to component j, $j \neq i$. The enabling guard of A will be denoted by g. When no participant list is given, then all participants are assumed to be existentially quantified. Shorthand notation $(x \dots)$ will be used for a participant list to indicate that x is a set of actual participant objects for certain participant roles, and that all other participants are existentially quantified. Similarly, notation $(x \dots; z \dots)$ will indicate that x is a set of actual participants for certain participant roles that were present already in layer S, and that z is a similar set for roles added in a component refinement.

## Persistence on External Interface Actions

Consider first component refinement $T^j$ for which interface action A is external. Such scenarios are obviously possible where (each refinement of) action A is disabled in $T^j$ at the moments when (a refinement of) A would be enabled in $T^i$. In the presence of several components to which A is external, the associated refinements may also 'conspire' in disabling A so that each of them would allow A intermittently, but their composition would never do this. Obviously, if $T^i$ imposes fairness requirements on A, these might in these cases not be satisfied in the composition T.

To formulate conditions under which these kinds of scenarios can be avoided, let $h_j(x)$ stand for the disjunction of the enabling conditions of all refinements of $A(x)$ in $T^j$. Here, x covers the whole participant list in layer S. If new participants have been added to the refinements, they are assumed to be existentially quantified in $h_j(x)$.

---

[8]Such actions are either private actions in component i, or newly introduced interface actions that contain only read accesses to variables in other components.

We now say that component refinement $T^j$ is *persistent* in allowing external interface action $A(x)$ for participants $x$ if there exist state predicates $q_j(x)$ and $p_j(x)$ for which the following conditions are satisfied by $T_0^j$:

$$\Box(h_j(x) \Leftrightarrow g(x) \wedge q_j(x)) \,, \tag{8.5}$$

$$\Box(p_j(x) \Rightarrow q_j(x)) \,, \tag{8.6}$$

$$\Box\Diamond g(x) \Rightarrow \Box\Diamond p_j(x) \,, \tag{8.7}$$

$$\textbf{stable } p_j(x) \textbf{ unless } \langle A(x) \rangle \,. \tag{8.8}$$

The intuition behind these predicates is as follows. The role of $q_j(x)$ is to express how the possibilities for executing (refinements of) action $A(x)$ have been constrained in $T^j$, as is shown by (8.5). Condition (8.6) then ensures that these constraints have no effect when predicate $p_j(x)$ is true. Finally, if the original guard of action $A(x)$ is repeatedly true, conditions (8.7) and (8.8) guarantee that $p_j(x)$ will eventually become true and also stay true, unless (some refinement of) action $A(x)$ is executed.

### Insistence on Local Interface Actions

Consider now component refinement $T^i$ for which interface action $A$ is local. The possibility for refining $A$ into several different actions with individual fairness requirements gives rise to further undesirable scenarios. This is because the other components might systematically disable $A$ at the moments when a particular refinement (with a fairness requirement) would be possible for $T^i$, but would still allow executing other refinements of $A$ infinitely often. The same phenomenon also arises, when new participants are added to $A$ in $T^i$ and fairness markings are associated with these.

To formulate conditions for avoiding such scenarios, let $B$ be a refinement of action $A$ in $T^i$, and let $h$ be its enabling condition. Furthermore, let $h_i$ stand for the disjunction of the enabling conditions of all refinements of action $A$ in $T^i$.

We now say that component refinement $T^i$ is *insistent* on local interface action $B$ for the participant roles of $x$ and $z$ if

$$\Box\Diamond h(x\ldots;z\ldots) \Rightarrow \Box\Diamond\langle B(x\ldots;z\ldots)\rangle \vee$$
$$\Diamond\Box(h_i(x\ldots) \Rightarrow h(x\ldots;z\ldots)) \tag{8.9}$$

is satisfied by $T_0^i$.

The intuitive meaning of this is that, if $B(x\ldots;z\ldots)$ is repeatedly enabled in $T_0^i$ without being executed, then eventually it is always enabled whenever any of the refinements of $A$ is enabled for $x$. Obviously, if $z$ is an empty list and $B$ is the only refinement of $A$ in $T^i$, then $h_i(x\ldots) \Leftrightarrow h(x\ldots;z\ldots)$, and the insistence condition (8.9) is therefore identically true.

## Robustness

A component refinement is now called *robust* if it is

- persistent in allowing all external interface actions, and
- insistent on local interface actions for those roles x (of old participants) and z (of new participants) for which fairness markings are given.

It is left as an exercise to the reader to show that, under the general assumptions presented above, robustness of component refinements is a sufficient condition for their composability (Exercise 8.3.3).

## Review Questions

QUESTION 8.3.1 What is the intuitive reason for the need of interfering component refinements?

QUESTION 8.3.2 Why is the independence condition for interput parameters needed?

QUESTION 8.3.3 What are all the conditions for robust component refinements?

## Exercises

EXERCISE 8.3.1 Do non-interfering component refinements always satisfy the robustness conditions?

EXERCISE 8.3.2 Show that the independence condition (8.3) on p. 281 for interput parameters is preserved by the requirement (8.4) on p. 282.

EXERCISE 8.3.3 Prove that the weakest composition of robust component refinements satisfies the liveness properties of the component refinements.

EXERCISE 8.3.4 Simplify the robustness conditions for component refinements for the case where all state variables are global, i.e., there are no objects.

EXERCISE 8.3.5 How could the persistence condition for external interface actions be modified to allow several refinements in the presence of existing fairness requirements also?

## 8.4 Interface Refinement

When interactions have been defined at a high level of abstraction, they need not be realistic for direct implementation. Therefore, the need may arise to refine 'abstract interactions' into more elementary 'concrete interactions'. Obviously, this can always be done when the total system is refined, but in this section we discuss how such an *interface refinement* can also be done in component refinements.

Above it was assumed that component refinements totally conform to the original partitioning of variables and actions into components. In interface refinement this assumption may need to be relaxed. Another interesting point is that, since both local and external interface actions can be refined in robust component refinements, an interface between two components can often be refined by refining either one of these components.

### 8.4.1 Goals for Interface Refinement

By interface refinement we understand refinements that affect interface actions and variables. The following important varieties of interface refinement can be distinguished:

- change of interface data representation,
- temporary disabling of interface actions, and
- refinement of atomicity of interactions.

Change of interface data representation means changing of interface variables and changing the parameters of interface actions. This can be done by data refinement (see Sect. 6.4.2, p. 186) and action transformations in component refinements.

Temporary refusal of external interface actions in robust component refinements was discussed in the previous section.

Refining the atomicity of an interaction means that an interface action is split into more elementary actions. The responsibilities for these can then be assigned to the different parties involved, which reflects the idea that an implementation of the original interaction needs some cooperation from all of them. Loosening of the required synchronization between the parties is often important in such refinements.

In the rest of this section we will mainly discuss the problems associated with atomicity refinement of interactions.

### 8.4.2 Changes in Responsibilities

Although each interface action is said to be executed by the component to which it is local, its implementation requires some cooperation from all components involved. In refining the atomicity of an interface action the roles of other components may therefore become explicit by actions that will be assigned to them, and this may also affect the partitioning of variables and actions. In other words, even when interface refinement takes place by component refinement, it may interfere with other components by assigning additional duties to them.

In terms of TLA, partitioning into components has no significance. Therefore, a refinement remains a refinement independently of a possible reallocation of responsibilities. This means that reallocation of responsibilities can be considered separately from the composability problem of component refinements, which was discussed in previous sections.

Obviously, for partitioning into components to have any significance, arbitrary changes to this partitioning should not be allowed. The relaxed principles that we adopt here are the following:

- Internal subdivisions within $X_i$ and $A_i$ can be changed in refinements of component $i$.
- Variables and actions of component $i$ can be moved to other components in refinements of component $i$.
- A component refinement may add new variables and new actions, possibly with associated fairness requirements, to other components also.
- Reallocations and additions to other components stay valid in composition with other component refinements.
- All changes in responsibilities honor the general properties required of partitionings, even when composed with refinements of other components.

To be more specific about honoring the general properties of partitionings, the responsibility for an action $A \in A_i$, for instance, cannot be moved to another component if it depends on variables in $X_i^{pvt}$. Similarly, a necessary condition for changing an interface variable to become private is that it belongs to the concealed subset $X_i^{cnc}$ (see Sect. 8.1.3, p. 266), and that existing external accesses of $x$ have been removed by data refinement and action transformations.

As an extreme example of changes in responsibilities, consider the following. If it is decided in an environment refinement that a real environment will be replaced by a simulated one, then all variables and actions of the environment part are moved to the system part. Such an environment refinement can then be composed with a system refinement, yielding a refined specification with a simulated environment.

Conversely, we can think of a system refinement that moves all its responsibilities to the environment. This would correspond to a situation where a separate system part will not be used, and everything is implemented by rules and activities imposed on the environment. This demonstrates that, although an interface refinement can be carried out as a refinement of one component, its feasibility cannot be judged without considering all parties concerned.

### 8.4.3 Example: Simplifying an Interface Action

In a high-level specification an interface action may directly execute some computation that an implementation should assign to private actions. As an example of this, consider a closed system consisting of an environment component (component 1) and a system component (component 2), where system variable $x \in X_2^{cnc}$ (initialized as 0) is used in layer S to accumulate information given by an environment action $A \in A_1^{ifc}$,

$$A(i : \mathbb{Z}) : \mathbf{T}$$
$$\rightarrow x' = f(i, x) ,$$

with f denoting some integer-valued function.

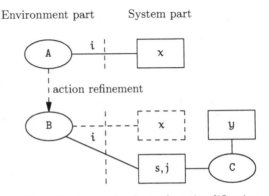

**Fig. 8.8.** Example of interface simplification

The problem with this interface is that all computing, i.e., evaluation of function f, is done by an environment action, which therefore needs access to the accumulated value x. A robust system refinement can, however, be given, which refines the interface so that variable x is effectively removed, and evaluation of f is moved to take place in a system action. This can be done as follows (see Fig. 8.8 for illustration).

As for variables, new system variables $s, j \in X_2^{ifc}$, $y \in X_2^{pvt}$ are introduced, initialized as true, 0, and 0, respectively. Interface action A, which is external to the system component, is refined into B,

$$B(i : \mathbb{Z}) : S.A(i)$$
$$\wedge s = \text{true}$$
$$\rightarrow j' = i$$
$$\wedge s' = \text{false} ,$$

and a new private system action C is introduced,

$$^{WF}C : S.Stutter$$
$$\wedge\ s = false$$
$$\rightarrow\ y' = f(j, y)$$
$$\wedge\ s' = true\ .$$

The fairness requirement in C ensures that this is, indeed, a robust component refinement of the system part. Therefore, if an environment refinement adds a fairness requirement on A, for instance, then the associated liveness property is preserved in the weakest composition with this system refinement.

Obviously, invariant $\Box(x = (\text{if } s = true \text{ then } y \text{ else } f(j, y)))$ now makes x redundant and, since x is concealed and an environment refinement cannot therefore introduce further dependences on it, it can be removed. Evaluation of function f has then been effectively moved from an environment action A to a system action C.

Although it is reasonable to make this interface refinement as a robust component refinement of the system part, the same transformation could, in fact, also be made as a robust (and non-interfering) environment refinement. In this case, even the fairness assumption on C could be omitted. However, assigning C to the responsibility of the system part, no further environment refinement could then add this fairness property, the purpose of which would be to prevent the system from stopping without executing C.

### 8.4.4 Example: Refinement of Communication

The normal method to refine the atomicity of an action A is to introduce new actions which, together with a refinement B of A, accomplish what was originally done by A alone. Compared to A, the enabling of B is then delayed until the new actions have done all the preparatory work that enables B to accomplish the job of the original A. Here we illustrate how this technique can be used for refining the atomicity of communication between components.

Consider the situation illustrated in the upper part of Fig. 8.9. There, the environment part gives an integer x to the system part in an atomic action A. This corresponds to the level of abstraction at which one usually thinks about communication between a user and an application program, for instance. For simplicity it is assumed here that action A updates no environment variables. Removing such restrictions will be discussed in the next subsection.

Since an implementation cannot be assumed to transmit arbitrary integers atomically, a refinement is needed where the digits of x are transmitted one by one. This can be expressed as a robust (and non-interfering) component refinement of the environment part as follows (see lower part of Fig. 8.9). The digits d of x are given to the system part by a new environment action D one by one. Once all of them have been transmitted, action B, which is a refinement of A, can reconstruct x from them. By proving the invariant that this integer is, indeed, x, the dependence of B on environment variables (shown

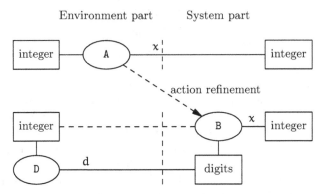

**Fig. 8.9.** Example of atomicity refinement

by a dashed line) can be removed, and B can be changed into a private action of the system part.

Unlike the refinement discussed in the previous subsection, this refinement cannot be made as a component refinement of the system part. The reason is that the responsibilities of one component cannot be taken over in a refinement of another component.

Thinking of A as an action where the user gives an integer to an application program, D describes the required user actions in an implementation, and B describes how x is reconstructed and given to the application program on the system side.

### 8.4.5 Loosening of Component Synchronization

In the example sketched in the previous subsection it was essential that action A did not update any environment variables. Otherwise the dependence of B on environment variables could not have been removed. In general, an interface action may update variables in all parties involved; an implementation may therefore need communication in each direction, and refinement of atomicity then needs loosening of synchronization between the components.

To sketch how this affects the refinement of interface atomicity, consider a situation where an interface action A models two-way communication between two components, updating variables x and y in them (see upper part in Fig. 8.10).

To get rid of synchronized updating of x and y, one of them (say, x) has to be transformed into a non-primitive state function, as discussed in Sect. 6.4.3 (p. 186). Therefore, let z be a new variable whose value will 'almost always' agree with that of x. The functions of action A can then be split into the following more elementary actions (see illustration in the lower part of Fig. 8.10): action C transmits the required values to component 2, action B is a refinement of A that updates y accordingly and computes the feedback to

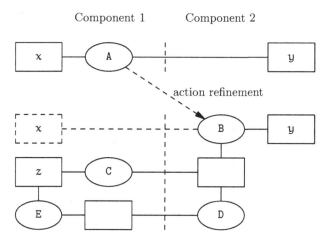

**Fig. 8.10.** Loosening of synchronization in two-way communication

be returned by a subsequent execution of action D to component 1, and action E finally updates z.

For the correctness of such a refinement (of component 1) it is essential that x has, indeed, become a non-primitive state function that needs no explicit representation, i.e., that x is used in component 1 only when its value is present in z. Another aspect that needs additional attention, in general, is that the enabling of A (and hence also of B) may depend on variables in component 2. Therefore, the new action C may also be executed in situations where A is not enabled, and its effects may therefore need to be canceled.

**Review Questions**

QUESTION 8.4.1 What are the specific goals in interface refinement?

QUESTION 8.4.2 What is the meaning of 'concealed' interface variables, and why are they needed?

**Exercises**

EXERCISE 8.4.1 Give a specification where a producer component produces a sequence of integers to be consumed by a consumer component, and refine this by component refinement into a form where communication takes place digit by digit.

## 8.5 Example: Reliable Channel

We conclude this chapter with an example that illustrates several aspects of the design method described in this book, including the use of robust compo-

nent refinements. In this example, a simple buffer is refined in several steps
into a reliable channel, which has a sending end and a receiving end, and
which uses two unreliable channels and an alternating bit protocol for the
communication between them.

### 8.5.1 Simple Buffer as an Abstract Channel

Let Buf be a layer that specifies a simple finite class Buffer with a local
variable y for storing a data value, with two states Set and Reset to indicate
whether y contains data or not, and with actions Put and Get for putting a
value in y and retrieving it from there:

$$\textbf{class } \text{Buffer} = \{y : \mathbb{U}; \textbf{ state } \text{Set}, \text{Reset}^*\} \,,$$

$$\text{Put}(b : \text{Buffer}; \ x : \mathbb{U}) : b.\text{Reset}$$
$$\rightarrow b.\text{Set}'$$
$$\wedge b.y' = x \,,$$

$$\text{Get}(b : \text{Buffer}; \ x : \mathbb{U}) : b.\text{Set}$$
$$\wedge x = b.y$$
$$\rightarrow b.\text{Reset}' \,.$$

In the following we will use layer Buf for different purposes at various
stages of the design. We will therefore utilize several copies $\text{Buf}_i$, $i = 1, 2, \ldots,$
of this layer, with independent but isomorphic classes $\text{Buffer}_i$.

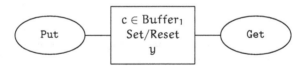

**Fig. 8.11.** Class $\text{Buffer}_1$ as an abstraction of a channel

At a high level of abstraction, class $\text{Buffer}_1$ in $\text{Buf}_1$ can be understood as
an abstraction of the kind of communication system that we intend to specify.
An object $c \in \text{Buffer}_1$ then models a channel into which single data items
can be put, and from which they can be taken out (see Fig. 8.11).

Since actions Put and Get alternate strictly for each $c \in \text{Buffer}_1$, this is
a model of reliable channels, which never lose their data. However, since no
fairness requirements are given at this stage, the data need not be taken out
of a channel.

Understanding this as a closed system, both of the actions are considered
to be environment actions. In the absence of system actions, channels are
therefore considered at this level as passive objects that can only store data

values. All their local variables are interface variables and, more specifically, we assume them to be concealed, so that no environment refinement is allowed to add further references to them. This is because the representations of these variables will be changed so that external read accesses might also interfere with the goals of the system refinements to be introduced below.

### 8.5.2 Adding the Two Ends

As the first step towards modeling of concrete channels, the simple buffers of class $Buffer_1$ are extended into aggregates, where two subobjects model the sending and receiving ends, respectively. For this purpose, layers $Buf_1$ and $Buf_2$ are imported to layer **Channels**, where class $Buffer_1$ is renamed as $Channel$ and extended by

$$\text{class } Channel = \{\ldots s, r : Buffer_2\} \,.$$

Subclasses $Channel.s$ and $Channel.r$ are assumed to be disjoint, and the complement set $(Buffer_2 \setminus Channel.s) \setminus Channel.r$ is assumed to be empty.

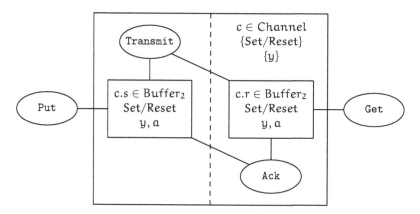

**Fig. 8.12.** A channel with two ends

The intuitive idea of this extension is as follows: a refined put action on a channel object $c \in Channel$ puts the value also to buffer $c.s$ in the sending end, an additional action $Transmit$ then copies it to buffer $c.r$ in the receiving end, and a refined get action on $c \in Channel$ takes the value (also) from $c.r.y$. Another additional action $Ack$ is needed to reset $c.s$. The situation is illustrated in Fig. 8.12.

The intended invariants for $c \in Channel$ are the following:

$$\Box(c.\text{Set} \Rightarrow c.s.\text{Set} \wedge c.y = c.s.y)\,, \qquad (8.10)$$

$$\Box(c.s.\text{Reset} \Rightarrow c.\text{Reset})\,, \qquad (8.11)$$

$$\Box(c.r.\text{Set} \Rightarrow c.\text{Set} \wedge c.y = c.r.y)\,, \qquad (8.12)$$

$$\Box(c.\text{Reset} \Rightarrow c.r.\text{Reset})\,. \qquad (8.13)$$

Since the value $c.y$ is needed only in state $c.\text{Set}$, these invariants make $c.y$ redundant, which is indicated by the braces around it in Fig. 8.12. (States $c.\text{Set}$ and $c.\text{Reset}$ will be made redundant at the next level of refinement, where variables $c.s.a$ and $c.r.a$ will also be added.)

The actions of this layer can now be given as follows:

$$\text{Put}(c : \text{Channel};\ x : \mathbb{U}) : \text{Buf}_1.\text{Put}(c, x)$$
$$\wedge\ \text{Buf}_2.\text{Put}(^*c.s,\ x)\,,$$

$$\text{Transmit}(^{\text{WF}}c : \text{Channel};\ x : \mathbb{U}) : \text{Buf}_1.\text{Stutter}$$
$$\wedge\ \text{Buf}_2.\text{Put}(^*c.r, x)$$
$$\wedge\ c.\text{Set}$$
$$\wedge\ x = c.s.y\,,$$

$$\text{Get}(c : \text{Channel};\ x : \mathbb{U}) : \text{Buf}_1.\text{Get}(c, x)$$
$$\wedge\ \text{Buf}_2.\text{Get}(^*c.r, x)\,,$$

$$\text{Ack}(^{\text{WF}}c : \text{Channel}) : \text{Buf}_1.\text{Stutter}$$
$$\wedge\ \text{Buf}_2.\text{Get}(^*c.s, c.s.y)$$
$$\wedge\ c.\text{Reset}\,.$$

Proving that invariants (8.10)–(8.13) are satisfied by the resulting system is left to the reader (Exercise 8.5.1). In particular, they guarantee that the value transmitted in action Transmit is the same as the one in $c.y$, and that there is no conflict in getting the same value from both $c$ and $c.r$ in action Get.

After this refinement, objects $c \in \text{Channel}$ are no longer purely passive objects, since the new actions Transmit and Ack are private actions of the system part. The new variables introduced for the subobjects $c.s$ and $c.r$ are all interface variables that are also accessed by the refined external interface actions Put and Get.

The resulting layer Channels is a robust system refinement of $\text{Buf}_1$, since the fairness requirements in Transmit and Ack guarantee that the persistence conditions on p. 284 are satisfied for the external interface actions Put and Get. This means that this system refinement is composable with any robust environment refinement of $\text{Buf}_1$, in particular with ones that would add fairness requirements on actions Put and Get.

### 8.5.3 Alternating Bits

States c.Set and c.Reset are still needed in layer **Channels** for distinguishing whether action **Transmit** or **Ack** should be executed in otherwise similar states. The technique of alternating bits is used to make these states redundant.

Layer **Channels** is therefore imported to layer **AB_Channels**, in which subclasses $Channel.s$ and $Channel.r$ are extended with 'alternating bits' $a$,

$$\textbf{class } Channel.s = \{\ldots\ a : \mathbb{B} := \text{true}\}\ ,$$
$$\textbf{class } Channel.r = \{\ldots\ a : \mathbb{B} := \text{false}\}\ ,$$

with the intended invariant that the state Set/Reset in c follows the corresponding state in either c.s or c.r, depending on whether the values of the alternating bits are different or the same:

$$\square(c.s.a \neq c.r.a \Rightarrow (c.Set \Leftrightarrow c.s.Set))\ , \tag{8.14}$$
$$\square(c.s.a = c.r.a \Rightarrow (c.Set \Leftrightarrow c.r.Set))\ . \tag{8.15}$$

Actions **Put** and **Get** are taken as default refinements, and actions **Transmit** and **Ack** are refined as follows:

$$Transmit(^{\text{WF}}c : Channel;\ x : \mathbb{U}) : \texttt{Channels.Transmit}(c, x)$$
$$\wedge\ c.s.a = \neg c.r.a$$
$$\rightarrow\ c.r.a' = \neg c.r.a\ ,$$

$$Ack(^{\text{WF}}c : Channel) : \texttt{Channels.Ack}(c)$$
$$\wedge\ c.s.a = c.r.a$$
$$\rightarrow\ c.s.a' = \neg c.s.a\ .$$

Proving that the intended invariants are satisfied is again left for the reader (Exercise 8.5.1).

With no refinements of interface actions, this is trivially a robust system refinement of **Channels** and also of **Buf**$_1$. Having made aggregates $c \in Channel$ superfluous as such, the refinement has also effectively partitioned the system part into two components, the sender part and the receiver part, which consist of objects in $Channel.s$ and $Channel.r$, respectively. As illustrated in Fig. 8.12 (p. 293), we choose to assign action **Transmit** to the former, and action **Ack** to the latter.

Writing out all actions of layer **AB_Channels** in full, and simplifying them on the basis of invariants (8.10) to (8.15), gives us actions

$$Put(c : Channel;\ x : \mathbb{U}) : c.s.Reset$$
$$\rightarrow\ c.s.Set'$$
$$\wedge\ c.s.y' = x\ ,$$

$$\text{Transmit}(^{\text{WF}}c : \text{Channel}; \ x : \mathbb{U}) : \text{c.s.Set}$$
$$\wedge \ \text{c.r.Reset}$$
$$\wedge \ x = \text{c.s.y}$$
$$\wedge \ \text{c.s.a} = \neg \text{c.r.a}$$
$$\rightarrow \ \text{c.r.Set}'$$
$$\wedge \ \text{c.r.y}' = \text{c.s.y}$$
$$\wedge \ \text{c.r.a}' = \neg \text{c.r.a} \ ,$$

$$\text{Get}(c : \text{Channel}; \ x : \mathbb{U}) : \text{c.r.Set}$$
$$\wedge \ x = \text{c.r.y}$$
$$\rightarrow \ \text{c.r.Reset}' \ ,$$

$$\text{Ack}(^{\text{WF}}c : \text{Channel}) : \text{c.s.Set}$$
$$\wedge \ \text{c.r.Reset}$$
$$\wedge \ \text{c.s.a} = \text{c.r.a}$$
$$\rightarrow \ \text{c.s.Reset}'$$
$$\wedge \ \text{c.s.a}' = \neg \text{c.s.a} \ .$$

Of these, Transmit and Ack are interface actions, which model synchronous communication between the two system components.

Notice that although states c.Set and c.Reset have become redundant, their representation depends on both c.s and c.r. It is therefore essential that the associated interface variable is concealed, so that no environment refinement can add any further testing of these states, since that would require synchronized access to both ends of the communication line.

### 8.5.4 Asynchronous Communication

Layer AB_Channels no longer has actions that would modify local variables in both ends of a channel. However, actions Transmit and Ack, which model reliable and synchronous communication, still need to access both ends at the same time. Our ultimate goal in this example is to derive a model of implementing each object $c \in \text{Channel}$ using two asynchronous and unreliable communication channels, one for data messages and the other for acknowledgements. First we add such data channels in a robust component refinement of the sender part.

Since an asynchronous channel can also be modeled as a simple buffer, we import in the next refinement step another copy $\text{Buf}_3$ of layer Buf, and use class $\text{Buffer}_3$ to represent data channels. In other words, objects $c \in \text{Channel}$ are extended with a component of class $\text{Buffer}_3$, c.dc:

$$\textbf{class } \text{Channel} = \{\ldots \ \text{dc} : \text{Buffer}_3\} \ .$$

The complement subclass of Channel.dc is assumed to be empty.

The idea of the refinement step is as follows. When in state Set, object c.s will put its data c.s.y and alternating bit c.s.a in the data channel c.dc by action Send, which is a specialization of Buf$_3$.Put for subclass Channel.dc. To model unreliability, this message may be lost from c.dc by action Lose_data, which is a specialization of Buf$_3$.Get for subclass Channel.dc.[9] Because of this unreliability, action Send has to be executed repeatedly, until an acknowledgement has been received from c.r. If not lost, the message is eventually received by c.r either by action Transmit or by action Omit_data. Of these, the former is a refinement of AB_Channels.Transmit and at the same time another specialization of Buf$_3$.Get for subclass Channel.dc. The latter is still another specialization of Buf$_3$.Get for subclass Channel.dc, and it is chosen if the message has already been received, which can be detected from the alternating bits.

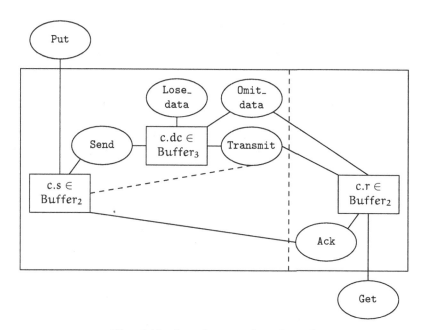

**Fig. 8.13.** Asynchronous data channel

This leads to the following action refinements and specializations:

$$\text{Send}(^{\text{WF}}\text{c} : \text{Channel}) : \text{AB\_Channels.Stutter}$$
$$\wedge \text{Buf}_3.\text{Put}(^*\text{c.dc}, (\text{c.s.y}, \text{c.s.a}))$$
$$\wedge \text{c.s.Set} ,$$

---

[9]For simplicity, this action is assumed to model both the disappearance of a message and the discarding of a corrupted message.

$$\text{Lose\_data}(c : \text{Channel}) : \text{AB\_Channels.Stutter}$$
$$\wedge \text{Buf}_3.\text{Get}(^*c.dc, c.dc.y) \,,$$

$$\text{Transmit}(^{\text{SF}}c : \text{Channel}; \; x : \mathbb{U}) : \text{AB\_Channels.Transmit}(c, x)$$
$$\wedge \text{Buf}_3.\text{Get}(^*c.dc, (x, \neg c.r.a)) \,,$$

$$\text{Omit\_data}(^{\text{WF}}c : \text{Channel}) : \text{AB\_Channels.Stutter}$$
$$\wedge \text{Buf}_3.\text{Get}(^*c.dc, (x, c.r.a))$$
$$\wedge c.r.\text{Reset} \,.$$

External interface actions Ack, Put, and Get are included as their default refinements, and Fig. 8.13 illustrates the resulting system. A dashed line indicates that object c.s is still a participant in action Transmit. With suitable invariants it can be shown, however, that this participation can be eliminated, as will be discussed below.

It is easy to check that this is a refinement, i.e., that the liveness properties for action Transmit have been preserved. Since robustness conditions are trivially satisfied, this is also a robust component refinement of the sender part. As for component structure, it is reasonable to consider that the data channels form a new component with a local action Lose_data, and that actions Transmit and Omit_data are moved to the responsibility of the receiver part.

Quite symmetrically, we can give a robust component refinement of the receiver part. Using another copy $\text{Buf}_4$ of layer Buf, acknowledgement channels are then appended to aggregates $c \in \text{Channel}$ as another component $ac : \text{Buffer}_4$. This gives us the following actions:

$$\text{Send\_ack}(^{\text{WF}}c : \text{Channel}) : \text{AB\_Channels.Stutter}$$
$$\wedge \text{Buf}_4.\text{Put}(^*c.ac, c.r.a)$$
$$\wedge c.r.\text{Reset} \,,$$

$$\text{Lose\_ack}(c : \text{Channel}) : \text{AB\_Channels.Stutter}$$
$$\wedge \text{Buf}_4.\text{Get}(^*c.ac, c.ac.y) \,,$$

$$\text{Ack}(^{\text{SF}}c : \text{Channel}) : \text{AB\_Channels.Ack}(c)$$
$$\wedge \text{Buf}_4.\text{Get}(^*c.ac, c.s.a) \,,$$

$$\text{Omit\_ack}(^{\text{WF}}c : \text{Channel}) : \text{AB\_Channels.Stutter}$$
$$\wedge \text{Buf}_4.\text{Get}(^*c.ac, \neg c.s.a)$$
$$\wedge c.s.\text{Set} \,.$$

Figure 8.14 illustrates the final composition, where the two component refinements are composed, and the component structure and responsibilities for actions are changed as suggested above. Since interface actions to the environment have not been touched, the resulting system is also a robust system

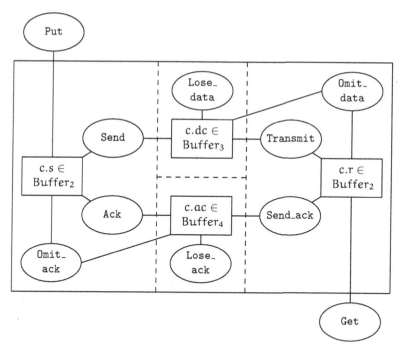

**Fig. 8.14.** Asynchronous implementation of a reliable channel

refinement of the original specification $Buf_1$. The goal of the refinements, i.e., distributed implementability, needs, however, further attention.

Distributed implementability of the resulting system requires, of course, that the participation of c.s and c.r be eliminated from actions `Transmit` and `Ack`, respectively. This simplification of actions requires appropriate safety properties, which guarantee that the data that are accessed in these participants can also be obtained from the messages. It is left as an exercise to the reader to formulate and prove such safety properties (Exercise 8.5.2), and to simplify the final actions accordingly (Exercise 8.5.3).

## Exercises

EXERCISE 8.5.1 Prove that the intended invariants are, indeed, satisfied in layers **Channels** (p. 294) and **AB_Channels** (p. 295).

EXERCISE 8.5.2 Formulate and prove invariants that capture the intentions of components c.dc and c.ac in the final component refinements.

EXERCISE 8.5.3 Write out and simplify the actions of the final layer to show their distributed implementability.

EXERCISE 8.5.4 Give a further refinement of the final layer, with the purpose that c.r would not send acknowledgement messages continually in state c.r.Reset, but only as a response to receiving a message by either Transmit or Omit_data.

## Bibliographic Notes

In state-based approaches, interfaces between components are given in terms of *shared variables*. Traditionally, components are understood in the literature as open systems, which can be specified separately. In composing state-based open systems one then has to specify how references to external variables are bound to variables that are local to other components.

An event-based open system, on the other hand, offers named events that can be synchronized with similar events in other components. This means that we then have *shared events*, which are executed jointly by the components concerned. This is the basic idea in *process-algebraic* approaches (see e.g. [86, 159, 160, 26]), which provide well-established and mathematically rigorous means to deal with composition of event-based open systems and with different kinds of equivalences between them.

In contrast to these approaches to *open-system composition*, the viewpoint of this chapter has been that of *closed-system partitioning*. It is pointed out that, since open systems have fixed interfaces (i.e., shared variables or shared events), the closed-system approach is necessary for interface refinement in the sense discussed here. Although actions in our approach correspond closely to shared events in event-based systems, each action is always assigned to a single component.

To some extent, the distinction between open and closed systems is, however, in the eye of the beholder. Consider process-algebraic specifications, for instance, where an isolated process is understood as an open system that can be composed with other processes. From the viewpoint of this book such a system could also be considered as a closed system, since it can be 'executed' by itself, i.e., with a generic environment that is the most nondeterministic allowed by the specification. Composition with other processes can then be interpreted as a superposition step where this nondeterminism is reduced.

In connection with LOTOS, the use of these kinds of composition steps has been called constraint-oriented specification style, since each process then adds some constraints to the original nondeterminism [26]. Using TLA, a similar specification style has been promoted by Herrmann and Krumm in cTLA [81, 82].

The idea of closed-system models is, of course, not new, and has been used in many areas of engineering. As already mentioned in Chap. 2, it has been advocated for operational specifications by Zave [195], for instance, and the idea has also been elaborated in more detail by Feather [54].

For further TLA-related discussion of interface refinement and of open-system vs. closed-system modeling, the reader is referred to Lamport's book [145], and to his comparative analysis of reasoning on open and closed systems [142]. Abadi and Lamport have also analyzed how a closed TLA specification can be 'opened' into a conjunction of open-component specifications, and have derived conditions for independent component refinements in such 'opened' systems [8]. In our terminology, their component refinements do not, however, allow disabling of external interface actions, which is essential for the methodology introduced here.

The idea of not 'opening' a closed system for component refinements seems to be new in this approach. The special case where no objects are present, and fairness requirements are therefore associated with entire actions only, was addressed earlier [125]. The discussion of interface refinement (Sect. 8.4) has also been adapted from there.

The discussion of design by non-interfering refinements and dealing with environment errors (Sects. 8.2.4 and 8.2.3) is based on [120]. The serializable database example, which had been used as a test case for comparing different specification formalisms [139], also appeared there in more detail. An early version of the incremental specification of the alternating bit protocol was given in [92].

# Part IV

Distributed and Real-Time Systems

# 9

# Distributed Systems

Reactive systems may be distributed systems, which consist of asynchronously communicating processes. Although some of the examples have already dealt with distributed systems, we address them more specifically in this chapter, and analyze how the action-system approach applies to their specification and design.

A distributed system consists of several concurrently operating execution agents, which will be called *processes* in the following. Processes will be modeled as objects, and actions are thought of as being executed cooperatively by their participant processes.

To be more specific, it will be assumed in this chapter that there are no global variables, that each object corresponds to a process, and that these are finite in number. Consequently, the number of actions in such a *distributed action system* – when instantiations for different participant combinations are considered as different actions – is then also finite. Each of these actions is also assumed to have a unique identification, by which it can be referred to in the handshake protocols between the concurrent processes.

The plan for the chapter is as follows:

- Reasoning in TLA is based on an *interleaving model*, where actions are executed one at a time. In Sect. 9.1 we analyze how this relates to a more realistic *distributed model*, which models *true concurrency*. Each action starts in this execution model with a synchronization of the participating processes, but concurrency is allowed between actions that have disjoint sets of participants. It is shown that an interleaving model also remains correct in this case, in the sense that – with a suitable definition of *observations* – it gives the temporal properties that can be observed.

- Action systems allow us to model distributed systems at a level where practical communication mechanisms are ignored. In Sect. 9.2 we demonstrate how refinement techniques can be used to lower the level of abstraction in distributed action systems, in order to reflect the possibilities of those communication primitives that are available in distributed programming.

- Fairness assumptions in action systems may be unrealistic for direct enforcement in distributed implementations. In Sect. 9.3 we therefore analyze such *uniform* fairness assumptions that are reasonable for uniform enforcement, even though only very weak assumptions can be made about the underlying 'fairness force' that is available in a truly distributed environment.
- Section 9.4 is devoted to a generic problem in distributed systems: how to coordinate concurrent processes without global synchronizations in situations where computing proceeds cyclically through a number of stages.

## 9.1 Interleaved Modeling of Concurrency

A well-known wisdom, attributed to Albert Einstein, is that a theory should be as simple as possible – but not any simpler. The theory presented in this book is simplified by being based on a purely sequential execution model: actions are selected for execution in a strictly sequential order. One may, however, doubt that this would make the theory too simple for the modeling of concurrency in distributed systems. These doubts are addressed in this section.

### 9.1.1 Theory and Reality

As discussed in Sect. 1.1 (p. 4), any theory is an abstraction of reality. The right question is not, however, whether a theory is truthful to how the reality behaves, but whether the results of reasoning in the theory conform to what we can observe of the reality. This is what we attempt to analyze in this section.

One should always be careful in distinguishing between a formal model of reality and the reality itself. In programming the danger for confusion is especially close, as was briefly discussed in Sect. 1.1.3 (p. 5), since the same program may be considered either as an abstract, machine-independent description of some computational phenomena, or as a description of the real phenomena that are caused by executing the program on a computer.

In order to understand the applicability of the theory presented in this book we need to take a closer look at some of its fundamental principles, and at their validity for 'real computations'. The first step in this direction is taken in this section by considering a model of distributed systems where concurrently executing processes may from time to time synchronize with each other to exchange information. It will be seen that such a more realistic view of distributed computations does not make the simple theory inapplicable. In the next section the discussion will be extended to a more basic level of abstraction, where synchronization is not possible, and all communication therefore takes place by asynchronous messages.

## 9.1.2 Interleaved Computations

Intuitively, time can be understood as a continuum, and physical phenomena can then be described in terms of continuous functions of time. A different view of reality is justified in computing, when the physical characteristics of computing devices are abstracted away.

### Discrete Event Sequences

Computational phenomena are usually modeled as sequences of *discrete events*, where each event takes place instantaneously. In sequential computing it is easy to get convinced of the validity of such modeling.

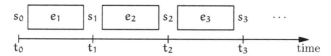

**Fig. 9.1.** Sequence of discrete events

Accepting the view that time is continuous in the real world, a sequential computation can be visualized in terms of distinct events $e_1, e_2, e_3, \ldots$, as shown in Fig. 9.1, where the direction of time is from left to right. During each event $e_i$, nothing certain is known about the state of the system, but at moments $t_0, t_1, t_2, \ldots$ between them all state variables can be observed, which gives us a state sequence $s_0, s_1, s_2, \ldots$. The durations of the events are finite and non-negative, but otherwise unknown and therefore arbitrary. Hence, the exact moments $t_i$ are also arbitrary with $t_i \leq t_{i+1}$ for all $i \geq 0$.

Modeling events $e_1, e_2, e_3, \ldots$ as actions then leads to an abstraction where TLA is applicable for reasoning on the behaviors $\langle s_0, s_1, s_2, \ldots \rangle$ that are possible in a system.

### Interleaving

When several threads of control are present, each of these can be thought of as a sequence of discrete events. The nondeterministic execution model of action systems makes it possible to model such computations by *interleaving*, i.e., so that events in different control threads are interleaved into some sequential order. Since nondeterminism allows arbitrary interleavings in an interleaving model, properties that hold for such a model then hold for all possible interleavings.

Interleaved modeling is obviously unfaithful to the reality of distributed systems, where no moments $t_i$, $i = 0, 1, \ldots$, would need to exist at which all processes would be in stable states at the same time. Similarly to the sequential case, a sequence of *local states*, $s_0^p, s_1^p, s_2^p, \ldots$, can be seen for each process p, but, except for the initial state, there need not be any situations where one of the combined local states $(s_i^p, s_j^q)$ would exist for two processes p and q.

For transformational systems (see Sect. 1.2.5, p. 11) interleaved modeling can, however, be justified by the fact that the final state of a terminating execution is independent of whether true concurrency is involved or one of the alternative interleavings is followed. This means that reasoning in terms of interleaving also gives correct results about the relation between initial and final states when the reality is not interleaved.

For reactive systems the situation is not as straightforward, since the very notion of behaviors refers to the global state at some moments $t_i$, $i = 0, 1, \ldots$. What is the meaning of a global state invariant, for instance, if there are no moments during execution, when a stable global state would exist? The situation is even more problematic for fairness properties, as will be seen below.

### 9.1.3 Distributed Execution Model

Doubts about the validity of the interleaving model lead us to consider a more realistic, non-interleaved execution model, which exhibits *true concurrency* for distributed action systems. It will then be shown that interleaving can still be used for reasoning on the temporal properties that can be observed of these distributed executions.

### Distributed Execution of Actions

To illustrate distributed execution of cooperative actions, consider a situation with three processes p, q, and r. We may then visualize actions $A(p, q)$, $B(q, r)$, and $C(p)$, for instance, to be executed as shown in Fig. 9.2, where the direction of time is again from left to right. Initially the processes are in some initial local states $s_0^p, s_0^q, s_0^r$, and each action modifies the local states of its participants only. Executions of actions are illustrated in the figure by polygons that extend vertically to the participants that are currently involved in these executions.

More generally, execution starts in some initial state and, whenever all participants of an action are free and this action is enabled for the combined local states of these processes, that action may be executed.[1] This execution is independent of what happens to other processes at the same time.

When a process is not engaged in an action, we can think that it may be communicating with other processes, trying to determine which actions would be enabled for it.[2] Once one or more enabled actions have been found,

---

[1] For simplicity we assume here that the guards have no quantified expressions, which would require communication with other processes also. Getting rid of quantified expressions will be discussed below in Sect. 9.2.6.

[2] As a special case, an action may have only one participant, in which case its enabledness can be found without communication with other processes.

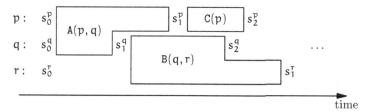

**Fig. 9.2.** Concurrent execution of actions

one of them may be started by a synchronized 'handshake', in which the participants get committed to the action.[3] After that, the participants may continue communicating with each other, in order to determine how their own local states should be updated. Finally, when a process has completed its role in an action, it releases itself from it and becomes ready for the next action.

When not constrained by a fairness scheduler, the selection between enabled actions is assumed to be arbitrary. Furthermore, execution need not obey *maximal parallelism*. That is, the existence of enabled actions need not imply that one of them would be immediately chosen. On the contrary, processes may wait arbitrarily long for further alternatives to become enabled, and – since fairness requirements are ignored – there is also the possibility not to choose any of them.

The reasons for not assuming maximal parallelism in the execution model are twofold. On one hand, maximal parallelism would mean that the durations of the participants' involvement in actions would affect which executions would be possible. On the other hand, executions that are not possible at one level of specification might then become possible in later refinements, which would undermine the very basis of the refinement methodology.

### Distributed Fairness Scheduling

In a sequential execution model it is easy to think of a fairness scheduler that monitors the enabling of fair actions and will eventually enforce their execution, when needed to avoid unfairness. For concurrently executable actions such monitoring is not directly possible. To check the enabledness of action $B(q,r)$, for instance, there must be a moment at which both $q$ and $r$ are not engaged in any action, but there need not exist any such moments, in general.

Assuming a truly distributed system, we can think that the processes communicate with a monitor by asynchronous messages, which transmit information about their involvement in actions and about their local states. With no access to a global clock, and with no assumptions about transmission delays,

---

[3]Here we assume a protocol by which the participants of an enabled action can achieve consensus about executing the action. This problem will be discussed in more detail in Sect. 9.3.

the monitor can then establish only a partial ordering of action executions, as determined by the participants' involvement in them.[4] In the situation of Fig. 9.2 (p. 309), for instance, messages from p and q would give the information that p's involvement in action $A(p, q)$ preceded action $C(p)$, and q's involvement in it preceded action $B(q, r)$. It would not, however, be possible for the monitor to determine the mutual order between $B(q, r)$ and $C(p)$, or the relative lengths of different participants' engagement in any of the actions.

Since it is impossible to monitor real enabling of actions in a distributed system, we assume a scheduler that monitors one of the *possible behaviors* that could have been obtained, had the actions been executed in some complete order that is consistent with the partial ordering observed. Constraining the future selection of actions, the scheduler can then control the execution so that the monitored behavior will turn out fair.

To be more specific, the scheduler could, for instance, keep track of the number of times that each fair action has been enabled in the monitored behavior without being executed. When this number exceeds some limit, the scheduler could direct the participants of this action to reduce their concurrent involvement in other actions so that the enabledness of this action can be continually checked, and the action can then also be executed when its enabling is found.

This kind of scheduling may obviously reduce the concurrency in an execution. In extreme cases a scheduler might then even force the execution to become purely sequential.

## Partial-order Executions

Having given an informal description of distributed executions by action systems, we now introduce a more precise notion of *partial-order executions*, in terms of which the crucial properties of distributed executions can be properly formulated. Compared to interleaved executions, partial-order executions can be characterized as follows:

- Instead of global states, partial-order executions deal with *local states* of processes. Initially, the combination of all local states has to satisfy the given initial condition.
- Like interleaved executions, partial-order executions consist of steps that satisfy actions. However, instead of relating global states to each other, steps now relate the combined local states of the participant processes only.
- Instead of a complete ordering of steps we have a partial ordering, which is determined by the order in which each process is involved in the steps.

---

[4]Here we assume conventions that make it possible to recover the order in which messages from the same process were sent.

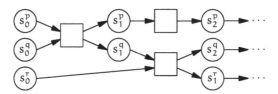

**Fig. 9.3.** Illustration of a partial-order execution

Figure 9.3 illustrates the partial-order execution that corresponds to the concurrent execution of actions in Fig. 9.2.

For simplicity we will assume in the following that the correspondence between steps and actions is unique in the sense that the identity of actions will not play any essential role in partial-order executions.

It should also be pointed out that the term 'behavior' is still used in its old meaning, and that no logical language will be introduced for expressing directly the properties of partial-order executions.

### 9.1.4 Fairness Paradox

For a given distributed execution, the particular behavior that can be monitored by a fairness scheduler is not uniquely determined. Suppose now that another process is also trying to check the fairness of a distributed execution in the same manner. Since this process may receive asynchronous messages in another order, there is no way to guarantee that it could keep track of the same behavior as the scheduler. The problem with this is that one of these orderings might be fair, while the other is unfair.

This dilemma in judging whether a distributed execution is fair or not is called the *fairness paradox*.

### Example

To illustrate the problem, consider the following situation. There are two processes p and q that belong to class P with a local Boolean variable b, which is initialized as false, and there are two actions: $A(x : P)$, which is always enabled and which complements the value of $x.b$, and $B(x, y : P)$, whose enabling guard is $x.b = y.b = true$.

Consider now the concurrent execution of actions illustrated in Fig. 9.4, where both $A(p)$ and $A(q)$ are executed infinitely often, but $B(p, q)$ is not executed at all. The question is whether this execution should be judged fair with respect to action $B(p, q)$ or not.

Independently of the durations of actions, this execution corresponds to the partial-order execution illustrated in Fig. 9.5, where processes p and q are never synchronized. The possible behaviors that are consistent with this

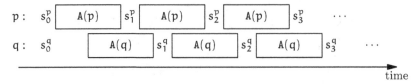

**Fig. 9.4.** Concurrent execution with no synchronizations

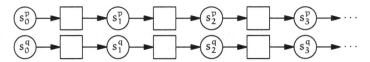

**Fig. 9.5.** Partial-order execution corresponding to Fig. 9.4

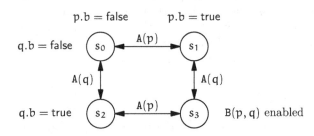

**Fig. 9.6.** State diagram for behaviors associated with Fig. 9.5

partial-order execution can be described in terms of the state-transition diagram in Fig. 9.6, where states $s_i$ stand for the four different combinations of values of p.b and q.b. State $s_0$ is the initial state (p.b = q.b = false), and action $B(p, q)$ is enabled only in state $s_3$ (p.b = q.b = true). Obviously, if one follows the behavior $\sigma = \langle s_0, s_1, s_3, s_2, s_0, s_1, s_3, s_2, \ldots \rangle$, for instance, the execution would be judged unfair with respect to $B(p, q)$, since state $s_3$ is visited infinitely often. Another possibility would, however, be behavior $\tau = \langle s_0, s_1, s_0, s_2, s_0, s_1, s_0, s_2, \ldots \rangle$, which does not visit state $s_3$ at all, and would therefore lead to the opposite conclusion.

## Equivalence Robustness

A behavior is said to *conform* to a partial-order execution if it is consistent with the partial ordering determined by the execution. Given a distributed system, each execution then determines an *equivalence class* of those behaviors that conform to the associated partial-order execution. In the above example, behaviors $\sigma$ and $\tau$ obviously belong to the same equivalence class, since they both conform to the partial-order execution in Fig. 9.5. Since this equivalence of $\sigma$ and $\tau$ depends crucially on action participants, it depends on such properties of action systems that fall outside of their TLA meanings.

A property $\Phi$ of behaviors is said to be *equivalence robust* (for a given distributed system) if the behaviors of the same equivalence class either all satisfy $\Phi$ or all satisfy $\neg\Phi$. It is easy to see that all safety properties that hold for (all behaviors in) an interleaving model of a distributed system are equivalence robust. The fairness paradox means that the same is not true for fairness properties, as was demonstrated above.

The fairness paradox seems to lead to a contradiction, since two observers of a distributed execution may base their observations on different behaviors of the same equivalence class, and may therefore be led to different conclusions about the satisfaction of a property. This dilemma has cast some doubts on whether the fairness properties of an interleaving model are at all applicable to distributed systems. In the following we will analyze this question in more detail.

### Note on Robust Relaxation of Properties

The quest for equivalence robustness might tempt us to use such relaxed properties that are guaranteed to be equivalence robust. Intuitively, it might seem natural to do this by accepting a property $\Phi$ to be satisfied for a behavior if at least one of the behaviors in the same equivalence class satisfies $\Phi$. After all, since an observer cannot have precise information about how a distributed execution has, in fact, proceeded, he/she could as well adopt the view which gives the most 'optimistic' results.[5]

For any property $\Phi$ of behaviors, let $\Phi^+$ therefore denote the *robust relaxation* of $\Phi$ defined for a given distributed system as follows: behavior $\sigma$ satisfies $\Phi^+$ if and only if there is a behavior $\tau$ that satisfies $\Phi$ and is equivalent to $\sigma$. Obviously, the robust relaxation of any property is equivalence robust.

This idea is not, however, useful for our purposes, since it would make it impossible to use the specification and design methods introduced in this book. To see this, consider a distributed system for which a relaxed state invariant $(\Box P)^+$ can be proved. The problem is that, when a refinement reduces nondeterminism, it may exclude the possibility for those behaviors that satisfy $\Box P$, and $(\Box P)^+$ would therefore no longer hold for the refined system (see Exercise 9.1.4).

### 9.1.5 Observations

For physical systems, observations are used to judge whether a theoretical model is acceptable or not. An observation *supports* a model if such properties are observed that agree with the model, and it *refutes* a model if a property

---

[5]Notice the analogy to serializable transactions in database theory, where transactions are serializable if and only if there is at least one sequential order in which they could have taken place with the same observable effects.

is observed that is in conflict with the model. A model can now be said to be correct if the following conditions hold:

- The model is supported by observations, i.e., it is possible to observe those properties that are present in the model.
- The model cannot be refuted by observations, i.e., one cannot observe properties that are in conflict with those in the model.

The notion of observations can also be applied in connection with formally defined systems. In our case, observations would model arrangements by which observations could be made at the implementation level.

Since the properties that are present in an interleaving model do not need to exist in distributed executions, the critical question is, what is meant by observing such properties. At first sight, the idea of a distributed fairness scheduler would seem to be based on observations. However, taking arbitrarily one of the equivalent behaviors that could have appeared, if no concurrency would have been present, can hardly be taken as observational evidence of all properties exhibited by this particular behavior. This is why we need to reconsider the notion of observations of distributed executions.

**Observations of Distributed Executions**

It seems reasonable to require that an observation of a distributed execution can observe only those combined local states that are actually realized in the handshakes for actions. Similarly, it seems reasonable to require that a more exact ordering of these partial states cannot be observed than what is determined by the partial ordering of action executions. How can it then be possible to observe arbitrary TLA properties?

Arrangements that make an observation possible in a closed system are always part of the total system, although they should not interfere with the observed phenomena more than what is necessary for making the observations. Combined local states that do not otherwise get realized can be observed by arrangements where additional participants are joined into actions, or auxiliary stuttering actions are added for some combinations of participants, in order to get them synchronized. Arrangements of this kind can be expressed by superposition that does not affect action guards or bodies, and therefore will not unduly interfere with the system observed. Partial-order executions in the systems obtained with this kind of superposition will be called *observations*.

The situation is, in fact, somewhat analogous to quantum-mechanical observations. The exact location of a particle, for instance, is not uniquely defined in quantum physics, except when an observation is made of it, which forces one of the possible locations to be realized. Similarly, an observation of a distributed system may force the global state to get realized, even if it would not otherwise appear in a distributed computation.

To be more precise, an observation $\omega$ of an individual concurrent execution is based on a partial order of local states, as determined by the observed system (with its fairness scheduler), together with those additional synchronizations that have been imposed on it by the observer. Let $\Sigma_\omega$ denote the set of behaviors that conform to this partial order. It is then reasonable to define that a property $\Phi$ has been observed in the particular concurrent execution if $\Phi$ is satisfied by all behaviors $\sigma \in \Sigma_\omega$.

As an extreme case, an observation may be *complete* in the sense that the complete global state gets realized between all actions. For a complete observation $\omega$, the set $\Sigma_\omega$ then consists of a single behavior, which makes it possible to observe any property $\Phi$ or its negation $\neg\Phi$.

### 9.1.6 Correctness of the Interleaving Model

With the above notion of observations, a fairness scheduler does not make an observation of the fairness properties that it is intended to enforce when it controls a system by monitoring a hypothetical behavior $\sigma$. By controlling the system in which all other possible observers are also included, it makes, however, all unfair observations impossible.

To show this, suppose that an observation $\omega$ observes a property that is in conflict with a fairness requirement F that a fairness scheduler is supposed to enforce. By definition, all behaviors in $\Sigma_\omega$ must then be in conflict with F. Since the fairness scheduler monitors the execution as affected by all observers, the behavior $\sigma$ monitored by it must also belong to $\Sigma_\omega$. Since $\sigma$ satisfies F by construction, we have a contradiction that proves our claim.

This allows us to conclude that the interleaving model is also a correct model for distributed systems.

### Review Questions

QUESTION 9.1.1 What is the reason for the desire to keep the interleaving model also for distributed computations?

QUESTION 9.1.2 Why is maximal parallelism inappropriate for an execution model for specifications?

QUESTION 9.1.3 How does a fairness scheduler judge the fairness of distributed executions?

QUESTION 9.1.4 What is meant by the fairness paradox, and why is it relevant for the correctness of the interleaving model?

QUESTION 9.1.5 What is meant by equivalence robustness? Which properties are guaranteed to be equivalence robust in an interleaving model?

QUESTION 9.1.6 Why can we not use robust relaxations of properties?

QUESTION 9.1.7 What do we mean by an observation of a distributed system?

QUESTION 9.1.8 Why is the interleaving model justified to be correct for distributed computations?

**Exercises**

EXERCISE 9.1.1 Give an example of a situation where a fairness scheduler may temporarily need to disallow maximal parallelism.

EXERCISE 9.1.2 Give a state invariant $\Box P$ that is not satisfied by the system discussed in Sect. 9.1.4 (p. 311), but the corresponding relaxed property $(\Box P)^+$ is satisfied.

EXERCISE 9.1.3 Show that $(\Box P)^+ \wedge (\Box Q)^+$ does not imply $(\Box(P \wedge Q))^+$.

EXERCISE 9.1.4 Give an example where a refinement invalidates the robust relaxation of a state invariant $(\Box P)^+$.

EXERCISE 9.1.5 Consider the situation that the distributed system discussed in Sect. 9.1.4 (p. 311) has another action $C(x, y : P)$ with enabling guard $x.b = y.b = \text{false}$. Is it now possible for a fairness scheduler to judge the execution illustrated in Fig. 9.4 (p. 312) to be fair with respect to both $B(p, q)$ and $C(p, q)$?

## 9.2 Modeling of Practical Mechanisms

Synchronizations are themselves an abstraction for which no primitive mechanisms are directly available for the processes in a distributed system. Basically, distributed computations have to be implemented as *asynchronous computations*, where only an asynchronous message passing mechanism is available for process communication. Programming environments may, however, offer some higher-level mechanisms that have been built on top of this basic facility.

In this section we investigate transformations by which an action system can be refined into a form that reflects the possibilities that are available in programming environments. Discussion of the implementation of fairness requirements will be postponed to the next section.

### 9.2.1 Refinements vs. High-level Mechanisms

In principle, there are two extreme alternatives in implementing a system that has been defined in terms of high-level concepts. One is to use the definition as a specification that needs to be tailored by refinement techniques into an implementable form. The other is to construct a general-purpose implementation of the high-level mechanisms that have been used. In general, a compromise is desirable, where the two ideas are combined in a balanced manner.

With the generality of distributed action systems it is obvious that no general-purpose implementation can totally remove the need for refinement techniques. For a general-purpose mechanism it may also be impossible to achieve the efficiency that would be possible for a more refined system. On the other hand, an implementation of a general multi-process synchronization mechanism could remove the need for repeatedly occurring standard refinements.

In each case, transformation into asynchronous computations can always be expressed as refinement by superposition. The difference is whether the superposition steps are given explicitly as part of system specification and design, or implicitly as part of the implementation of a general-purpose mechanism.

### 9.2.2 Decentralized Evaluation of Guards

An action system will be called *centralized* if its object structure reflects the processes in a distributed implementation, but the actions do not obey the constraints imposed by the interaction and communication mechanisms that are available in the intended implementation environment. Imposing such constraints by suitable transformations will be called *decentralization*.

An intuitively natural goal in decentralization is that each process be able to evaluate its own readiness to participate in actions independently of other processes. Next we introduce some concepts that are useful in analyzing how this requirement can be met.

### Non-participant Parameters

Concerning non-participant parameters, direct implementability of an action requires that each of these can be interpreted as output from one of the participants to the others. This means that each such parameter be assigned to one of the participants, and that the value of the parameter be uniquely determined by the local variables of that participant. In other words, each non-participant parameter should be understood as a shorthand for an expression that involves local variables of a single participant only.

In the rest of this chapter we will always assume this to be the case.

**Local, Shared, and Global Guard Expressions**

An expression in a guard is said to be *local* to a participant if it depends, in addition to local variables of that process, only on the identities of the other participants (see Sect. 5.3.1, p. 136).

An expression that depends on the local variables of several participants is said to be *shared*. Shared expressions can be evaluated jointly by the participants in question.

When not local or shared, an expression in a guard is said to be *global*. In the absence of global variables, global expressions are made possible only by quantification.

For instance, if an action has participant roles p and q, guard expression

$$p.next = q.id$$

is local to p, since it refers only to the identity of q, expressions

$$p.x > q.x \,,$$
$$f(p) \wedge (g(p) \vee h(q))$$

are shared by p and q, and

$$\forall r \in P : r.x \geq p.x$$

is global.

**Separable Guards**

The guard of an action is said to be *separable* if it contains no global expressions, and each atomic logical expression in it is local to a single participant.

In the above example, $f(p) \wedge (g(p) \vee h(q))$ would be a separable guard, whereas $p.x > q.x$ would not.

By transformation into a disjunctive form, a separable guard of an action with $n$ participants can always be put into the disjunctive form

$$(p_{11} \wedge \cdots \wedge p_{1n}) \vee \cdots \vee (p_{k1} \wedge \cdots \wedge p_{kn}) \,,$$

where each atomic expression $p_{ij}$ is local to participant $j$. An action with a separable guard can therefore be implemented as a collection of actions with identical bodies, one action for each disjunct in the disjunctive form of the guard. For instance, an action with guard $f(p) \wedge (g(p) \vee h(q))$ can be implemented as two actions with guards $f(p) \wedge g(p)$ and $f(p) \wedge h(q)$, respectively.

When this transformation is used in a situation where the original action has fairness markings, the associated liveness properties are preserved if each of the new actions is given the corresponding fairness markings. The resulting liveness properties may, however, then be stronger than those originally required.

### 9.2.3 Modeling of Implementations

To be able to transform an action system into a form that can be implemented in a distributed fashion, we also need to understand how distributed implementations can be modeled as action systems.

#### Atomic Actions in Concurrent Processes

As already discussed in Chap. 2, atomicity of actions means that, once started, an action will eventually be completed without any interference from outside of the action itself.

Within each process in a distributed system, any deterministic, terminating, and non-communicating piece of code can be understood as a private action that has only one participant. A potentially non-terminating loop, on the other hand, can be understood as a repeatedly executed private action, with the loop condition as part of its guard.

A communication event can be understood to start a new atomic action. If nondeterminism is involved in the selection between several alternative communication events, each of these alternatives will then start a different atomic action.

For instance, in the select statement of Ada, a process may be prepared for several different communication events at the same time, in which case each of these would start a different atomic action (see process ACTIONS in Table 2.2, p. 51). Still another alternative action could in this kind of a situation be a private action that corresponds to a timeout event, and which can be selected if no communication event has taken place within a specified deadline.

#### Classification of Communication Mechanisms

A mechanism for process communication is an *interaction mechanism* if it allows immediate feedback from other participants within the same atomic action. Using an interaction mechanism, an atomic action can update the local states of the participating processes on the basis of the local states of the other participants.

*Ada rendezvous* and the interaction mechanism in CSP-like languages, like *Occam*, are examples of two-process interaction mechanisms, which will be discussed in more detail below.

Communication mechanisms where the roles of *sender* and *receiver* processes are clearly separated from each other are *message passing mechanisms*. This separation of roles means that the sender cannot get any feedback from the receiver(s) within the same action.[6]

---

[6]The enabling of a message passing event may depend on the state(s) of the receiver(s), which then provides a primitive form of feedback, but, once such an event takes place, the sender's state is updated independently of the receivers' states.

A message passing mechanism is *synchronous* or *asynchronous* depending on whether the sending and receiving of a message takes place in a single atomic event or not.[7]

As has already been mentioned, asynchronous message passing is a basic mechanism on which other mechanisms can be implemented. Synchronous message passing can be considered as the simplest abstraction that provides a primitive form of synchronization between processes.

Somewhat different communication paradigms are offered by *shared memory* and *remote procedure calls*. In this context they can, however, be considered as variations of an asynchronous message passing mechanism, which will be discussed in more detail below.

**Two-process Interaction Mechanisms**

The *rendezvous* or entry mechanism in Ada (see the example discussed in Sect. 2.4.2, p. 49) is a two-process interaction mechanism. As illustrated in Fig. 9.7, one of the two processes acts as a 'caller' that may invoke an accept statement within the code of a 'callee' process. This invocation is similar to a procedure call – except that the callee must be prepared to accept the call – and parameters may also be associated with it. After the callee has executed this accept statement, return parameters may be transmitted to the caller, and both processes will then proceed concurrently according to their own control threads.

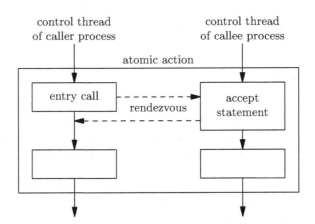

**Fig. 9.7.** Ada rendezvous as a two-process action

---

[7]Notice that the words 'asynchronous' and 'synchronous' are multiply overloaded in information technology. In this context they have nothing to do with whether the actual transmission lines are synchronous or asynchronous in the sense that these words are used in telecommunications literature, or with the synchrony hypothesis discussed in Sect. 1.2.5 (p. 11).

Considering rendezvous as an atomic action, the guard of the action requires that both processes are prepared for the rendezvous. That is, the control threads of both processes have proceeded to a place where the rendezvous can take place, and the local guarding condition, which is possible in Ada only on the callee's side, is true.

With the assumption that an accept statement contains no further entry calls, and that its execution will always be completed successfully, the body of the action can be understood to consist of the accept statement itself, and arbitrary (deterministic, terminating, and non-communicating) subsequent code within both processes. In addition, if the rendezvous starts a sequence of interaction events between the same pair of processes, these may also be included in the same action.

Instead of a symmetric way to access the local states of the two processes, as in action systems, only the state of the callee is directly visible within an accept statement. The relevant local variables in the caller's state have to be made accessible through parameters that are given in the entry call. Feedback from the accept statement to the callee can also take place through the return parameters of the entry call.

The Ada rendezvous mechanism is asymmetric with respect to the two participants, requiring that the caller can be prepared for at most one rendezvous (and possibly also a private timeout action) at a time, whereas the callee may have several concurrently enabled accept alternatives in a select statement (see example in Table 2.2, p. 51).

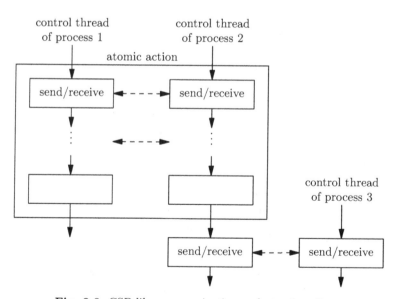

**Fig. 9.8.** CSP-like communication and atomic actions

In a similar manner, various CSP-like languages allow synchronous interaction by events in which messages can be sent in both directions. Such an event and its immediate consequences in both processes, including possible continued communication between the two processes, can be considered to constitute a single atomic action as outlined in Fig. 9.8.

In principle, the CSP mechanism is more symmetric than Ada rendezvous. However, to avoid complex handshake procedures between processes, it may be required that one of the partners is designated as the 'active' partner (or caller), which is allowed to be ready for at most one interaction at a time, while the 'passive' partner (callee) may have several alternatives.

Notice that languages like Ada and CSP do not provide any explicit support for the notion of actions. For instance, no syntactic correspondence exists between entry calls and the matching accept statements in Ada, or between the interaction points in CSP processes. Instead, the same entry call (or interaction point in an active partner) may give rise to different actions, depending on the accept statement (or interaction point in the passive partner) that will respond to it.

As for fairness issues, programming languages usually do not guarantee any kind of fairness in the nondeterministic selection between different alternatives.

### Message Passing

*Synchronous message passing* mechanisms allow a sender process to update a receiver's local state by a data value (message). The receiver is then needed as a participant in the action, but it is a 'passive' participant that may only affect the enabling of the action. That is, synchronous message passing requires synchronization between the communicating processes, but allows no feedback from the receiver.

Synchronous message passing may also allow *broadcast communication* with one sender and multiple receivers in one action. This is an exception to having only two-process actions at an implementation level.

*Asynchronous message passing* mechanisms have the additional restriction that explicit joint actions between sender and receiver processes are not possible. Instead, a communication event needs an intermediate auxiliary participant – a *channel* or a *message buffer* – to which a sender first gives a message (as in synchronous communication), and which then transmits the message to a receiver (or multiple receivers) in a separate event (or events).

Additional characteristics may be associated with the auxiliary participants in asynchronous message passing. These may have *bounded capacity* for storing undelivered messages. They may be *unreliable*, in which case messages may be lost or corrupted. Also, they need not be *order-preserving*, that is, messages need not be delivered in the same order in which they were sent.

## Other Communication Mechanisms

Communication through *shared memory* is similar to asynchronous message passing in the sense that a shared memory behaves as an intermediary between senders and receivers. It offers, however, flexible possibilities to build powerful higher-level communication mechanisms. A well-known example of this is the *Linda* approach, where versatile possibilities are provided for storing and retrieving tuples in a shared memory.

*Remote procedure call* mechanisms can be understood as conventions by which processes can use asynchronous message passing to invoke procedures in each other, and to receive the associated return values.

The notion of multi-process actions has also given rise to proposals for higher-level mechanisms that support *multi-process interactions* directly, by using general handshake algorithms for multi-process synchronization.

Various fairness notions have also been studied that can be supported in connection with multi-process interactions. The basic idea then is that all processes are provided with a uniform view of the sequence of events in the system. That is, one ensures that they can all monitor the same behavior that conforms to the distributed computation in question, and that they cooperate in making this behavior fair.

### 9.2.4 Constraints for Implementable Actions

To sum up, direct implementability of actions (in terms of the available communication mechanisms) imposes constraints of the following kinds:

- Usually only two-process communication is supported in programming languages for distributed systems. To reflect this, actions cannot have more than two participants.
- Processor topology may impose restrictions on the processes that can directly communicate with each other. This means that it need not be possible for all pairs of processes to have joint actions with each other.
- The guards of two-participant interactions need to be conjunctions of local expressions, which can be evaluated separately by the participants. To allow direct transformation into this form, the guards of actions must be separable.
- Asymmetry in interaction mechanisms may impose restrictions on the set of actions for which a process can be ready at the same time.
- In message passing mechanisms, receiver processes are passive participants that cannot affect the updating of the sender's local state. This causes asymmetry in what can be done in action bodies.
- Asynchronous message passing requires the introduction of auxiliary intermediate participants (asynchronous channels, message buffers, or shared memory), which are only passive participants in actions.

### 9.2.5 Example: Distributed Exchange Sort

The simple example of distributed sorting, which was already discussed in Sect. 5.6.5 (p. 156), will be used in the following to illustrate various transformations that can be used for the decentralization of actions.

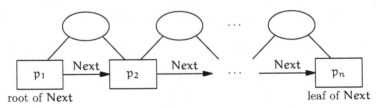

**Fig. 9.9.** Processes and communication actions in distributed exchange sort

To repeat the problem, we have $n$ processes $p \in P$, $|P| = n \geq 1$, each with one number $p.x$. The processes have been arranged as a sequence, where each $p$ can communicate directly only with its immediate neighbors as visualized in Fig. 9.9. The neighbor relation Next will now be represented in terms of local attributes $p.next$ and $p.prev$ in the processes, so that

$$p \cdot \text{Next} \cdot q \Leftrightarrow p.next = q.id \wedge q.prev = p.id \ ,$$

and $p.prev = q.next = \textbf{none}$ for the root $p$ and the leaf $q$ of Next. For simplicity, predicates $p.root$ and $p.leaf$ will be used as shorthand for $p.prev = \textbf{none}$ and $p.next = \textbf{none}$, respectively.

The purpose of the actions is to sort the numbers into an ascending order so that $p.next = q.id$ implies $p.x \leq q.x$. As was already discussed in Sect. 5.6.5 (p. 156), this can be done by action

$$^{\text{WF}}\text{Exchange}(p, q : P) : p.next = q.id$$
$$\wedge \ p.x > q.x$$
$$\rightarrow \ p.x' = \min(p.x, q.x)$$
$$\wedge \ q.x' = \max(p.x, q.x) \ .$$

An additional action that would use the final number $p.x$ in process $p$ for some purpose could have a global condition

$$\forall q \in P : (q \cdot \text{Next}^+ \cdot p \Rightarrow q.x \leq p.x) \wedge (p \cdot \text{Next}^+ \cdot q \Rightarrow p.x \leq q.x) \qquad (9.1)$$

in its guard. As such this would, however, require $p$ to communicate with all other processes $q \in P$.

The initial layer with the above action Exchange will be denoted by Sort. It is pointed out that our aim in the following refinements of this layer is only to demonstrate various kinds of transformations, not to derive optimal solutions for the distributed sorting problem.

## 9.2.6 Getting Rid of Global Guards

In high-level specifications it is often convenient to use global guards. A distributed implementation then requires transformation into a form with only shared or local guard expressions.

Consider the situation that an action $A(p : P)$ has a global guard $g$. Superposition can then be used for introducing a local condition $p.h$ with an intended invariant

$$\Box(p.h \Rightarrow g) .$$

Strengthening the guard $g$ into $p.h$ would obviously make it local, and would also preserve all safety properties. Preservation of liveness properties would need to be proved in the usual manner.

### Example

As an example, consider the global expression (9.1), expressing that process $p$ in the sorting example already has its final number.

The form of this expression suggests using local variables $p.\mathsf{max\_left}$ and $p.\mathsf{min\_right}$ to indicate the 'knowledge' of process $p$ about the largest number to its left, and the smallest number to its right, respectively. Special values '$\top$' and '$\bot$' can be used to indicate the lack of such knowledge, with the idea that '$\top$' ('$\bot$') is in arithmetic comparisons larger (smaller) than any other value.

More precisely, the intended invariants can then be given as

$$\Box(p.\mathsf{root} \Rightarrow p.\mathsf{max\_left} = \bot) ,$$

$$\Box(\neg p.\mathsf{root} \Rightarrow p.\mathsf{max\_left} = \top \vee p.\mathsf{max\_left} = \max_{q.\mathsf{Next}^+ p} (q.x)) ,$$

$$\Box(p.\mathsf{leaf} \Rightarrow p.\mathsf{min\_right} = \top) ,$$

$$\Box(\neg p.\mathsf{leaf} \Rightarrow p.\mathsf{min\_right} = \bot \vee p.\mathsf{min\_right} = \min_{p.\mathsf{Next}^+ q} (q.x)) .$$

These invariants can be imposed initially by setting $p.\mathsf{max\_left}$ as '$\bot$' or '$\top$', depending on whether $p$ is the leftmost process or not, and correspondingly $p.\mathsf{min\_right}$ as '$\top$' or '$\bot$', depending on whether $p$ is the rightmost process or not.

During a computation these invariants can be maintained, and the 'knowledge' expressed by them can be increased by refining action **Exchange** into

$$^{\mathrm{WF}}\mathbf{Exchange}(p, q : P) : \mathsf{Sort.Exchange}(p, q)$$
$$\rightarrow \text{ if } q.\mathsf{min\_right} \neq \bot \text{ then}$$
$$p.\mathsf{min\_right}' = \min(p.x, q.\mathsf{min\_right})$$
$$\wedge \text{ if } p.\mathsf{max\_left} \neq \top \text{ then}$$
$$q.\mathsf{max\_left}' = \max(q.x, p.\mathsf{max\_left}) .$$

In addition, we have to ensure that this 'knowledge' will eventually be spread out to all processes. Intuitively this means that each process that already has such knowledge is required to make sure that its neighbors will also get it. This can be achieved, for instance, by the following new actions:

$$^{\mathrm{WF}}\mathsf{Spread\_right}(p,q:P) : \mathsf{Sort.Stutter}$$
$$\wedge\; p.\mathsf{next} = q.\mathsf{id}$$
$$\wedge\; p.\mathsf{max\_left} \neq \top$$
$$\wedge\; q.\mathsf{max\_left} = \top$$
$$\rightarrow\; q.\mathsf{max\_left}' = \max(p.\mathsf{x}, p.\mathsf{max\_left})\;,$$

$$^{\mathrm{WF}}\mathsf{Spread\_left}(p,q:P) : \mathsf{Sort.Stutter}$$
$$\wedge\; p.\mathsf{next} = q.\mathsf{id}$$
$$\wedge\; p.\mathsf{min\_right} = \bot$$
$$\wedge\; q.\mathsf{min\_right} \neq \bot$$
$$\rightarrow\; p.\mathsf{min\_right}' = \min(q.\mathsf{x}, q.\mathsf{min\_right})\;.$$

With the given fairness requirements, the 'knowledge' expressed by the local variables $p.\mathsf{max\_left}$ and $p.\mathsf{min\_right}$ will eventually be maximized, and the local expression

$$p.\mathsf{max\_left} \leq p.\mathsf{x} \leq p.\mathsf{min\_right} \tag{9.2}$$

will then imply the global expression (9.1).

Obviously, the solution so obtained could be streamlined, for instance, by combining actions $\mathsf{Spread\_right}$ and $\mathsf{Spread\_left}$.

### 9.2.7 Dealing with Non-separable Guards

Because of the condition $p.\mathsf{x} > q.\mathsf{x}$, the guard of action $\mathsf{Sort.Exchange}$ is not separable.[8] Separability can be imposed, however, by moving this non-separable condition to be evaluated in the body, and letting the body do a stuttering execution, if this is not true.

In general, given an action $A$ with a guard $g$ that consists of a separable part $g_s$ and a non-separable part $g_n$, i.e., $g = g_s \wedge g_n$, this modification can be expressed as a stuttering relaxation of $A$ (see Sect. 6.4.4, p. 187) that allows stuttering under the condition $g_s \wedge \neg g_n$. As discussed in Sect. 6.4.4, if there are fairness requirements on $A$, this modification gives proof obligations for their preservation.

---

[8]Notice, however, that for a finite range of numbers $p.\mathsf{x} > q.\mathsf{x}$ could also be made separable. For the range $\{0, 1, 2\}$, for instance, it could be expressed as $(p.\mathsf{x} \geq 1 \wedge q.\mathsf{x} = 0) \vee (p.\mathsf{x} = 2 \wedge q.\mathsf{x} \leq 1)$.

## Example

In the distributed sorting example the separable (in this case even local) and non-separable parts of the guard are

$$g_s(p, q) \Leftrightarrow p.next = q.id ,$$
$$g_n(p, q) \Leftrightarrow p.x > q.x ,$$

and the stuttering relaxation of action Sort.Exchange is after straightforward simplification as follows:

$$Order(^{WF}p, q : P) : p.next = q.id$$
$$\rightarrow \ p.x' = \min(p.x, q.x)$$
$$\wedge \ q.x' = \max(p.x, q.x) .$$

Obviously, without the given change in the fairness marking, sorting would not need to be completed. With this stronger fairness requirement, preservation of liveness properties can be shown using the safety property that the non-separable condition $g_n(p, q)$ can be turned from true to false only by this action itself,

$$\textbf{stable } g_n(p, q) \textbf{ unless } \langle Order(p, q) \rangle .$$

With a separable guard the action has now become implementable with CSP-like communication mechanisms, for instance.

A layer where sorting is accomplished with this Order action will be denoted by $Sort_1$ in the following.

### 9.2.8 Imposing a Policy

In general, a nondeterministic model allows a large number of executions, many of which may be inefficient, either for a given implementation environment or by any reasonable metrics.

For instance, the technique that was described for making guards separable introduces additional stuttering executions of actions. Theoretically, fairness requirements can still guarantee that these cause no harm, but a direct implementation might involve a lot of unnecessary communication.

By a policy we mean here constraints by which nondeterminism is decreased for efficiency reasons. Such policies can be imposed by superposition. For instance, stuttering executions of an action can often be avoided by introducing new variables with suitable invariants.

## Example

As an example, consider action $Sort_1$.Order, which is always enabled for two neighboring processes – until possibly permanently disabled by an additional global condition that could be superposed on it – and can therefore cause a lot of unnecessary communication.

With some 'knowledge' about each other's numbers, some unnecessary stuttering executions can be avoided. Such information can be maintained by remembering the numbers that the neighbors had in previous exchange actions. For this purpose we can introduce additional variables p.x_left and p.x_right with the intended invariant

$$p.next = q.id \land p.x > q.x \Rightarrow p.x > p.x\_right \lor q.x < q.x\_left .$$

With '$\top$' and '$\perp$' as above, the invariant can be enforced by initializing p.x_left and p.x_right as '$\top$' and '$\perp$', respectively, and augmenting the body of $Sort_1$.Order with 'assignments'

$$\land p.x\_right' = \max(p.x, q.x)$$
$$\land q.x\_left' = \min(p.x, q.x) .$$

Strengthening the guard with conjunct

$$p.x > p.x\_right \lor q.x < q.x\_left$$

will then remove only stuttering executions.

### 9.2.9 Asymmetry in Invoking Actions

As discussed in Sect. 9.2.4 (p. 323), an asymmetric interaction mechanism may have the restriction that an active partner can be ready for at most one interaction at a time.

Such asymmetry can be enforced in joint actions by designating the active partner for each two-process action, and constraining nondeterminism so that no other actions are enabled for a process for which some action with active partnership is enabled. Notice that the active partner need not be statically determined, but may also depend on the current state.

### Example

Suppose that an active partner in exchange actions may be ready to communicate in only one direction at a time. If no exchange of numbers is needed in that direction, the direction can be changed only if the action permits stuttering.

Let the direction in which a process is ready to communicate be indicated by the local states

state Look_left, Look_right .

The desired effect is then obtained by refining action $Sort_1$.Order as follows:

$$\texttt{Order}(^{\text{WF}}\texttt{p}, \texttt{q} : \texttt{P}) : \texttt{Sort}_1.\texttt{Order}(\texttt{p}, \texttt{q})$$
$$\wedge\, \texttt{p.Look\_right}$$
$$\wedge\, \texttt{q.Look\_left}$$
$$\rightarrow\ \text{if}\ \neg\texttt{p.root}\ \text{then}\ \texttt{p.Look\_left}'$$
$$\wedge\ \text{if}\ \neg\texttt{q.leaf}\ \text{then}\ \texttt{q.Look\_right}'\,.$$

It is easy to see that the liveness properties of the system are preserved if the leftmost process is initialized to look to the right, and the rightmost process is initialized to look to the left.

Since at most one interaction is now enabled for any process $\texttt{p} \in \texttt{P}$, much freedom is left for designating the active partner in the above action $\texttt{Order}$. For instance, it could always be the left partner $\texttt{p}$, or it could also be the odd-numbered process in the sequence.

There is one problem, however, to be noticed. By having also added state changes to stuttering executions of action $\texttt{Sort}_1.\texttt{Order}$, these executions no longer stutter. The above fairness requirement therefore disallows permanent disabling of the action even when the sorting has been finished. This could be avoided by giving a stronger guard, where an additional conjunct remains true at least as long as the numbers have not been sorted, but will eventually turn false.

### 9.2.10 Decoupling of Effects

Message passing mechanisms do not permit events where the state change in the sender would depend on the state of the receiver. Therefore, such effects in the two partners of an action may need to be decoupled into separate actions.

### Example

Consider action $\texttt{Sort}_1.\texttt{Order}$, where the state changes in the participants depend on both of them.

To decouple the effects in the two participants we can think of splitting the action into three parts:

- **Send**, where one of the participants sends a message about its number $x$ to its partner,
- **React**, where the partner changes its number $x$, if necessary, and returns a message with its old number $x$ to the first participant, and
- **Complete**, where the first participant changes its number $x$, if necessary.

For simplicity, we can always think of the left participant to be the initiator that starts this sequence of actions.

Unfortunately, no refinement can possibly decouple the changes in $\texttt{p.x}$ and $\texttt{q.x}$ into different actions. We can, however, use the technique introduced in Sect. 6.4.3 (p. 186) for refinement of atomicity. That is, we can mimic $\texttt{p.x}$ by a new variable p.y, which is initialized with the same value and will 'almost always' agree with p.x.

Let class P therefore be extended into

**class** $P = \{\ldots y : \mathbb{U}; \textbf{state } \mathsf{Passive}^*, \mathsf{Active}; \mathsf{from\_left}, \mathsf{from\_right} : \mathbb{U}(\bot)\}$,

where y is the new variable to be used instead of x, states Active and Passive indicate whether the process has initiated communication with its right neighbor or not, and from_left and from_right are for storing messages from the two neighbors.

Actions for this superposition step can now be given as follows:

$$\mathsf{Send}(^{\mathrm{WF}}p, q : P) : \mathsf{Sort}_1.\mathsf{Stutter}$$
$$\wedge\, p.next = q.\textbf{id}$$
$$\wedge\, p.\mathsf{Passive}$$
$$\wedge\, p.\mathsf{from\_left} = \bot$$
$$\rightarrow\ q.\mathsf{from\_left}' = p.y$$
$$\wedge\, p.\mathsf{Active}',$$

$$\mathsf{React}(^{\mathrm{WF}}p, q : P) : \mathsf{Sort}_1.\mathsf{Order}(p, q)$$
$$\wedge\, q.\mathsf{Passive}$$
$$\wedge\, q.\mathsf{from\_left} \neq \bot$$
$$\rightarrow\ q.y' = \max(q.y, q.\mathsf{from\_left})$$
$$\wedge\, p.\mathsf{from\_right}' = \min(q.y, q.\mathsf{from\_left})$$
$$\wedge\, q.\mathsf{from\_left}' = \bot,$$

$$\mathsf{Complete}(^{\mathrm{WF}}p) : \mathsf{Sort}_1.\mathsf{Stutter}$$
$$\wedge\, p.\mathsf{Active}$$
$$\wedge\, p.\mathsf{from\_right} \neq \bot$$
$$\rightarrow\ p.y' = p.\mathsf{from\_right}$$
$$\wedge\, p.\mathsf{from\_right}' = \bot$$
$$\wedge\, p.\mathsf{Passive}'.$$

One of the intended invariants for this step is

$$\Box(p.x = (\text{if } p.\mathsf{from\_right} = \bot \text{ then } p.y \text{ else } p.\mathsf{from\_right})). \tag{9.3}$$

It expresses the purpose of the transformation, which is to change variables p.x into non-primitive state functions that are not needed in an implementation, since their values can always be obtained from other variables, i.e., from p.y and p.from_right. Checking that (9.3) is, indeed, satisfied is left to the reader (Exercise 9.2.4). Since this allows us to eliminate p.x and q.x from action React, actions Send and React can be interpreted as synchronous message passing actions, to be executed by participants p and q, respectively.

The correctness of the transformation requires us, of course, to prove that liveness properties have also been preserved in it (Exercise 9.2.5).

### 9.2.11 Discussion

Various problems in the decentralization of actions have been illustrated in this section by representative examples. The techniques of superposition and elimination of variables have shown their power and feasibility in carrying out such transformations in a well-managed manner.

In particular, transformations for decoupling of effects are important if the actions of a centralized specification have participants that cannot have actions with each other in an implementation. The example in Sect. 9.2.10 (p. 329) demonstrates such decoupling under the assumption that synchronous message passing can be used. With only asynchronous message passing, neighboring processes $p, q \in P$ could not participate in the same actions, which would lead to the need for an auxiliary participant to represent a communication channel (see Exercise 9.2.8). An example of using this technique was discussed already in Sect. 8.5 (p. 291).

When a variable $p.x$ is turned into a 'ghost' variable, its representation function is not, in general, local to process $p$ itself, as it was in the simple situation of Sect. 9.2.10. This means that other actions that utilize the value of $p.x$ may not have any decentralized possibilities to access it. This usually leads to temporary disabling of such actions, which means that the preservation of their liveness properties may also give further proof obligations.

### Review Questions

QUESTION 9.2.1 What is the significance of separable guards? Why is it possible for a separable guard to contain arbitrary logical connectives?

QUESTION 9.2.2 How is nondeterminism present in programming languages for distributed systems?

QUESTION 9.2.3 What is the difference between synchronous interactions and synchronous message passing mechanisms?

QUESTION 9.2.4 When concurrent processes are modeled as action systems, why is it possible that the effects of the same piece of code are included in several different actions?

QUESTION 9.2.5 What kind of asymmetry is often present in the mechanisms for synchronous interaction, and what is the reason for this?

**Exercises**

EXERCISE 9.2.1 Consider an Ada process (i.e., a 'task') that contains a non-terminating loop with two alternatives for an interaction in each cycle:

```
loop
    select accept entry_1 do ··· end; ··· ; – – alternative 1
        or accept entry_2 do ··· end; ··· ; – – alternative 2
    end select;
end loop;
```

Discuss how this code can be reflected in an action-system model, and which kinds of fairness requirements could be enforced by a compiler. Why would weak fairness properties be sensitive to whether the alternatives are thought of as single actions or as sequences of several actions?

EXERCISE 9.2.2 Give a high-level description of an exchange sort system where an additional action forces each process to enter a final state after the sorting has been finished. Combine different techniques demonstrated in this section to obtain an 'efficient' specification that could be directly implemented with synchronous message passing mechanisms. Show that the construction is correct, and write out its final actions.

EXERCISE 9.2.3 Show that the liveness properties of the original layer Sort are preserved in the construction of layer Sort₁ in Sect. 9.2.7 (p. 326).

EXERCISE 9.2.4 Formulate and prove the intended invariants for the construction in Sect. 9.2.10 (p. 329). In particular, show that invariant (9.3) is satisfied.

EXERCISE 9.2.5 Show that the construction in Sect. 9.2.10 (p. 329) also preserves liveness properties.

EXERCISE 9.2.6 Concerning the construction in Sect. 9.2.10 (p. 329), consider allowing p to respond to the left after initiating communication to the right, i.e., leaving condition q.Passive out from the guard of React. What kind of errors would this allow, and how would this be reflected in an attempt to prove the necessary invariants?

EXERCISE 9.2.7 Consider the possibility of allowing either one of the two partners to initiate a communication event in the construction in Sect. 9.2.10 (p. 329).

EXERCISE 9.2.8 Change the construction in Sect. 9.2.10 (p. 329) to one where the resulting actions can be implemented using an asynchronous message passing mechanism. Would the representation function for p.x still allow other actions to access its value at any time?

## 9.3 Uniform Fairness Assumptions

Fairness is a basic 'force of nature' that forces actions into execution in our theory. As a theoretical notion it is an abstraction of the reality, in which no such force is available for explicit utilization. The validity of all fairness assumptions therefore needs to be checked. For distributed systems this leads to specific questions, since the interleaving model with its fairness notions is an even 'more theoretical' model for them than for non-distributed systems, as is apparent from the analysis in Sect. 9.1.

For an asynchronous message passing mechanism, for instance, a primitive 'fairness force' can be assumed to ensure only that every message will eventually be delivered. Even this is often an unrealistic assumption of the underlying physical reality, in which case a communication protocol is required to guarantee that no incorrect messages are delivered, and that all messages will eventually be delivered. Furthermore, only *probabilistic* enforcement of such properties is possible in practice, which guarantees them with probability 1, but still leaves the theoretical possibility for unfair or otherwise incorrect behaviors with probability 0 (see Sect. 2.3.9, p. 45).

In this section we analyze which kinds of basic fairness assumptions are reasonable for uniform enforcement in distributed action systems, even though only very weak assumptions can be made about the 'fairness force' that is available for doing this.

### 9.3.1 Enforcement of Fairness Properties

Theoretically, the underlying primitive fairness force could be utilized to construct a fairness scheduler for an arbitrary distributed action system. As discussed in Sect. 9.1.3 (p. 309), such a general-purpose implementation of multiprocess actions would rely on a protocol for the processes to communicate with each other and with the scheduler.

On the other hand, as discussed in Sect. 9.2, refinement techniques can be used to refine a system into the level of basic implementation mechanisms, for which some fairness assumptions are directly available, and no additional scheduling would then be needed. This latter approach would mean that multiprocess actions are effectively used only in high-level specifications.

A compromise between the two extremes is also possible. Instead of supporting arbitrary fairness requirements, general-purpose conventions on handshaking protocols and scheduling algorithms can be utilized to ensure some *uniform fairness properties*, which are independent of the specification in question and its specific fairness requirements. Refinement techniques can then be used to refine specifications to a level where the required properties are guaranteed by these uniform properties. In particular, such refinements may add temporary disabling of actions that might 'compete' with a given fair action.

The purpose of this section is to analyze uniform fairness assumptions that are reasonable for enforcement in arbitrary distributed action systems.

We will not, however, go into any details of how they could be enforced by explicit protocols and scheduling algorithms.

### 9.3.2 Basic Actions and Action Fairness

Given an action $A$ in a distributed action system, and a set $x$ of possible participants for it, $A(x)$ will now be called a *basic action*.[9] Whenever there is no danger for confusion, the word 'action' will denote basic actions in the following.

Assuming a finite number of processes, the number of basic actions is also finite. They will be denoted in the following by $A_1(x_1), \ldots, A_n(x_n)$, or simply by $A_1, \ldots, A_n$, when the participants are of no interest.

To allow each process to evaluate independently its own readiness to participate in actions, the guards of all actions $A_i$ are assumed in the following to be conjunctions of local conditions in the participants. Obviously, such a readiness can change only as a result of executing an action in which the process itself participates. As a consequence, an enabled action cannot be disabled without some of its participants participating in an action.

The fairness requirements that are expressible in distributed action systems are strong and weak fairness requirements with respect to basic actions or some disjunctions of them. The assumption of weak (strong) fairness with respect to each action would give us simple uniform fairness assumptions, which we call *weak (strong) action fairness*, and abbreviate as WAF (SAF):

$$\text{WAF} \triangleq \text{WF}(A_1) \wedge \cdots \wedge \text{WF}(A_n) , \tag{9.4}$$

$$\text{SAF} \triangleq \text{SF}(A_1) \wedge \cdots \wedge \text{SF}(A_n) . \tag{9.5}$$

These would obviously be very strong assumptions, which would not be realistic for distributed implementation.

### 9.3.3 Example: Dining Philosophers

The well-known dining philosophers problem will be used in the following to illustrate the kinds of refinements that are useful in making the fairness requirements of a specification implementable by general-purpose protocols.

The problem is formulated as follows. There are $n$ philosophers $p_i$, $i = 0, \ldots, n - 1$, $n > 1$, sitting around a table, and there are $n$ forks $f_i$, $i = 0, \ldots, n - 1$, one between each two neighboring philosophers (see Fig. 9.10). The main work of philosophers is to think, but they also need to eat every now and then. Therefore, an unbounded amount of spaghetti is provided, but, for eating spaghetti, a philosopher needs both of the two forks that are next to him. This has the consequence that it is not possible for any two neighboring

---

[9]Non-participant parameters can be omitted, because of the assumption that their values are uniquely determined by a single participant (see Sect. 9.2.2, p. 317).

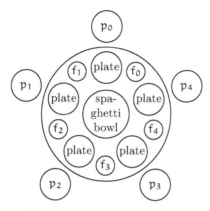

**Fig. 9.10.** Five dining philosophers

philosophers to eat at the same time. The problem is to coordinate the system so that no philosopher will starve.

The philosophers and the forks are modeled as processes $p \in P$ and $f \in F$, respectively. The topology of the processes can be expressed as follows: the philosophers form a ring, where $p.next$ and $p.prev$ indicate the neighbors[10] on the right and on the left of $p$, respectively, and $p.left$ and $p.right$ indicate the two forks associated with $p$. A Boolean variable $p.hungry$, initialized as false, will indicate whether philosopher $p$ is hungry or not.

The lives of the philosophers can now be described in a high-level model Life by two actions:

$$\text{Think}(^{\text{WF}}p : P) : \neg p.hungry$$
$$\rightarrow p.hungry' = \text{true} \,,$$

$$\text{Eat}(^{\text{WF}}p : P;\ l, r : F) : l = p.left$$
$$\wedge r = p.right$$
$$\wedge p.hungry$$
$$\rightarrow p.hungry' = \text{false} \,.$$

Obviously, the fairness requirements in this specification imply the desired liveness property that every philosopher eats infinitely often. It is not, however, obvious how this property can be enforced in a distributed implementation. To be more precise, it would be the task of a fairness scheduler to eventually stop the continual eating of philosophers $p_0$ and $p_2$, for instance,

---

[10]Although these neighbor relations are not utilized in the actions to be given in the text, they are introduced to indicate potential partners of direct communication. Obviously, other possibilities for such communication relations could also be assumed.

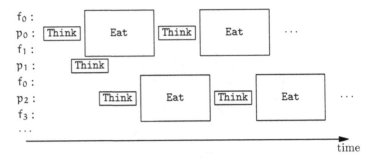

**Fig. 9.11.** A concurrent execution scenario, where philosopher $p_1$ starves

if forks $f_1$ and $f_2$ would not otherwise become simultaneously available for philosopher $p_1$ (see the scenario in Fig. 9.11). In the absence of such a fairness scheduler, similar disabling has to be built explicitly into the system, in which case some more primitive assumptions are sufficient to guarantee fair execution of eating actions.

### 9.3.4 Insufficiency of Fundamental Liveness

As discussed in Sect. 2.3.6 (p. 43), *fundamental liveness (FL)* is a natural basic fairness assumption for deterministic systems. Disregarding the partitioning of actions into system and environment actions, the meaning of this is: if something can happen, then something will eventually happen. For the situation discussed in this section, FL can be formalized as weak fairness with respect to the disjunction of all basic actions $A_i$, $i = 1, \ldots, n$:

$$FL \stackrel{\Delta}{=} WF(A_1 \vee \cdots \vee A_n) \,. \tag{9.6}$$

We start with two observations about the (non-)applicability of FL as a fundamental assumption for distributed systems. Firstly, it is easy to think about poorly designed communication protocols that do not enforce even FL. For instance, if there are three actions $A(p, q)$, $B(q, r)$, and $C(r, p)$, which are all continually enabled, there is a possibility for infinite communication scenarios that do not lead to a consensus between the three processes $p$, $q$, and $r$ about the selection of the next action. Still, FL would require one of them to be executed. This shows, in fact, that there exists no reasonable fairness notion that could be attributed directly to the underlying reality of distributed systems.

Secondly, although anything weaker than FL does not seem useful, FL is clearly insufficient for distributed systems, and somewhat stronger assumptions are therefore needed. For instance, if the processes of a system are completely independent, FL does not ensure progress in each of them. In that situation it would be natural to strengthen FL into separate FL assumptions for each process, the meaning of which is: if a process can continually do something, it will eventually do something.

More formally, if $A_p$ denotes the disjunction of all basic actions in which process p is a participant, such *weak liveness* of all processes is defined as

$$WL \triangleq \bigwedge_p WF(A_p) \, , \tag{9.7}$$

and the corresponding *strong liveness* of all processes is

$$SL \triangleq \bigwedge_p SF(A_p) \, . \tag{9.8}$$

In any behavior that conforms to the scenario of Fig. 9.11 (p. 336), action Eat is continually enabled for philosopher $p_1$ after his thinking action, but no more actions are executed for him. This shows that even WL is too strong to be taken as a basic assumption in the general case – not to speak about SL, which is even stronger.

This scenario also demonstrates that WL cannot, in general, be enforced without reducing concurrency. The notions of WL and SL will, however, be used in Sect. 9.3.9 in a context where such problems do not arise.

### 9.3.5 Weak Interaction Fairness

In the absence of nondeterminism, FL is equivalent to WAF (9.4). In general, WAF is stronger than FL, but also stronger than WL. In searching for a suitable basic fairness notion for distributed systems we look, however, for a condition of the form (9.4), where the conjuncts $WF(A_i)$ are appropriately weakened.

The reason for the difficulties in ensuring $WF(A)$ for a basic action A is that the participants of A may be engaged in other actions instead, as was illustrated in the scenario of Fig. 9.11. It seems reasonable, however, to assume that all participants of A cannot stay idle indefinitely, if A is continually enabled.

This leads to the following definition of *weak interaction fairness* with respect to a basic action A, denoted by $WIF(A)$:

- A behavior satisfies $WIF(A)$ for a basic action A if it cannot be the case that, from some point on, A is continually enabled, but none of its participants is involved in any action.

Unlike $WF(A)$ and $SF(A)$, $WIF(A)$ is not a TLA property of behaviors in isolation from the basic actions of the system and of their participants. In Sect. 9.3.8 we will, however, introduce a transformation after which $WIF(A)$ can be expressed as an ordinary weak fairness property in the transformed system.

The uniform fairness property that we can now take as the basic liveness assumption in distributed action systems is $\mathrm{WIF}(A_i)$ with respect to all basic actions $A_i$, $i = 1, \ldots, n$, called *weak interaction fairness* (WIF):

$$\mathrm{WIF} \triangleq \mathrm{WIF}(A_1) \wedge \cdots \wedge \mathrm{WIF}(A_n) \,. \tag{9.9}$$

Obviously, WIF implies that, for any set of enabled actions, either an action of this set will eventually be executed, or one of their participants gets involved in some other action. Therefore, WIF implies FL, and in the case of independent processes also WL. It is also easy to see that, unlike with WL, scheduling with the WIF property never leads to conflict with full use of maximal parallelism.

For the basic form of the dining philosophers example given in Sect. 9.3.3 (p. 334), WIF enforces an infinite number of eating actions, but allows the starvation of any individual philosopher.

### 9.3.6 Outline for Enforcing WIF

Presenting WIF as the basic liveness property for distributed action systems is actually quite a strong statement, since it is not a trivial task to design a truly distributed communication protocol that guarantees uniform enforcement of $\mathrm{WIF}(A)$.

If a centralized scheduler can be used, the task is, however, not difficult at all. When idle, each process can evaluate its readiness to participate in actions and send this information to the scheduler, which can then select actions for execution and inform the participants about this. Since the scheduler continually has information about the processes' readiness to participate in actions, it is easy to select actions in such a way that the WIF property is guaranteed.

In the absence of a centralized scheduler, processes can broadcast their readiness messages to other processes concerned, which makes it possible for some of them to detect actions that are enabled. The main problem in this is that overlapping sets of participants may lead to mutually contradictory suggestions for action selection. Even when only asynchronous messages are available for communication, it is possible to resolve such conflicts by designating one of the participants of each action as its 'master', and letting the masters of competing actions negotiate and agree on the selection. Correct and efficient organization of such a distributed negotiation is more difficult than ensuring WIF by the result, and will not be discussed here.

An intermediate situation is one where messages are transmitted through a broadcast channel (like Ethernet, for instance). This imposes a unique ordering on all messages, and this same order will then be recognized by all processes. No designated masters are then needed for actions, and any participant can suggest an enabled action to be executed. When conflicting suggestions arise, the unique ordering of messages can be utilized to make the processes accept or refuse these suggestions in a consistent manner, and so that the WIF property will also be guaranteed.

### 9.3.7 Philosophers with Counters on the Forks

Two enabled actions are said to be *competing* if their participant sets overlap. In the absence of competition, WIF eventually forces an enabled action into execution. When designing a system for WIF, one should therefore design it so that, if a continually enabled fair action is not executed, WIF is also sufficient to ensure that all competition will eventually be eliminated for it.

As an example, consider the competition between the eating actions of two neighboring philosophers. For any philosopher $p \in P$, elimination of competition means that the eating actions of both neighbors must eventually become disabled, unless p itself gets a chance to eat.

One possibility to enforce this is to add counters l_count and r_count to the forks, indicating the number of times they have been used as left forks and right forks, respectively, and maintaining some bound $k, k > 0$, for the differences of these numbers.[11] The eating actions can then be refined into

$$Eat(^{WF}p : P; \, l, r : F) : Life.Eat(p, l, r)$$
$$\wedge \; l.l\_count - l.r\_count < k$$
$$\wedge \; r.r\_count - r.l\_count < k$$
$$\rightarrow \; l.l\_count' = l.l\_count + 1$$
$$\wedge \; r.r\_count' = r.r\_count + 1 \, ,$$

and invariants

$$\square(p.left.l\_count = p.right.r\_count) \, , \tag{9.10}$$
$$\square(|f.l\_count - f.r\_count| \le k) \tag{9.11}$$

will then be satisfied for all philosophers and forks, respectively.

Because of the topology of the processes, a deadlock in the system would imply that the difference $f.l\_count - f.r\_count$ is either k for all forks f, or $-k$ for all of them, both of which situations would violate invariant (9.10). (Checking this is left as an exercise to the reader; see Exercise 9.3.6.) Therefore, WIF forces an infinite number of eating actions to be executed and $\sum_f f.l\_count$, for instance, will then grow unboundedly.

On the other hand, the invariants also imply that for two neighboring forks l and r, the difference $|l.l\_count - r.l\_count|$ never exceeds k. (Checking this is left as an exercise to the reader; see Exercise 9.3.6.) Therefore, for two arbitrary forks this difference can never exceed $n/2 * k$. This means also that every individual philosopher must eat infinitely often.

Considering the situation from the viewpoint of a single enabled eating action, the counters ensure eventual elimination of competition: unless a given eating action is executed, the two potentially competing eating actions will eventually become permanently disabled.

---

[11]Obviously, only the differences of these counters are needed, but the proofs are easier with separate counters.

### 9.3.8 Monitoring of Actions Reconsidered

When the execution of actions is monitored for scheduling purposes, as discussed in Sect. 9.1.3 (p. 309), the monitored sequence may contain both the handshakes for actions and also the events where a process releases an action. Such a sequence corresponds, in fact, to a behavior in a modified action system that can be obtained from the original by simple superposition, and which models concurrency in a simple manner.

To be more specific, let $S$ be an arbitrary distributed action system (in which all fairness requirements are irrelevant, for the moment), and let $S^*$ be the distributed action system obtained from it as follows. As for variables, each process (i.e., each class) in $S$ is extended with a Boolean variable $b$, initialized as false, to indicate whether the process is currently engaged in an action or not. As for actions, each action $A$ (with $k$ participants in classes $P_1, \ldots, P_k$) is refined into

$$A^*(p_1 : P_1, \ldots, p_k : P_k) : S.A(p_1, \ldots, p_k)$$
$$\wedge \neg p_1.b \wedge \cdots \wedge \neg p_k.b$$
$$\rightarrow \; p_1.b' = \text{true}$$
$$\cdots$$
$$\wedge p_k.b' = \text{true} ,$$

and a new action $R$ is added for each process class $P$ to model the event that a process $p \in P$ is released from some action:

$$R(^{WF}p : P) : S.\text{Stutter}$$
$$\wedge p.b$$
$$\rightarrow \; p.b' = \text{false} .$$

Monitoring an arbitrary concurrent execution in a distributed action system $S$ would then yield a refined behavior $\sigma^*$ in system $S^*$, instead of the corresponding behavior $\sigma$ in $S$, as illustrated in Fig. 9.12. The fairness assumption in action $R$ models the requirement that each participant is eventually released from executing an action. Enforcing further fairness properties on behaviors $\sigma^*$ would impose further liveness properties on the corresponding behaviors $\sigma$ that can be generated.

### 9.3.9 WIF and Beyond

There is now a simple relationship between scheduling on the basis of behaviors $\sigma^*$, which relate to the transformed distributed action system $S^*$, and enforcing WIF for the corresponding behaviors $\sigma$ in the original system $S$:

- An implementation of a distributed action system $S$ satisfies WIF iff the associated behaviors in $S^*$ satisfy WAF.

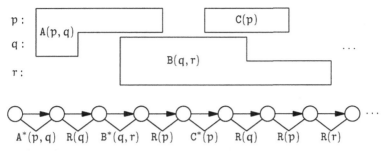

**Fig. 9.12.** Example of concurrent execution of actions in a system S, with a corresponding behavior in S*

Showing this is left as an exercise for the reader (Exercise 9.3.9).

Other reasonable uniform fairness notions, which are stronger than WIF, but not in conflict with maximal parallelism, can now also be formulated as follows:

- An implementation of a distributed action system S is said to satisfy *weak process fairness* (WPF) iff the associated behaviors in S* satisfy WL (see the definition (9.7) of WL on p. 337).
- An implementation of a distributed action system S is said to satisfy *strong process fairness* (SPF) iff the associated behaviors in S* satisfy SL (see the definition (9.8) of SL on p. 337).
- An implementation of a distributed action system S is said to satisfy *strong interaction fairness* (SIF) iff the associated behaviors in S* satisfy SAF.

This list was given in an increasing order of strength. Therefore, the implications shown in Fig. 9.13 hold for all action systems (see Exercise 9.3.10).

$$
\begin{array}{ccc}
\text{SAF} & \Rightarrow & \text{WAF} \\
\Downarrow & & \Downarrow \\
\text{SIF} & & \text{WIF} \\
\Downarrow & & \Uparrow \\
\text{SPF} & \Rightarrow & \text{WPF}
\end{array}
$$

**Fig. 9.13.** Implications between different uniform fairness notions

## Review Questions

QUESTION 9.3.1 What is meant by uniform fairness properties, and how can they be utilized?

QUESTION 9.3.2 What is meant by basic actions?

QUESTION 9.3.3 What are the definitions of FL and WL, and are they too weak or too strong to be used as basic fairness assumptions on distributed action systems?

QUESTION 9.3.4 Why is it not possible to say that WIF is a basic 'law of nature' in distributed systems?

QUESTION 9.3.5 Do the fairness notions of this section allow scheduling with maximal parallelism?

QUESTION 9.3.6 In which sense does the transformation of action systems in Sect. 9.3.8 (p. 340) reflect concurrency?

**Exercises**

EXERCISE 9.3.1 Give a model for the situation where several sender processes share the same communication channel for messages. Discuss the need and feasibility of associated fairness assumptions.

EXERCISE 9.3.2 Give a formal definition of WIF (see Sect. 9.3.5, p. 337).

EXERCISE 9.3.3 Outline a centralized scheduler that guarantees WIF (see Sect. 9.3.6, p. 338).

EXERCISE 9.3.4 Outline a communication protocol that ensures FL (see Sect. 9.3.4, p. 336) with maximal parallelism without using a centralized scheduler. Hint: since it does not matter for FL how competition conflicts are resolved, this can be done simply by assigning priorities to actions.

EXERCISE 9.3.5 What is the minimum number of philosophers that eat infinitely often under WIF in the basic version of the dining philosophers example in Sect. 9.3.3 (p. 334)?

EXERCISE 9.3.6 Check the reasoning for the construction in Sect. 9.3.7 (p. 339).

EXERCISE 9.3.7 Formulate a solution for the dining philosophers problem that is based on the following idea. A number of tokens is associated with the forks, eating is allowed only with at least one token on the left fork, and each eating action transfers one token from the left fork to the right fork. Is WIF now sufficient for preventing starvation?

EXERCISE 9.3.8 If fairness requirements are associated with actions in a distributed system S, are these always feasible for the transformed system S*, discussed in Sect. 9.3.8 (p. 340)?

EXERCISE 9.3.9 Show that WIF in a distributed action system S is equivalent to WAF in the transformed system S*, as claimed in Sect. 9.3.9 (p. 340).

EXERCISE 9.3.10 Prove that the implications in Fig. 9.13 (p. 341) hold for all action systems, but none of these can be replaced by an equivalence (for arbitrary action systems).

EXERCISE 9.3.11 Why are WL and SL not the same as WPF and SPF, respectively?

EXERCISE 9.3.12 Prove that WL implies WPF, but even SIF does not imply WL.

## 9.4 Generic Example of Coordination

Computing often proceeds through cyclic stages. In a centralized system, as defined in Sect. 9.2.2 (p. 317), all processes can enter the next stage in a synchronized fashion, when the previous stage has been completed. Compared to this, a distributed system offers the flexibility that consecutive stages can overlap: some processes can already enter the next stage while some others are still completing their parts in the previous stage. This must, however, be done in a coordinated manner.

A general solution to this generic problem in the coordination of distributed processes will be discussed in this section.

### 9.4.1 Cyclic Stages

Consider a situation where, according to a global view, computation proceeds cyclically through a sequence of stages $1, 2, \ldots, k, 1, 2, \ldots$ . In a distributed implementation one may then have processes $p \in P$ that cycle through corresponding local stages $1, \ldots, k, 1, \ldots$ and communicate with each other only when they are in the same stage.

For simplicity we will assume that $k = 2$ in the following, and an integer-valued local variable $p.stage$ will be used to indicate the local stage of process $p$.

Figure 9.14 gives an example of a scenario for how the processes in a distributed implementation may then proceed. The direction of time is from left to right and, for each process $p_1, \ldots, p_4$, the moments are shown when it enters the next stage 1 or 2. Obviously, some of the processes may already

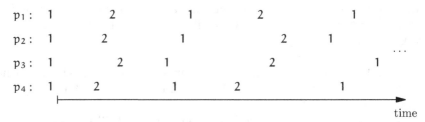

**Fig. 9.14.** Coordinated stages in four processes

communicate with each other in a new stage, while some others are still doing that in the previous stage.

The processes must, however, be coordinated so that two processes in the same stage are also within the same cycle of stages. In other words, if an imaginary local counter p.i (initialized as 0) is incremented each time when the local stage p.stage changes, two processes can be in the same stage only when these counters have the same values. Obviously, if the maximum difference of these imaginary counter values is guaranteed never to exceed 1, then p.stage = q.stage implies p.i = q.i for p, q ∈ P.

As for externally visible actions, by which the processes of the system communicate with the environment, these must be constrained to be executed in a fashion that would also be possible in a centralized implementation. This is the case if the executions of such externally visible actions of one stage always precede those of the next stage.

The situation can be understood as a relaxation of *barrier synchronization*, in which processes are prevented from proceeding beyond a 'barrier', until all processes have reached it. In our situation, where the barrier corresponds to entering the next stage, we do allow processes to proceed beyond it, as long as this has no effect on the resulting externally visible behavior.

### 9.4.2 Critical Moments and Actions

Since there is no global indication of the two stages, we have to examine more closely how the local stages are allowed to change. As indicated by the dashed and solid vertical lines in Fig. 9.15, the system should repeat the following cycle of states, where every second state overlaps with the succeeding one:

$$(\forall p : p.stage = 1) \rightarrow (\exists p : p.stage = 2) \rightarrow$$
$$(\forall p : p.stage = 2) \rightarrow (\exists p : p.stage = 1) \rightarrow$$
$$(\forall p : p.stage = 1) \rightarrow \cdots .$$

For each stage those moments are significant at which the last process enters the stage. In Fig. 9.15 these *critical moments* have been marked by

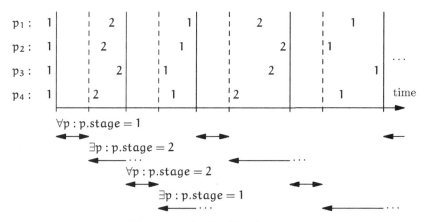

**Fig. 9.15.** Cycle of local stages

solid vertical lines. To guarantee correct operation, the processes have to be coordinated so that no *critical actions* of a new stage are executed before this moment. By critical actions we mean

- actions in which a process exits a stage and enters the next one, and
- externally visible actions in which a process communicates with the environment.

Allowing no process to exit a stage before the critical moment guarantees that the difference between two imaginary counter values p.i never exceeds 1. Disallowing externally visible actions before the critical moment then ensures that the overlap of local stages has no effect on the externally visible behavior of the system.

### 9.4.3 Global Guards for Critical Actions

The guard of each critical action requires an expression that is turned true at the critical moment, and stays true at least until all critical actions of the current stage have been executed. Obviously, the local stages of the processes cannot be directly used for this purpose.

The desired expressions can be obtained with the aid of two local Boolean variables p.a and p.b in each process $p \in P$. If they are all initialized as false, and if p.b (p.a,) is complemented each time when p enters stage 2 (1), then these variables have the same values in all processes during the intervals shown in Fig. 9.16. Furthermore, process p is in stage 1 (2) exactly when $p.a = p.b$ ($p.a \neq p.b$), which shows that variables p.stage can be omitted.

Now, process p is in stage 1, and all other processes have also entered this stage (although they may have exited it already), if and only if

$$p.a = p.b \land \forall q \in P : q.a = p.a ,$$

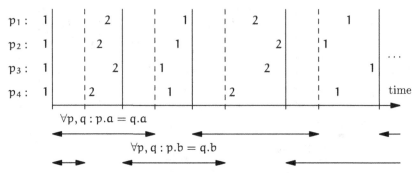

**Fig. 9.16.** Global conditions for critical actions

and the corresponding situation exists for stage 2 when

$$p.a \neq p.b \land \forall q \in P : q.b = p.b \ .$$

This gives the desired global conditions that can be used in the guards of critical actions in the two stages.

Decentralization of actions can then take place with the techniques described in Sect. 9.2 (p. 316). In particular, one can get rid of the global conditions in guards, as shown in Sect. 9.2.6 (p. 325).

### 9.4.4 Example: Repeated Exchange Sort

Related to the sorting example of Sect. 9.2.5 (p. 324), consider its generalization to repeated sorting, where the sorted numbers are to be given as output in critical actions, and a new set of numbers is to be obtained as input in the same actions.

Obviously, a crucial correctness condition here is that the numbers of different sets of numbers do not get mixed. The sorting and output of one set of numbers, as well as the input of the next set, can be considered to constitute a single stage of computation. The computation then alternates between the stages of dealing with odd-numbered sets and even-numbered sets.

The only critical actions are now those in which the sorted numbers are given as output and new numbers are accepted as input. These actions obviously satisfy both conditions for criticality.

For odd-numbered sets of numbers the required actions can now be given in a centralized form as follows:

$^{WF}\text{Exchange1}(p, q : P) :$ p.next = q.id
$$\land \text{ p.a} = \text{p.b}$$
$$\land \text{ q.a} = \text{q.b}$$
$$\land \text{ p.x} > \text{q.x}$$
$$\rightarrow \text{ p.x}' = \min(\text{p.x}, \text{q.x})$$
$$\land \text{ q.x}' = \max(\text{p.x}, \text{q.x}) \,,$$

$^{WF}\text{Proceed1}(p : P; \text{ u}, v : \mathbb{Z}) :$ p.a = p.b
$$\land \forall q \in P : \text{q.a} = \text{p.a}$$
$$\land \forall q \in P : \text{q} \cdot \text{Next}^+ \cdot \text{p} \Rightarrow \text{q.x} \leq \text{p.x}$$
$$\land \forall q \in P : \text{p} \cdot \text{Next}^+ \cdot \text{q} \Rightarrow \text{p.x} \leq \text{q.x}$$
$$\land \text{ u} = \text{p.x}$$
$$\rightarrow \text{ p.x}' = v$$
$$\land \text{ p.b}' = \neg\text{p.b} \,.$$

For even-numbered sets the corresponding actions are

$^{WF}\text{Exchange2}(p, q : P) :$ p.next = q.id
$$\land \text{ p.a} \neq \text{p.b}$$
$$\land \text{ q.a} \neq \text{q.b}$$
$$\land \text{ p.x} > \text{q.x}$$
$$\rightarrow \text{ p.x}' = \min(\text{p.x}, \text{q.x})$$
$$\land \text{ q.x}' = \max(\text{p.x}, \text{q.x}) \,,$$

$^{WF}\text{Proceed2}(p : P; \text{ u}, v : \mathbb{Z}) :$ p.a $\neq$ p.b
$$\land \forall q \in P : \text{q.b} = \text{p.b}$$
$$\land \forall q \in P : \text{q} \cdot \text{Next}^+ \cdot \text{p} \Rightarrow \text{q.x} \leq \text{p.x}$$
$$\land \forall q \in P : \text{p} \cdot \text{Next}^+ \cdot \text{q} \Rightarrow \text{p.x} \leq \text{q.x}$$
$$\land \text{ u} = \text{p.x}$$
$$\rightarrow \text{ p.x}' = v$$
$$\land \text{ p.a}' = \neg\text{p.a} \,.$$

To prevent mixing between numbers in different sets, the exchange actions check that processes p and q are in the same stage. The guards of the critical actions Proceed1 and Proceed2 contain several global conditions: the ones checking that all processes have entered the stage of process p, and the ones checking that p.x already has the final value. The value p.x is made available as output as parameter u, the next number is input as parameter v, and either p.a or p.b is complemented, as required of an action that changes the local stage.

Transforming these actions into a form with only shared guards is left as an exercise for the reader (Exercise 9.4.3).

**Review Questions**

QUESTION 9.4.1 How does the coordination problem discussed in this section relate to barrier synchronization?

**Exercises**

EXERCISE 9.4.1 Prove that introducing variables p.a and p.b, as shown in Sect. 9.4.3 (p. 345), has the effect that the maximum difference between the values in p.i is 1.

EXERCISE 9.4.2 Generalize the discussion in this section to cyclic computations with more than two stages. Give a generic specification layer on which solutions to specific problems of this kind can be superposed.

EXERCISE 9.4.3 Transform the actions in the repeated exchange sort example of Sect. 9.4.4 (p. 346) into a form with no global guards.

# Bibliographic Notes

Abstract execution models for concurrent computations were pioneered in 1962 by Petri, whose goal then was to define a notion of abstract machines that would be suited for describing physical implementations of automata [168]. Both *true concurrency* and *interleaving* can be assumed in connection with Petri nets. The former seems more natural for their original philosophy, but the latter is often preferred because of its mathematical simplicity and adequacy for most practical purposes.

The basic notion of Petri nets has been extended in various ways, making them better suited for modeling at higher levels of abstraction. Distributed action systems, for instance, can be translated in a natural manner into high-level Petri nets [94]. In fact, when joint action systems were first introduced [20], their execution model was explained in terms of such nets. Since Petri-net theory and other approaches to distributed computing have been developed rather independently, the reader should be warned of the fact that some terms, like 'liveness', have different meanings in Petri nets and in temporal-logic-based theories.

Event ordering in distributed systems, which is essential for *interleaving semantics*, was first discussed by Lamport [136]. An early example of interleaving models is the one presented by Lynch and Fischer [149]. The problem of recording global states in transaction-based distributed systems according to such an ordering was formulated and solved by Fischer et al. [56]. An algorithm for monitoring distributed systems by 'global snapshots' was developed by Chandy and Lamport [34]. A clear exposition of this algorithm was given by Dijkstra [45], and a chapter is devoted to it in Chandy and Misra's textbook [36].

In contrast to interleaved models, the idea of true concurrency leads to *partial-order semantics*. Partial-order and interleaving semantics were compared by Reisig for CSP-like languages [176]. The fairness notion suggested there for partial-order semantics corresponds to weak interaction fairness (WIF).

The idea of synchronizing concurrent computations in a distributed setting arose in Hoare's work on CSP [85, 86]. For efficiency reasons, communication constructs were asymmetric in [85], so that input commands could be guarded, but output commands could not. This restriction was removed in the more theoretical treatise [86]. Generalizations to multi-process synchronization were introduced by several authors, for instance in *joint actions* by Back and Kurki-Suonio [18], in the work on Raddle by Forman and Attie [14, 59, 60], in *shared actions* by Ramesh and Mehndiratta [175], in *Script* by Francez and Hailpern [64], and in the *multiway rendezvous* by Charlesworth [38]. For more information about this development, the interested reader is referred to a paper by Evangelist et al. [53], and to a book on *IP (Interacting Processes)* by Francez and Forman [63].

As for the Linda paradigm for asynchronous communication, the reader is referred to [32].

CSP soon inspired studies of the associated implementation issues. An early analysis of the problems of output guards was given by Bernstein [24]. The important subproblem of implementing reliable broadcast protocols in unreliable networks was solved by Chang and Maxemchuk [37]. Algorithms for implementing two-party interactions in asynchronous networks were given, for instance, by Schneider [179], by Buckley and Silberschatz [31], and by Bagrodia [23]. The more general problem of implementing multi-party interactions was studied, for instance, by Ramesh [174], by Chandy and Misra [36], by Bagrodia [22], and by Joung and Smolka [101]. For the special case of Ethernet-like broadcast networks the problem was studied by Back and Kurki-Suonio [18]. A good review of these implementation algorithms can be found in Francez and Forman [63]. A comprehensive analysis of the complexity of implementing multi-party interactions has been given by Joung and Smolka [102].

Research on fairness issues in distributed programs was also inspired by CSP and by the subsequently developed 'real' programming languages that were influenced by it, like Occam [87] and Ada [10]. Hoare's discussion of fairness in [85] witnesses of the transformational paradigm of the time, where program termination is the only logical property that is affected by fairness. Rejecting the use of fairness for termination proofs, he considers it from the viewpoint of efficiency, and suggests that "an efficient implementation should try to be reasonably fair and should ensure that an output command is not delayed unreasonably often after it first becomes executable." An extensive treatment of fairness from the viewpoint of program termination in CSP-like languages has been given in a textbook by Francez [61].

As was shown in this section, there are different possibilities for the uniform fairness notions that could be used for reasoning on distributed systems. The one chosen in UNITY [36] was weak action fairness (WAF). Kuiper and de Roever were the first to analyze alternative uniform fairness notions for CSP-like languages [117]. The language-independent analysis in Sect. 9.3.9 (p. 340) is taken from Back and Kurki-Suonio [19].

The problems in fair scheduling of distributed processes have been discussed, for instance, by Attie et al. [16]. Most scheduling algorithms that have been published in the literature, and which allow maximal parallelism, support weak interaction fairness (WIF); see e.g. [63]. The algorithm in [18] ensures strong interaction fairness (SIF) with probability 1, but the broadcast channel that is assumed there is, in fact, a simple centralized resource.

The kind of 'conspiracy' that is demonstrated by the dining philosophers example can be avoided only if the scheduler is allowed to reduce parallelism in the system. This technique was used by Attie et al. in a scheduling algorithm for WAF [15]. It is also needed for implementing *hyperfairness*, a conspiracy-resistant and equivalence-robust fairness notion proposed in [16].

All this raises questions about the limits of implementability of different fairness notions. An early impossibility result for distributed systems was Lehmann's and Rabin's proof that there is no truly distributed, deterministic, and symmetric solution to the dining philosophers problem [148]. In the absence of centralized agents or resources, either the symmetry between the processes has to be broken, or the implementation needs to be randomized.

The implementability of different fairness notions by deterministic algorithms and without reducing parallelism was first studied by Tsay and Bagrodia [189], and more extensively by Joung [99], who also gave a necessary and sufficient condition for such implementability. Applying this criterion, he showed that, of the fairness notions discussed in Sect. 9.3.9 (p. 340), weak process fairness (WPF) is the strongest that is implementable in the general case. For two-party interactions even strong process fairness (SPF) is implementable, whereas SIF is also unimplementable in this case. In [98] Joung gives, however, randomized algorithms with which SIF can be implemented with probability 1.

The fairness paradox was first noted by Apt et al. [12], and equivalence robustness was then given as one of the criteria for an acceptable fairness notion. The relevance of this requirement was questioned in [19], where equivalence robust completions of non-robust fairness notions were suggested. A more detailed analysis of such completions was given by Francez et al. [62]. Further work on robust completions and their implementability has been done by Joung [100]. Solving the fairness paradox by the modified notion of observations described in Sect. 9.1.5 (p. 313) was outlined in [129] and presented explicitly in [126].

The idea of refining an action system into a form where it is implementable in a distributed fashion was used by Back and Kurki-Suonio [20]. Extending this design method to deal with fairness properties has been discussed in [122, 133, 131]. In [109], Kellomäki has studied how message passing protocols can be derived from collective behaviors by superposition.

Proof methods for the generic coordination problem discussed in Sect. 9.4 (p. 343) have been developed by Elrad and Francez [52], and by Stomp and de Roever [185].

Distributed implementation of the repeated exchange sort example provided the initial inspiration for the superposition-based development method of this book, which was first presented in [20]. The same example was also used by Kurki-Suonio in formalizing the notion of 'knowledge' in the development of distributed systems [118]. The epitomical example of dining philosophers, originally due to Dijkstra [42], has been used in analyzing different fairness notions for distributed systems, for instance in [18, 19, 16].

# 10

# Real Time

Real-time properties are often critical for the correct behavior of reactive systems. Therefore, it is important for a specification and modeling formalism to be able to deal with them also.

In this chapter we investigate how the modeling of real time can be added to action systems and the action language, and how real-time properties can then be enforced in specifications. The plan for the chapter is as follows:

- In Sect. 10.1 we show how time can be superposed on action systems, and how temporal requirements can then be expressed. Introduction of time also leads to the counterintuitive possibility for behaviors in which an infinite number of actions are executed in finite time. The consequences of this phenomenon are also discussed in this section.
- In Sect. 10.2 generic classes are introduced for the modeling of *periodic* and *aperiodic events* in a real-time system. This demonstrates how object-oriented modeling concepts can be useful for logical modeling even when no object structure can be recognized in the system to be modeled.
- Section 10.3 extends the approach to *hybrid systems* that also have continuously changing state functions. This makes it possible to model physical phenomena in control applications, for instance.

## 10.1 Modeling of Real-Time Properties

Modeling of real-time properties is based on treating time as a special state function, whose value increases monotonically. In contrast to ordinary state functions, its value is intuitively understood to grow continuously, not in discrete steps.

### 10.1.1 Introducing a Clock

As a continuous state function, time is not directly available in actions as such. Instead, we introduce a *clock* as a state variable in which the current time is recorded in actions.

The clock variable will be denoted by $\Omega$, and its value is assumed to be a non-negative real number,[1] initialized as 0. Intuitively, $\Omega$ records time from the beginning of a behavior.

Variable $\Omega$ is assumed to be introduced in a simple specification layer Time. To update the clock reading, this layer has just one action,

$$\texttt{Record}(\tau : \mathbb{R}) : \tau \geq \Omega$$
$$\rightarrow \Omega' = \tau \, ,$$

where the parameter $\tau$ gives the new clock reading. Reflecting monotonic growth of time, step invariant

$$\square[\Omega \leq \Omega'] \tag{10.1}$$

now holds, which means that clock $\Omega$ is never turned backward.

### 10.1.2 Timing of Actions

A specification without the clock variable $\Omega$ is called *non-timed*. Composing non-timed specifications with layer Time gives *timed* specifications.

In composing a non-timed specification S with Time we adopt the following conventions. For each action S.A we include in the composition the synchronization of S.A and Time.Record. In addition, we include 'as such' the non-synchronized action Time.Record, which is 'almost stuttering' in the sense that the only variable affected by it is the clock $\Omega$. By excluding non-synchronized refinements of actions S.A we achieve the situation that recording of the current time is enforced in all actions.

Fairness requirements for the synchronized actions are taken directly from S. Since the enabling of the actions of layer S is not affected, all properties of layer S are then preserved in this composition.

The principle of recording the current time in all actions is also extended to refinements of timed specification layers, so that each action will always have Time.Record as its ancestor. In addition, there will always be the default refinement of action Time.Record, which in further refinements and compositions takes the role that the stuttering action has in non-timed specifications.

---

[1] If one wishes to have a countable set instead, real numbers can be replaced by some countably infinite but dense subset, for instance by rational numbers. (A set of numbers S is dense if, for each pair $x, y \in S, x < y$, there is a number $z$ that lies between them, $x < z < y$.)

Each action in a timed specification then has parameter $\tau$, which indicates the time at which it is executed. For simplicity, the execution of an action is thought to take place instantaneously at that moment.[2]

Notice that the causality between time – as indicated by clock readings – and events is now in some sense the converse of how one usually thinks about real-time systems: in our models observable events do not take place because time passes, but the passing of time is noticed as a result of an observable event. In other words, no 'force' is postulated to make time proceed as such. It is still only fairness that can force actions to be executed, and the proceeding of time can be observed in the value of $\Omega$ as a consequence of this.

### 10.1.3 Real-Time Properties

Behaviors in timed specifications will be called *timed behaviors*. In addition to non-real-time properties, timed behaviors also have *real-time properties*, in which clock values $\Omega$ (i.e., execution moments of actions) can be referenced.

As far as non-real-time properties are concerned, the composition of a non-timed specification S with Time is obviously equivalent to S. That is, their non-real-time properties are the same.

Non-trivial real-time properties can be added to a specification by further superposition that constrains the execution moments of actions, typically by giving lower and/or upper bounds for the parameter $\tau$. Facilities to do this in a convenient manner will be introduced below.

Obviously, adding upper bounds for $\tau$ to fair actions leads to proof obligations for the preservation of liveness properties, since this is an essential strengthening of their guards.

Real time cannot be referenced directly in this approach; it is available only indirectly through the clock. In isolation from actions, the clock is not updated, and time itself therefore remains outside the formalism. For instance, we cannot express the intuitively natural property that time will grow unboundedly. Instead, we can express whether clock readings will exceed any finite bound when an infinite number of actions is executed.

For simplicity of presentation, suppose that there is an auxiliary variable $\tau_A$ for each action A, recording the most recent execution moment of A. That is, an 'assignment'

$$\tau'_A = \tau$$

is assumed in the body of A. To indicate that A has not been executed, initialization of $\tau_A$ with some negative value can be assumed.

As an example, let A and B be two actions whose executions are known to strictly alternate, A representing a stimulus, and B being the response to it.

---

[2]From the viewpoint of concurrent executions, as discussed in Chap. 9, the parameter $\tau$ can be understood as the start time of an action. When needed, durations of actions can be explicitly built into a model, for instance using the kind of transformations discussed in Sect. 9.3.8 (p. 340).

The *bounded response property* that a response must always follow within a deadline d from a stimulus can now be expressed as

$$\langle A \rangle \rightsquigarrow \langle B \wedge \Omega' \leq \tau_A + d \rangle . \tag{10.2}$$

Formally (10.2) is a liveness property. However, in the presence of (10.1) on p. 354, i.e., the safety property that the clock is never turned backward, this liveness property is equivalent to the conjunction of the liveness property that each stimulus leads to a response,

$$\langle A \rangle \rightsquigarrow \langle B \rangle , \tag{10.3}$$

and the safety property that a response never comes too late,

$$\square[B \Rightarrow \Omega' \leq \tau_A + d] . \tag{10.4}$$

In general, it is characteristic to many 'real-time liveness properties' that they add safety properties to the corresponding non-real-time liveness properties from which all timing constraints have been deleted.

### 10.1.4 Enforcing Real-Time Properties

Enforcing an earliest execution moment t for an action is straightforward by strengthening its guard by conjunct $\tau \geq t$. With latest execution moments or *deadlines* the situation is more complex, since a deadline can no longer be met after executing any action with $\tau$ exceeding this deadline. Therefore, when a deadline t is set for some action, the execution of all actions must be prevented for $\tau > t$, until the deadline has been removed.

### Deadlines

Technically, deadlines for action execution can be introduced by superposition as follows:

- Deadlines that are manipulated in layer S are real numbers that can be assigned only to new variables introduced for that purpose in layer S, and to an implicitly introduced multiset-valued variable $\Delta_S$, which is normally initialized as empty. A specification is assumed to be such that this 'type correct' use of deadlines can be checked.
- Setting of a deadline will be expressed in an action body as

$$x' = \Delta\_\mathrm{on}(d) ,$$

where d is a real number, and x is a new variable for storing deadlines in this layer. The effect will correspond to assignments

$$x' = \max(\tau + d, \tau)$$
$$\wedge \, \Delta_S' = \Delta_S + \{\max(\tau + d, \tau)\} ,$$

which prevent the setting of any deadlines to the past. If several $\Delta\_$on expressions are given in the same body of an action, all associated deadlines are added to $\Delta_S$.

- The guards of all actions, including the special action `Record`, are implicitly strengthened by an additional conjunct[3]

$$\tau \leq \min(\Delta_S) .$$

- Removing a deadline from $\Delta_S$ will be expressed in an action body as

$$\Delta\_\text{off}(x) ,$$

where $x$ is a variable for storing deadlines of this layer. The effect will correspond to assignment

$$\Delta_S' = \Delta_S - \{x\} .$$

If several $\Delta\_$off expressions are given in the same body, all associated deadlines are removed from $\Delta_S$.

- No explicit use of variable $\Delta_S$ is allowed; the value of $\Delta_S$ can be updated only by the use of $\Delta\_$on and $\Delta\_$off.

With the above conventions, variable $\Delta_S$ is an implicit variable that cannot be explicitly used in actions, and there is no need to use it in the formulation of real-time properties, either. In the following, we will use $\Delta$ to denote collectively the set of all deadlines in the variables $\Delta_S$ of all layers $S$.

## Basic Invariants

Disallowing the introduction of deadlines that have already been passed leads to state invariant

$$\Box(\Omega \leq \min(\Delta)) . \tag{10.5}$$

Step invariant (10.1) on p. 354 also gets the slightly stronger form

$$\Box[\Omega \leq \Omega' \leq \min(\Delta)] . \tag{10.6}$$

Since real-time properties are introduced by superposition, it is clear that this does not affect any safety properties. With liveness properties the situation is obviously different. For instance, if a fair action is given an earliest execution moment which exceeds a deadline that is never removed from $\Delta$, the action will continually stay disabled, and the associated fairness property therefore cannot be satisfied.

---

[3]The minimum of an empty multiset is assumed to exceed any real number.

## Example

To achieve the bounded response property (10.2) on p. 356, actions A and B
can be extended with

$$x' = \Delta\_\text{on}(d)$$

and

$$\Delta\_\text{off}(x) \, ,$$

respectively, where x is a new state variable. Obviously, this enforces the required safety property (10.4) on p. 356, but does not guarantee the associated
non-real-time liveness property (10.3).

### 10.1.5 Note on Implementing Deadlines

In a specification it is possible to enforce step invariant (10.6) simply by
adding the associated constraints to all guards, as was done implicitly above.
Operationally this means that the clock reading – and therefore time itself
– is not allowed to grow beyond a deadline, until this deadline and all lower
deadlines, if any, have been removed from $\Delta$. This is associated with reversing
the intuitive causality between time and events, which was already referred
to above.

From the viewpoint of implementation, on the other hand, the clock $\Omega$ is
different from other state variables. In particular, an implementation cannot
stop or slow down the proceeding of time, and thereby affect clock readings
and enforce the satisfaction of (10.6). There are, however, other means that an
implementation can use to impose upper bounds for the execution moments
of actions.

The simplest possibility is to make sure that the code between setting
and removing a deadline is short enough. Another possibility is to use *clock
interrupts* and *timeouts* to trigger actions for which deadlines have been set.

In each case, if an implementation allows behaviors where the execution
moments of actions, i.e., the new clock readings $\Omega'$, do not satisfy (10.6), the
implementation is incorrect. Obviously, with short deadlines in a specification
and inefficient hardware for implementation, it may be impossible to satisfy
the real-time properties of a given specification.

### 10.1.6 Finite Variability

Intuitively, time grows unboundedly. Therefore, clock readings should also
grow unboundedly in infinite behaviors. Superposing time on an action system
does not, however, enforce this property, as was explained above.

The property that clock readings will eventually exceed any real number
T can be expressed as

$$\forall T > 0 : \Diamond(\Omega > T) \, . \tag{10.7}$$

Terminating behaviors – i.e., those that end in indefinite stuttering – cannot, however, satisfy this property, since $\Omega$ is updated only in non-stuttering actions (including non-stuttering executions of the 'almost stuttering' action Record). Therefore, (10.7) is too strong a requirement, in general.

Since a non-stuttering step can be expressed as $\langle \mathbf{T} \rangle$, it would seem natural to weaken (10.7) into requiring

$$\Box\Diamond\langle \mathbf{T} \rangle \Rightarrow \forall T > 0 : \Diamond(\Omega > T) , \tag{10.8}$$

which expresses that executing an infinite number of non-stuttering actions forces the clock reading to eventually exceed any finite bound. This property disallows an infinite number of changes within any finite time interval, and is therefore called *finite variability*.

### 10.1.7 Zeno Behaviors

Although finite variability (10.8) cannot be violated in the reality of implementations, it can be violated in specifications. This happens, for instance, when an infinite number of actions can be executed with the same parameter value $\tau$. Since the possible clock readings form a dense set (see footnote 1, p. 354), (10.8) need not hold even when each action increments the clock by a non-zero amount.

One possibility to enforce finite variability in specifications also would be to require each action to increment $\Omega$ by at least some minimum amount, which amount may even be left unspecified. We consider this solution, however, inelegant for specifications, especially since it would complicate dealing with deadlines. Furthermore, the mere possibility for violating finite variability need not be considered an error in specifications, since an implementation need not implement all behaviors that a specification allows.

However, if some deadline is never removed from $\Delta$, there is no possibility for (10.7) to hold. If there are actions that stay enabled in this situation and can be executed infinitely many times, then (10.8) does not hold, either.

This leads us to the notion of *Zeno behaviors*, which originates in the famous paradoxes of the Greek philosopher Zeno of Elea. The most well known of his paradoxes on infinity was formulated in terms of a running competition between Achilles and a tortoise:

- Even though Achilles is much faster than the tortoise, he can never catch it for the following reason. Once Achilles has covered the distance to the tortoise, the tortoise will have advanced some distance away from its previous position, and the same procedure must be repeated. This leads to an infinite number of steps, in which Achilles will never catch the tortoise.

In our terminology, Zeno's scenario for Achilles and the tortoise does not satisfy finite variability (10.8). The question that is essential for us here is whether Achilles is forced to follow this infinite scenario, or if there are other options for him. It is not, in fact, harmful for a specification to allow this kind of behaviors also, as long as it is also always possible to continue in a way that satisfies (10.8).

The condition that there always exists an option that does not violate (10.8) will be called the *real-time feasibility condition*, and it can be formalized as the possibility property (see Sect. 3.5.12, p. 98) that it is always possible for $\Omega$ to grow beyond any bound. In conclusion, if this possibility property is satisfied, violation of finite variability (10.8) does not make a specification infeasible for implementation. On one hand, impossible behaviors will automatically be absent from any implementation and, on the other hand, this feasibility condition guarantees that no implementation can ever find itself in a state where an impossible continuation would be required.

Since possibility properties are properties of a system, not of behaviors, we define *non-Zenoness* of timed behaviors as

$$\forall T > 0 : \Diamond \Box \min(\Delta) > T . \tag{10.9}$$

This formalizes the property that deadlines, if there are any, will always grow beyond any bound. A behavior that does not satisfy (10.9) is called a *Zeno behavior* in the following. Absence of Zeno behaviors is a somewhat stronger requirement than the above possibility property, under which real-time specifications are feasible.[4]

### 10.1.8 Relative Safety Properties

Like non-real-time properties, real-time properties may be safety properties, liveness properties, or conjunctions of these.

From a practical viewpoint, a real-time property that is a pure liveness property is somewhat artificial. For instance, the property that there will eventually be an action A that is followed by an action B within a given deadline is a pure liveness property, since any prefix of a behavior can be extended into one that satisfies it. Such a property does not, however, seem to be very useful in practice.

With an intuitive understanding of safety properties one might argue that reasonable real-time properties, like the bounded response property discussed in Sect. 10.1.3 (p. 355), would be safety properties. The reasoning behind this argument would run as follows: if such a property is violated, the violation will become apparent within a finite time. For instance, if some occurrence of action A is not followed by B within a given deadline, this becomes apparent after waiting for the duration of the deadline.

The above argument is, however, insufficient for making a property a safety property, since waiting for a finite time need not correspond to a finite number of actions, because (10.7) on p. 358 need not be satisfied, as was discussed

---

[4]Notice that a proof of this possibility property (see Sect. 3.5.12, p. 98) effectively requires us to find a certain kind of refinement that satisfies (10.9).

above. The informal reasoning is, however, correct in the following sense: under the assumption that (10.7) holds, bounded response properties, for instance, have the character of safety properties. Therefore, they can be called *relative safety properties*, i.e., safety properties relative to the liveness property (10.7). Formally, such a relative safety property can be expressed as a conjunction of (10.7) and a safety property.

This shows that the proof techniques for safety properties are widely applicable in proving real-time properties.

### 10.1.9 Example: Gas-burner Revisited

As an example let us return to the gas-burner example of Chap. 2. The non-timed specification given there will be denoted as **Burner**. The following real-time properties, where $d_1$, $d_2$, and $d_3$ are some constants, will now be imposed on the composition of **Burner** and **Time**:

- The maximum time for the system to stay continuously in state **Starting** (see Fig. 2.5, p. 38) is $d_1$,

$$\text{Starting} \rightsquigarrow \langle \neg\text{Starting}' \wedge \Omega' \leq \tau_{\text{Start\_s}} + d_1 \rangle \, .$$

- If the flame goes off in state **Ignited**, this state is exited within $d_2$ time units,

$$\text{Ignited} \wedge \neg\text{flame} \rightsquigarrow \langle \text{Idle}' \wedge \Omega' \leq t_{\text{Flame\_off}} + d_2 \rangle \, ,$$

where $t_{\text{Flame\_off}}$ denotes the time when the flame has first gone off after state **Ignited** was entered – or actually the time when this was recognized by action **Flame_off_s**.[5]

- Once in state **Idle**, the minimum time to stay in this state is $d_3$,

$$\square[\text{Idle} \Rightarrow \Omega' \geq \max(\tau_{\text{Stop\_s}}, \tau_{\text{Close\_s}}, 0) + d_3] \, .$$

To enforce these real-time properties, three new variables are introduced, in addition to $\tau_{\text{Start\_s}}$, $\tau_{\text{Stop\_s}}$, $\tau_{\text{Close\_s}}$, and $t_{\text{Flame\_off}}$ referred to above:

- variable **d_started** to store the deadline for exiting state **Starting**,
- Boolean variable **b** to register flame failure in state **Ignited**, and
- variable **d_fail** to store the deadline for exiting state **Ignited** in the case of flame failure.

---

[5] Since we have no possibility to record the exact time when the environment action **Flame_off_e** was executed, the maximum lag between it and action **Flame_off_s** needs to be taken into account in determining an appropriate value for $d_2$. To be exact, similar lags may also apply to determining the values of the other parameters.

Some of the system actions are now refined to use these variables as follows:

$$^{\text{SF}}\texttt{Start\_s}(\tau : \mathbb{R}) : \texttt{Burner.Start\_s}$$
$$\wedge \texttt{Time.Record}(\tau)$$
$$\wedge \tau \geq \max(\tau_{\texttt{Stop\_s}}, \tau_{\texttt{Close\_s}}, 0) + d_3$$
$$\rightarrow \tau'_{\texttt{Start\_s}} = \tau$$
$$\wedge \texttt{d\_started}' = \Delta\_\texttt{on}(d_1) ,$$

$$^{\text{SF}}\texttt{Ign\_off\_s}(\tau : \mathbb{R}) : \texttt{Burner.Ign\_off\_s}$$
$$\wedge \texttt{Time.Record}(\tau)$$
$$\rightarrow \texttt{b}' = \texttt{false}$$
$$\wedge \Delta\_\texttt{off}(\texttt{d\_started}) ,$$

$$^{\text{SF}}\texttt{Stop\_s}(\tau : \mathbb{R}) : \texttt{Burner.Stop\_s}$$
$$\wedge \texttt{Time.Record}(\tau)$$
$$\rightarrow \tau'_{\texttt{Stop\_s}} = \tau$$
$$\wedge \Delta\_\texttt{off}(\texttt{d\_started}) ,$$

$$^{\text{SF}}\texttt{Flame\_off\_s}(\tau : \mathbb{R}) : \texttt{Burner.Flame\_off\_s}$$
$$\wedge \texttt{Time.Record}(\tau)$$
$$\rightarrow \text{if Ignited} \wedge \neg \texttt{b} \text{ then}$$
$$(\texttt{b}' = \texttt{true}$$
$$\wedge t'_{\texttt{Flame\_off}} = \tau$$
$$\wedge \texttt{d\_fail}' = \Delta\_\texttt{on}(d_2)) ,$$

$$^{\text{SF}}\texttt{Close\_s}(\tau : \mathbb{R}) : \texttt{Burner.Close\_s}$$
$$\wedge \texttt{Time.Record}(\tau)$$
$$\rightarrow \tau'_{\texttt{Close\_s}} = \tau$$
$$\wedge \text{if b then } \Delta\_\texttt{off}(\texttt{d\_fail}) .$$

All other actions are taken as their default refinements.

It is left for the reader to check that this system generates no Zeno behaviors (Exercise 10.1.1), and that the above real-time requirements are satisfied (Exercise 10.1.2).

### Review Questions

QUESTION 10.1.1  What is meant by real-time properties in our theory?

QUESTION 10.1.2  When deadline variables $\Delta_\text{S}$ are introduced by superposition, why do we need to distinguish between variables $\Delta_\text{S}$ for different layers S?

QUESTION 10.1.3 Why is it reasonable to allow specifications in which all behaviors need not satisfy finite variability?

QUESTION 10.1.4 What are the differences between finite variability (10.8), p. 359, non-Zenoness (10.9), p. 360, and the satisfaction of the real-time feasibility condition given in Sect. 10.1.7?

QUESTION 10.1.5 Why are bounded response properties not safety properties?

QUESTION 10.1.6 Why are the proof techniques for safety properties also useful for bounded response properties?

### Exercises

EXERCISE 10.1.1 Show that the action system in Sect. 10.1.9 (p. 361) generates no Zeno behaviors.

EXERCISE 10.1.2 Show that the action system in Sect. 10.1.9 (p. 361) satisfies the real-time requirements given for it.

## 10.2 Periodic and Aperiodic Events

Typically, the purpose of real-time systems is to monitor and control something that happens in the real physical world. The speed of natural phenomena is then essential in determining the frequency with which interactions between a computer and its environment need to take place. For instance, measurements of a physical quantity may need to be made frequently enough in order to be able to control this quantity by changing some associated physical parameters.

This leads to the idea of *periodic events*, which are triggered at a given frequency by the proceeding of time. In contrast, *aperiodic events* are ones that are triggered as a reaction to something that has happened in the system.

In this section we discuss the use of generic, abstract classes in the modeling of periodic and aperiodic events. The layer in which these classes are defined will be called Events.

### 10.2.1 Periodic Events

Each periodic event can be associated with an object p of class Per with two states:

$$\textbf{class } \mathsf{Per} = \{\textbf{state } \mathsf{Passive}^*, \mathsf{Active} \textbf{ where}$$
$$\mathsf{Active} = \{\mathsf{d}, \mathsf{t} : \mathbb{R}\}\} \, .$$

When Active, an object p ∈ Per has attributes d and t, where d is the length of the period for triggering the event, and t is the time for which the next execution of the event has been scheduled.

Activation of a periodic event with a given length of period and a given delay for its first execution takes place by action

$$\texttt{Activate}(p : \mathsf{Per};\ \tau, period, delay : \mathbb{R}) : \texttt{Time.Record}(\tau)$$
$$\land\ p.Passive$$
$$\land\ period > 0$$
$$\land\ delay > 0$$
$$\rightarrow\ p.Active'$$
$$\land\ p.d' = period$$
$$\land\ p.t' = \Delta\text{-on}(delay)\ .$$

When active, the repeated triggering of a periodic event is modeled by action

$$\texttt{Trigger}(^{\text{WF}}p : \mathsf{Per};\ \tau : \mathbb{R}) : \texttt{Time.Record}(\tau)$$
$$\land\ p.Active$$
$$\land\ \tau = p.t$$
$$\rightarrow\ \Delta\text{-off}(p.t)$$
$$\land\ p.t' = \Delta\text{-on}(p.d)$$

and, finally, action

$$\texttt{Passivate}(p : \mathsf{Per};\ \tau : \mathbb{R}) : \texttt{Time.Record}(\tau)$$
$$\land\ p.Active$$
$$\rightarrow\ p.Passive'$$
$$\land\ \Delta\text{-off}(p.t)$$

can passivate the event.

Notice that, if no constraints are given for the parameters in these actions, Zeno behaviors are also possible, in which new events are always scheduled in front of an already existing one. As such these Zeno behaviors are not, however, harmful in the sense discussed in Sect. 10.1.7 (p. 359).

### 10.2.2 Aperiodic Events

Similarly to periodic events, each aperiodic event can be associated with an object a of class Aper, in which attribute a.t indicates the time for which the next execution of an active event has been scheduled, and no attribute for a period is needed:

$$\textbf{class } \mathsf{Aper} = \{\textbf{state } Passive^*, Active \textbf{ where}$$
$$Active = \{t : \mathbb{R}\}\}\ .$$

Scheduling of an aperiodic event with a given delay can now take place by action

$$
\begin{aligned}
\texttt{Schedule}(a : \texttt{Aper}; \; \tau, \texttt{delay} : \mathbb{R}) &: \texttt{Time.Record}(\tau) \\
&\wedge a.\texttt{Passive} \\
&\wedge \texttt{delay} > 0 \\
&\rightarrow \; a.\texttt{Active}' \\
&\wedge a.t' = \Delta\_\texttt{on}(\texttt{delay})
\end{aligned}
$$

and its execution is modeled by action

$$
\begin{aligned}
\texttt{Execute}(^{\texttt{WF}}a : \texttt{Aper}; \; \tau : \mathbb{R}) &: \texttt{Time.Record}(\tau) \\
&\wedge a.\texttt{Active} \\
&\wedge \tau = a.t \\
&\rightarrow \; p.\texttt{Passive}' \\
&\wedge \Delta\_\texttt{off}(a.t) \, .
\end{aligned}
$$

Finally, descheduling of an event without execution is modeled by action

$$
\begin{aligned}
\texttt{Deschedule}(a : \texttt{Aper}; \; \tau : \mathbb{R}) &: \texttt{Time.Record}(\tau) \\
&\wedge a.\texttt{Active} \\
&\rightarrow \; p.\texttt{Passive}' \\
&\wedge \Delta\_\texttt{off}(a.t) \, .
\end{aligned}
$$

Similarly to actions for periodic events, these actions also give rise to Zeno behaviors, which are not harmful as such.

### 10.2.3 Example: Toy Car

As an example we discuss the specification of control software for a simple mobile robot, a toy car that moves along a tape on the floor. As input the control software receives readings from an odometer and from sensors that sense the relative position of the car with respect to the tape. The outputs control engine speed and the steering of the car. In addition, there is a switch to start and stop the car. For simplicity, a constant target speed will be assumed.

The specification will be given in layers illustrated in Fig. 10.1. Layer Basis simply models unconstrained reading of sensors and setting of control parameters. Logic superposes on this the logical sequencing of these actions, whereas Algorithms adds the algorithms for determining the control parameters. Real time and periodic execution of these actions are finally imposed using composition with layer Events.

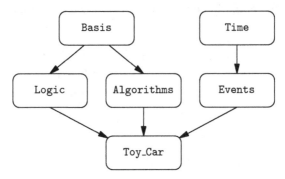

**Fig. 10.1.** Layers in the toy-car specification

## Basis

In the first specification layer, `Basis`, we include four real-valued variables for recording the readings of the two sensors and the settings of the two control parameters as follows:

- variable r_dist is used for the distance driven after the previous odometer reading,
- variable r_tape is used for the position of the car with respect to the tape,
- variable c_engine is used for the control parameter for engine speed,
- variable c_steer is used for the control parameter for steering.

Three actions are included in this layer: one for resetting all four variables as 0, one for reading the two sensors, and one for setting the two control parameters:

$$\text{Clear}: \mathbf{T}$$
$$\rightarrow\ r\_dist' = 0$$
$$\wedge\ r\_tape' = 0$$
$$\wedge\ c\_engine' = 0$$
$$\wedge\ c\_steer' = 0\ ,$$

$$\text{Read}(x, y : \mathbb{R}): \mathbf{T}$$
$$\rightarrow\ r\_dist' = x$$
$$\wedge\ r\_tape' = y\ ,$$

$$\text{Set}(x, y : \mathbb{R}): \mathbf{T}$$
$$\rightarrow\ c\_engine' = x$$
$$\wedge\ c\_steer' = y\ .$$

At this level, all three actions are always enabled, and no constraints are imposed on the parameters that indicate the values of sensor readings and control parameters.

## Logic

Layer Logic imposes logical control on driving, without paying attention to the required control algorithms. The state of the system is extended with nested state machines as follows (see Fig. 10.2):

$$\textbf{state } \text{Off}^*, \text{On } \textbf{where}$$
$$\text{On} = \{\textbf{state } \text{Reading}^*, \text{Setting}\}.$$

Here,

- states Off and On model the status of the main switch on the car, and
- states Reading and Setting model whether the sensors are to be read or the control parameters are to be set.

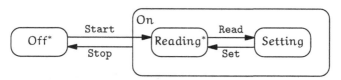

**Fig. 10.2.** Logical control on driving

Starting the car takes place by turning the main switch from Off to On. Defining this action as (the only) refinement of **Basis.Clear** makes sure that old sensor readings and control parameter values are then cleared:

$$\text{Start} : \text{Basis.Clear}$$
$$\wedge \text{ Off}$$
$$\rightarrow \text{ On.Reading}'.$$

Stopping the car is modeled simply by a new action

$$\text{Stop} : \text{Basis.Stutter}$$
$$\wedge \text{ On}$$
$$\rightarrow \text{ Off}'$$

and, in order to follow the control flow indicated in Fig. 10.2, actions Read and Set of layer **Basis** are refined as follows:

$$^{WF}\text{Read}(x, y : \mathbb{R}) : \text{Basis.Read}(x, y)$$
$$\wedge \text{ On.Reading}$$
$$\rightarrow \text{ On.Setting}' ,$$

$$^{WF}\text{Set}(x, y : \mathbb{R}) : \text{Basis.Set}(x, y)$$
$$\wedge \text{ On.Setting}$$
$$\rightarrow \text{ On.Reading}' .$$

The fairness requirements in these ensure that they are executed alternatingly as long as the system is in state On.

### Algorithms

Algorithms for determining the control values for engine speed and steering are introduced in layer **Algorithms**, independently of the drive states introduced above. Because of friction, three different states are distinguished in movement control by an enumeration variable $m\_state$:

$$m\_state : \{power\_up, moving, normal\} .$$

The value of $m\_state$ will be $power\_up$, when no movement has been sensed, $moving$, when movement has just been sensed, and $normal$ otherwise.

For steering we will use the so-called PID algorithm, which will not be explained here. For the purposes of this presentation it is only important that it needs two additional variables, $r\_tape\_old$ and $r\_tape\_ma$, for recording the previous reading of the tape position and the moving average of $n$ most recent readings, respectively, where $n$ is some constant.

Action **Clear** of **Basis** now needs to be refined to initialize the new variables also:

$$\text{Clear} : \text{Basis.Clear}$$
$$\rightarrow \ r\_tape\_old' = 0$$
$$\wedge \ r\_tape\_ma' = 0$$
$$\wedge \ m\_state' = power\_up .$$

Actions **Read** and **Set** are refined so that the former updates the newly introduced variables, and the latter determines the control parameters using certain control functions f and g and some limit value $max$:

$$\text{Read}(x, y : \mathbb{R}) : \text{Basis.Read}(x, y)$$
$$\rightarrow \ m\_state' = \text{if } (x = r\_dist = 0) \text{ then } power\_up$$
$$\text{else if } (x > r\_dist = 0) \text{ then } moving$$
$$\text{else } normal$$
$$\wedge \ r\_tape\_ma' = ((n - 1) \times r\_tape\_ma - r\_tape)/n$$
$$\wedge \ r\_tape\_old' = r\_tape ,$$

$\mathrm{Set}(x, y : \mathbb{R}) : \mathrm{Basis.Set}(x, y)$

$\qquad \wedge x = \text{if } |r\_tape| > max \text{ then } 0$

$\qquad \text{else } f(m\_state, c\_engine, r\_dist)$

$\qquad \wedge y = g(r\_tape, r\_tape\_old, r\_tape\_ma)$ .

## Composed Specification

The final specification of the toy car is obtained by composing the aspects specified independently in layers Logic and Algorithms with the generic layer Events appropriately.

In order to model the reading of sensors as a periodic event, we constrain class Per of layer Events to be a singleton class, and associate the only object $p \in$ Per with the execution of action Read. Similarly, the class Aper of aperiodic events is also constrained into a singleton class, and the setting of control parameters is associated with its only object $a \in$ Aper.

Action Logic.Start must now be synchronized with Algorithms.Clear. Since this action also needs to activate the reading of sensors, synchronization with Events.Activate is also needed for the periodic event $p \in$ P. This leads to action

$\qquad \mathrm{Start}(p : \mathrm{Per}; \ \tau : \mathbb{R}) : \mathrm{Logic.Start}$

$\qquad\qquad \wedge \mathrm{Algorithms.Clear}$

$\qquad\qquad \wedge \mathrm{Events.Activate}(p, \tau, q, d)$ ,

where q and d are suitable constants for the length of the period and for the delay for the first execution, respectively.

Similarly, action Logic.Read must be synchronized both with action Algorithms.Read and with action Events.Trigger, which triggers the periodic event for reading the sensors. In an implementation this will be immediately followed by the setting of the control parameters. This can be modeled here by letting this action also schedule an aperiodic event for this setting with some delay $e$, which must be less than the period d, $0 < e < d$. This leads to action[6]

$\qquad {}^{\mathrm{WF}}\mathrm{Read}(p : \mathrm{Per}; \ a : \mathrm{Aper}; \ \tau, x, y : \mathbb{R}) : \mathrm{Logic.Read}(x, y)$

$\qquad\qquad\qquad \wedge \mathrm{Algorithms.Read}(x, y)$

$\qquad\qquad\qquad \wedge \mathrm{Events.Trigger}(p, \tau) \ \&$

$\qquad\qquad\qquad \mathrm{Events.Schedule}(a, \tau, e)$ .

As for action Logic.Set, it must be synchronized with Algorithms.Set. Since synchronization is also needed with executing the aperiodic event that was scheduled for the setting of the control parameters, we get

---

[6]It is obvious that combining actions for two different event objects, as done here, does not affect any essential safety properties.

$${}^{\text{WF}}\text{Set}(a:\text{Aper}; \ \tau, x, y : \mathbb{R}) : \text{Logic.Set}(x, y)$$
$$\wedge \ \text{Algorithms.Set}(x, y)$$
$$\wedge \ \text{Events.Execute}(a, \tau) \ .$$

Finally, action Logic.Stop needs to be synchronized with descheduling of further reading of sensors and setting of control parameters. Since the latter event is scheduled only when in state Setting, this leads to two different actions:

$$\text{Stop1}(p:\text{Per}; \ \tau : \mathbb{R}) : \text{Logic.Stop}$$
$$\wedge \ \text{Algorithms.Stutter}$$
$$\wedge \ \text{Events.Passivate}(p, \tau)$$
$$\wedge \ \text{Reading} \ ,$$

$$\text{Stop2}(p:\text{Per}; \ a:\text{Aper}; \ \tau : \mathbb{R}) : \text{Logic.Stop}$$
$$\wedge \ \text{Algorithms.Stutter}$$
$$\wedge \ \text{Events.Passivate}(p, \tau) \ \&$$
$$\text{Events.Deschedule}(a, \tau)$$
$$\wedge \ \text{Setting} \ .$$

The condition $e < d$ is now sufficient to guarantee that the real-time properties of the final system are not in conflict with the strict alternation of actions Read and Set, as required in layer Logic. The fairness requirements on the resulting actions Read and Set are then sufficient to guarantee the preservation of the liveness properties of both Logic and Events.

### Discussion

In addition to demonstrating the use of objects to represent periodic and aperiodic events, this is another example of aspect-oriented specification. In particular, it shows how the scheduling of actions can be separated from other concerns in the design.

To illustrate how the actions of the resulting system contain conjuncts that originate in different specification layers, we write out the final action Read in its complete form (simplifications are indicated by enclosing superfluous conjuncts in braces):

$${}^{\text{WF}}\text{Read}(p:\text{Per}; \ a:\text{Aper}; \ \tau, x, y : \mathbb{R}) : \text{On.Reading}$$
$$\{\wedge \ p.\text{Active}\}$$
$$\{\wedge \ a.\text{Passive}\}$$
$$\{\wedge \ e > 0\}$$
$$\wedge \ \Omega \leq \tau \leq \min(\Delta)$$
$$\wedge \ \tau = p.t$$

$\rightarrow$ On.Setting$'$
$\wedge$ r_dist$'$ = x
$\wedge$ r_tape$'$ = y
$\wedge$ m_state$'$ =
    if (x = r_dist = 0) then power_up
    else if (x > r_dist = 0) then moving
    else normal
$\wedge$ r_tape_ma$'$ =
    $((n-1) \times$ r_tape_ma $-$ r_tape$)/n$
$\wedge$ r_tape_old$'$ = r_tape
$\{\wedge$ a.Active$'\}$
$\wedge$ $\Delta$_off(p.t)
$\wedge$ p.t$'$ = $\Delta$_on(p.d)
$\wedge$ a.t$'$ = $\Delta$_on(e)
$\wedge$ $\Omega'$ = $\tau$ .

The simplifications are based on the following observations. On account of invariants

$$\square(\text{On} \Leftrightarrow \text{p.Active}) ,$$
$$\square(\text{On.Setting} \Leftrightarrow \text{a.Active}) ,$$

which can be easily proved for the single events $p \in$ Per, $a \in$ Aper, the two-state structures in Per and Aper are superfluous. Similarly, condition $e > 0$ can be omitted from the action, since the assumptions on $e$ make it identically true.

Notice that, instead of constraining classes Per and Aper into singleton classes, we could have introduced and used singleton subclasses $P \subseteq$ Per and $A \subseteq$ Aper. In that case the actions of the final layer would have been specializations for these subclasses. However, this would have left the possibility for other periodic and aperiodic events to give rise to Zeno behaviors. Although not harmful in the sense discussed in Sect. 10.1.7 (p. 359), the resulting system would not have been a refinement of layer Logic, since its liveness properties would not have been satisfied by these Zeno behaviors.

## Exercises

EXERCISE 10.2.1 Give scenarios where periodic or aperiodic events give rise to Zeno behaviors. What is the minimum number of events needed for these, if strong fairness assumptions are used in actions Trigger and Execute?

EXERCISE 10.2.2 What would happen if condition $e < d$ did not hold in the toy-car example?

## 10.3 Hybrid Systems

In addition to state functions whose values change in discrete events, modeling of a physical environment may involve continuous functions of time. A system with both kinds of state functions is called a *hybrid system*.

### 10.3.1 Real-Time Functions

A *real-time function (RT function)* is a function of time t, where $0 \leq t < \infty$. Time t is assumed to proceed continuously, even though only discrete values of it are recorded in the clock $\Omega$. In this subsection we consider how RT functions can be generated by behaviors.

#### Continuous Time

Continuous time t is itself a simple RT function, which can be defined in a trivial manner using the clock variable $\Omega$ as follows.

In each state $s_i$ of a behavior $\langle s_0, s_1, s_2, \ldots \rangle$, the clock variable $\Omega$ shows the moment of time $t_i = s_i[\![\Omega]\!]$ at which state $s_i$ was entered. Using $\delta$ to denote the time that has elapsed since that moment, we have in each state $s_i$ a function of $\delta$, denoted by $\overline{\Omega}$, which can be understand to express continuous real time in state $s_i$:

$$\overline{\Omega}(\delta) \stackrel{\Delta}{=} t_i + \delta .$$

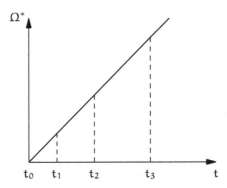

**Fig. 10.3.** Real time as an RT function $\Omega^*$

As illustrated in Fig. 10.3, a continuous RT function $\Omega^*(t)$ can now be constructed piecewise from functions $\overline{\Omega}(\delta)$ in the different states, so that in each interval $(t_i, t_{i+1})$ the value of $\Omega^*(t)$ is determined by the function $\overline{\Omega}$ in state $s_i$ as $\Omega^*(t) = \overline{\Omega}(t - t_i)$. Obviously, $\Omega^*(t) = t$ is then trivially true for each interval $(t_i, t_{i+1})$.

In the following we generalize this construction for arbitrary functions of state variables and the time $\delta$ that has elapsed in the current state $s_i$.

## Time-dependent State Functions

*Time-dependent state functions*, or *TD functions* for short, are defined by expressions that depend on state variables and on $\delta$, and which are defined for all non-negative real values of $\delta$. In the following, TD functions will be denoted by using a bar on top of identifiers.

In each state $s$, all state variables have fixed values. A TD function $\bar{f}$ then determines in each state $s$ a function of $\delta$, $s[\![\bar{f}]\!]$, which is defined for all values $\delta \geq 0$. For instance, if $a$ and $b$ are state variables, then expression

$$\bar{f} \triangleq a + b \times \delta \tag{10.10}$$

is a TD function, which in each state $s$ determines a linear function $s[\![\bar{f}]\!]$ of $\delta$,

$$s[\![\bar{f}]\!](\delta) = s[\![a]\!] + s[\![b]\!] \times \delta .$$

This means that, in each state $s$, $\bar{f}$ determines a unique value $s[\![\bar{f}]\!](t - s[\![\Omega]\!])$ for any $t$, $t \geq s[\![\Omega]\!]$, as illustrated in Fig. 10.4.

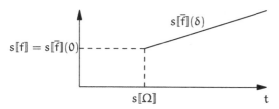

**Fig. 10.4.** Illustration of a TD function $\bar{f}$ in state $s$

Intuitively, a TD function $\bar{f}$ has value $s[\![\bar{f}]\!](0)$ at the moment when state $s$ is entered, but its value changes after that according to $s[\![\bar{f}]\!](\delta)$. Using the corresponding unbarred symbol $f$ to denote $\bar{f}(0)$, i.e.,

$$s[\![f]\!] \triangleq s[\![\bar{f}]\!](0) ,$$

$f$ is an ordinary state function connected with $\bar{f}$ by the invariant

$$\Box(f = \bar{f}(0)) .$$

A truth-valued TD function $\bar{P}$ will be called a *TD predicate*.

## Action Intervals

Let $\sigma = \langle s_0, s_1, \ldots \rangle$ be a timed behavior with clock readings $t_i = s_i[\![\Omega]\!]$ in its states, $t_0 \leq t_1 \leq \cdots$. *Action intervals* $T_i$, $i = 0, 1, \ldots$, for behavior $\sigma$ are then defined either as closed time intervals $[t_i, t_{i+1}]$ or semiclosed intervals $[t_i, \infty)$, depending on whether $\sigma$ ends with indefinite stuttering in state $s_i$ or not. In other words,

$$T_i \triangleq \begin{cases} \{t \in \mathbb{R} \mid t_i \le t \le t_{i+1}\}, & \text{if } \exists j : j > i \wedge s_j \ne s_i , \\ \{t \in \mathbb{R} \mid t_i \le t\}, & \text{if } \forall j : j > i \Rightarrow s_j = s_i . \end{cases}$$

Within an action interval $T_i$, time t is assumed to go through all values in $T_i$, with all state variables – including the clock $\Omega$ – staying unchanged. Final stuttering steps give rise to intervals where $\overline{\Omega}$ grows unboundedly, but all state variables stay unchanged. For behaviors that satisfy the finite variability condition (10.8) on p. 359, action intervals $T_i$ cover together all values $0 \le t < \infty$.

Notice that it is also possible for an action interval $T_i$ to consist of a single value $t_i$, when $t_{i+1} = t_i$. In particular, intermediate stuttering steps generate such singular intervals, but final stuttering steps do not.

### Generation of Real-Time Functions

Given a behavior $\sigma$, a TD function $\overline{f}$ can be used for piecewise definition of a *real-time function* $f^*(t)$, or *RT function* for short,

$$f^*(t) \triangleq s_i[\![\overline{f}]\!](t - t_i) , \quad \text{for } t \in T_i . \tag{10.11}$$

Figure 10.5 illustrates an RT function $f^*(t)$ generated by a TD function $\overline{f}$ that is always linear.

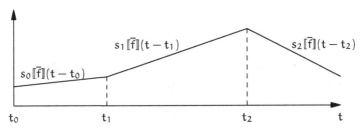

**Fig. 10.5.** Illustration of an RT function, determined by a TD function $\overline{f}$

For the endpoints $t_i$ of action intervals, (10.11) need not determine unique values for $f^*(t)$. However, if the step invariant

$$\Box[\overline{f}(\Omega' - \Omega) = \overline{f}'(0)] \tag{10.12}$$

holds, then the different values always agree, and $f^*(t)$ is uniquely defined also for all endpoints $t = t_i$. For behaviors that satisfy the finite variability condition, $f^*(t)$ is then uniquely defined for all values $t \ge 0$.

A truth-valued RT function $P^*(t)$ will be called an *RT predicate*.

## 10.3.2 Approximation of Physical Quantities

Intuitively, the state of a closed hybrid system (which also includes the cooperating environment) has two kinds of variables: those whose values change only at discrete moments of time (the discrete state), and those whose values change continuously with time (the continuous state).

Hybrid models are useful for real-time systems that control physical quantities $\hat{f}$ associated with some real physical phenomena. The controlled quantities $\hat{f}$ are real-time functions that are governed by the laws of nature, but can also be affected by changes in the discrete state of the control system. In life-critical systems physical phenomena impose critical safety requirements for the total system. The purpose of the control system then is to achieve some goal without violating these safety requirements.

In principle, a physical quantity $\hat{f}$ to be controlled is not explicitly accessible to a real-time system. In each discrete state it can, however, be approximated by a TD function $\overline{f}$. This $\overline{f}$ needs to be updated frequently enough in actions that take observations of $\hat{f}$ as input.

In general, an approximation $\overline{f}$ may need to be associated with other TD functions by which its precision can be managed. For instance, one may have a TD function $\overline{f}$ and a constant $\epsilon$ for which the laws of nature and the properties of the control system are sufficient to guarantee that

$$\forall t \geq 0 : |\overline{f}(t) - f^*(t)| \leq \epsilon ,$$

i.e., that the RT function generated by $\overline{f}$ never differs more than $\epsilon$ from the real value $\hat{f}(t)$.

## 10.3.3 Real-Time Invariants

For an RT predicate $P^*(t)$ it is natural to interpret the informal statement '$P^*(t)$ is always true' as

$$\forall t \geq 0 : P^*(t) . \tag{10.13}$$

Using $\overline{P}(\delta)$ to denote the TD predicate that generates $P^*(t)$, and P to denote the ordinary state predicate defined by

$$\Box(P \Leftrightarrow \overline{P}(0)) ,$$

the state invariant $\Box P$ is, in general, insufficient to guarantee (10.13), since the value of $P^*(t)$ may change at some point of time without any action taking place at that moment. This is illustrated in Fig. 10.6, where P is always true, but $P^*(t)$ is temporarily false between $t_1$ and $t_2$ and also becomes permanently false after the last non-stuttering action at time $t_n$.

For this reason we introduce notation $\Box_t P^*(t)$ to denote that $P^*$ is a *real-time invariant*, or *RT invariant* for short, with the following formal meaning:

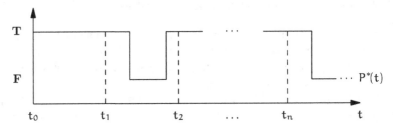

**Fig. 10.6.** Illustration of a situation where $\Box P$ holds but $\Box_t P^*(t)$ does not

$$\Box_t P^*(t) \overset{\Delta}{=} \forall \delta : (\delta \geq 0 \wedge \neg \bar{P}(\delta) \rightsquigarrow \langle \Omega' < \Omega + \delta \rangle) \,. \qquad (10.14)$$

This can be read as follows: if a state is entered where the TD predicate $\bar{P}(\delta)$ is false for some value $\delta \geq 0$, then some action will necessarily be executed at an execution moment $\tau$ where $\tau < \Omega + \delta$. It can easily be seen that this condition prevents the phenomena illustrated in Fig. 10.6, thereby guaranteeing that $P^*(t)$ stays true for all values $t \geq 0$.

Obviously, $\Box_t P^*(t)$ implies $\Box P$ for the associated ordinary state predicate P.

Notice that this definition of RT invariance can also be used when it has not been shown that $P^*(t)$ would be uniquely defined for the endpoints of all action intervals $T_i$.

### 10.3.4 Monotonic Time-dependent State Functions

A TD function $\bar{f}$ is *nondecreasing* in state s if the current state function $s[\![\bar{f}]\!]$ cannot decrease with time. Correspondingly, it is *nonincreasing* if $s[\![\bar{f}]\!]$ cannot increase with time:

$$s[\![\mathrm{NonDec}(\bar{f})]\!] \overset{\Delta}{=} 0 \leq \delta_1 \leq \delta_2 \Rightarrow s[\![\bar{f}]\!](\delta_1) \leq s[\![\bar{f}]\!](\delta_2) \,,$$
$$s[\![\mathrm{NonInc}(\bar{f})]\!] \overset{\Delta}{=} 0 \leq \delta_1 \leq \delta_2 \Rightarrow s[\![\bar{f}]\!](\delta_1) \geq s[\![\bar{f}]\!](\delta_2) \,.$$

When nonincreasing but not nondecreasing, a TD function is *decreasing*:

$$s[\![\mathrm{Dec}(\bar{f})]\!] \overset{\Delta}{=} s[\![\mathrm{NonInc}(\bar{f})]\!] \wedge \neg s[\![\mathrm{NonDec}(\bar{f})]\!] \,.$$

A TD function $\bar{f}$ is *monotonic* if it is either nondecreasing or nonincreasing in each state, i.e.,
$$\Box(\mathrm{NonDec}(\bar{f}) \vee \mathrm{NonInc}(\bar{f})) \,.$$

An RT function $f^*(t)$ that is generated by a monotonic TD function $\bar{f}$ is *piecewise monotonic*, i.e., either nondecreasing or nonincreasing within each action interval $T_i$. In particular, a linear TD function $\bar{f}$ (see (10.10) on p. 373) always yields a piecewise linear RT function $f^*(t)$.

All these terms apply also to TD predicates, when false is interpreted to be less than true. Obviously, an RT predicate that is generated by a monotonic TD predicate can change its value at most once within any action interval. In Fig. 10.6 (p. 376) the value of $P^*(t)$ changes twice within action interval $[t_1, t_2]$, which shows that the associated TD predicate $\overline{P}$ is neither nondecreasing nor nonincreasing in state $s_1$ and therefore not monotonic.

When real phenomena are monitored with sufficiently frequent actions, the associated quantities $\hat{f}(t)$ can be approximated by linear TD functions $\overline{f}$, which yield piecewise linear RT functions $f^*(t)$. Inequalities on linear TD functions lead to monotonic TD predicates (Exercise 10.3.1). This is one reason why monotonic TD predicates are an important special case.

### 10.3.5 Regular Real-Time Predicates

An RT predicate $P^*(t)$ is called *regular* if it is generated by a monotonic TD predicate $\overline{P}$, and is uniquely defined also for the endpoints of all action intervals:

$$\Box(\mathrm{NonDec}(\overline{P}) \vee \mathrm{NonInc}(\overline{P}))\,,$$

$$\Box[\overline{P}(\Omega' - \Omega) = \overline{P}'(0)]\,.$$

For a regular RT predicate $P^*(t)$, the RT invariance condition (10.14) on p. 376 can be simplified into

$$\Box_t P^*(t) \Leftrightarrow \Box P \wedge (\mathrm{Dec}(\overline{P}) \rightsquigarrow \langle \mathbf{T} \rangle)\,, \tag{10.15}$$

which can be read as follows: the associated ordinary state predicate $P$ is invariantly true, and the system does not halt in any state where the current TD predicate $\overline{P}(\delta)$ is decreasing (i.e., would turn false after some time $\delta$).

This simplifies RT invariants for regular RT predicates into ordinary state invariants and simple liveness properties.

### 10.3.6 Example: Gas Burner as a Hybrid System

As an example we discuss hybrid properties of the real-time gas burner of Sect. 10.1.9 (p. 361). These properties will be utilized for adjusting the constants $d_1$, $d_2$, and $d_3$ in the actions properly.

#### Constraint on Gas Leakage

The real phenomenon behind the critical requirements for the gas-burner system is the increase and decrease of gas concentration in the air. Ignoring again the lag between the flame going off and the system recognizing this, predicate

$$\mathsf{Leak} \triangleq \mathsf{flow\_s} \wedge \neg\mathsf{flam\_s}$$

is true when the gas concentration increases. A primary requirement is that this concentration does not exceed some critical value.

Instead of describing the associated physical phenomena directly, we start with the following requirement, which could be derived from such a description under suitable assumptions on gas flow and ventilation: during each continuous time interval of length $T^*$, $T^* \geq 60$, the accumulated leakage time $L^*$ (i.e., the total time when Leak is true) does not exceed $T^*/20$.

Assuming that the measuring of a time interval $T^*$ and the associated leakage time $L^*$ starts at an arbitrary moment, these are nondecreasing, piecewise linear RT functions, and the given requirement is

$$\forall t > 0 : T^*(t) \geq 60 \Rightarrow T^*(t) \geq 20 \times L^*(t) .$$

Defining RT predicate $Q^*(t)$ as

$$Q^*(t) \overset{\Delta}{=} T^*(t) \geq 60 \Rightarrow T^*(t) \geq 20 \times L^*(t) , \qquad (10.16)$$

this requirement can be formulated as an RT invariance

$$\Box_t Q^*(t) . \qquad (10.17)$$

### Regular RT Predicate

As defined in (10.16), $Q^*(t)$ has a unique value for all $t, t \geq 0$, but it is not piecewise monotonic and therefore not regular. For instance, if leakage stops for good at moment $t_i$ when $T^*(t_i) = 40$ and $L^*(t_i) = 4$, then $Q^*(t_i)$ is true, but will turn false when $T^*(t) = 60$, and again true when $T^*(t) = 80$, as shown in Fig. 10.7. More generally, if $T^*(t) < 60$ but $L^*(t) > 3$, then $Q^*(t)$ will necessarily turn false when $T^*(t) = 60$.

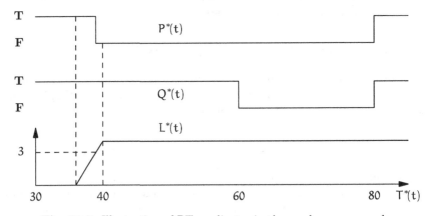

**Fig. 10.7.** Illustration of RT predicates in the gas-burner example

Instead of $Q^*(t)$, we can, however, consider the modified RT predicate $P^*(t)$,

$$P^*(t) \stackrel{\Delta}{=} L^*(t) \geq 3 \Rightarrow T^*(t) \geq 20 \times L^*(t) , \tag{10.18}$$

which turns false in such a situation already when $L^*(t)$ exceeds 3. Requirement (10.17) can then be replaced by an equivalent requirement

$$\Box_t P^*(t) . \tag{10.19}$$

It is left as an exercise for the reader to show that (10.19) is, indeed, equivalent to (10.17) (Exercise 10.3.4). It is also left as an exercise to the reader to show that $P^*(t)$ is regular (Exercise 10.3.5), which then allows us to use (10.15) on p. 377 for proving (10.19).

## Instrumenting the Gas Burner

In order to find conditions that guarantee (10.19), the TD predicate $\overline{P}$ associated with the RT predicate $P^*(t)$ has to be safely approximated in terms of state variables in the action system. In the following this will be done by 'instrumentation' that adds new variables without otherwise affecting any behaviors.

First we notice that $\overline{P}(\delta)$ can be decreasing only if the state is Starting, or if the state is Ignited and flam_s = false. In both cases, fairness forces some (system) action to be executed eventually. Therefore, on account of (10.15) on p. 377, RT invariance of $P^*(t)$ reduces to proving the associated ordinary invariance

$$\Box(L \geq 3 \Rightarrow N \geq 19 \times L) , \tag{10.20}$$

where $N$ and $L$ are ordinary state functions, and non-leakage time $N = T - L$ has been used instead of the total elapsed time $T$.

Obviously, $L$ and $N$ can be safely approximated in (10.20) by any $l$ and $n$ that approximate them from above and below, respectively. For simplicity we take $n$ to measure time spent in state Idle only, and $l$ to measure time spent either in state Starting or in state Ignited with b = true.

In order to express these state functions $l$ and $n$ in terms of state variables, we introduce two state variables $l_{acc}$ and $n_{acc}$, which are initialized as 0, and are updated only in connection with system actions. When the measurement is going on, the formulas for $l$ and $n$ are then

$$l = l_{acc} + (\text{if Starting then } \Omega - \tau_{Start\_s}$$
$$\text{else if Ignited} \wedge b \text{ then } \Omega - t_{Flame\_off}$$
$$\text{else } 0) ,$$

$$n = n_{acc} + (\text{if Idle then } \Omega - \max(\tau_{Stop\_s}, \tau_{Close\_s}, 0) \text{ else } 0) .$$

In addition, auxiliary state variables p and i are introduced to indicate measuring as follows. Variable p (initialized as false) indicates whether the measuring of l and n has started, and variable i (initialized as 0) counts the number of times that state Idle has been entered with p = true.

It should be possible to start the measurement of l and n at an arbitrary moment. For safe approximation of n and l it is, however, sufficient to do this only in connection with action Start_s. For this purpose, a Boolean parameter q is added to this action, indicating that the measurement should start, if not already started.

Denoting the specification layer in Sect. 10.1.9 (p. 361) by Timed_Burner, this instrumentation can be given by the following refinements of system actions:

$$^{SF}\text{Start\_s}(q : \mathbb{B}; \ \tau : \mathbb{R}) : \text{Timed\_Burner.Start\_s}(\tau)$$
$$\to \ p' = \text{if } q \wedge \neg p \text{ then true else false}$$
$$\wedge \ i' = \text{if } p \text{ then } i + 1 \text{ else } 0$$
$$\wedge \ n'_{\text{acc}} = \text{if } p \text{ then}$$
$$n_{\text{acc}} + \tau - \max(\tau_{\text{Stop\_s}}, \tau_{\text{Close\_s}}, 0)$$
$$\text{else } 0 \ ,$$

$$^{SF}\text{Ign\_off\_s}(\tau : \mathbb{R}) : \text{Timed\_Burner.Ign\_off\_s}(\tau)$$
$$\to \ l'_{\text{acc}} = \text{if } p \text{ then } l_{\text{acc}} + \tau - \tau_{\text{Start\_s}} \text{ else } 0 \ ,$$

$$^{SF}\text{Stop\_s}(\tau : \mathbb{R}) : \text{Timed\_Burner.Stop\_s}(\tau)$$
$$\to \ l'_{\text{acc}} = \text{if } p \text{ then } l_{\text{acc}} + \tau - \tau_{\text{Start\_s}} \text{ else } 0 \ ,$$

$$^{SF}\text{Close\_s}(\tau : \mathbb{R}) : \text{Timed\_Burner.Close\_s}(\tau)$$
$$\to \ l'_{\text{acc}} = \text{if } p \wedge b \text{ then}$$
$$l_{\text{acc}} + \tau - t_{\text{Flame\_off}}$$
$$\text{else } 0 \ .$$

## Adjusting Deadlines and Delays

On the basis of how system actions can follow each other it is easy to check that the above instrumentation gives safe approximations of L and N. For a safe adjustment of constants $d_1$, $d_2$, and $d_3$ we now have to find under which conditions invariant

$$\square(l \geq 3 \Rightarrow n \geq 19 \times l) \tag{10.21}$$

can be guaranteed to be true.

For this we need bounds for the values of $l_{\text{acc}}$ and $n_{\text{acc}}$. The following bounds can be derived from a worst-case scenario, and can be proved to be invariantly true (Exercise 10.3.6):

$$\Box(p \wedge \text{Idle} \Rightarrow l_{\text{acc}} \leq (i+1) \times (d_1 + d_2) \wedge n_{\text{acc}} \geq i \times d_3),$$
$$\Box(p \wedge \text{Starting} \Rightarrow l_{\text{acc}} \leq i \times (d_1 + d_2) \wedge n_{\text{acc}} \geq i \times d_3),$$
$$\Box(p \wedge \text{Ignited} \Rightarrow l_{\text{acc}} \leq i \times (d_1 + d_2) + d_1 \wedge n_{\text{acc}} \geq i \times d_3).$$

From the definitions of state functions $l$ and $n$ we now get the following bounds for $l$ and $n$:

$$\Box(l \leq (i+1) \times (d_1 + d_2) \wedge n \geq i \times d_3).  \tag{10.22}$$

From (10.22) we can check for which values of $d_1$, $d_2$, and $d_3$ the property (10.21) is true. For simplicity, assume that $d_1 + d_2 \leq 1$. Then $l \geq 3$ implies that $i \geq 2$, and we also have

$$n - 19 \times l \geq i \times d_3 - 19 \times (i+1)$$
$$= i \times (d_3 - 19) - 19$$
$$\geq 2 \times (d_3 - 19) - 19 \qquad \text{(provided that } d_3 \geq 19)$$
$$= 2 \times d_3 - 57.$$

This shows that conditions $d_1 + d_2 \leq 1$ and $d_3 \geq 28.5$ are sufficient to ensure that the system satisfies (10.21) and hence also the required real-time invariance property (10.19) on p. 379.

## Review Questions

QUESTION 10.3.1  Give an informal explanation of how TD functions, RT functions, and associated ordinary state functions relate to each other.

QUESTION 10.3.2  Under which condition do action intervals cover all non-negative real numbers?

QUESTION 10.3.3  What are the situations in which a TD function $\overline{f}$ does not generate a uniquely defined RT function $f^*(t)$ for all $t \geq 0$?

QUESTION 10.3.4  What is the intuitive meaning of a real-time invariant $\Box_t P^*(t)$, explained in terms of the associated TD predicate $\overline{P}(\delta)$?

QUESTION 10.3.5  Is a monotonic TD function $\overline{f}$ either nondecreasing in each state or nonincreasing in each state?

QUESTION 10.3.6  When is an RT predicate called regular, and what is the significance of this property?

**Exercises**

EXERCISE 10.3.1 Show that if two monotonic TD functions $\bar{f}$ and $\bar{g}$ are linear, then $\bar{f} \geq \bar{g}$ is a monotonic TD predicate.

EXERCISE 10.3.2 Show that if TD predicates $\bar{P}$ and $\bar{Q}$ are both nondecreasing (or nonincreasing) in a state $s$, then so also are $\bar{P} \wedge \bar{Q}$ and $\bar{P} \vee \bar{Q}$.

EXERCISE 10.3.3 Show that the definition of an RT invariant (10.14) on p. 376 reduces to (10.15) on p. 377 for regular RT predicates.

EXERCISE 10.3.4 Show that requirement (10.19) on p. 379 is equivalent to (10.17) in the gas-burner example.

EXERCISE 10.3.5 Show that RT predicate (10.18) on p. 379 is regular.

EXERCISE 10.3.6 Check the correctness of the bounds and calculations that were used in enforcing (10.21) on p. 380 in the gas-burner example.

## Bibliographic Notes

For a representative collection of papers where various formal approaches were extended to deal with real time, the reader is referred to [40]. In particular, it contains a paper by Abadi and Lamport [7], where TLA was first used for the specification of real-time systems, and on which many of the ideas in this chapter are based.

A method for incremental modeling of real-time systems with action systems was first developed without explicit facilities to enforce real-time properties [122, 133]. The form used here is mainly from Kurki-Suonio and Katara [128], where the toy-car example was also used. A similar presentation was included in [126].

The notion of relative safety properties is due to Henzinger [80].

For extensions and adaptations of various formal approaches to deal with hybrid systems, the reader is referred to [72]. Among others, this collection contains a paper by Lamport [140], where TLA is used for hybrid systems, and a paper where action systems are extended to deal with hybrid systems [121]. The gas-burner example, first discussed by Hansen et al. [75], has been used in several early papers on hybrid systems.

Comparing to other approaches with similar ideas, one characteristic feature in the approach of this book is that fairness is used as the fundamental 'execution force' in real-time and hybrid specifications also. The contrast between this approach and a more conventional philosophy of time was discussed in [123]. For instance, the approach described by Maler et al. [150] is based on temporal logic, but does not use fairness for enforcing real-time properties.

The convention of introducing the execution moments of actions as additional parameters also distinguishes this presentation from related formalisms described in the literature. Usually 'tick' actions (i.e., actions that correspond to `Time.Record`) are not synchronized with other actions, which means that the clock is advanced only in actions that have no other effects. The choice made here has an effect on the enabling of actions and helps in keeping fairness assumptions as the only 'force' behind liveness properties.

# Part V

# Epilogue

# 11

# Reexamining the Theory

The aim of this book has been to improve our understanding of how to develop manageable specifications for complex reactive systems. Different aspects of a comprehensive theory, as outlined in Sect. 1.2 (p. 8), have been discussed, ranging from logical foundations to model-oriented abstractions. The main contribution of the approach is its support for structuring specifications in a manner that is guided by the logical properties of behaviors, rather than by the architectural structure of system implementations. As illustrated by several examples, this deviation from the conventional wisdom is crucial for incremental development of specifications.

An inevitable consequence of this change in the underlying way of thinking is that the presented theory is not just formalization of established concepts and practices. Although this may make the presented ideas somewhat hard to adopt, they do not, however, contain anything radically new. For instance, the history of temporal logic in system specification [170, 151, 172, 152, 153] dates back to 1977, and that of TLA [138, 141, 144, 145], action-oriented execution models [20, 36], and superposition [48, 20, 36, 105] to the 1980s. Here we have only made an effort to show how a comprehensive practical theory can be built on these ideas.

Although we have used the term 'practical theory', the emphasis of this book has not been on tools, but on such conceptual understanding of reactive systems that is needed in their specification, design, and maintenance. Different aspects of this have been addressed in the previous chapters. The main viewpoint has been that of operational modeling. The key ideas have been formulated in an 'abstract' form, and we have by purpose avoided discussing how they are supported in the DisCo tools [4, 49], for instance, which were developed in conjunction with the theory. This reflects the opinion that tools are subsidiary to theoretical understanding, not the other way around.

In this concluding chapter we reiterate briefly some of the key aspects of the theory, with the hope that the reader can then better distinguish the essential underlying ideas from the more arbitrary decisions that had to be made in the writing of this book.

## 11.1 Basic Principles

Theories cannot be judged in isolation from the purposes for which they are intended. In particular, it makes a big difference whether reactive systems are thought of as 'natural phenomena' to be observed and verified to satisfy given requirements, or as artifacts to be constructed for purposes that evolve or are initially not fully understood. Obviously, the viewpoint of this theory is the latter. In this section we review briefly some of the basic principles of operational modeling that this has led to.

### 11.1.1 Dynamic Behaviors

In object-oriented programming, the word 'behavior' is often used to denote just the 'methods' of an object, since these determine how an object will react to different requests. One of the key principles then is that an object encapsulates both state and behavior.

The background of such a notion of behavior is in an algorithmic view of software, with *transformational semantics* given separately to each method. This view is not, however, well suited for describing how a system actually behaves. In particular, such a static view of objects does not give a natural basis for specifying or reasoning on collective behaviors. To compensate for this, various formalisms have been introduced in practice to describe dynamic *scenarios* (i.e., examples or patterns of collective behaviors) that should be possible in the system.

In contrast to this traditional view, the theory presented in this book is based on *reactive semantics*, where dynamic properties are not added to a basically transformational view as an afterthought. Instead, the very meaning of a system is understood in terms of the dynamic behaviors that it can generate. As a consequence, behaviors can no longer be encapsulated in objects, since they are collective phenomena to which all objects of a system may contribute.

This fundamental principle is reflected in all parts of the theory, ranging from the underlying logic to the operational execution model, and to language principles.

### 11.1.2 Closed-system Modeling

With focus on dynamic behaviors, an operational model needs to be closed in the sense that it models both the system to be implemented and its assumed environment. When collective behaviors are modeled in this fashion, it is natural to treat the system to be implemented and its environment in a homogeneous manner.

For the underlying execution model this means that it should be suited for modeling not only algorithmic processes but also nondeterministic choices. The latter are needed especially in the modeling of environment behavior, but are also otherwise useful at the level of specifications. In the presence of nondeterminism, fairness assumptions are a natural notion for expressing liveness requirements.

In order to be able to separate the system to be implemented from its assumed environment, each action in a closed-system model has to be assigned to the responsibility of one of the cooperating parties. This partitioning of responsibilities is considered here to be external to the theory itself, although it is important for validating whether a model does what it is intended to do, for deciding on the refinements that may be needed to achieve implementability on an intended hardware/software platform, and, of course, for an implementation itself.

Since a closed-system specification determines all possible scenarios for collective behaviors, it also gives a formal basis for constructing test cases for system testing.

### 11.1.3 Action Orientation

From the viewpoint of traditional software-engineering methods, the action-oriented execution model of this theory may be considered an obstacle. In particular, no general rules can be given to transform arbitrary action systems into efficient implementations, which means that the gap between specifications and implementations cannot be overcome in a straightforward manner.

However, as stated above, the main purpose of this theory is not to model implementations as such, but to aid in developing manageable specifications for complex systems. From this viewpoint the action-oriented execution model has two major advantages. Firstly, it has an intuitively natural relationship to the underlying logic, which makes it easy to alternate between the viewpoints of operational execution and of formal properties. Secondly, it is eminently suited for the superposition-based development method, which would lead to unnecessary complexities in connection with more traditional execution models.

For these reasons the action-oriented execution model is essential in making the different components of the theory fit together in a natural manner. It affects, however, the module structure of the resulting specifications, which will be discussed below in Sect. 11.2.

### 11.1.4 Abstractions

The main enemy in software engineering is complexity, which has increased not only with system size, but also as a result of a paradigm shift from algorithmic computing to reactive systems [193]. As stated by Dijkstra [47]: "Because we are dealing with artifacts, all unmastered complexity is of our own making ..., so we had better learn how not to introduce such complexity in the first place."

The most powerful weapon to fight complexity is our mental capability for abstraction. For reactive systems this means that we need means to consider them at varying levels of abstraction. To serve their purpose, these abstractions must capture the meaning of a system correctly, not only as more or less truthful descriptions of the intended system, as is often thought.

The theory presented here provides such abstractions of the system under specification and design, as has been discussed by Kurki-Suonio and Mikkonen [130, 131, 132]. The levels of abstraction are also associated with an incremental specification method in a natural manner. The approach can therefore be called *abstraction-based*, in contrast to *component-based* approaches, in which the specification and design process is guided by the architectural structure of the intended implementation entities. This contrast will be elaborated in more detail below in Sect. 11.2.

Correct abstractions are useful not only in specification and design, but for any purposes where human understanding of complex systems is needed. In the DisCo project, Mikkonen et al. have studied the use of hierarchical abstractions in the management of *evolving* software systems [156, 157, 5], and Aaltonen has utilized them in reverse engineering of a distributed switching system – an industrial evaluation of this work was given in [88] – as well as in generating test cases for system testing [2, 1].

### 11.1.5 Preexistence of Variables

In programming it is natural to think that variables come into existence by declarations or by their first uses. Variables that have not yet been added to a system are therefore nonexistent. In logic the situation is different: the existence of a variable is independent of whether anything is said about it.

The need for correct abstractions of systems under specification leads also in operational models to the logical view of variables. Since abstractions are models of the final system, we have to think that each variable of the final system 'preexists' in each abstraction, even when nothing is said about it. In other words, saying nothing of a variable does not mean its nonexistence, but that no constraints are given for its values in behaviors.

Similarly, subclasses of a class also need to 'preexist' before anything has been said about them. As a consequence, introducing a subclass also introduces implicitly the associated complement subclass, even if nothing is explicitly said about it.

This may sound like overemphasizing a slight difference in the way of thinking in logics and in programming. In connection with multiple inheritance this makes, however, a difference that cannot be ignored in reasoning. The reason for this is that for any two classes it is important to know whether their intersection is empty or not – independently of whether their multiple inheritance has already been explicitly utilized.

### 11.1.6 Connection Between Variables and Actions

Another difference from conventional thinking is that variables have no significance as such; they get their meanings only through the actions that deal with them.[1] This means that variables and the associated actions must always be introduced together.

For incremental specification and for the correctness of abstractions this is a crucial point. In particular, if new ways to update previously introduced variables could be added at lower levels of abstraction, this would immediately invalidate previous abstractions. Nondeterminism is obviously essential for introducing actions at levels where their effects cannot yet be specified in a deterministic manner.

### 11.1.7 Composition of Closed Systems

In 'classical' object-oriented modeling, systems are constructed by composing them from components, which may be individual objects or (open) subsystems that consist of several interacting objects. Reusability is mainly achieved at the level of classes, which are reusable patterns for objects with similar properties.

From the viewpoint of such component-based architectures, composition of closed systems may sound self-contradictory. How can several closed systems be parts of a larger closed system, and how can a single closed system be reused in different contexts? With a slight change of viewpoint, composition and reuse are, however, natural ideas also for closed-system models:

- The closed systems to be composed can be understood as *projections* of the resulting system. Each of them describes the same closed system, but concentrates on different (possibly overlapping) aspects of it.
- Instead of composing specific systems from specific objects or subsystems, one can compose *patterns* for systems from subpatterns [154, 113]. The same pattern[2] can be reused in different contexts, to generate either patterns or specific systems.

Following these ideas, conventional composition has been generalized in this theory into more general *synthesis*, where modules are patterns rather than specific systems, and the patterns to be composed need not model components that would correspond to disjoint implementation entities in the synthesized system.

---

[1]As pointed out in Sect. 6.3.3 (p. 182), this does not apply to variables that are introduced as immutable constants, describing some fixed parameters of the problem.

[2]This conforms to the usage of the word 'pattern' in object-oriented design. Obviously, a specific system is a special case of a pattern, where no further freedom is left for the designer.

## 11.2 Two Dimensions of System Architecture

As has been pointed out several times in this book, software-engineering methods are affected by the basic philosophy that is adopted, which may be either transformational (algorithmic) or reactive. In this section this question is analyzed in more detail in the light of two orthogonal dimensions of specification architectures, as discussed in [155, 104].

### 11.2.1 Vertical Architectures

Executions of a system can be understood as state sequences that start from an initial state and (possibly) end in a final state. The transformational philosophy leads to specifying them in terms of a precondition (P), which is assumed to be satisfied in the initial state, and the intended postcondition (Q), which should be satisfied in the final state (see Fig. 11.1). An implementation of such a specification generates, in general, state sequences with intermediate states. The contributions of a conventional component to these sequences correspond to subsequences (V) with transformational specifications of their own, i.e., with their own preconditions ($P_V$) and postconditions ($Q_V$), as illustrated in Fig. 11.2.

**Fig. 11.1.** Illustration of a transformational specification

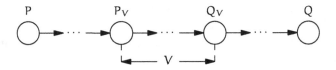

**Fig. 11.2.** Vertical slice in a state sequence

In general, the component structure of a system then induces a nested structure of subsequences of states. Since this results in vertical slicing of graphical illustrations, the components will be called *vertical modules* in the following, and structuring a system in terms of them will be called *vertical architecture*.

With this philosophy, the goal of a specification method is to find a suitable component structure and associated subspecifications ($P_V, Q_V$) in terms of which the original specification (P, Q) is implementable. Determining and implementing such subspecifications can be seen as an application of the *divide-and-conquer* approach to deal with complexity.

## 11.2.2 Horizontal Architectures

In the reactive philosophy, a specification determines behaviors, which may also be nonterminating. As discussed extensively in this book, a natural module of a specification then corresponds to a projection of the intended behaviors on a given subset of variables (see Fig. 11.3, where H denotes such a projection of a behavior).

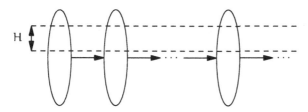

**Fig. 11.3.** Horizontal slice in a state sequence

In general, the module structure of a specification then induces a nested structure of projections. Since this results in horizontal slicing of graphical illustrations, such modules will be called *horizontal modules* in the following, and structuring a system in terms of them will be called *horizontal architecture*.

With this philosophy, the idea of a specification method is to find suitable projections of collective behaviors, in terms of which the total specification can be constructed incrementally. The main tool for dealing with complexity is then *abstraction*, as was discussed above.

## 11.2.3 Orthogonality of the Two Dimensions

In good programming practice, variables are encapsulated in the (vertical) modules to which they belong. If X denotes the set of variables encapsulated in such a module, then the vertical slices of behaviors that are generated by the module also determine uniquely the horizontal slices for the set X. The reader may therefore ask whether there is any essential difference between the two kinds of modules.

Instead of asking whether a module *is* a vertical or horizontal module, the right question is, however, for which purpose it is a *natural* module. Individual objects, for instance, are usually not natural modules for reasoning on collective behaviors, but they may be realistic units of implementation.

The contrast between the two kinds of modules is illustrated by the two 'cakes' in Fig. 11.4. The slices shown in the left-hand cake indicate a given vertical architecture, where each variable is encapsulated in one of the slices. A horizontal architecture, on the other hand, is illustrated by the layers in the cake on the right, where each layer may extend over several (possibly all)

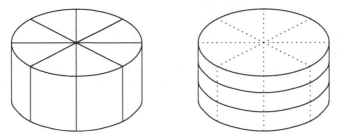

**Fig. 11.4.** Illustration of vertical vs. horizontal modularity

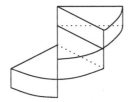

**Fig. 11.5.** Vertical slices as horizontal layers

vertical slices. The concerns addressed by such layers are therefore often called *crosscutting concerns*.

As shown by Fig. 11.4, the two dimensions of architecture are independent of each other and can therefore be understood as *orthogonal* dimensions. This does not, however, exclude the reduced possibility of treating a basically vertical architecture also in a horizontal manner, which was referred to above. Instead of addressing crosscutting concerns, the layers then specify behaviors from the viewpoints of the individual vertical modules only, as illustrated in Fig. 11.5. This is, in fact, how collective behaviors are often defined and reasoned about in formal approaches to component-based and other vertically structured systems.

### 11.2.4 Notes on Current Practice

The mechanisms for modularity in programming languages provide powerful support for vertical architectures. Therefore, traditional specification and design methods are also based on the vertical view. The need for taking a horizontal view has, however, also been recognized in practice. In current design methods this dimension is, however, taken as an auxiliary viewpoint, which is either appended to a vertically structured specification, or used informally in its construction. As such the role of the horizontal view is secondary, although it then also provides valuable information for checking whether the design satisfies the intentions of the designer. In UML, for instance, this viewpoint of dynamic scenarios is applied in *sequence diagrams* and *use cases* [191].

More effectively, the horizontal dimension is utilized in *design patterns* [65], which can be understood as horizontal modules on which applications are to be superposed [154]. The same holds also for *middleware* systems like *CORBA* [181]. Jackson's *problem frames* [89] are another proposal to guide developers to focus on the horizontal dimension.

In programming languages the horizontal dimension is emerging in terms of *aspect-oriented programming* [115, 51, 183], where an additional structure of aspects is imposed on top of a vertical structure of objects.

### 11.2.5 Comparing the Two Kinds of Modularity

The main properties and relative advantages of the two kinds of architecture can be summarized as follows:

- Vertical and horizontal architectures are associated in a natural manner with *transformational* and *reactive* semantics, respectively.
- For state sequences in behaviors, vertical architectures induce nesting of *subsequences* of states, whereas horizontal architectures induce nesting of *projections* to subsets of variables.
- In the vertical dimension, modularity can be expressed in terms of *open systems*, whereas *closed-system* modularity is natural for the horizontal dimension.
- *Sequential composition* and *subroutine invocation* are natural operations for the composition of vertical modules, whereas *parallel composition* and *superposition* take analogous roles for the synthesis of horizontal modules.[3]
- From the viewpoint of formal methods, vertical modularity supports *stepwise refinement* of complete specifications, whereas horizontal modularity supports *incremental* derivation of specifications.
- In managing the complexity of system design, vertical modularity is associated with the *divide-and-conquer* approach, whereas horizontal modularity makes effective use of *abstractions*.
- Vertical modularity is good for systems and components with fully given and stable specifications, whereas horizontal modularity has advantages in dealing with *evolving* systems and with systems that are under construction and not yet completely understood.
- Vertical modularity is strongly supported by current languages and tools, whereas support for horizontal modularity is only emerging and still very weak.
- Vertical modularity has proved essential in *implementation* technology, whereas the main advantages of horizontal modularity seem to be in *specification*.

---

[3]Notice, however, that subclassing can be understood as superposition on class definitions also in the context of vertical modularity.

## 11.2.6 Combining the Two Dimensions

In the theory presented in this book, the primary dimension of modularity is horizontal. That is, the specification process for reactive systems is suggested to proceed incrementally in terms of horizontal layers. The justification for this is that the primary concern in specification is the meaning of a system, and horizontal modularity is the natural one for reactive semantics.

The vertical dimension has a secondary role in this approach, and is reflected in the high-level view taken of the object structure in an eventual implementation. This object structure does not, however, remove the gap that still exists between the resulting action-oriented specifications and their implementation with currently available tools. If the horizontal structure corresponds to a well-specified architectural pattern, as described in [95], for instance, this gap need not be a problem. In the worst case the horizontal structure of a specification may, however, totally disappear from an implementation.

As mentioned above, a kind of opposite approach is taken in aspect-oriented programming, which aims at supporting horizontal modularity at the level of programming languages. Based on conventional programming languages, crosscutting concerns are addressed in these approaches as a kind of afterthought, added on top of vertical module structures. Even though these ideas seem like a major step in utilizing the horizontal dimension in implementations, they do not reflect the fact that horizontal views are most important in early stages of specification and design.

Obviously, combining the two architectural dimensions in an optimal fashion in the specification, design, and implementation of software requires better tool support than what is available, yet. An interesting direction for further research therefore is to investigate how the currently used design methods and programming systems could be extended or modified so that the horizontal structure of aspect-oriented specifications could be effectively utilized with them. For some promising efforts in this direction the reader is referred to the use of *AspectJ* [114, 13] by the DisCo group [3] and by Sihman and Katz [182], of UML [191] by Hammouda et al. [74], by Katara and Katz [103], and by Pitkänen and Selonen [169], and of *OMG Model Driven Architecture* [165] by Mikkonen et al. [158].

# References

1. Timo Aaltonen. Defining observation objectives for reactive and distributed systems. In Alexandre Petrenko and Andreas Ulrich, editors, *Formal Approaches to Software Testing*, number 2931 in Lecture Notes in Computer Science, pages 101–113. Springer, Berlin Heidelberg New York, 2003.
2. Timo Aaltonen and Joni Helin. Formal basis for testing with joint-action specifications. In Rob Hierons and Thierry Jéron, editors, *Proceedings of Formal Approaches to Testing 2002 (FATES'02), A Satellite Workshop of CONCUR'02*, pages 65–77, 2002.
3. Timo Aaltonen, Joni Helin, Mika Katara, Pertti Kellomäki, and Tommi Mikkonen. Coordinating aspects and objects. In Antonio Brogi and Jean-Marie Jacquet, editors, *Electronic Notes in Theoretical Computer Science*, volume 68. Elsevier, 2003.
4. Timo Aaltonen, Mika Katara, and Risto Pitkänen. DisCo toolset – the new generation. *Journal of Universal Computer Science*, 7(1):3–18, 2001. http://www.jucs.org.
5. Timo Aaltonen and Tommi Mikkonen. Managing software evolution with a formalized abstraction hierarchy. In Danielle C. Martin, editor, *Proc. 8th IEEE International Conference on Engineering of Complex Computer Systems, ICECCS 2002*, pages 224–231. IEEE Computer Society, 2002.
6. Martín Abadi and Leslie Lamport. The existence of refinement mappings. *Theoretical Computer Science*, 82(2):253–284, May 1991.
7. Martín Abadi and Leslie Lamport. An old-fashioned recipe for real time. *ACM Transactions on Programming Languages and Systems*, 16(5):1543–1571, September 1994. An earlier version appeared in [40], pages 1–27.
8. Martín Abadi and Leslie Lamport. Conjoining specifications. *ACM Transactions on Programming Languages and Systems*, 17(3):507–534, May 1995.
9. Jean-Raymond Abrial. *The B-Book: Assigning Programs to Meanings*. Cambridge University Press, 1996.
10. *Ada Programming Language*. ANSI/MIL-STD-1815A-1983.
11. Bowen Alpern and Fred B. Schneider. Defining liveness. *Information Processing Letters*, 21(4):181–185, October 1985.
12. Krzysztof R. Apt, Nissim Francez, and Shmuel Katz. Appraising fairness in languages for distributed programming. *Distributed Computing*, 2(4):226–241, 1988.

13. AspectJ home page, `http://aspectj.org`.

14. Paul C. Attie. A guide to Raddle 87 semantics. Technical Report STP-340-87, Microelectronics and Computer Technology Corp., 1988.

15. Paul C. Attie, Ira R. Forman, and Eliezer Levy. On fairness as an abstraction for the design of distributed systems. In *Proc. 10th International Conference on Distributed Computing Systems (ICDCS)*, pages 150–157. IEEE Computer Society, 1990.

16. Paul C. Attie, Nissim Francez, and Orna Grumberg. Fairness and hyperfairness in multiparty interactions. *Distributed Computing*, 6:245–254, 1993.

17. Ralph-Johan Back. Refinement calculus, part II: parallel and reactive programs. In Jaco W. de Bakker, Willem-Paul de Roever, and Grzegorz Rozenberg, editors, *Stepwise Refinement of Distributed Systems*, number 430 in Lecture Notes in Computer Science, pages 67–93. Springer, Berlin Heidelberg New York, 1989.

18. Ralph-Johan Back and Reino Kurki-Suonio. Distributed cooperation with action systems. *ACM Transactions on Programming Languages and Systems*, 10(4):513–554, 1988.

19. Ralph-Johan Back and Reino Kurki-Suonio. Serializability in distributed systems with handshaking. In Timo Lepistö and Arto Salomaa, editors, *Automata, Languages and Programming*, number 317 in Lecture Notes in Computer Science, pages 52–66. Springer, Berlin Heidelberg New York, 1988.

20. Ralph-Johan Back and Reino Kurki-Suonio. Decentralization of process nets with a centralized control. *Distributed Computing*, 3:73–87, 1989. An earlier version appeared in *Proc. 2nd ACM SIGACT-SIGOPS Symposium on Principles of Distributed Computing*, pages 131–142, 1983.

21. Ralph-Johan Back and Joakim von Wright. *Refinement Calculus, a Systematic Introduction*. Springer, Berlin Heidelberg New York, 1998.

22. Rajive Bagrodia. Process synchronization: design and performance evaluation of distributed algorithms. *IEEE Transactions on Software Engineering*, 15(9):1053–1065, September 1989.

23. Rajive Bagrodia. Synchronization of asynchronous processes in CSP. *ACM Transactions on Programming Languages and Systems*, 11(4):585–597, October 1989.

24. Arthur J. Bernstein. Output guards and nondeterminism in "Communicating Sequential Processes". *ACM Transactions on Programming Languages and Systems*, 2(2):234–238, April 1980.

25. Daniel G. Bobrow, Linda G. DeMichiel, Richard P. Gabriel, Sonya E. Keene, Gregor Kiczales, and David A. Moon. Common Lisp object system specification. *ACM Sigplan Notices*, 23 (Special Issue), September 1988.

26. Tomasso Bolognesi and Ed Brinksma. Introduction to the ISO specification language LOTOS. *Computer Networks and ISDN Systems*, 14:25–59, 1987.

27. Egon Börger and Robert Stärk. *Abstract State Machines, a Method for High-Level System Design and Analysis*. Springer, Berlin Heidelberg New York, 2003.

28. Luc Bougé and Nissim Francez. A compositional approach to superimposition. In *Proc. 15th ACM Symposium on Programming Languages*, pages 240–249. ACM, 1988.

29. Per Brinch Hansen, editor. *The Origin of Concurrent Programming: From Semaphores to Remote Procedure Calls*. Springer, Berlin Heidelberg New York, 2002.

30. Manfred Broy and Ernst Denert, editors. *Software Pioneers: Contributions to Software Engineering*. Springer, Berlin Heidelberg New York, 2002.

31. Gael N. Buckley and Abraham Silberschatz. An effective implementation for the generalized input–output construct of CSP. *ACM Transactions on Programming Languages and Systems*, 5(2):223–235, April 1983.

32. Nicholas Carriero and David Gelernter. Linda in context. *Communications of the ACM*, 32(4):444–459, April 1989.

33. K. Mani Chandy. Concurrent programming for the masses. In *Proc. 4th Annual ACM Symposium on Principles of Distributed Computing*, pages 1–12. ACM, 1985. Invited address in 3rd Annual ACM Symposium on Principles of Distributed Computing.

34. K. Mani Chandy and Leslie Lamport. Distributed snapshots: determining global states of distributed systems. *ACM Transactions on Computer Systems*, 3(1):63–75, February 1985.

35. K. Mani Chandy and Jayadev Misra. Another view of "fairness". *ACM Software Engineering Notes*, 13(3):20, July 1988.

36. K. Mani Chandy and Jayadev Misra. *Parallel Program Design, a Foundation*. Addison-Wesley, 1988.

37. Jo-Mei Chang and Nicholas F. Maxemchuk. Reliable broadcast protocols. *ACM Transactions on Computer Systems*, 2(3):251–273, August 1984.

38. Arthur Charlesworth. The multiway rendezvous. *ACM Transactions on Programming Languages and Systems*, 9(2):350–366, July 1987.

39. Ole-Johan Dahl, Bjørn Myhrhaug, and Kristen Nygaard. Simula 67 common base language. Technical Report S-22, Norwegian Computer Center, 1970.

40. Jaco W. de Bakker, Cornelis Huizing, Willem-Paul de Roever, and Grzegorz Rozenberg, editors. *Real-Time: Theory in Practice*. Number 600 in Lecture Notes in Computer Science. Springer, Berlin Heidelberg New York, 1992.

41. Edsger W. Dijkstra. Cooperating sequential processes. In F. Genuys, editor, *Programming Languages*, pages 43–112. Academic, 1968. Reprinted in [29], pages 65–138. The original report EWD123 is also available at http://www.cs.utexas.edu/users/EWD/indexBibTeX.html.

42. Edsger W. Dijkstra. Hierarchical ordering of sequential processes. *Acta Informatica*, 1:115–138, 1971. Appeared also in *Operating Systems Techniques*, C. A. R. Hoare and Ronald H. Perrott, editors, pages 72–93, Academic, 1972, and reprinted in [29], pages 198–227. The original report EWD310 is also available at http://www.cs.utexas.edu/users/EWD/indexBibTeX.html.

43. Edsger W. Dijkstra. Guarded commands, nondeterminacy and the formal derivation of programs. *Communications of the ACM*, 18(8):453–457, August 1975. Available at http://raw.cs.berkeley.edu/Papers/DijkstraGC.pdf. The original report EWD472 is also available at http://www.cs.utexas.edu/users/EWD/indexBibTeX.html.

44. Edsger W. Dijkstra. *A Discipline of Programming*. Prentice Hall, 1976.

45. Edsger W. Dijkstra. The distributed snapshot of K. M. Chandy and L. Lamport. In Manfred Broy, editor, *Control Flow and Data Flow*, pages 513–517. Springer, Berlin Heidelberg New York, 1985.

46. Edsger W. Dijkstra. Position paper on "fairness". *ACM Software Engineering Notes*, 13(2):18–20, April 1988. The original report EWD1013 is also available at http://www.cs.utexas.edu/users/EWD/indexBibTeX.html.

47. Edsger W. Dijkstra. The tide, not the waves. In Peter J. Denning and Robert M. Metcalfe, editors, *Beyond Calculation: the Next Fifty Years of Computing*, pages 59–64. Copernicus, Springer, Berlin Heidelberg New York, 1997.

48. Edsger W. Dijkstra and Carel S. Scholten. Termination detection for diffusing computations. *Information Processing Letters*, 11(1):1–4, August 1980.

49. DisCo home page, http://disco.cs.tut.fi.

50. Desmond Francis D'Souza and Alan Cameron Wills. *Objects, Components, and Frameworks with UML: the Catalysis Approach*. Addison-Wesley, 1998.

51. Tzilla Elrad, Robert E. Filman, and Atef Bader. Aspect-oriented programming. *Communications of the ACM*, 44(10):29–32, October 2001.

52. Tzilla Elrad and Nissim Francez. Decomposition of distributed programs into communication-closed layers. *Science of Computer Programming*, 2(3):155–173, December 1982.

53. Michael Evangelist, Nissim Francez, and Shmuel Katz. Multiparty interactions for interprocess communication and synchronization. *IEEE Transactions on Software Engineering*, 15(11):1417–1426, November 1989.

54. Martin S. Feather. Language support for the specification and development of composite systems. *ACM Transactions on Programming Languages and Systems*, 9(2):198–234, April 1987.

55. Martin S. Feather. Constructing specifications by combining parallel elaborations. *IEEE Transactions on Software Engineering*, 15(2):198–208, February 1989.

56. Michael J. Fischer, Nancy D. Griffeth, and Nancy A. Lynch. Global states of a distributed system. *IEEE Transactions on Software Engineering*, 8(3):198–202, May 1982.

57. Robert Floyd. Assigning meanings to programs. In J. T. Schwartz, editor, *Mathematical Aspects of Computer Science*, number 19 in Symposium on Applied Mathematics, pages 19–32. American Mathematical Society, 1967. Available at http://raw.cs.berkeley.edu/Papers/FloydMeaning.pdf.

58. Charles L. Forgy and John McDermott. OPS, a domain independent production system language. In *Proc. 5th International Joint Conference on Artificial Intelligence*, pages 933–939. Morgan Kaufmann, 1977.

59. Ira R. Forman. Raddle, an informal introduction. Technical Report STP-182-85, Microelectronics and Computer Technology Corp., 1986.

60. Ira R. Forman. Design by decomposition of multiparty interactions in Raddle 87. In *Proc. 5th International Workshop on Software Specification and Design*, pages 2–10. IEEE Computer Society, 1989.

61. Nissim Francez. *Fairness*. Springer, Berlin Heidelberg New York, 1986.

62. Nissim Francez, Ralph-Johan Back, and Reino Kurki-Suonio. On equivalence completions of fairness assumptions. *Formal Aspects of Computing*, 4(6):582–591, 1992.

63. Nissim Francez and Ira R. Forman. *Interacting Processes, a Multiparty Approach to Coordinated Distributed Programming*. Addison-Wesley, 1996.

64. Nissim Francez and Brent Hailpern. Script: a communication abstraction mechanism. In *Proc. 2nd ACM SIGACT-SIGOPS Symposium on Principles of Distributed Computing*, pages 213–227. ACM, 1983.

65. Erich Gamma, Richard Helm, Ralph Johnson, and John Vlissides. *Design Patterns, Elements of Reusable Object-Oriented Software*. Addison-Wesley, 1995.

66. Stephen J. Garland and John V. Guttag. An overview of LP, the Larch prover. In Nachum Dershowitz, editor, *Proc. 3rd International Conference on Rewriting Techniques and Applications*, number 355 in Lecture Notes in Computer Science, pages 137–151. Springer, Berlin Heidelberg New York, 1989.

67. Adele Goldberg and David Robson. *Smalltalk-80: the Language and its Implementation*. Addison-Wesley, 1983.

68. Herman H. Goldstine and John von Neumann. Planning and coding problems for an electronic computer instrument. In Abraham Haskel Taub, editor, *John von Neumann: Collected Works*, volume 5, pages 80–235. Pergamon, 1963. Originally three reports prepared for U. S. Army Ord. Dept. at the Institute for Advanced Study, Princeton University, 1947–48.

69. Michael J. C. Gordon. HOL: a proof generating system for higher-order logic. In Graham M. Birtwistle and P. A. Subrahmanyam, editors, *VLSI Specification, Verification and Synthesis*, pages 73–128. Kluwer, 1988.

70. James Gosling, Billy Joy, Guy Steele, and Gilad Brancha. *The Java Language Specification*. Addison-Wesley, second edition, 2000.

71. David Gries. *The Science of Programming*. Springer, Berlin Heidelberg New York, 1981.

72. Robert L. Grossman, Anil Nerode, Anders P. Ravn, and Hans Rischel, editors. *Hybrid Systems*. Number 736 in Lecture Notes in Computer Science. Springer, Berlin Heidelberg New York, 1993.

73. Nicolas Halbwachs. *Synchronous Programming of Reactive Systems*. Kluwer, 1992.

74. Imed Hammouda, Johannes Koskinen, Mika Pussinen, Mika Katara, and Tommi Mikkonen. Adaptable concern-based framework specialization in UML. In *Proc. 19th IEEE International Conference on Automated Software Engineering*, pages 78–87. IEEE Computer Society, 2004.

75. Kirsten M. Hansen, Anders P. Ravn, and Hans Rischel. Specifying and verifying requirements of real-time systems. *ACM Software Engineering Notes*, 16(5):44–54, December 1991.

76. David Harel. Statecharts: a visual formalism for complex systems. *Science of Computer Programming*, 8:231–274, 1987.

77. David Harel, Hagi Lachover, Amnon Naamad, Amir Pnueli, Michal Politi, Rivi Sherman, Aharon Shtull-Trauring, and Mark Trakhtenbrot. STATEMATE: a working environment for the development of complex reactive systems. *IEEE Transactions on Software Engineering*, 16(4):403–414, April 1990.

78. David Harel and Amir Pnueli. On the development of reactive systems. In K. R. Apt, editor, *Logics and Models of Concurrent Systems*, volume F-13 of *NATO ASI Series*, pages 477–498. Springer, Berlin Heidelberg New York, 1985.

79. Eric Hehner. *The Logic of Programming*. Prentice Hall, 1984.

80. Thomas A. Henzinger. Sooner is safer than later. *Information Processing Letters*, 43(3):135–141, September 1992.

81. Peter Herrmann, Günter Graw, and Heiko Krumm. Compositional specification and structured verification of hybrid systems in cTLA. In *Proc. 1st IEEE International Symposium on Object-Oriented Real-Time Distributed Computing*, pages 335–340, 1998.

82. Peter Herrmann and Heiko Krumm. A framework for modeling transfer protocols. *Computer Networks*, 34(2):317–337, August 2000.

83. C. A. R. Hoare. An axiomatic basis for computer programming. *Communications of the ACM*, 12(10):576–580, 1969. Reprinted in *Communications of the ACM*, 26(1):100–106, January 1983, and in [30], pages 367–383. Available also at http://raw.cs.berkeley.edu/Papers/HoareAxioms.pdf.

84. C. A. R. Hoare. Proofs of correctness of data representation. *Acta Informatica*, 1(4):271–281, 1972. Reprinted in [30], pages 385–396.

85. C. A. R. Hoare. Communicating sequential processes. *Communications of the ACM*, 21(8):666–677, August 1978. Reprinted in [29], pages 413–443.

86. C. A. R. Hoare. *Communicating Sequential Processes*. Prentice Hall, 1985.

87. Inmos Ltd. *Occam Programming Language*. Prentice Hall, 1985.

88. Seppo Isojärvi. DisCo and Nokia: experiences of DisCo with modeling real-time system in multiprocessor environment. FMEIndSem'97, Otaniemi, Finland, February 20, 1997.

89. Michael Jackson. *Problem Frames: Analyzing and Structuring Software Development Problems*. Addison-Wesley, 2001.

90. Ivar Jacobson, Grady Booch, and James Rumbaugh. *The Unified Software Development Process*. Addison-Wesley, 1999.

91. Hannu-Matti Järvinen. *The Design of a Specification Language for Reactive Systems*. Number 95 in Publications. PhD Thesis, Tampere University of Technology, 1992.

92. Hannu-Matti Järvinen and Reino Kurki-Suonio. DisCo specification language: marriage of actions and objects. In *Proc. 11th International Conference on Distributed Computing Systems*, pages 142–151. IEEE Computer Society, 1991.

93. Hannu-Matti Järvinen, Reino Kurki-Suonio, Markku Sakkinen, and Kari Systä. Object-oriented specification of reactive systems. In *Proc. 12th International Conference on Software Engineering*, pages 63–71. IEEE Computer Society, 1990.

94. Kurt Jensen. *Coloured Petri Nets – Basic Concepts, Analysis Methods and Practical Use, Volume 1: Basic Concepts*. Springer, Berlin Heidelberg New York, 1992.

95. Jyke Jokinen, Hannu-Matti Järvinen, and Tommi Mikkonen. Incremental introduction of behaviors with static software architecture. *Computer Standards & Interfaces*, 25(3):215–222, June 2003.

96. Cliff B. Jones. *Systematic Software Development Using VDM*. Prentice Hall, 2nd edition, 1990. Available at http://www.cs.man.ac.uk/fmethods/people/cbj-research-other.html.

97. Cliff B. Jones. The early search for tractable ways of reasoning about programs. *IEEE Annals of the History of Computing*, 25(2):26–49, April–June 2003.

98. Yuh-Jzer Joung. Two decentralized algorithms for strong interaction fairness for systems with unbounded speed variability. *Theoretical Computer Science*, 243(1–2):307–338, July 2000.

99. Yuh-Jzer Joung. On fairness notions in distributed systems, part I: a characterization of implementability. *Information and Computation*, 166(1):1–34, April 2001.

100. Yuh-Jzer Joung. On fairness notions in distributed systems, part II: equivalence-completions and their hierarchies. *Information and Computation*, 166(1):35–60, April 2001.

101. Yuh-Jzer Joung and Scott A. Smolka. Coordinating first-order multiparty interactions. *ACM Transactions on Programming Languages and Systems*, 16(3):954–985, May 1994.

102. Yuh-Jzer Joung and Scott A. Smolka. A comprehensive study of the complexity of multiparty interaction. *Journal of the ACM*, 43(1):75–115, January 1996.

103. Mika Katara and Shmuel Katz. Architectural views of aspects. In *Proc. 2nd International Conference on Aspect-Oriented Software Development*, pages 1–10. ACM, 2003.

104. Mika Katara, Reino Kurki-Suonio, and Tommi Mikkonen. On the horizontal dimension of software architecture in formal specifications of reactive systems. In *FOAL 2004 Proceedings, Foundations of Aspect-Oriented Languages Workshop at AOSD 2004*, pages 37–43. Technical Report TR 04-04, Department of Computer Science, Iowa State University, 2004.

105. Shmuel M. Katz. A superimposition and control construct for distributed systems. *ACM Transactions on Programming Languages and Systems*, 15(2):337–356, April 1993.

106. Shmuel M. Katz and Joseph Gil. Aspects and superimpositions. In *ECOOP'99 Aspect-Oriented Programming Workshop*, number 1743 in Lecture Notes in Computer Science, pages 308–309. Springer, Berlin Heidelberg New York, 1999.

107. Pertti Kellomäki. *Mechanical Verification of Invariant Properties of DisCo Specifications*. Number 218 in Publications. PhD Thesis, Tampere University of Technology, 1997.

108. Pertti Kellomäki. Verification of reactive systems using DisCo and PVS. In John Fitzgerald, Cliff B. Jones, and Peter Lucas, editors, *FME'97: Industrial Applications and Strengthened Foundations of Formal Methods*, number 1313 in Lecture Notes in Computer Science, pages 589–604. Springer, Berlin Heidelberg New York, 1997.

109. Pertti Kellomäki. Deriving message passing protocols from collective behavior. In Bernd Kleinjohann, editor, *Architecture and Design of Distributed Embedded Systems, Proc. IFIP WG10.3/WG10.4/WG10.5 International Workshop on Distributed and Parallel Embedded Systems (DIPES 2000)*, pages 183–192. Kluwer, 2001.

110. Pertti Kellomäki. A structural embedding of Ocsid in PVS. In Richard J. Boulton and Paul B. Jackson, editors, *Theorem Proving in Higher Order Logics*, number 2152 in Lecture Notes in Computer Science, pages 281–296. Springer, Berlin Heidelberg New York, 2001.

111. Pertti Kellomäki. Composing distributed systems from reusable aspects of behavior. In *Proc. ICDCS'02 Workshops*, pages 481–486. IEEE, 2002.

112. Pertti Kellomäki. An annotated specification of the consensus protocol of Paxos using superposition in PVS. Technical Report 36, Tampere University of Technology, Institute of Software Systems, 2004. Available at `http://www.cs.tut.fi/ohj/reports.html`.

113. Pertti Kellomäki and Tommi Mikkonen. Design templates for collective behavior. In Elisa Bertino, editor, *ECOOP 2000 – Object-Oriented Programming*, number 1850 in Lecture Notes in Computer Science, pages 277–295. Springer, Berlin Heidelberg New York, 2000.

114. Gregor Kiczales, Erik Hilsdale, Jim Hugunin, Mik Kersten, Jeffrey Palm, and William G. Griswold. An overview of AspectJ. In Jørgen Linskov Knudsen, editor, *ECOOP 2001*, number 2072 in Lecture Notes in Computer Science, pages 327–353. Springer, Berlin Heidelberg New York, 2001.

115. Gregor Kiczales, John Lamping, Anurag Mendhekar, Chris Maeda, Cristina Lopes, Jean-Marc Loingtier, and John Irwin. Aspect-oriented programming. In

Mehmed Aksit and Satoshi Matsuoka, editors, *ECOOP '97 – Object-Oriented Programming*, number 1241 in Lecture Notes in Computer Science, pages 220–242. Springer, Berlin Heidelberg New York, 1997.

116. James C. King. A program verifier. In *Information Processing '71, Proc. IFIP World Congress 71*, pages 234–249. Elsevier, 1971.

117. Ruurd Kuiper and Willem-Paul de Roever. Fairness assumptions for CSP in a temporal logic framework. In Dines Bjørner, editor, *Formal Description of Programming Concepts II*, pages 159–167. North-Holland, 1983.

118. Reino Kurki-Suonio. Towards programming with knowledge expressions. In *Proc. 13th ACM Symposium on Principles of Programming Languages*, pages 140–149. ACM, 1986.

119. Reino Kurki-Suonio. Modular modeling of temporal behaviors. In Setsuo Ohsuga, Hannu Kangassalo, Hannu Jaakkola, Koichi Hori, and Naoki Yonezaki, editors, *Information Modelling and Knowledge Bases III*, pages 283–300. IOS, 1992.

120. Reino Kurki-Suonio. Operational specification with joint actions: serializable databases. *Distributed Computing*, 6(1):19–37, 1992.

121. Reino Kurki-Suonio. Hybrid models with fairness and distributed clocks. In Robert L. Grossman, Anil Nerode, Anders P. Ravn, and Hans Rischel, editors, *Hybrid Systems*, number 736 in Lecture Notes in Computer Science, pages 103–120. Springer, Berlin Heidelberg New York, 1993.

122. Reino Kurki-Suonio. Stepwise refinement of real-time systems. *IEEE Transactions on Software Engineering*, 19(1):56–69, January 1993.

123. Reino Kurki-Suonio. Real time: further misconceptions (or half-truths). *IEEE Computer*, 27(6):71–76, June 1994.

124. Reino Kurki-Suonio. Fundamentals of object-oriented specification and modeling of collective behaviors. In Haim Kilov and William C. Harvey, editors, *Object-Oriented Behavioral Specifications*, pages 101–120. Kluwer, 1996.

125. Reino Kurki-Suonio. Component and interface refinement in closed-system specifications. In Jeannette M. Wing, Jim Woodcock, and Jim Davies, editors, *FM'99 – Formal Methods, Volume I*, number 1708 in Lecture Notes in Computer Science, pages 134–154. Springer, Berlin Heidelberg New York, 1999.

126. Reino Kurki-Suonio. Action systems in incremental and aspect-oriented modeling. *Distributed Computing*, 16(2–3):201–217, September 2003.

127. Reino Kurki-Suonio and Hannu-Matti Järvinen. Action system approach to the specification and design of distributed systems. In *Proc. 5th International Workshop on Software Specification and Design*, pages 34–40. IEEE Computer Society, 1989.

128. Reino Kurki-Suonio and Mika Katara. Logical layers in specifications with distributed objects and real time. *Computer Systems Science & Engineering*, 14(4):217–226, July 1999.

129. Reino Kurki-Suonio and Tommi Mikkonen. Abstractions of distributed cooperation, their refinement and implementation. In Bernd Krämer, Naoshi Uchihira, Peter Croll, and Stefano Russ, editors, *Proc. International Symposium on Software Engineering for Parallel and Distributed Systems, PDSE'98*, pages 94–102. IEEE Computer Society, 1998.

130. Reino Kurki-Suonio and Tommi Mikkonen. Liberating object-oriented modeling from programming-level abstractions. In Jan Bosch and Stuart Mitchell, editors, *Object-Oriented Technology*, number 1357 in Lecture Notes in Computer Science, pages 195–199. Springer, Berlin Heidelberg New York, 1998.

131. Reino Kurki-Suonio and Tommi Mikkonen. Harnessing the power of inter-action. In Hannu Jaakkola, Hannu Kangassalo, and Eiji Kawaguchi, editors, *Information Modelling and Knowledge Bases X*, pages 1–11. IOS, 1999.

132. Reino Kurki-Suonio and Tommi Mikkonen. From program construction to abstraction engineering. In Yulin Feng, David Notkin, and Marie-Claude Gaudel, editors, *Proc. Conference on Software: Theory and Practice, 16th IFIP World Computer Congress 2000*, pages 861–868. Publishing House of Electronics Industry, 2000.

133. Reino Kurki-Suonio, Kari Systä, and Jüri Vain. Real-time specification and modeling with joint actions. *Science of Computer Programming*, 20:113–140, 1993.

134. Simon S. Lam and A. Udaya Shankar. Protocol verification via projections. *IEEE Transactions on Software Engineering*, 10(4):325–342, July 1984.

135. Leslie Lamport. The TLA web page, http://research.microsoft.com/users/lamport/tla/tla.html.

136. Leslie Lamport. Time, clocks, and ordering of events in a distributed system. *Communications of the ACM*, 21(7):558–565, July 1978.

137. Leslie Lamport. "Sometime" is sometimes "not never": on the temporal logic of programs. In *Proc. 7th ACM Symposium on Principles of Programming Languages*, pages 174–185. ACM, 1980.

138. Leslie Lamport. A simple approach to specifying concurrent systems. *Communications of the ACM*, 32(1):32–45, January 1989.

139. Leslie Lamport. Critique of the "Lake Arrowhead three". *Distributed Computing*, 6(1):65–71, 1992.

140. Leslie Lamport. Hybrid systems in TLA$^+$. In Robert L. Grossman, Anil Nerode, Anders P. Ravn, and Hans Rischel, editors, *Hybrid Systems*, number 736 in Lecture Notes in Computer Science, pages 77–102. Springer, Berlin Heidelberg New York, 1993.

141. Leslie Lamport. The temporal logic of actions. *ACM Transactions on Programming Languages and Systems*, 16(3):872–923, May 1994.

142. Leslie Lamport. Composition: a way to make proofs harder. In Willem-Paul de Roever, Hans Langmaack, and Amir Pnueli, editors, *Compositionality: the Significant Difference*, number 1536 in Lecture Notes in Computer Science, pages 402–423. Springer, Berlin Heidelberg New York, 1998.

143. Leslie Lamport. Proving possibility properties. *Theoretical Computer Science*, 206(1–2):341–352, October 1998.

144. Leslie Lamport. Specifying concurrent systems with TLA$^+$. In Manfred Broy and Ralf Steinbrüggen, editors, *Calculational System Design*, pages 183–247. IOS, 1999.

145. Leslie Lamport. *Specifying Systems: the TLA$^+$ Language and Tools for Hardware and Software Engineers*. Addison-Wesley, 2002.

146. Leslie Lamport and Lawrence C. Paulson. Should your specification language be typed? *ACM Transactions on Programming Languages and Systems*, 21(3):502–526, May 1999.

147. Kevin Lano. *Formal Object-Oriented Development*. Springer, Berlin Heidelberg New York, 1995.

148. Daniel J. Lehmann and Michael O. Rabin. On the advantages of free choice: a fully distributed symmetric solution to the dining philosophers problem. In *Proc. 8th ACM Symposium on Principles of Programming Languages*, pages 133–138, 1981.

149. Nancy A. Lynch and Michael J. Fischer. On describing the behavior and implementation of distributed systems. *Theoretical Computer Science*, 13(1):17–43, 1981.

150. Oded Maler, Zohar Manna, and Amir Pnueli. From timed to hybrid systems. In Jaco W. de Bakker, Cornelis Huizing, Willem-Paul de Roever, and Grzegorz Rozenberg, editors, *Real-Time: Theory in Practice*, number 600 in Lecture Notes in Computer Science, pages 447–484. Springer, Berlin Heidelberg New York, 1992.

151. Zohar Manna and Amir Pnueli. How to cook a temporal proof system for your pet language. In *Proc. 10th ACM Conference on Principles of Programming Languages*, pages 141–154. ACM, 1983.

152. Zohar Manna and Amir Pnueli. *The Temporal Logic of Reactive and Concurrent Systems, Specification*. Springer, Berlin Heidelberg New York, 1992.

153. Zohar Manna and Amir Pnueli. *Temporal Verification of Reactive Systems, Safety*. Springer, Berlin Heidelberg New York, 1995.

154. Tommi Mikkonen. Formalizing design patterns. In *Proc. 1998 International Conference on Software Engineering, ICSE 98*, pages 115–124. IEEE Computer Society, 1998.

155. Tommi Mikkonen. The two dimensions of an architecture. In *WICSA1, First Working IFIP Conference on Software Architecture*, 1999. Position paper, available at http://www.ece.utexas.edu/~perry/prof/wicsa1/.

156. Tommi Mikkonen and Hannu-Matti Järvinen. Specifying for releases. In *International Workshop on Principles of Software Evolution (in ICSE 98)*, pages 118–122, 1998.

157. Tommi Mikkonen, Eero Lähde, Marko Siiskonen, and Juhapekka Niemi. Managing software evolution with the service concept. In Takuya Katayama, Tetsuo Tamai, and Naoki Yonezaki, editors, *Proc. International Symposium on Principles of Software Evolution*, pages 46–50. IEEE Computer Society, 2000.

158. Tommi Mikkonen, Risto Pitkänen, and Mika Pussinen. On the role of architectural style in model driven development. In Flavio Oquendo, Brian Warboys, and Ron Morrison, editors, *Software Architecture, Proceedings of the First European Workshop on Software Architecture, EWSA 2004*, number 3047 in Lecture Notes in Computer Science, pages 74–87. Springer, Berlin Heidelberg New York, 2004.

159. Robin Milner. *A Calculus of Communicating Systems*. Number 92 in Lecture Notes in Computer Science. Springer, Berlin Heidelberg New York, 1980.

160. Robin Milner. *Communication and Concurrency*. Prentice Hall, 1989.

161. Carroll Morgan. *Programming from Specifications*. Prentice Hall, 1990.

162. F. Lockwood Morris and Cliff B. Jones. An early program proof by Alan Turing. *IEEE Annals of the History of Computing*, 6(2):139–143, April–June 1984.

163. Peter Naur. Proof of algorithms by general snapshots. *BIT*, 6:310–316, 1966.

164. Ernst-Rüdiger Olderog and Krzysztof R. Apt. Fairness in parallel programs: the transformational approach. *ACM Transactions on Programming Languages and Systems*, 10(3):420–455, July 1988.

165. OMG Model Driven Architecture, http://www.omg.org/mda/.

166. Sam Owre, John M. Rushby, and Natarajan Shankar. PVS: a prototype verification system. In Deepak Kapur, editor, *Automated Deduction – CADE-11*, number 607 in Lecture Notes in Computer Science, pages 748–752. Springer, Berlin Heidelberg New York, 1992.

167. Lawrence C. Paulson. *Isabelle: a Generic Theorem Prover.* Number 828 in Lecture Notes in Computer Science. Springer, Berlin Heidelberg New York, 1994.

168. Carl Adam Petri. *Kommunikation mit Automaten.* Number 2 in Schriften des IIM. Institut für Instrumentelle Mathematik, Universität Bonn, 1962. English translation *Communication with automata* by C. F. Greene, Supplement 1 to Technical Report RADC-TR-65-377, Vol. 1, Rome Air Development Center, Griffiss Air Force Base, January 1966.

169. Risto Pitkänen and Petri Selonen. A UML profile for executable and incremental specification-level modeling. In Thomas Baar, Alfred Strohmeier, and Ana Moreira, editors, ⟨⟨*UML*⟩⟩ *2004 – The Unified Modeling Language,* number 3273 in Lecture Notes in Computer Science, pages 158–172. Springer, Berlin Heidelberg New York, 2204.

170. Amir Pnueli. The temporal logic of programs. In *Proc. 18th IEEE Symposium on Foundations of Computer Science,* pages 46–57. IEEE Computer Society, 1977.

171. Amir Pnueli. The temporal semantics of concurrent programs. *Theoretical Computer Science,* 13:45–60, 1981.

172. Amir Pnueli. Applications of temporal logic to the specification and verification of reactive systems: a survey of current trends. In Jaco W. de Bakker, Willem-Paul de Roever, and Grzegorz Rozenberg, editors, *Current Trends in Concurrency,* number 224 in Lecture Notes in Computer Science, pages 510–584. Springer, Berlin Heidelberg New York, 1986.

173. Precise UML Group home page, http://www.cs.york.ac.uk/puml/.

174. S. Ramesh. A new and efficient implementation of multiprocess synchronization. In *PARLE: Parallel Architectures and Languages Europe, Vol. 2,* number 259 in Lecture Notes in Computer Science, pages 387–401. Springer, Berlin Heidelberg New York, 1987.

175. S. Ramesh and S. L. Mehndiratta. A methodology for developing distributed algorithms. *IEEE Transactions on Software Engineering,* 13(8):967–976, 1987.

176. Wolfgang Reisig. Partial order semantics versus interleaving semantics for CSP-like languages and its impact on fairness. In Jan Paredaens, editor, *Automata, Languages and Programming,* number 172 in Lecture Notes in Computer Science, pages 403–413. Springer, Berlin Heidelberg New York, 1984.

177. James Rumbaugh, Ivar Jacobson, and Grady Booch. *The Unified Modeling Language Reference Manual.* Addison-Wesley, 1999.

178. Markku Sakkinen. A critique of the inheritance principles of C++. *Computing Systems,* 5(1):69–110, Winter 1992. Corrigendum in *Computing Systems,* 5(3):361, Summer 1992.

179. Fred B. Schneider. Synchronization in distributed programs. *ACM Transactions on Programming Languages and Systems,* 4(2):179–195, April 1982.

180. Fred B. Schneider and Leslie Lamport. Another position paper on "fairness". *ACM Software Engineering Notes,* 13(3):18–19, July 1988.

181. Jon Siegel. *CORBA 3 Fundamentals and Programming.* John Wiley, second edition, 2000.

182. Marcelo Sihman and Shmuel Katz. Superimpositions and aspect-oriented programming. *The Computer Journal,* 46(5):529–541, September 2003.

183. Yannis Smaragdakis and Don Batory. Mixin layers: an object-oriented implementation technique for refinements and collaboration-based designs. *ACM*

*Transactions on Software Engineering and Methodology*, 11(2):215–255, April 2002.

184. Mike Spivey. *The Z Notation: a Reference Manual.* Prentice Hall, second edition, 1992. Available at `http://spivey.oriel.ox.ac.uk/~mike/zrm/`.

185. Frank A. Stomp and Willem-Paul de Roever. Designing distributed algorithms by means of formal sequentially phased reasoning (extended abstract). In Jean-Claude Bermond and Michel Raynal, editors, *Proc. 3rd International Workshop on Distributed Algorithms*, number 392 in Lecture Notes in Computer Science, pages 242–253. Springer, Berlin Heidelberg New York, 1989. Full text appeared as Report 89-8, University of Nijmegem.

186. Bjarne Stroustrup. *The C++ Programming Language.* Addison-Wesley, second edition, 1991.

187. Kari Systä. A graphical tool for specification of reactive systems. In *Proc. Euromicro'91 Workshop on Real-Time Systems*, pages 12–19, 1991.

188. Antero Taivalsaari. On the notion of inheritance. *ACM Computing Surveys*, 28(3):438–479, September 1996.

189. Yih-Kuen Tsay and Rajive Bagrodia. Some impossibility results in interprocess synchronization. *Distributed Computing*, 6(4):221–231, 1993.

190. Alan Turing. Checking a large routine. In *Report on Conference on High Speed Automatic Calculating Machines*, pages 67–69. Cambridge University Mathematical Laboratory, Cambridge, June 1949. Available at `http://www.turingarchive.org/browse.php/B/8`. Reprinted with typographical corrections and comments in [162].

191. UML$^{TM}$ Resource Page, `http://www.uml.org/`.

192. Peter Wegner. Dimensions of object-based language design. *ACM Sigplan Notices*, 22(12):168–182, December 1987. In *Proc. OOPSLA'87, Object-Oriented Programming Systems, Languages and Applications*.

193. Peter Wegner. Why interaction is more powerful than algorithms. *Communications of the ACM*, 40(5):80–91, May 1997.

194. Mark Weiser. Programmers use slices when debugging. *Communications of the ACM*, 25(7):446–452, July 1982.

195. Pamela Zave. An operational approach to requirements specification for embedded systems. *IEEE Transactions on Software Engineering*, 8(3):250–269, May 1982.

# Index

# Monographs in Theoretical Computer Science · An EATCS Series

K. Jensen
**Coloured Petri Nets**
*Basic Concepts,* Analysis Methods
and Practical Use, Vol. 1
2nd ed.

K. Jensen
**Coloured Petri Nets**
Basic Concepts, *Analysis Methods*
and Practical Use, Vol. 2

K. Jensen
**Coloured Petri Nets**
Basic Concepts, Analysis Methods
and *Practical Use,* Vol. 3

A. Nait Abdallah
**The Logic of Partial Information**

Z. Fülöp, H. Vogler
**Syntax-Directed Semantics**
Formal Models Based
on Tree Transducers

A. de Luca, S. Varricchio
**Finiteness and Regularity
in Semigroups and Formal Languages**

E. Best, R. Devillers, M. Koutny
**Petri Net Algebra**

S. P. Demri, E. S. Orlowska
**Incomplete Information:
Structure, Inference, Complexity**

J. C. M. Baeten, C. A. Middelburg
**Process Algebra with Timing**

L. A. Hemaspaandra, L. Torenvliet
**Theory of Semi-Feasible Algorithms**

E. Fink, D. Wood
**Restricted-Orientation Convexity**

Zhou Chaochen, M. R. Hansen
**Duration Calculus**
A Formal Approach to Real-Time
Systems

M. Große-Rhode
**Semantic Integration
of Heterogeneous Software
Specifications**

# Texts in Theoretical Computer Science • An EATCS Series

J. L. Balcázar, J. Díaz, J. Gabarró
**Structural Complexity I**

M. Garzon
**Models of Massive Parallelism**
Analysis of Cellular Automata
and Neural Networks

J. Hromkovič
**Communication Complexity
and Parallel Computing**

A. Leitsch
**The Resolution Calculus**

A. Salomaa
**Public-Key Cryptography**
2nd ed.

K. Sikkel
**Parsing Schemata**
A Framework for Specification
and Analysis of Parsing Algorithms

H. Vollmer
**Introduction to Circuit Complexity**
A Uniform Approach

W. Fokkink
**Introduction to Process Algebra**

K. Weihrauch
**Computable Analysis**
An Introduction

J. Hromkovič
**Algorithmics for Hard Problems**
Introduction to Combinatorial
Optimization, Randomization,
Approximation, and Heuristics
2nd ed.

S. Jukna
**Extremal Combinatorics**
With Applications
in Computer Science

P. Clote, E. Kranakis
**Boolean Functions
and Computation Models**

L. A. Hemaspaandra, M. Ogihara
**The Complexity Theory Companion**

C. S. Calude
**Information and Randomness.**
An Algorithmic Perspective, 2nd ed.

J. Hromkovič
**Theoretical Computer Science**
Introduction to Automata,
Computability, Complexity,
Algorithmics, Randomization,
Communication and Cryptography

A. Schneider
**Verification of Reactive Systems**
Formal Methods and Algorithms

S. Ronchi Della Rocca, L. Paolini
**The Parametric Lambda Calculus**
A Metamodel for Computation

Y. Bertot, P. Castéran
**Interactive Theorem Proving
and Program Development**
Coq'Art: The Calculus
of Inductive Constructions

L. Libkin
**Elements of Finite Model Theory**

M. Hutter
**Universal Artificial Intelligence**
Sequential Decisions
Based on Algorithmic Probability

G. Păun, G. Rozenberg, A. Salomaa
**DNA Computing**
New Computing Paradigms
2nd corr. printing

W. Kluge
**Abstract Computing Machines**
A Lambda Calculus Perspective

J. Hromkovič, R. Klasing, A. Pelc,
P. Ružička[†], W. Unger
**Dissemination of Information
in Communication Networks**
Broadcasting, Gossiping, Leader
Election, and Fault Tolerance

R. Kurki-Suonio
**A Practical Theory
of Reactive Systems**
Incremental Modeling
of Dynamic Behaviors